teach
yourself ...

Netscape
Communicator
4.0

*teach
yourself ...*

Netscape Communicator 4.0

*by
Kevin Reichard
and Ted Stevenson*

A Subsidiary of Henry Holt
and Company, Inc.

First Edition—1997

Printed in the United States of America.

Library of Congress Cataloging-in-Publication Data

Reichard, Kevin.
    Teach yourself ... Netscape Communicator / by Kevin Reichard, Ted Stevenson.
        p.   cm.
    ISBN 1-55828-541-5
    1. Netscape Communicator. 2. Internet (Computer network)—Computer programs. 3. World Wide Web (Information retrieval system)—Computer programs. I. Stevenson, Ted. II. Title.
    TK5105.883.N48R43   1997   97-20211
    005.7'13769—dc21   CIP

10 9 8 7 6 5 4 3 2 1

MIS:Press books are available at special discounts for bulk purchases for sales promotions, premiums, fund-raising, or educational use. Special editions or book excerpts can also be created to specification.

For details contact: Special Sales Director
                       MIS:Press
                       a subsidiary of Henry Holt and Company, Inc.
                       115 West 18th Street
                       New York, New York 10011

Associate Publisher: *Paul Farrell*

Managing Editor: *Shari Chappell*   **Copy Edit Manager:** *Karen Tongish*
Editor: *Laura Lewin*   **Copy Editor:** *Winnifred Davis*

Production Editor: *Kitty May*

Contents

Introduction: Welcome to Netscape Communicator! ix

SECTION 1: INTRODUCING NETSCAPE COMMUNICATOR 1
Chapter 1: Netscape Communicator and the Internet 3
    The On Ramp 4
    Your Link to the Web 4
    The Internet 4
    The World Wide Web 7
    Netscape Communicator and Operating Systems 11
    The New Communicator: Navigator and More 14
    Where Can I Get Communicator? 16
    Grabbing Communicator from the Web 17
    Summary 17

Chapter 2: Installing and Using Netscape Communicator .19
    Laying the Groundwork 20
    The Internet and Your Connection 20
    Downloading Netscape Communicator 36
    Installing Communicator 40
    Before You Upgrade 41
    Installing Netscape Communicator on Windows 95 .41
    Installing Netscape Communicator under Windows 3.1 44
    Installing Netscape Communicator on the Macintosh 46
    Installing Netscape Communicator on a UNIX System 47
    A Tour of Netscape Communicator 48
    Highlighting Text 52
    Frames 53
    Using the Component Bar 54
    Your Maiden Voyage 56
    Toolbar Buttons 62
    Pulldown Menus 63
    The Hidden Pop-Up Menu 96
    About: Your Setup 99
    Summary 101

Chapter 3: Customizing Netscape Communicator and Netscape Navigator 103
    Configuring Netscape Navigator 104
    Using Preferences 106
    The Appearance Panel 106
    The Advanced Panel 137
    Summary 148

Chapter 4: Cruising the Web with Navigator 149
    Jumping on the On Ramp of the Information Superhighway 150
    Bookmarks 155

The Bookmarks Window 158
Going Back in History 167
Working in Kiosk Mode 169
Forms and Netscape Navigator 170
Some Cool Web Sites 173
Using Internet Search Engines 185
Using Netscape Navigator Locally 192
Summary 194

Chapter 5: FTP and Navigator **195**
Grabbing Files the Old-Fashioned Way with FTP .196
How Do I Grab a File? 197
Saving the File 203
Uploading Files 208
Summary 209

Chapter 6: Gopher and Navigator **211**
Living History: Gopher, the Archie Crew, and Older Utilities 212
What Is Gopher? 212
Using a WAIS Server 219
Summary 220

SECTION 2: NETSCAPE COMPOSER **221**
Chapter 7: Creating Your Own HTML Documents **223**
Netscape Composer 224
An HTML Overview 224
Adding More Spice to Your Page 230
Help from the Web 231
The Composer Toolbars 235
The Composer Menus 239
Composer's Properties Dialog Boxes 244
Advanced Page Authoring 252
Using the Spell Checker 267
Publishing Your Composer Documents 268
Summary 271

SECTION 3: NETSCAPE MESSENGER **273**
Chapter 8: Electronic Mail: Your Interactive Link with the World **275**
Electronic Mail: Reach Out and Touch Someone 276
How Electronic Mail Works 277
Netscape Messenger 279
Setting Up Mail Preferences 279
Sending and Receiving Mail 286
Creating and Sending an E-Mail Message 290
Searching Through Mail 294
Message-Composition Options 298
Linking to Web Documents 311
Linking to Discussion Postings 312
vCard Business Cards 312
Sorting Through Messages 314
Summary 316

Chapter 9: Advanced Messenger Topics 319
The Netscape Messenger Toolbar 320
Running Through the Pull-down Menus 321
Other Mail-Configuration Options 339
Welcome to the Working Week 341
Working with the Address Book 344
Working Offline 351
Security and E-Mail 355
E-Mailing to Links on the Web 360
Summary 361

SECTION 4: MULTIMEDIA 363
Chapter 10: Audio and Video with RealPlayer 365
Video and Audio on the Web 366
Getting RealPlayer 367
Summary 371

Chapter 11: Other Netscape Plug-Ins 373
Plugging More into Netscape Communicator 374
Virtual-Reality Plug-Ins 374
Formatted-Page Plug-Ins 376
Multimedia Plug-Ins 382
Audio Players 386
Remote-Computing Plug-Ins 389
Miscellaneous Plug-Ins 390

Chapter 12: Push Me, Pull You 393
Push Technology: Direct to You 394
Summary 400

SECTION 5: NETSCAPE COLLABRA 401
Chapter 13: Netscape Collabra 403
Using the Usenet 404
What Is the Usenet? 404
How the Usenet Works 409
An Introductory Usenet News Session 412
Netscape News and Graphics 422
Some Newsgroup Topics 424
Internal Discussion Groups 428
Summary 431

Chapter 14: Advanced Collabra Topics 433
The Netscape Message Center Window 434
The Netscape Discussion Window 437
Using the Right-Hand Mouse Button 439
Advanced Collabra Setup Options 442
Connecting to Multiple Servers 444
Working Offline 446
Maneuvering through the Message Maze 450
Organizing and Managing Groups 456
Nontext Message Content 461
Summary 463

SECTION 6: NETSCAPE CONFERENCE 465
Chapter 15: Using Netscape Conference 467
Hardware You'll Need 468
Configuring Conference 468
Making a Call 470
Setting Call Options 471
Audio Adjustments 471
Alternate Dialing Methods 473
Voice Mail 477
The Netscape Conference Tools 480
Summary 488

SECTION 7: NETSCAPE COMMUNICATOR PRO COMPONENTS 489
Chapter 16: Using Netscape Calendar 491
Scheduling by Computer 492
An Overview of Netscape Calendar 492
The Calendar Toolbar 496
Calendar's Working Views 499
Setting Calendar Preferences 499
Printing 501
Drag-and-Drop Scheduling 504
Linking Tasks to Entries 506
Group Scheduling 506
Working Offline 508
Summary 511

Chapter 17: IBM Host on Demand 513
Mainframe Connectivity 513
Summary 515

SECTION 8: SECURITY 517
Chapter 18: Security and Communicator 519
Security and the Internet 520
Netscape Communicator, Proxies, and SOCKS 526
Mail and Security 530
Java: Brewing a Revolution 532
Summary 535

Appendix A: For More Information 537
Books 537
Magazines 538

Appendix B: Netscape Communicator and UNIX 539
Running Netscape Communicator with Command-Line Options 540
Changing Fonts 542
Other UNIX Issues 542

Glossary 545

Index 553

Welcome to Netscape Communicator!

Welcome to Netscape Communicator! You're in for a fantastic journey through one of the most exciting developments of the 20th Century: The Internet, that worldwide network of interconnected computers. It's hard to throw a dead cat these days without hitting some reminder of the growing interest of the Internet in our daily lives, whether it is that steady stream of electronic mail from your co-workers and friends from around the world or the opening of yet another cybercafe that offers metered Internet access and a decent cafe au lait.

It all smacks of hype. Indeed, it's hard to find a more hyped development in the 1990s than the Internet. However—to the amazement of many—the Internet continues to grow and prosper with each passing day, decreasing the likelihood that it will become the electronic equivalent of a mood ring or Chia Pet. In short, the Internet is here to stay.

As is Netscape Communicator, the amazing set of Web tools from Netscape Communications. Netscape Communicator and its predecessor, Netscape Navigator, have fueled the amazing growth of the Internet, combining ease of use with enough power to placate even the most finicky users. That such power exists isn't surprising—after all, there's a lot of very powerful software out there, much of it far too esoteric for the average user. However, when you combine that power with ease of use, it's an unbeatable combination. Yes, the Internet can be a rather complex place, and Internet veterans (a.k.a. NetHeads) sometimes forget that new users (a.k.a. newbies) really don't know their way around the Internet and aren't familiar with things like FTP file transfers or POP3 mail servers.

To a large extent, Netscape Communicator hides those nasty details. Yes, you'll need to master a certain number of Internet details as you set up Netscape Communicator (which, obviously, is one of the reasons you bought this book). But once you're connected and configured, using Netscape Communicator is simply a matter of pointing and clicking as you navigate the wide-open spaces of the Web.

A NEOPHYTE'S INTRODUCTION TO THE INTERNET

If you are a true newbie, you'll probably want to read this section. If you're already familiar with the Internet, you can skip ahead to the next section.

The Internet is an entity that—on some levels, anyway—defines easy characterization. On one hand, it's a disservice to speak of the Internet as a coherent entity, because it really isn't. Rather, it's an amorphous entity that you can't really get your arms around. When looked at logically and analytically, the Internet is merely a collection of telephone lines and computer servers. Yes, there are some really neat things happening that makes those telephone lines and computer servers work so well, but that's not what intrigues most of us. In a way, you can think of the Internet as a giant interstate highway system (yes, there is a lot of truth to the *information superhighway* analogy); construction workers and transit planners might be dazzled by the details of the road-work, but for the rest of us, a freeway is merely a means of getting from one place to another.

That is why we're intrigued by the content that sits on these computer servers. This content is the reason why we cruise the Internet, looking for information or entertainment. On that level, the Internet has the potential to transform personal communications as significantly the printing press and television did. Thanks to the Internet, anyone can be a publisher, broadcaster, or columnist; we need only post our stuff to the Internet and try to entice others to visit.

NOTE Take this with a large grain of salt. Yes, there's a ton of new information, data, and opinions on the Web, but a lot of it is dreck. Also, despite illusions of freedom on the Internet, remember that the entities controlling its day-to-day administration include AT&T and MCI, two multinational firms that aren't particularly well-known for benevolence toward the grass roots.

What sources of new information are out there? Consider the Internet Movie Database (*http://www.imdb.com/*). As its home page shows (see Figure I.1), the service is the sum of its users' contributions, aided by a few cinema buffs who patiently track down the cast listings of such obscure films as *Chilly Scenes of Winter*. Actually, this is a good example of the strengths and weaknesses of Internet information. The Internet Movie Database says that *Head Over Heels* is also known as *Chilly Scenes of Winter*. In truth, the two movies are different. After the original *Head Over Heels* flopped in the theaters, it was re-edited and changed, and released under the title *Chilly Scenes of Winter*, the title of the Ann Beattie novel upon which it was based. The two movies are not the same. The lesson here is that Internet data can't always be counted upon as being 100-percent accurate.

Figure I.1 *The home page for the Internet Movie Database.*

Despite this caveat, the fact that so many people can now participate in a truly mass media is an exciting development, one that can give rise to a chorus of voices that would have been unheard in the past. And you can share in that excitement, thanks to Netscape Communicator.

The Sum of Its Parts

On a more practical level, the Internet can be an important part of your life when it comes to routine, day-to-day activities. Viewed on this level, the Internet is actually a set of many different services, emanating from different servers. The following services make up the Internet:

- The *World Wide Web*, or WWW, is the flashiest part of the Internet so far, and the most popular reason to use Netscape Communicator. The Web incorporates text, graphics, and multimedia files to bring you an interactive document that's linked to other Internet resources. (We'll spend a lot more time explaining the Web elsewhere in this book.) Netscape Navigator, a component of Netscape Communicator, is a Web browser, which takes the information from the World Wide Web and formats it on your computer.

- *Electronic mail,* or e-mail, is the most popular service of the Internet, and it was the original rationale for the Internet. Basically, electronic mail allows you to send text messages and files to other Internet users, including users of commercial on-line services with gateways to the Internet. Netscape Communicator contains a powerful electronic-mail module, which is the subject of Chapter 8.

- *Newsgroups* contain extended discussions of a specific topic. There are literally thousands of newsgroups, ranging from relatively esoteric discussions (such as *sci.anthropology*) to general discussions of trivial and important topics (your view will determine which camp *alt.alien.visitors* falls into). Netscape Communicator contains a useful newsreader, which will be covered in Chapter 13.

- *Gophers* are servers on the Internet that present their wares via menus; you merely move through the menus in a hierarchical fashion. Gopher servers have no flashy graphics or multimedia images, but they do present an awful lot of good, text-based information (including many government-document archives) that is accessible only via Gopher servers. Chapter 6 covers how you can access Gopher servers via Netscape Communicator.

- *FTP* (File Transfer Protocol) is an older method of connecting to other computers to upload and download files. As you use Netscape Communicator more, you'll probably download many files from Web sites, and you may be using FTP to transfer the files. Chapter 5 covers FTP.

- *Push technology* brings the content of the Web to you automatically so that you don't have to forage through search engines and endless links to find the information you need. Netscape Communicator's push component is called Netcaster, and it's discussed in Chapter 12.

- The use of *audio* and *video* on the Internet has exploded, thanks to great new tools from Progressive Networks called RealAudio and RealVideo. We cover both in Chapter 10.

The Internet offers other services, but they are largely inconsequential—at least for now. The point is that the Internet is a collection of many different services and that you can use these services with Netscape Communicator.

Connecting to the Internet

To take advantage of these services, you need to connect to the Internet. Basically, Netscape Communicator is only a small portion of what you'll need to set up. In this book, there will be a discussion of getting your computer connected to the Internet so that you can take advantage of Netscape Communicator. This discussion begins in Chapter 1.

NETSCAPE COMMUNICATOR AND VARIOUS OPERATING SYSTEMS

Netscape Communicator is available for the Windows 95, Windows 3.x, Windows NT, Macintosh, and UNIX/X Window System operating systems. (Only NCSA Mosaic is available on as many operating-system platforms.) Basically, these versions are identical, although they all have slightly different install procedures.

In this book, we'll spend most of our time discussing the Windows 95 and Windows 3.x versions. However, there will be coverage of the Macintosh version when appropriate (during discussion of installation, for instance), and when a feature isn't present in every version of Netscape Communicator, it will be noted.

Also, our coverage will focus on the "pure" Netscape Communicator as it comes directly from Netscape Communications. Many vendors ship Netscape Communicator as part of a larger software suite, while Netscape itself sells Netscape Communicator commercially under the *Netscape Communicator Personal Edition* moniker. Because of the lag time between shipping dates and releases, you may not be using the most recent version of Netscape Communicator if you buy it as part of a larger software package (for instance, the Apple Internet Connection Kit includes only Netscape Navigator). Often these software package feature their own setup and configuration routines. There's no way to cover all of these installation routines, so our focus will be on the core package and not on its many commercial permutations.

Netscape Communicator Versions

We'll be focusing on version 4.0 of Netscape Communicator, the most recent when this book was written.

This isn't to say that this book won't be extremely valuable if you're using an older version of Netscape Navigator. The many things that make the World Wide Web unique—the HTTP addressing schemes, the mechanics of responding to a Web page—remain the same, no matter what version of Netscape Communicator you're using. We'll try to point out features that are new in version 4.0, while keeping coverage universal enough to benefit any Netscape Communicator user.

How This Book Is Organized

This book is broken into three sections: Introducing Netscape Communicator, Netscape Composer, Netscape Messenger, Multimedia, Netscape Collabra, Netscape Conference, Netscape Communicator Pro Components, and Security. The chapters break down as following:

- Chapter 1 introduces Netscape Communicator and the Internet, focusing on such things as URLs, connectivity schemes, and general Internet concepts.

- Chapter 2 focuses on obtaining and installing Netscape Communicator. It will help you take your first tentative steps on the World Wide Web and will provide thorough run-through of the Netscape Communicator menu schemes.

- Chapter 3 takes the Netscape Communicator education further with a look at configuration options.

- Chapter 4 focuses on some Netscape Communicator tools (such as frames and bookmarks), and highlights some interesting Internet sites.

- Chapter 5 teaches you how to obtain software via the File Transfer Protocol (FTP).

- Chapter 6 discusses using Netscape Communicator with Gopher servers.

- Chapter 7 shows you how to create your own Web pages using Netscape Composer.

- Chapter 8 shifts the discussion to Netscape Messenger, which is used to send and receive Internet electronic mail.

- Chapter 9 covers advanced Netscape Messenger components and configuration issues.

- Chapter 10 discusses RealPlayer, the multimedia tool from Progressive Networks that plays RealAudio and RealVideo files.

- Chapter 11 lists other plug-ins, software programs that extend Communicator's capabilities and enhance your Internet experiences.

- Chapter 12 explained push technology and how it's implemented in Netscape Netcaster.

- Chapter 13 introduces Netscape Collabra in the context of Usenet newsgroups. The Usenet is the world's largest discussion group, and Collabra is a powerful way of reaching Usenet users around the globe.

- Chapter 14 covers advanced Collabra functions, such as configuration and using Collabra for private discussions within an intranet. It also covers the newsreading function in Netscape Communicator.

- Chapter 15 explains Netscape Conference's features, ranging from phone calls to whiteboard and chat capabilities.

- Chapter 16 covers Netscape Calendar, a tool for organizing your schedule and meshing it with other users in your workgroup.

- Chapter 17 covers IBM Host on Demand, which opens a TN3270 session on a remote mainframe.

- Chapter 18 examines the tricky area of security and the Internet, focusing on the tools provided in Netscape Communicator.

- A glossary defines many of the terms used throughout the book.

CONVENTIONS USED IN THE BOOK

This book uses the following formatting conventions:

- New concepts or terms are noted by *italic* type. Many of these terms are defined in the glossary.
- Direct commands and menu choices are set in **bold** type.
- Command lines that are to be typed directly after a DOS command prompt are noted by `monospaced` type.

REACHING THE AUTHORS

You can drop us a line via Internet electronic mail at *reichard@mr.net*. We'll try to answer as many of your questions as possible. There's a Web page devoted to this book at *http://www.kreichard.com*.

Introducing Netscape Communicator

Welcome to the new world of Netscape Communicator and its various components! This section will introduce Netscape Communicator and provide some in-depth coverage of Netscape Navigator, the world's most popular Web browser.

In Chapter 1, we'll cover Netscape Communicator and the Internet, briefly explaining how the Internet works and how Netscape Communicator can help you master the Internet.

Chapter 2 is a beefy look at installing and configuring Netscape Communicator. It also covers some rudimentary tasks, like a first excursion onto the World Wide Web with Navigator.

Chapter 3 covers Netscape Communicator's various customization options, detailing how to make Netscape Navigator and other Communicator components do what you want.

Chapter 4 gets to why you bought this book: it teaches you how to cruise the Web.

Chapters 5 and 6 describe FTP and Gopher—two older Internet tasks that can still come in handy from time to time.

CHAPTER 1

Netscape Communicator and the Internet

Welcome to the Internet and Netscape Communicator! This chapter introduces some key concepts that you'll use to surf the Net, including:

- Connecting to the Net
- TCP/IP and more network voodoo
- URL addresses explained
- Web servers and you
- IP addresses
- Intranets

THE ON RAMP

In this chapter, we'll cover the basics of the Internet, then move to a specific discussion of Netscape Communicator and your computer. During the course of this discussion, we'll occasionally descend into some Internet jargon, some of which is on the technical side. Be warned that there is Internet jargon, and there is *Internet jargon* of a more serious sort. Here, we'll give you the jargon that you'll need to deal with and avoid the stuff that only a serious and dedicated NetHead would love.

We'll begin with a general description of the Internet, followed by a look at how Netscape Communicator fits into the Internet.

YOUR LINK TO THE WEB

Netscape Communicator won't do a whole lot of good if it's not running on a *network* of some sort. This network will probably be the Internet, but Netscape Communicator can also be used on a corporate network that's not connected to the rest of the world. (The trendy term for this is *intranet*, which we'll explain later.) Still, since Netscape Communicator will probably be connected to the Internet, that aspect of Netscape Communicator connectivity will be covered here. (The topic of connecting Netscape Communicator to local and network files will be covered in Chapter 4.)

It's best to begin with an overview of the Internet and your computer's place in it.

THE INTERNET

A lot has been written about the Internet in the last couple of years—enough to prop up the economy of a Third World country. Still, despite the gallons of ink and tons of newsprint, people still have a somewhat amorphous view of the Internet. Yes, it seems to be pervasive in our society (although perhaps not as important as the Web fetishists from the likes of *Wired* magazine would have us believe), but for many, the Internet is a little too large for them to get their arms around.

Basically, the Internet is a collection of computer networks that speak the same underlying language—*Transmission Control Protocol/Internet Protocol*, more commonly known as TCP/IP. This *networking protocol* is one of many ways that computers can speak to one another. (You may have used some of the other protocols if you've worked with computers before; computers connected by Novell NetWare speak one protocol, while Macintoshes connected with AppleTalk speak another protocol.) These networks, when viewed together, are referred to as the *Internet*. As far as networking protocols go, TCP/IP is considered the most common denominator—it's not necessarily as complex as other networking protocols (such as the aforementioned NetWare), but it has the advantage of being supported on virtually every kind of computer, from Cray supercomputers to Macintoshes to personal computers running Windows.

HOT LINK

To use Netscape Communicator on the Internet, your computer will need to speak TCP/IP on some level. This is discussed in Chapter 2.

In addition to its collection of networks, the Internet also consists of a collection of services, including:

- The World Wide Web
- The Usenet newsgroups
- Gopher servers
- Electronic mail
- FTP servers
- Chat services

Each of these services can be accessed on some level by Netscape Communicator, as you learned in the Introduction. Accordingly, each will be covered in its own section to varying levels of detail. But before we discuss the services, we'll discuss the Internet itself.

IP Addresses

With such a common denominator, computers on the Internet can directly speak to one another, as one computer will make a request to another computer. How does your computer know how to speak directly to another computer? Because every computer on the Internet has a distinct *Internet Protocol* (or IP) address. This address always looks like:

xxx.xxx.xxx.xxx

where numbers take the place of *x*. These addresses are assigned by an Internet standards group. The addresses are coordinated on an international level to make sure that two computers aren't assigned the same IP address.

Your computer will need an IP address to be part of the Internet. This means that you'll need Internet access of some sort. For example, you might have Internet access at work, and so your IP address will be assigned through your company. Some of you will sign up for Internet access through a *service provider*, which will probably assign you a new IP address each time you login the Internet. (Both methods will be covered in Chapter 2 in some detail.) There's really no advantage to either method.

Internet Connections

Armed with this IP address, your computer literally becomes part of the Internet. This connection is maintained by networking software of some sort that speaks TCP/IP.

What kind of software you use will depend on your operating system and your personal preferences. Windows 95 has TCP/IP connectivity tools built directly into it. Windows 3.1 and Macintosh users can easily obtain the tools needed for these connections. We'll cover all three operating systems and their setup in Chapter 2. The thing to remember here is that Netscape Communicator doesn't provide the tools for connecting to the Internet (unless you've purchased the Personal Edition, which can be a very evil way of connecting to the Internet)—you'll need to go out and get the tools if your operating system doesn't have them.

THE WORLD WIDE WEB

Netscape Navigator began life as a *Web browser*—a piece of software designed to view World Wide Web pages on the Internet. The latest version, expanded to Netscape Communicator, transcends this original design, offering mail and news capabilities in addition to the Web usage.

However, you'll use Netscape Navigator primarily to view Web pages. Basically, a Web page is a computer file stored on a remote computer called a *Web server*. This server takes a request from Netscape Navigator to pass along a file. This file can be straight text, or it can be formatted in the HyperText Markup Language (known more informally as HTML). This format takes the form of tags that accompany text. Netscape Navigator takes these tags and makes them into the rich, graphical environment you associate with the Internet. As such, it could be formatted with *links* to other Web pages or contain graphics and maps. These HTML files aren't written for a particular operating system; they're written to work with any Web browser on any operating system. Figure 1.1 shows a typical Web page, and Figure 1.2 shows the underlying HTML file that goes across the Internet.

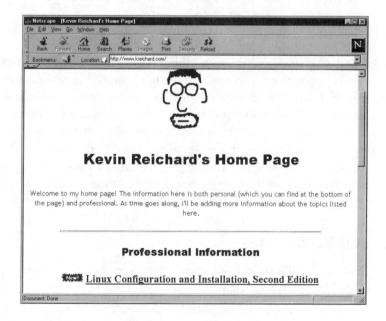

Figure 1.1 *A rendered Web page.*

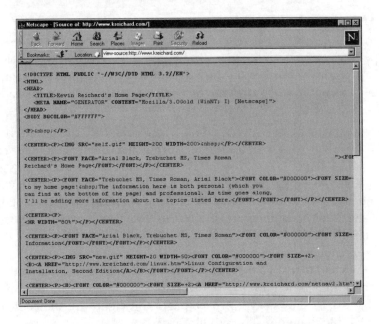

Figure 1.2 *The underlying HTML code for the page shown in Figure 1.1.*

A Web page really isn't analogous to anything else. Sure, it's like a computer text file in some ways, but the typical text file doesn't contain direct links to other documents or embedded graphics. Anything is fair game when it comes to the content of a Web page. You can have Web pages devoted to serious topics like government data and software support or frivolous topics like exploding heads, or live-action shots of fish tanks or coffee machines. There are millions of Web pages out there, and part of the pure delight of perusing the Web is the serendipity when you go through a series of links and find a slew of unexpected surprises along the way. Yes, this voyage is essentially linear—you're really just moving from Web page to Web page—but the ease of movement and the flashy graphics make the journey much richer than reading a book.

URLs and Web Pages

With millions and millions of Web pages, Netscape Navigator needs a way to find them and keep track of them.

Each Web page has a unique Uniform Resource Locator, or URL. Only one page can exist at a URL. The various portions of a URL tell Netscape Navigator and the Internet where to look for the file, as well as what sort of data is contained in the file. Look at the following URL, which connects you to the home page for one of the authors of this book:

http://www.kreichard.com

When you break down this address, you see that it has several distinct parts:

- *http* tells Netscape Navigator to use the HyperText Transfer Protocol (HTTP) to transfer the file to your computer.

- *www* is short for World Wide Web. Most, but not all, Web pages begin with *www.*

- *kreichard* is the unique name of the organization that hosts the Web page.

- *com* tells us that a commercial entity hosts the Web site.

There can be many variations. The "official" URL types are listed in Table 1.1.

Table 1.1 *The Official URL Types.*

TYPE	EXPLANATION
http	Transfers Web pages in the HyperText Transfer Protocol with a Web server.
mail	Sends electronic mail to a mail server.
news	Reads Usenet newsgroups from a news server.
ftp	Begins File Transfer Protocol (FTP) sessions with an FTP server.
gopher	Connects to a Gopher server.
telnet	Initiates telnet session with a remote computer.

This is how you get a wide assortment of URLs, such as the following:

http://www.mr.net

http://ourworld.compuserve.com:80/homepages/reichard/

ftp://ftp.microsoft.com

news:comp.answers

The *com* designation used in our earlier example stands for a commercial entity. Other Web sites may be located in other commercial or noncommercial entities that specialize in Internet access (*net*), colleges (*edu*), the military (*mil*), non-commercial (*org*), or governmental bodies (*gov*). In addition, the end of a URL may have a reference to the originating country. Web sites in Canada typically end with a *ca,* while British sites end with *uk* and German sites end with *de.* If a URL lacks such a designation, it's assumed that it's located in the United States (for, as we all know, the United States is the center of the universe).

When you look closely at *http://www.kreichard.com,* you'll see that it contains some elements that don't make any sense, specifically the colon and the two slashes. Don't worry—it's not supposed to make sense. You don't need to understand the format; all you need to do is make sure that the data is entered properly.

Paths on the Straight and Narrow

Take a close look at the address:

http://ourworld.compuserve.com:80/homepages/reichard/

It is complicated and a pain to type. However, it explains a few things about Web sites and how they are organized.

A Web site is merely a computer hooked to the Internet that distributes Web pages to people like you. In the above example, the actual server's address is:

ourworld.compuserve.com

The other elements provide additional information about the Web page you want. The *80* tells the Web browser to use a specific port on the Web server (this is relatively unimportant for you to know, so don't bother committing any brain cells to long-term memory here). The remainder, */homepages/reichard/,* tells you that the file you want is called **reichard**, and it's stored in a directory called **homepages**. DOS and UNIX users will instantly recognize that the remainder is part of a pathname identifying exactly where the desired file is in the server's directory structure. (This web site doesn't actually exist, by the way.)

In some ways, we're getting ahead of ourselves here. You'll learn more about the Web and its conventions after you've learned more about Netscape Navigator and actually had a chance to use it.

Intranets

There's one problem with connecting to the world at large—security. Many companies are finding that it's not worth the hassle to connect their networks to the outside world, for fear some hacker will swoop in and trash valuable corporate data. (Never mind that this is a relatively rare occurrence. Here, perception is far more compelling than reality.)

However, that doesn't mean that these companies are not using Netscape Communicator. Instead of connecting their networks to the outside, they are merely keeping them local and using Netscape Communicator to distribute data throughout the enterprise. A Web server is a Web server, whether it's located down the hall in the IS department or in some closet halfway across the world. In these situations, companies are said to be setting up *intranets* (as opposed to *Internet*—get it?) and using Netscape Communicator to communicate with internal network servers.

In these instances, you might use Netscape Communicator a little differently that you would on the Web, and this primarily affects how URLs are set up. If you do have an intranet, you probably have an IS department that's available to handle any questions you may have about URL addressing. In many other ways, however, the way you use Netscape Communicator will be the same on intranets and the Internet, so this book won't distinguish between the two.

NETSCAPE COMMUNICATOR AND OPERATING SYSTEMS

On the surface, Netscape Communicator doesn't appear to be overly complex software. Conceptually, it isn't—it's merely a program that translates the coded text sent over the Internet into a form you can read on your local computer.

The transaction is actually pretty simple. You load Navigator on your computer. It sends a message to a preselected Internet *server,* asking the server for a specific document. The server then sends out the document to your computer in text form. It's then up to your computer to take this text and use local resources (e.g., fonts, colors) to turn the page into graphical format.

 You'll learn how to change fonts and colors in Chapter 3.

HOT LINK

This reliance on local resources is one of the great strengths of the Internet (it cuts down on the traffic sent over the Net). It also means that Web pages can look slightly different, depending on which computer and Web browser is doing the work. In Figures 1.3, 1.4, and 1.5, the same Web page is shown rendered on three different copies of Netscape Communicator.

Figure 1.3 *A Web page rendered on Windows 95, using Navigator.*

Figure 1.4 *The same Web page rendered on Linux, using Navigator.*

Figure 1.5   *The same Web page rendered on the Macintosh, using Navigator.*

One of the best things about Netscape Communicator is that there are versions for many different operating systems—even operating systems like Linux and IBM OS /2. Communicator is offered for the following operating systems:

Windows 95

Windows NT 3.51 and 4.0

Windows 3.1 and 3.11

OS/2 Warp

Linux

BSD Unix 3.0

SCO Unix

Apple Macintosh OS 7.1 and higher (68K)

Apple Macintosh OS 7.1 and higher (PowerPC)

Digital Alpha (Digital Unix 3.2 and higher)

Digital Alpha (Windows NT 3.51 and 4.0)

Hewlett-Packard (HP-UX 9.03, 9.05, 10.x and higher)

IBM RS/6000 (AIX 4.1 and higher)

Silicon Graphics (Irix 5.3, 6.2 and higher)

Sun SPARC (Solaris 2.4 and higher)

Sun SPARC (Sun OS 4.1.3 and 4.1.4)

Even though the focus is on Netscape Communicator for Windows and Macintosh users, that doesn't mean that users of older versions of Netscape Navigator can't benefit from this book. Most of the basic functions described here—especially the material found in Chapters 1–4—applies to older versions of Netscape Navigator.

THE NEW COMMUNICATOR: NAVIGATOR AND MORE

As you learned in the Introduction, the new Netscape Communicator is much more than an update of the Navigator Web browser—it's a set of powerful tools that can extend your computing power on the Internet. Yes, there's a new version of Netscape Navigator, which you've already seen in action throughout this chapter, but Netscape Communicator also includes several other components:

- **Netscape Messenger** manages electronic-mail and Usenet newsgroup messages. It's shown in Figure 1.6. Most users will want to use this feature for their electronic-mail management; in addition, the newsgroup features can be applied both to the global Usenet and to locally run newsgroups on an intranet.

- **Netscape Composer** is meant for creating and editing HTML (Web) pages. You can use it to import existing Web pages, or you can create a page from scratch. While Netscape Composer doesn't have the advanced functionality of a Hot Dog or even Microsoft Front Page, it does work for most basic Web-page needs. It's shown in Figure 1.7.

- **Netscape Conference** is a tool for placing phone calls via the Internet. It can also be used for videoconferencing and whiteboard functions. It's shown in Figure 1.8.

- **Netscape Collabra** is Web-based groupware.

- **Netscape Calendar** is a new calendar and scheduling program that's part of the Professional Edition.

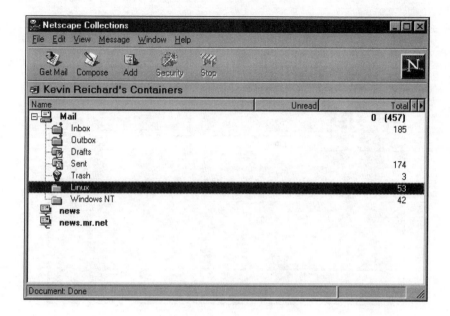

Figure 1.6 Netscape Messenger.

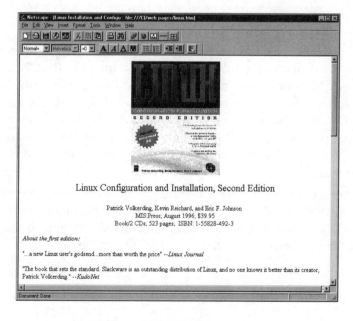

Figure 1.7 Netscape Composer.

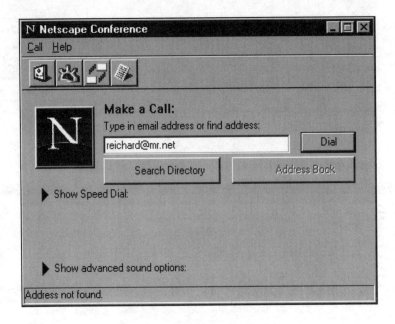

Figure 1.8 *Netscape Conference.*

WHERE CAN I GET COMMUNICATOR?

Whenever you deal with the Internet, there are a ton of Catch-22s. Unless you already own Netscape Communicator, you'll find that getting Netscape Communicator is more of a problem than you anticipated. Yes, you can buy Netscape Communicator at your local computer store, but it's not necessarily going to be the most recent version (in our experience, retail versions of Netscape products tended to lag behind the most recent versions by two to three months).

Your bet is to grab Netscape Communicator directly from the Internet. It doesn't matter if you're directly connected to the Internet or indirectly like using America Online, Prodigy, or CompuServe). All you need is the ability to transfer a file to your hard drive.

GRABBING COMMUNICATOR FROM THE WEB

Many of you are already connected to the Internet and using a Web brov
like Netscape Navigator or Microsoft Explorer, or a commercial service
CompuServe, Prodigy, or America Online. In these cases, you can use the (
nection to grab Netscape Communicator directly from the Netsc
Communications Web site.

You'll want to connect to the Netscape Communications home p;
home.netscape.com. To do that, enter the following URL in your browser's URL f

http://home.netscape.com

This connects you to the Netscape home page.

On this page, you'll see some sort of announcement regarding the r
recent version of Netscape Communicator. In the past, it was a button lab
Netscape Now! that was directly linked to a Web page that guided you thrc
the download process. Click on this button or one like it. If past proced
are any guide, you begin by choosing your operating system. Click on
appropriate OS, and then follow the directions for downloading your
copy. Your Web browser may prompt you for a course of action when
begin the download; you'll want to save the file to disk. It doesn't really
ter where you store this file on your hard drive, just be warned that it ca
as large as 5 megabytes, depending on the version you download.

After you download the file, you can sever your connection to
Internet. Armed with a copy of Netscape Communicator, you're ready fo
next big step: actually installing and configuring Netscape Communic
the topic of the next chapter.

SUMMARY

This short introductory chapter explains some of the key concepts under
the Internet, the World Wide Web, and Netscape Communicator. Conne
to the Internet isn't very difficult, but you do need to know about ;
things—like TCP/IP, IP addresses, and Web servers—before you can full
Netscape Navigator.

In the next chapter, we'll discuss how to acquire Netscape Navigat'
alternative means, as well as how to use Netscape Navigator and how t
around using pull-down menus, directory buttons, and the toolbar.

CHAPTER 2

Installing and Using Netscape Communicator

Now it's time to get to the specifics—installing and using Netscape Communicator. In this long chapter, you'll cover the following topics:

- Connecting to the Internet
- Setting up Windows 95 to connect to the Internet
- Setting up Trumpet Winsock under Windows
- Grabbing Windows 95, Windows 3.1, Macintosh, and UNIX versions of Netscape Communicator
- Touring the main elements of Communicator

- Frames
- Going though the pulldown menus
- Entering a URL

LAYING THE GROUNDWORK

Now that you know all there is to know about the Internet—just kidding!—it's time to prepare your computer for installing and running Netscape Communicator. In most cases, it will be a matter of making sure that your computer is connected correctly to the Internet. If it is, you can grab Communicator directly from Netscape Communications.

THE INTERNET AND YOUR CONNECTION

Back in the Dark Ages of computing, connectivity to the Internet was something of a status symbol, as self-proclaimed Net Geeks controlled the action. Today, it's remarkably simple to connect to the Internet for computer users of all sorts, as you don't need to be a Net Geek to cruise the Web with Communicator.

How you connect to the Internet will vary in the specifics. Generally, however, there are two major types of Internet connections: *direct* and *dial-up*. Each type will be covered here.

A Direct Connection to the Internet

When you have a direct connection to the Internet, your computer system has a full-time, open network connection to the Internet. In this instance, your computer is running either TCP/IP or Novell Netware networking software that connects directly to a server on your network, which then maintains the full-time Internet link.

If you've been around computing at all, you realize that talk of networking software and servers entails some serious dollars. Generally, only corporations maintain direct Internet links, although there are some serious net surfers who make the requisite investments. And if you have a dedicated link to the Internet, chances are that you're not going to need an introductory look at connecting to the Internet with Netscape Communicator, as is the case with this book—so we're not going to explain more about dedicated links. Suffice it to say that if you've got a dedicated link to the Internet, you've already got a system administrator who can help you set up Netscape Communicator to work with your network.

If you're a home user, you won't want to pursue a direct connection to the Internet, unless you're ready to pony up hundreds of dollars for specialized networking equipment. Instead, you'll either have or want to purchase a dial-up connection to the Internet, one that combines a modem, networking software, and Netscape Communicator to forge your way across the World Wide Web.

Dial-Up Connections to the Internet

The more common connectivity method for the Internet is a dial-up account with an Internet service provider, and this is the route you'll want to pursue.

Basically, a dial-up account lets you temporarily become part of the Internet. Your computer will be running special software that accomplishes this. When you make a connection, most often the Internet server will assign you an *IP address* that temporarily establishes your computer as part of the Internet. When you're finished with your business on the Web, the IP address is then assigned to another user. In Internet parlance, these IP addresses are *dynamically* assigned, as they'll usually be different every time you connect to the Internet.

These connections occur using two different kind of networking protocols: The older Serial Line Internet Protocol (SLIP) or the newer Point-to-Point Protocol (PPP). PPP is preferable, as it's easier to set up and use, and it's maintenance-free. Virtually all service providers support PPP.

This special software differs by operating system:

- Windows 3.1 or Windows for Workgroups will need either a Winsock manager like Trumpet Winsock or a full-featured TCP/IP package from the likes of NetManage (sold under the Chameleon name). However, full-featured TCP/IP can cost upwards of $500—a rather steep price for getting on the Internet. You're better off with Trumpet Winsock, which you can grab from *http://www.trumpet.com.au, ftp://jazz.trumpet.com.au,* or *ftp://ftp.trumpet.com.* At the time this book was written, the latest version of Trumpet Winsock was 3.0d, and its filename was **twsk30d.exe**. It supports both SLIP and PPP. We'll explain how to use Trumpet Winsock later in this chapter.

- Windows 95 and Windows NT 4.0 Workstation/Server users can use the operating system's built-in SLIP and PPP tools. Later in this chapter, we'll explain how to set this up. Also, Windows 95/NT users can use the Trumpet Winsock to connect to the Internet, but this means using the Windows 3.1 version of Netscape Communicator instead of the Windows 95/NT version. (We'll explain this further later in this chapter.)

- Macintosh users will need MacTCP, which includes MacPPP or MacSLIP. This software comes directly from Apple and is distributed in many ways. If you're already using America Online, you can download this software from the software libraries (keyword: AppleComputer). If you're connected to the Internet, you can use FTP to grab this software from *ftp.info.apple.com/Apple_Support_Area/Apple_SW_Updates/ US/Macintosh/Networking-Communications/Open_Transport/* (yes, amazingly enough, this is the URL!). Setting this up can be rather simple, but if the notion of setting up a networking connection with your Macintosh is daunting, you should check out one of several books on using MacTCP, such as Adam Engst's *Internet Starter Kit.* (As a matter of fact, this book is an excellent place to start, and since it has all the software you need, the book is a good investment.)

If the past is any guide, Netscape Communicator will be sold commercially through retail outlets like CompUSA and Software Etc. This version may or may not include networking software.

N O T E

What Is a Service Provider?

If you don't yet own networking software, you may be able to get some through your service provider. An *Internet service provider* maintains a computer system that allows you to connect directly to the Internet using a dial-up connection. There are literally hundreds of service providers in the United

States (indeed, it's been a growth industry all on its own), and they range from giants like Netcom and PSI to smaller, regional outfits like Minnesota Regional Network.

Choosing a service provider will take a little research on your part, as pricing schedules and services vary widely. Some national service providers, such as Portal or Netcom, maintain local dial-up connections in hundreds of North American cities. Other regional service providers, such as the Minnesota Regional Network, maintain dial-up lines for a small set of cities in a limited geographical area. At the bottom of the food chain are small service providers that set up shop in a single city. Prices vary, as some small service providers allow unlimited access for less than $30 a month, while other larger providers may charge upwards of $50 a month.

Also, the major online networks (CompuServe, America Online, Microsoft Network) are converting their services to be Internet access points. In the past, you were forced to use a proprietary Web browser through these services. If you live in an area that isn't served by an Internet service provider, you may want to see if you can get straight Internet access through an online network's 800-number access. This will be a little more expensive than a service provider would charge, but at least you'd have reliable Internet access without long-distance charges.

If you have access to the Web and want to check out some listings of Internet service providers, enter one of the following URLs in your Web browser:

- *http://thelist.com*
- *http://www.primus.com/providers*
- *http://www.stars.com/Vlib/Misc/Providers.html*
- *http://union.ncsa.uiuc.edu/HyperNews/get/www/leasing.html*
- *http://budgetweb.com/budgetweb/*
- *http://budgetweb.com/hndocs/list.shtml*
- *http://www.yahoo.com/Business_and_Economy/Companies/ Internet_Services/Web_Presence_Providers/*

TIP

How do you evaluate a service provider? Well, a good tip is to avoid a service provider that's located in someone's basement or garage. (Yes, they exist.) Another way is to ask how many modems the service provider has. A larger outfit like Netcom has a rather large number of access points, while a small service provider will have a limited number of modems. This becomes a problem when you try to access your service provider during high-usage times, such as right away in the morning (when everyone is checking their electronic mail) or in the shank of the evening.

When you sign up for an Internet account, you should get a listing of relevant Internet addresses and servers from your service provider. You'll need these to set up your computer. In the next two sections, we'll discuss how to set up your computer for the Internet.

Setting Up a Winsock and TCP/IP Connection

Here, we'll assume that you already have grabbed Trumpet Winsock from the Internet. (Again, you can grab it from *http://www.trumpet.com.au* or *ftp://ftp.trumpet.com.*) You'll also need the PKZip or WinZip utility to *unzip* the file.

N O T E

Yes, this is a conundrum—how can you get on the Internet without having an Internet setup? The thing to remember about the Internet is that it's really not for the pure beginner, as it involves a little bit of telecommunications savvy and some basic computer skills.

Still, this doesn't answer the question of where you can get Trumpet Winsock. Since you need a modem to get on the Internet, you can use that modem to get this software. Many large bulletin-board systems feature Trumpet Winsock. In addition, the major online services (CompuServe, America Online, Prodigy) also have Trumpet Winsock in their software libraries.

In fact, it might be a good idea to join an online service on a limited basis, if only to be able to grab the Internet software you need. They all have membership plans where you get between 4 and 10 free hours when you sign up—which is plenty of time to get the software you need and then cancel your membership.

It's easiest to put the downloaded **twsk30d.exe** file in its own directory, along with the **pkunzip.exe** or **unzip.exe** file used to unzip it.

Basically, there are only a few things you need to do to set up Trumpet Winsock in the configuration screen shown in Figure 2.1:

- You'll need to enter the **Name Server** (also known as the Domain Name Server, or DNS) of your service provider. This information should have been provided when you signed up for Internet access.

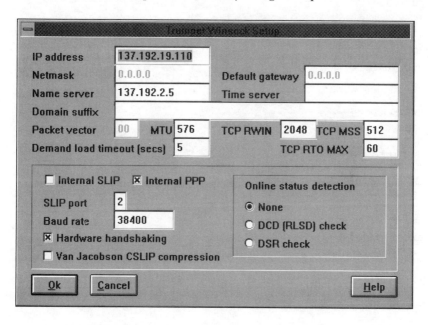

Figure 2.1 *The setup screen for Trumpet Winsock.*

- You'll need to specify whether you use SLIP or PPP for connectivity. The default is SLIP, although most users will want to use PPP.
- You'll need to tell Trumpet Winsock which comm (or serial) port your modem uses; Trumpet Winsock uses the term **SLIP port** to set the comm port. The default is COM1.

Trumpet Winsock uses scripts to login to Internet servers. These scripts dial the number and either pass along your username and password or prompt you to do so. The default login script is stored in the filename **login.cmd**, but you'll want to change it. Here's a script that will connect your computer to an Internet server, prompt you for a username and password, and then initiating the PPP connection:

```
output atdtxxxxxxx\13
input 60 CONNECT
output \13
input 30 Username:
username <username>
output \u\13
input 60 Password:
password <password>
output \p\13
output ppp\13

input 30 Your IP address is
#
# parse address
#
address 30
input 30 \n
#
# we are now connected, logged in and in ppp mode.
#
display \n
display Connected.  Your IP address is \i.\n
```

The only customization you need to make to this script is to enter the phone number of your service provider in the first line, in the place of *xxxxxxx*. If you're using SLIP instead of PPP, you'll want to change this line:

```
output ppp\13
```

to:

```
output slip\13
```

Store the script under the name of **login.cmd** in the Trumpet directory, in the place of the existing **login.cmd** command.

To test the script, select **Login** from the Dialer menu. This command runs the **login.cmd** script. If everything works as it should, you should have a working link to the Internet and the underlying network tool needed to run Netscape Communicator. There are some other things you can do to customize Trumpet Winsock, such as telling it to connect to the Internet automatically every time you load the software, but basically your work with Trumpet Winsock is done.

 You can use Trumpet Winsock to connect to the Internet under Windows 95. However, if you use Trumpet Winsock you'll need to use the Windows 3.1 (i.e., the 16-bit) version of Windows 95.

N O T E

Setting Up the TCP/IP PPP Connection in Windows 95

Windows 95 was one of the most-hyped events in computer history, so you're excused if you're really sick about hearing about it. If you're a user, however, you're probably not concerned about the hype; rather, you're concerned about connecting to the Internet. It's really not a difficult task—but it's not necessarily simple, either. Just involved.

Windows 95 features built-in networking for direct connections to an Internet service provider. This means that you won't need separate networking software (such as Trumpet Winsock) to connect to the Internet. It does mean, however, that you'll need to do some preliminary configuration work with Windows 95 before you can use *any* Internet software, much less Netscape Communicator. This is work you'll have to do no matter what, even if your PC came preloaded and configured with Windows 95.

By and large, the instructions here also apply to Windows NT 4.0 configuration, for either the Workstation or Server versions.

N O T E

Under the Surface

Configuring the Internet connection with Windows 95 is basically a three-step procedure:

- Installing a modem
- Installing and configuring TCP/IP
- Installing dial-up connections

Installing a Modem

Windows 95 likes to know what kind of modem in installed on your computer. Generally speaking, you can get by if your system assumes that there's a generic Hayes-compatible modem, but this won't allow you to take advantage of specific features found on various modems (such as fax capabilities, which can also be utilized under Windows 95). If you installed Windows 95 from scratch or configured Windows 95 on a PC where it was preinstalled, the setup procedure attempted to detect and install a modem.

If you skipped this step, you'll need to install a modem. First, open **Control Panel** and then select **Modems**. When you choose **Add**, Windows 95 will attempt to find a modem. If it cannot—which is sometimes the case with older or off-brand modems—you'll need to find your modem in a list of modems, or else find a listing that's close to your modem. (When in doubt, choose the Generic Hayes configuration.) If you choose a generic listing, you'll need to go through the settings and make sure they're appropriate for your modem, such as the *port*, the maximum speed, the connection preferences (data bits, parity and stop bits), and port settings.

Basically, this process is pretty self-explanatory; follow the instructions, and then you're ready to move on to a larger and somewhat more complicated task: Installing and configuring the networking components.

Installing and Configuring TCP/IP

As you learned in Chapter 1, TCP/IP is the lingua franca of the Internet, and to get on the Internet you're going to need to add TCP/IP to your system.

First, you need to check if TCP/IP and dial-up networking are already installed. You can do so by opening the My Computer window. If TCP/IP and dial-up networking were installed, there would be a folder called Dial-Up Networking near the bottom of the window. (If you installed Microsoft Plus!, dial-up networking would be automatically installed.)

Assuming that networking isn't already installed, your next step is to install it. From the Control Panel window under My Computer, you'll want to double-click on the icon entitled **Network**. This brings up a window like the one shown in Figure 2.2.

You want to add a network protocol, so you'll want to press the Add button. Windows 95 will respond with a dialog box that asks you for the type of network you want to install (as shown in Figure 2.3). You'll want to choose client.

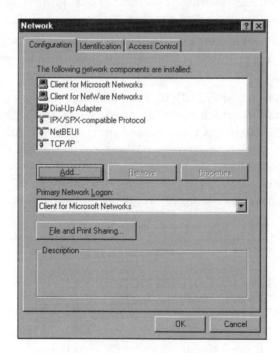

Figure 2.2 *The Network window.*

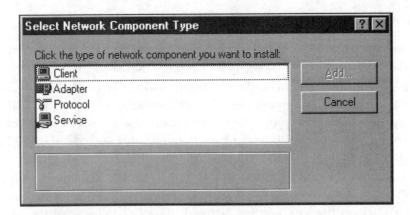

Figure 2.3 *The Select Network Component dialog box.*

You'll be presented with another dialog box entitled Select Network Client. Here, you'll select **Microsoft** under the list of manufacturers, followed by **Client for Microsoft Networks**. At the end of this process, select **OK**, which will return you to the Network dialog box.

You're not through yet; as a matter of fact, you're just beginning. You've just installed some preliminary networking software that's needed before you can run TCP/IP.

Your next step is install TCP/IP. With the Network dialog box still open, press the **Add** button, which brings up the Select Network Component Type dialog box again. Highlight **Protocol** and then select the **Add** button. You'll see a dialog box entitled Select Network Protocol that lists manufacturers and network protocols. Highlight **Microsoft** and then double-click on **TCP/IP**. You'll be returned to the Network dialog box, and you'll see that **TCP/IP** appears at the bottom of the list of installed components.

Don't close that Network dialog box quite yet; you'll still need it for the next step in the installation process.

Installing Dial-Up Connections

Now that the networking protocol is installed, you'll need to tell Windows 95 that you want to connect to the Internet via a dial-up connection.

Basically, you'll need to tell Windows 95 what device you want to use for Internet connectivity. Begin by clicking on the **Add** button, which brings up the now-familiar Select Network Component Type dialog box. Select **Adapter** and then click on the **Add** button. In the resulting dialog box, Select Network Adapters, choose **Microsoft** from the list of manufacturers and then **Dial-Up Adapters** under the list of network adapters. This brings you back to the Network dialog box. Don't close this dialog box, as you'll need to begin there for your next task.

Take a break, grab a cup of coffee or tea, and then get prepared for the final stretch.

Configuring Your Dial-Up Connection

Now you're ready to tell Windows 95 how to connect to the Internet. Here, we're going to assume that you're using a PPP connection to the Internet. If you have a choice between SLIP and PPP, you'll definitely want to go with PPP.

Under the Network dialog box, you'll want to select **TCP/IP** from the list of installed components and then press the **Properties** box. This brings up a dialog box entitled TCP/IP Properties (as shown in Figure 2.4), where you'll do a lot of work.

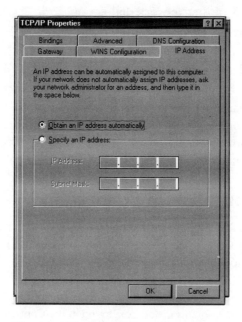

Figure 2.4 *The TCP/IP Properties dialog box.*

Begin with the IP Address page. If you have a dynamically allocated IP address from your service provider, you'll want to make sure that the **Obtain an IP address automatically** line is checked. If your service provider or your network administrator gives you a specific IP address to use every time you log on the Internet (which probably won't happen), you'll want to make sure that the **Specify an IP address** line is selected, with the proper information filled in the IP Address and Subnet Mask lines. (If you're told to use a specific IP address, you'll be given this information.)

You can ignore the WINS Configuration page, as well as the Gateway and Advanced pages.

Under DNS Configuration, you'll need to select **Enable DNS** and enter your host address, the domain, and the Domain Name Server address provided by your service provider or your network administrator. Actually, all you really need to enter is a single DNS address, but most service providers provide two or more DNS addresses.

Finally, under Bindings, you'll want to make sure that the **Client for Microsoft Networks** box is selected.

After all of this is done, press the **OK** button at the bottom of the page. This brings you back to the Network dialog box.

Finally, there are a few things you'll want to do before leaving the Network dialog box.

First, make sure that **Client for Microsoft Networks** is showing as your **Primary Network Logon**. If not, click on the list of choices and highlight it.

Next, select **Identification** and enter information in the three available fields. If you're doing only dialup networking, you can pretty much enter anything you want—but you do need to enter something. Press the **OK** button and close the Network dialog box.

Setting Up Your Dial-Up Connection

You're now ready to tell Windows 95 how to actually connect to the Internet. If you open the My Computer window, you'll see that there's a folder on the bottom of the window entitled Dial-Up Networking.

N O T E

If the Dial-Up Networking icon isn't there, you'll need to install it. Open the Add/Remove Programs dialog box, found in the Control Panel window. Select **Windows Setup** and then select **Communications**, followed by pressing the **Details** button. There should be four components listed. Make sure that the **Dial-Up Networking** line is checked. Select **OK** and close all the dialog boxes.

There should be an icon entitled **Make New Connection** in the Dial-Up Networking box. Double-click on this icon, which brings up a dialog box shown in Figure 2.5.

Windows 95 automatically inserts My Connection in the Type a name for the computer you are dialing field; unless you have a good reason, you should leave this title as it is. If you've installed a modem successfully (it seems like hours since you entered this information earlier in this chapter!), it will appear in the Select a modem: field.

After selecting **Next**, you'll see a dialog box entitled Make New Connection, where you enter the phone number of your service provider.

After choosing **Next**, you'll be congratulated for setting up a dialup connection, and prompted to press **Finish** to end this chore. A new icon called **My Connection** (or whatever you named your connection) appears in your Dial-Up Networking window.

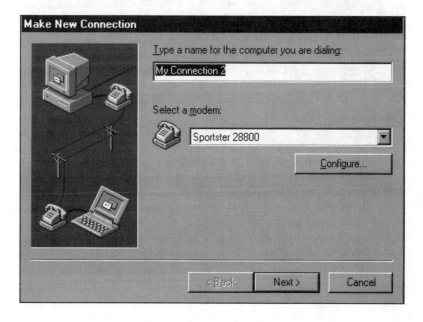

Figure 2.5 *The Make New Connection dialog box.*

Trying a Connection

Now you're ready to prepare for a connection. First, you'll need to make sure that a few things are set properly.

Highlight the **My Connection** icon and then select **Properties** from the File menu. Then select the **Configure** button under the modem type, which brings a window named Your Modem Properties (where **Your Modem** is the name of your modem). Under **Options**, make sure that the **Bring up terminal window after dialing** box is selected. Select **OK** and then **OK** again when the My Connection dialog box appears.

Now, hold your breath and double-click on the **My Connection** icon. This brings up a dialog box called Connect To, as shown in Figure 2.6. Enter your user name and password, and then press the **Connect** button.

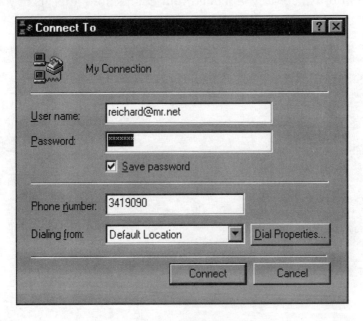

Figure 2.6 *The Connect To dialog box.*

If all goes well, you'll see a window called Connecting to My Connection on the screen and hear a dial tone on your modem, followed by a phone number being dialed and then a connection to your service provider. A screen entitled Post-Dial Terminal Screen appears (as shown in Figure 2.7), where you enter your username, password, and whatever information your service provider requires. After you're through, press the **F7** button. After some networking information is traded, you should see a window that says **Connected to My Connection**, which tells you at what speed you are connected, as well as a line that tells you how long you've been connected. When you're through with the Internet, press the **Disconnect** button.

You could also edit a connection script for connecting automatically to the Internet. Example scripts can be found in the /system32/ras directory, along with instructions on how to program and set up your own script.

There you are! Now it's time to actually download Netscape Communicator.

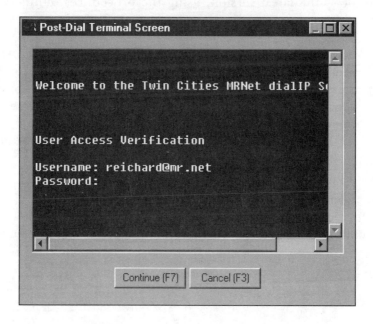

Figure 2.7 *The Post-Dial Terminal Screen.*

Downloading Netscape Communicator

Netscape Communications makes copies of Netscape Communicator free of charge via the Internet. This applies only for personal, evaluation, or student usage; corporate users must license Netscape Communicator.

Having said that, however, Netscape Communicator does make it simple for you to download a copy from the Internet. If you're already connected to the Internet and have a Web browser (as in the case of Windows 95 users, who have Microsoft's Internet Explorer handy), you can point your browser to:

http://home.netscape.com

or

ftp://ftp.netscape.com/pub/navigator/

and download the latest version, using the procedures outlined on the Netscape Web pages.

NOTE   During the download process, you're asked to select a site from where you want to download Netscape Communicator. The instructions say to pick a site close to you, but this advice doesn't make any sense when you stop and consider that the Internet is a worldwide phenomenon and distance is usually irrelevant. Instead of choosing a close site, choose a site that's probably not very busy; delays in downloads usually occur because of overworked servers, not because of overwhelmed phone lines.

If you're relatively conversant with the Internet and use Windows 95, you can use the ftp tool to grab Netscape Communicator. To do so, open a MS-DOS window while connected to the Internet and type the following command line:

```
C:\WINDOWS> ftp
ftp>
```

From this prompt you can connect to the Netscape ftp server at *ftp://ftp.netscape.com/pub/navigator/*. (Actually, the following instructions apply to *any* FTP connection, not just the one found in Windows 95.) The beginning of the transaction is shown in Figure 2.8.

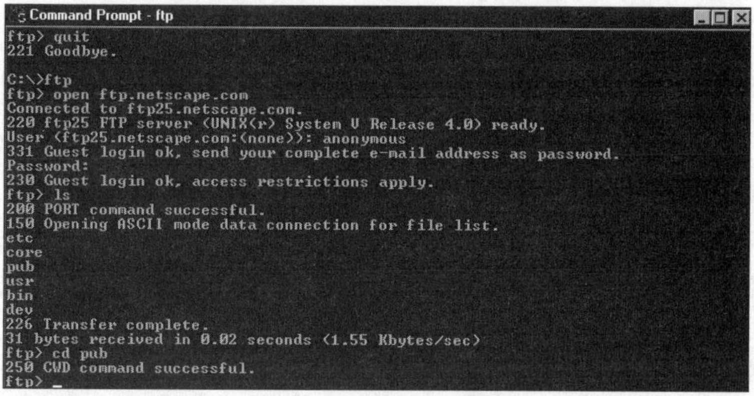

Figure 2.8 Using FTP to get Netscape Communicator.

The thing to note here is that you should supply *anonymous* as a user name, and type in your e-mail address as your password.

After you're in the server, you'll need to make your way to the proper sub-directory. Do so by entering the following command lines:

```
ftp> cd pub
ftp> cd communicator
ftp> cd 4.0
ftp> cd current
ftp> ls
```

At this point there should be a listing of operating systems something like the following:

```
mac
unix
windows
```

You'll need to select which operating system to go for. To switch to the windows directory, you'd use the following command line:

```
ftp> cd windows
```

Call up a listing of the contents of the current directory with the following command line:

```
ftp> ls
200 PORT command successful
150 Opening ASCII mode data connection for file list

...

226 Transfer complete
```

This will give you a listing of the files in the directory. There should also be a README file of some sort that will explain the files. Generally speaking, Netscape places a **32** somewhere in the filename to denote a 32-bit version (such as **c32e40b.exe**) and a **16** to denote the 16-bit version (such as **c16e40b.exe**). (Your filenames are guaranteed to be different. These are merely examples.)

Now you're ready to transfer the file to your computer. First, tell your computer that you want to download a binary file and not a text file with the following command line:

```
ftp> binary
200 Type set to I.
```

You'll then grab the file, which will be stored on your system's current directory. If you're using Windows 95, you'll probably want to download the file entitled **c32e40.exe**, the 32-bit version of Netscape Communicator. Do so with the following command line:

```
get c32e40.exe
```

After the file is transferred to your computer, you can end your FTP session with the following command line:

```
ftp> quit
221 Goodbye.

C:\WINDOWS>
```

Using Navigator to Download Communicator

Many of you will be upgrading from older editions of Netscape Navigator, and so you'll be using it to download Communicator. For the most part, these upgrades are simple (we cover the issues in a later section entitled "Before You Upgrade," but there are a few things that you'll need to note before you download.

Netscape Communicator has grown to the point where the downloaded files are *huge*—between three and seven megabytes in size. This can take a while, so you don't want to have any interruptions as you download. One potential problem is if you have Netscape Navigator set up to automatically check for mail, that checking can interrupt or even sever the downloading. You don't want this to happen when you've spent 45 minutes downloading a large file! In such a case, you'll need to turn off automatic mail checking before starting the download procedure.

Which Version to Download?

When you download Netscape Communicator from the Internet via a Web browser, you're asked to provide your operating system and location before a list of download sites is displayed.

This is a simplistic approach to determining which version of Netscape Communicator you should download, or how you may need to adjust your own computer setup. This is where we need to use some computerese for a minute.

The difference between the Windows 3.1 and Windows 95 versions of Netscape Communicator lies in how they're programmed. Windows 3.1 is a 16-bit operating system, while Windows 95 is (mostly) a 32-bit operating system.

N O T E To use Netscape Communicator under Windows 95, you'll need to use a 32-bit TCP/IP stack. If you're using the network tools included in Windows 95, you are indeed using a 32-bit TCP/IP stack. If you're using Trumpet Winsock as your Internet connection tool, you're using a 16-bit networking stack and must use the 16-bit version of Netscape Communicator.

In addition, Netscape Communications now offers different configurations of Netscape Communicator to download. You can download the minimum Netscape Communicator configuration, which includes Netscape Navigator as well as mail and news functions. If you want the Netscape plug-ins (like Live3D), you'll want to download the standard configuration. If you want page-editing capabilities, you'll want to download the Gold configuration. If you want everything, you'll want to download the Pro edition.

INSTALLING COMMUNICATOR

Now that you've set up your computer and your Internet connection, it's time to install and configure Netscape Communicator. How you do so will depend on how you've acquired it (via the Internet, directly from Netscape Communications, or through a third-party vendor) and the operating system you're using.

Under most circumstances, installing Netscape Communicator is a pretty straightforward procedure. We'll guide you through Netscape Communicator installation on Windows 3.x, Windows 95, and Macintosh platforms here, under the premise that you've already grabbed it via the Internet or gotten a copy from a friend.

WARNING When you install Netscape Communicator, make sure that there's no other programs running on your system. In addition, if you're using a virus checker, disable it while you install.

BEFORE YOU UPGRADE

If you're upgrading from a previous version of Netscape Navigator, you should back up your important files before actually installing the new software. For Windows 3.x users, this means copying your mail and news directories into new directories, as well as these files: **bookmark.htm**, **address.htm**, **cookies.txt**, and **netscape.ini**. For Windows 95/NT users, it means copying your mail and news directories into new directories, as well as these files: **bookmark.htm**, **address.htm**, and **cookies.txt**. For Macintosh users, this means copying your mail and news directories into new directories, as well as these files: **bookmark.htm**, **address.htm**, and **cookies.txt**. For UNIX users, this means copying your mail and news directories into new directories, as well as these files: **bookmark.htm**, **address.htm**, and **cookies.txt**.

These measures are preventative more than anything else; generally speaking, Netscape Communicator doesn't trash existing configurations, but if you have these files and directories stored in nonstandard locations, you'll want to make sure that they're not accidentally trashed in the Netscape installation.

After you have installed the new version, you can copy the files back into their appropriate places.

INSTALLING NETSCAPE COMMUNICATOR ON WINDOWS 95

You'll start with the large, executable file you've grabbed online. Depending on which Web browser you use, this file will either be in a compressed or an uncompressed form. (After you download Netscape Communicator, watch closely. If a bunch of files and an MS-DOS window appear on your screen, you'll know that your existing Web browser has allowed the file to become uncompressed. If you download Netscape Communicator from an FTP site using FTP software, the file will be compressed.)

NOTE   If you're unfamiliar with some of the conventions of Windows 95 usage, you may want to look at the documentation or a good book before installing Netscape Communicator.

Installation is easiest if you put the downloaded file in its own folder. To set this up, use the Windows Explorer to create a folder (using the **New Folder** command under the File menu). It doesn't really matter where this folder is located, as Netscape Communicator will automatically install to the Windows directory anyway. When this book was written, **c32e40.exe** was the compressed file containing Netscape Communicator. (Your version number may be different. However, the installation procedures should be quite similar to what's described here.)

You can stay within Windows Explorer to install Netscape Communicator by simply clicking on **c32e40.exe** or its shortcut. (When you move files around under Windows Explorer, you may get shortcuts to files instead of actual files. For our purposes, it doesn't really matter which you use.) After you click on the filename, you'll get a small dialog box informing you that Netscape Communicator will be installed, while also confirming that you want to continue. Since you do, you can click on the **Yes** button.

After the files are extracted, the Windows 95 InstallShield Wizard is launched. This wizard oversees the Netscape Communicator installation. There's nothing especially remarkable about this opening screen. Choosing **Next>** will get you to a dialog box that controls the destination location of Netscape Communicator files. The default under Netscape Communicator and Windows 95 is to install to the Program Files folder, with a full pathname of **C:\Program Files\Netscape\Communicator**.

 This location is different than the default locations found in previous versions of Netscape Navigator.

N O T E

Unless you have a problem with this (such as lack of space on a disk drive), you'll want to use that default. (If you do have a problem, choose the **Browse...** button. This brings up the Windows 95 directory chooser, from where you can select a new folder.) If you're comfortable with the directory location, select **Next>**. Netscape Communicator then installs, letting you know when the installation process is complete. In addition, you'll be asked if you want to read the **README.TXT** file before you run Netscape Communicator. It's always a good idea to browse through this folder, as it contains last-minute information about Netscape Communicator.

A Netscape Communicator folder appears on your Windows 95 desktop, along with a shortcut. Clicking on the shortcut or choosing the **Netscape Communicator** icon from the Netscape Communicator folder will launch Netscape Communicator. And with that, the installation process is complete, although you will be asked if you agree to a Netscape Communicator license before running the software. When you do run the software, it will look like Figure 2.9.

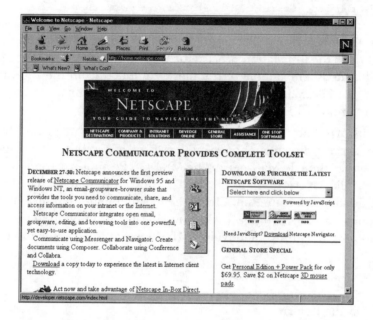

Figure 2.9 Netscape Communicator running under Windows 95.

A small component bar will also appear at the bottom right of your screen, as shown in Figure 2.10.

Figure 2.10 The Netscape Communicator component bar.

That's all there is to installing Netscape Communicator under Windows 95. You're now ready for an explanation of how Netscape Communicator works, followed by a quick tour of the Internet; you can jump ahead to the section entitled "A Tour of Netscape Communicator."

INSTALLING NETSCAPE COMMUNICATOR UNDER WINDOWS 3.1

The installation process for Windows 3.1 and Netscape Communicator is pretty close to the installation process for Windows 95. We'll use the filename of **c16e40.exe** as an example of the file we grabbed from the Internet, and we'll use the File Manager program (found in the Main program group) found in Windows 3.1.

As with Windows 95, you'll want to place **c16e40.exe** in its own directory, either an existing directory or one you've created expressly for Netscape. (You can use either the File Manager or the MS-DOS Prompt program to create a directory called **Netscape.**) You'll need to uncompress the **c16e40.exe** file. You can do so by selecting **Run...** from the **File** menu in Program Manager, or else by opening a DOS window (using the MS-DOS Prompt program found in the Main program group) and typing **n16e40.exe** at the command line:

```
C:\NETSCAPE> c16e40.exe
```

followed by the **Return** key.

If you use the Run... command, Windows 3.1 will open a DOS window and list filenames; if you use the command line, the window will already be open, and the list of filenames will scroll by. If you're using the Run... command, the window will close; if you've opened a DOS window, you'll need to type the following command line to close the window:

```
C:\NETSCAPE> exit
```

followed by the **Return** key.

This step merely uncompresses the files found in the **c16e40.exe** archive. The next step is actually installing the program from the uncompressed files.

This time, you'll want to use the **Run...** command found under the File menu in the Program Manager to run the **setup.exe** program that was part of the Netscape Communicator archive. This is a Windows program that guides you through installation. There's not a lot to this program: It asks you where you want to install the program and in which program group you want to store the Netscape Communicator icons, followed by the display of a license agreement. (In fact, it's basically the same as the procedures explained in the preceding coverage of installing Netscape Communicator under Windows 95.)

Once Netscape Communicator is installed, your work may not be through, due to some flaws in the Windows 3.1 setup.

Using the Microsoft 32-Bit Extensions

The Windows operating system is a *16-bit operating system*, which means that it processes 16 bits at a time. Netscape Communicator was written to work with a *32-bit operating system*, which means that you might need to make some changes with Windows 3.1. (You don't need to go through these hoops if you're using Windows NT or Windows 95.)

Basically, the changes involve grabbing and installing the 32-bit extensions to Windows, which Microsoft calls *Win32s*. These extensions to the operating system allow 32-bit applications to be run in the 16-bit Microsoft Windows operating system. Some hardware manufacturers who preload Windows, such as Epson, include the Win32s because of the needs of bundled software. You'll need to determine if you already have the 32-bit extensions installed. If not, you'll need to get them from Microsoft and install them.

TIP

Here's an easy way to see if you're got the Microsoft 32-bit extensions to Windows 3.1 loaded. Open the Games program group in the Program Manager. If there's an icon for a game called Freecell, double-click on the icon. If the game run, then you have the 32-bit extensions.

If you don't have Freecell, it doesn't necessarily mean that you don't have Win32s. You can always see if there is a file named **WIN32S.INI** in the **\WINDOWS\SYS-TEM** directory. If you're running Windows for Workgroups, you can see if there's a file named **WIN32S16.DLL** in the **\WINDOWS\SYSTEM** directory.

If your system lacks Win32s, you'll need to go out and get them. First off, you'll need a fairly recent version (1.20 or better). The most widely distributed of the Win32 extensions can be found in the archived file **PW1118.EXE**. Microsoft offers these extensions free of charge, and they post them in several places in the electronic world, including:

Internet: Connect via FTP to *ftp.microsoft.com*. The file **PW118.EXE** is in the **\SOFTLIB\MSLFILES** directory.

CompuServe: GO MSL to the Microsoft Software Library, where you can download the file **PW1118.EXE**. After you download the file, place it in its own directory and then run it from a DOS command line:

```
C:\DOWNLOAD\>PW1118.EXE
```

assuming, of course, that you've placed the file in a directory called **DOWNLOAD**.

The Microsoft Download Service (MSDL), which is essentially a bulletin-board service (BBS) of Microsoft software. You use your modem and telecomm software (such as the Terminal package found in Windows 3.1) to call 206/936-6735; once connected, you download the file named PW1118.EXE.

Once you download this software from these sources, you don't have to do much else, as it automatically installs.

INSTALLING NETSCAPE COMMUNICATOR ON THE MACINTOSH

When you grab Netscape Communicator from the Internet or purchase it in a store, you're going to need to make sure that you're using the proper version for your Macintosh, as the older 680 × 0-based Macs use a different version than the newer PowerPC-based Macs.

The installation begins when you double-click on the **Installer** icon. The installation process is rather streamlined: All you need to do it sit back and agree with the defaults as they whiz by.

After you've installed Netscape Communicator, a new window appears on your local computer containing a Netscape Communicator icon. Use MacTCP to connect to the Internet, double-click on the **Netscape Communicator** icon, and off you go.

INSTALLING NETSCAPE COMMUNICATOR ON A UNIX SYSTEM

Netscape Communicator is precompiled for many UNIX variants, including:

- Linux
- BSD Unix 3.0
- SCO Unix
- Digital Unix 3.2 and higher
- HP-UX 9.03, 9.05, 10.x and higher
- AIX 4.1 and higher
- Irix 5.3, 6.2 and higher
- Sun Solaris 2.4 and higher)
- Sun OS 4.1.3 and 4.1.4
- SCO OpenServer Release 5, version 3.2
- SCO Unixware 2.1
- Sun Solaris x86 2.4 AIX

You'll need to make sure that you're grabbing the correct version for your UNIX version. If you're using a version of UNIX outside the above list, you're basically out of luck, since Netscape Communicator isn't available in source-code format for compiling on your own system. However, most users should fall somewhere on the list of supported UNIX variants.

Installing on a UNIX system is pretty much dependent on the UNIX variant you're using. After you download the proper version, you should place the archived file in its own directory (it doesn't matter what the name is) and then type the following command line:

```
$ zcat filename.tarZ | tar xvf-
```

This breaks the archive into assorted files. One of these files should be called **README**. This file will contain installation procedures specific to your variant of UNIX. You will probably need to move some files around, but you shouldn't need to do much customization before using Netscape Communicator.

A Tour of Netscape Communicator

Now that you've installed Netscape Communicator, you need to learn how to use it. In the rest of this chapter, we'll cover the basics of Netscape Communicator usage.

What Goes Where

No matter what version of Netscape Communicator you're using—Windows 3.1, Windows 95, Macintosh, Linux—it looks the same and acts the same, for the most part. With Netscape Communicator, what you see *really* is what you get: The various parts of the window provide the tools you'll use most often. Go ahead and launch Netscape Communicator. The default is to first load Netscape Navigator when Communicator is started (you can change this, as you'll see in Chapter 3). The rest of this chapter will cover Netscape Navigator; the other components will be covered throughout the course of the book. You can basically break down a Netscape Communicator window—either the Web browser, mail client, Calendar, Collabra, Conference, or newsreader—into these main areas by looking at a typical Netscape Navigator window, going from the top of the window to the bottom (as illustrated in Figure 2.11).

- A **titlebar** is at the top of the window, providing the name of the Web page.
- **Pulldown menus** control Netscape Communicator settings and allow you to perform basic actions. They follow the interface guidelines provided by your operating system; for instance, the Windows 3.1 and Windows 95 versions have a File menu as the first menu on the left.

Figure 2.11 *The parts of a Netscape Navigator window illustrated.*

- **Toolbar buttons** provide shortcuts to basic Netscape Communicator commands. These will be covered at the end of this chapter. The thing to note here is that there are really no *buttons* as such when you first look at the interface; instead, the buttons become highlighted when you place the cursor over them (shades of Microsoft Internet Explorer!).These buttons can be hidden or displayed by placing the cursor over the textured areas at the right of the toolbar, or else you can use the menu choices under the View menu to hide or display them. There are actually three separate toolbars (in order): the Navigation Toolbar (which provides access to buttons that perform specific commands), the Location Toolbar (which controls the Bookmarks button and the location text field), and the Personal Toolbar. You can change the order of the toolbars by selecting a toolbar with the left mouse button and then moving the toolbar to a new location within the set of toolbars. You cannot, however, move a toolbar to a different portion of the Netscape Navigator interface; they must remain below the pulldown menus and above the content area. (The Personal Toolbar can be edited using the Bookmarks function, which you'll cover in Chapter 4, and the toolbar appearances can be changed, as you'll see in Chapter 3.)

Something new in Netscape Navigator 4.0 is the presence of tabs to the left of the toolbars; these tabs control whether or not the toolbars are visible. (The View pulldown menu does the same thing, as you'll see later in this chapter.) When the tabs are vertical, the toolbar is visible (obviously!), but when the tabs are horizontal, the toolbar is hidden. To change the status of the toolbar, click on the tab.

The Macintosh version of Netscape Navigator doesn't allow for a Personal Toolbar.

MACINTOSH

- **Popdown menus** provide shortcuts to your list of bookmarks and to Web resources maintained on the Netscape Communications server. These menus can be hidden or displayed by placing the cursor over the textured areas at the right of the toolbar.

- A **location text field** is where you enter URL addresses. When you enter a new URL, the label of the field changes from **Location** to **Go to**, and when the new Web page is through loading, the field label changes to **Netsite**. When you're through entering the new address, press **Enter**. If you're using a Windows version of Netscape Communicator, you can pull down a history of past URLs you've entered by selecting the arrow at the right of the field. This history spans sessions, which means that if you quit Netscape Communicator and start it again at a later date, the history will include the previously visited Web sites.

- A **URL link icon** appears to the left of the location text field. If you position the cursor above this icon, the cursor changes from an arrow to a hand. This means that the URL in the location text field can be dragged and dropped to the Bookmarks file (do so by dragging and dropping to the Bookmarks icon to the left of the URL link icon) to the Windows 95/NT desktop, where the URL will be converted to a shortcut, or to Netscape Composer, where the URL will be edited. As you drag and drop, you'll notice that the cursor changes from a hand to an arrow attached to a little link. If you move the link to an area that can't accept its input, the cursor changes to a small circle with a line through it.

Win95

This option is available only in the Windows 95/NT version of Netscape Navigator.

- The **status indicator** (which is the Netscape Communications corporate logo—the *N* on the right of the screen) tells you when a page or file is being transferred; you'll know because there's a little animation playing when the transaction is taking place. Clicking on the **N** will connect you immediately to the Netscape Communications home page, *http://home.netscape.com.*

- A **page display** shows the actual Web page. There are different elements to this page display—text, pictures, and graphical elements like lines and bullets. Like any other window in your operating system, the content area may have vertical and horizontal scrollbars if the contents of the content area exceed the boundaries of the page. The differently colored and underlined text is a *link* to another Web page; when you place the mouse pointer over the link, the actual location of the Web page is displayed at the bottom of the page. To move to that link, you simply click over the underlined and colored text. You can change the settings for this text (as well as the background of the content area), as you'll see in Chapter 3. You can also treat the text as any other text by highlighting it and cutting and pasting it between applications and to your operating system's clipboard. (We'll cover this later in this chapter.)

- If a page is too large to fit in the window, then **scrollbar**s will appear at the right and/or the bottom of the window, which you can then use to scroll through the page. A page display can be divided into different sections, called *frames*, which we'll cover in a following section.

MACINTOSH

You can hide the scrollbars by typing **Control-Option-h** when using the Macintosh version of Netscape Navigator. If you're working on a page with frames, **Control-Option-h** will hide the scrollbars in a selected frame. To display the scrollbars, use **Control-Option-j**.

- The bottom of the window is devoted to a **control bar**, which has several elements. A lock on the bottom left of the screen and on the menu bar tells you whether or not the document is secure. If the lock is closed, the document is secure. If the lock is open, the document is not secure. (Older versions of Netscape Navigator used a key and a blue bar on the top of the page area to denote if a document was secure. The key and blue bar are now obsolete.)

- A **progress bar** appears on the bottom of the screen when you're connecting to a Web site and transferring a Web page. It shows what percentage of a Web page has already been loaded, as well as the percentage of an image as it loads.

- A **status message** tells you what part of the page is being transferred and how much is left to be transferred. You're also told when a document is through loading. In addition, when you place the mouse pointer over a link, the full URL of the link is displayed at the bottom of the screen.

To make the control bar appear and disappear, type **Ctrl-Alt-S**.

N O T E

If you don't get enough information from the status message, try typing **Ctrl-Alt-T** as a Web page is loading. You'll get a ton of information about the current transfer, including how many connections you're using to grab a Web page, how many active URLs make up a Web page, and what system sockets are used in the process of a transfer.

N O T E

In the rest of this chapter, we'll tour Netscape Navigator.

HIGHLIGHTING TEXT

The page display is the heart of Netscape Navigator, and it's here where you'll view Web pages. Basically, a Web page is a combination of text and graphics. The text is like any other text found in the computer world. Graphics are usually smaller files that are rendered locally by Netscape Navigator and displayed.

Since the text on a Web page is like the other text used by your computer and its operating system, you can cut and paste it between applications. You can select it like any other text, with the mouse pointer. (One note: You don't have a cursor to show you where the highlighted part begins and ends—you'll need to use the mouse to select the text.) After you select text with the mouse pointer, you can use the commands under the Edit menu to copy it to your operating-system clipboard; from there it can be pasted into other applications. (If you're using the Windows 95/NT version of Netscape Navigator, you can drag the selected text to another open application.) Alternately, you can select text by clicking at the beginning of a chunk of text, then moving the cursor to the end of the text you want selected and clicking on the left mouse button while pressing the **Shift** key.

FRAMES

One of the most used features in Netscape Navigator is *frames*. Basically, frames allow the content area to be broken into different areas. In most ways, these different areas form their own Web page, complete with scrollbars and individual links. When you clink on a link in a frame, only the content of that frame will change. A page with three distinct frames—a listing of contents to the left of the screen, a text introduction on the top right of the screen, and ads on the bottom right of the screen—is shown in Figure 2.12.

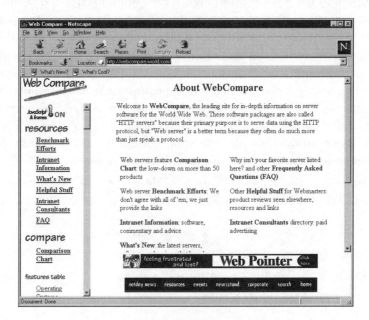

Figure 2.12 *A page with three frames.*

When a Web page is sent to you, the frames are set in specific sizes. You can change the size of a frame by positioning the mouse pointer on the border between the areas, holding down the left mouse button and then dragging the border to where you want the new frame to be.

Frames are important when you're trying to save Web pages to disk or maneuver between them. Only one frame can be active at a given time. When you move your cursor somewhere over a Netscape Navigator Web page and then click with the left mouse button, you'll notice that the border around the frame becomes darker, and keyboard input (if any) goes to that frame. If you want to save a page to disk—a procedure that's covered later in this chapter—you'll need to make sure that your desired frame is active. Similarly, if you're moving between pages within a frame, you'll need to make sure that the frame is active before using the Back and Forward buttons, as you'll learn about later in this book. To reload a frame but not the entire Web page, click on the right mouse button and select **Reload Frame** from the resulting pop-up menu.

USING THE COMPONENT BAR

The component bar was shown in Figure 2.10 when used as a floating palette (that is, as a small window that can be positioned anywhere on the page). It's designed as a shortcut to the most used elements of Netscape Communicator.

The component bar can also be attached (or *docked*, in Netscape lingo) to a Netscape Communicator window, as shown in Figure 2.13. To do this, you need to click on the **Netscape logo** on the component bar when it's used as a floating palette, or else select **Dock Component Bar** from the Communicator menu. The component bar will then attach to the bottom right of a Netscape Communicator window. To place the component bar on the desktop, select **Show Component Bar** from the Communicator menu.

There are four icons on the component bar. These can't be changed. They are (from left to right; see Figures 2.10 or 2.13 for a representation):

- Browser (Web browser, or Netscape Navigator)
- Inbox (electronic mail)
- Discussions (Usenet newsgroups or Collabra)
- Editor (HTML editor)

Selecting one of the icons will launch the corresponding application.

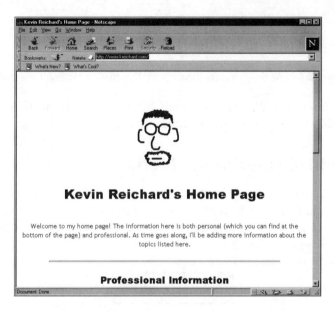

Figure 2.13 *The component bar attached to a window.*

To move the component bar, place the cursor on the bottom left of the bar and then drag the component bar to the new location.

If you select the right mouse button when the cursor is above the bottom left of the component bar, you can change the settings. There are only three: whether or not the component bar is always on the top of the screen, no matter what applications are running (the default is Always on top); whether or not text is shown on the component bar (the default is not to show the text); and if the icons are displayed horizontally or vertically (the default is to display them horizontally).

The Component Bar and Mail Notification

If you've set up Netscape Messenger to automatically poll your mail server for mail (a topic you'll cover in Chapter 8), the notification can take place on the component bar and the Windows 95 screen (the latter will be covered in the next session). When you do have mail waiting, the Inbox icon on the task changes to the icon shown in Figure 2.14.

Figure 2.14 The component bar indicating that there is mail on the server.

When you press on the icon, your mail Inbox opens. From there, you can select **Get Mail** to grab your mail from the mail server.

Another Mail-Notification Method

There's one more Netscape Communicator screen element. If you've set up Netscape Messenger to automatically poll your mail server for mail (a topic you'll cover in Chapter 8), the notification takes place on the Windows 95/NT taskbar, as shown in Figure 2.15.

Figure 2.15 You have mail!

The small, hard-to-discern icon next to the Dial-Up Networking icon indicates that there are mail messages waiting for you on your mail server. If you click on the little icon, your mail Inbox opens. From there, you can select **Get Mail** to grab your mail from the mail server.

One More Mail-Notification Tool

Netscape Communicator features a separate application for checking mail. Netscape Mail Notification doesn't require that other Netscape components be running, and it can be set to check for mail at specific intervals. If there's mail on the mail server, it will inform you. (It's like the **biff** and **xbiff** applications from the UNIX world.)

YOUR MAIDEN VOYAGE

This concludes our brief tour of the Netscape Communicator interface. To get around on the Internet, however, all you need is to know is how to enter a URL—which is what we'll show you right here.

Your First URL

When you load Netscape Communicator, you are connected initially to the Netscape Communications home page, *http://home.netscape.com.* (Yes, you can change this, as you will see in Chapter 3.) As you can see in Figure 2.16, this address is already entered in its own line.

Figure 2.16 *The URL address highlighted.*

You'll also note that *http://home.netscape.com* is highlighted. To move to another point on the Web, you'll need to replace *http://home.netscape.com* with a new URL. Move your mouse pointer over the address and delete it, using the **BackSpace** or **Delete** keys. After the old address is erased, you can enter the new address. Here's an address you can use to begin your maiden journey on the Web:

http://www.kreichard.com

When you're through typing, hit the **Enter** key.

The bottom of the Netscape Communicator screen tells you the status of connecting to this Web page. This information is rather precise, informing you about the download of each portion of the Web page (text and individual graphics). Additionally, the cursor will turn into an hourglass, telling you that a Web-page transfer is taking place, and the **Reload** button on the toolbox changes to a **Stop** icon (as shown in Figure 2.17). Use this button to stop the page from being downloaded to your system.

Figure 2.17 *The Stop icon.*

As the Web page *http://www.kreichard.com* is transferred to your system, you'll see text appear from top to bottom on your page, followed by graphics. The end result is shown in Figure 2.18.

Figure 2.18 *The Kevin Reichard home page.*

Admittedly, the page at http://www.kreichard.com isn't a great work of art, but that makes it somewhat typical of the offerings of the Internet and the World Wide Web. The important thing to note here is the layout of the Web page and what you can do.

Some URL Tips

In the earliest days of the World Wide Web, there was some concern that the format used for URLs would be too obscure to be practical. And it was true that using the earliest Web browsers could be an infuriating experience, requiring absolute precision when typing in obscure and long URLs.

Today, you still need a certain amount of precision when it comes to entering URLs, but Netscape Navigator makes it a little easier to enter a URL without too much typing.

The first method is URL completion. Say that you've visited a site regularly—for example, *http://www.kreichard.com*—and you go once again to visit it. As you get to the point where you've typed *http://www.k*, Netscape Navigator automatically finishes *http://www.kreichard.com* on the URL line, with *reichard.com* highlighted. Netscape Navigator will analyze what you've entered and try to logically complete the URL. If instead you had wanted to enter the URL *http://www.kentucky.com*, you could just keep on typing.

The second method is working from the name of a site and not the entire URL. For instance, you can enter just *kreichard* and Netscape Navigator will search for *www.kreichard.com*. Be warned that this method works only for Web sites (*www*) that end with *com*.

What Can Go Wrong?

There are actually a few things that can go wrong when you're connecting to a Web page. *Wrong* perhaps isn't the right word, but there are a few error messages you can receive when a Web page isn't accessible.

Netscape Navigator returns *error messages* in the form of dialog boxes with only one choice: **OK**. The most common error is that a Web page doesn't exist at a specified address. The error message is short and sweet, shown in Figure 2.19. This message tells you that the Web server (in this case, *http://www.kreichard.com*) exists, but the document you requested (*cigars.htm*) doesn't. Don't automatically assume that the Web page you want doesn't actually exist, however; it could be that there's a typo in the Web address you've entered. It's rather easy to have a typo in an address, thanks to the strange formatting used by URL formats. Something as simple as using a comma instead of a period will generate an error.

A simple typo may lead to another common error message, informing you that the Web server itself doesn't exist—or rather, that it doesn't have a DNS entry (as shown in Figure 2.20.). This message can also be generated because of a dropped connection to the Internet.

There's also one more error message you may run into that has nothing to do with typos or nonexistent servers. When a connection to a Web server takes too long, Netscape Communicator will cut the connection and inform you that the connection has been timed out. As the Internet gets more popular, there will be times when there's so much traffic on the network that connections become slower than you'd like—so slow that it's really impossible to make some connections. In these cases, there's not a lot you can do, except log off the Internet and try again during a less busy time.

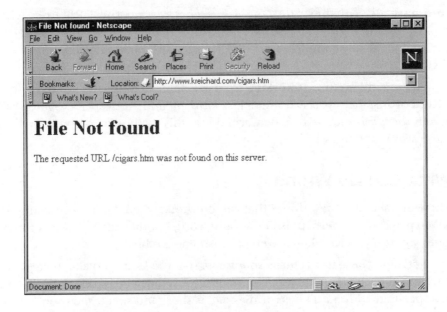

Figure 2.19 *A message telling you that a Web page doesn't exist.*

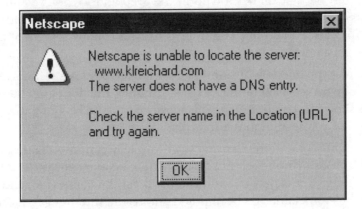

Figure 2.20 *Another common error message.*

Jumping from Page to Page

Assuming that the Web page found at *http://www.kreichard.com* loads properly, it's time to explain exactly what sorts of things you can do with it. This home page contains *links* to other Web pages, and it's really easy to follow them.

How can you tell a link? Because it will be underlined and in a blue color. Basically, a link is a convenience to you. Instead of typing a long Web address in Netscape Communicator (say, *http://www.kreichard.com/linux.html*), you can click on the highlighted text *Linux Configuration and Installation, Second Edition*, and you'll automatically be loading that page onto your computer.

HOT LINK

You can control how these links appear, as you'll see in Chapter 3.

It's these links that make jumping around the Internet so fascinating, and also such a potential waste of time. Don't like what you see on the screen? Click on a link and go somewhere else. Find a list of interesting-looking sites? It's really simple to hop from site to site. These links also lead to instant gratification: You can jump to a linked site even before the current page totally loads.

Of course, you can make a link too quickly. Then, you'll want to go back and revisit a Web site. You can do so in two ways:

- Click on the **Back** button on the toolbar. This brings you back to the page you just left. If you're using a page with frames, you'll need to make sure that a desired frame is active before you click on the Back button.

- Pull down the list of URLs you've visited. You'll notice that there's an arrow next to where you entered a URL, in the location text field. Click on this arrow, and you'll see a list of Web pages you've visited. Highlight the desired page, and you'll see it reappear on your screen.

When you revisit a Web site, you'll notice that it reloads quickly into Netscape Navigator. This isn't because Netscape Navigator hasn't grown magically faster—Netscape Navigator keeps a copy of recently accessed Web pages on your hard drive. (You'll learn more about this in Chapter 3.)

You can move between links via the keyboard; press the **Tab** button to move you to the next link on a page.

TOOLBAR BUTTONS

As you learned earlier, Netscape Navigator features a toolbar row, which places icons on their own row, representing frequently used actions. Instead of pulling down a menu or two to locate a function, you can use one of the preconfigured toolbar icons. (No, you can't edit the row of icons; the only changes you can make are whether both pictures and text are displayed. You'll see how to make these changes in Chapter 4.)

Most of the icons are self-evident; for instance, the Reload icon reloads the current page, and the Home icon connects you to the Netscape Home Page. However, there are a few things you'll want to note:

- Placing the mouse pointer over the Back and Forward icons displays where you would go if you pressed on the icon.

- There are actually keyboard equivalents for the Back and Forward icons: Use **Alt-←** (for **Back**) and **Alt-→** (for **Forward**).

- Placing the mouse pointer over the Back and Forward icons and pressing either mouse button brings up a list of the pages that you've already visited; you can then choose a page from this list instead of having to go through the hassle of opening the History window and making a selection there.

- The Search icon connects you with the Netscape Communications search page, which lists the four major search engines (Excite, Lycos, Infoseek, and Yahoo) and allows you to search them for phrases. In addition, other search tools are listed. Be warned that these companies pay Netscape for the privilege of being on this page, and they may not represent the best search choices for your particular situation.

- The Guide icon opens a set of resources maintained by Netscape Communications: The Internet, People, Yellow Pages, What's New, and What's Cool. Each has a specialty:

    The Internet summons a page of Internet resources. People links to search engines specializing in names and addresses (Bigfoot, Four11, IAF, InfoSpace, Switchboard, and WhoWhere).

Yellow Pages summons a list of search engines specializing in business information.

What's New links to a page of new Web resources.

What's Cool summons a page of "cool" Web sites.

Be warned that these aren't necessarily the best or the coolest resources on the Internet—they're the ones that have ponied up a payment to Netscape Communications in order to be listed on these pages.

Break out the cigars! *Now* it's time to learn a little more about Netscape Navigator, starting with its pulldown menus.

PULLDOWN MENUS

There are six pulldown menus:

- File
- Edit
- View
- Go
- Communicator
- Help

A *pulldown menu* gives you access to another set of commands. When you move your mouse pointer over the menu and click the left mouse button (or, in the case of the Macintosh, the *only* mouse button), a menu appears, with some of the menu choices sitting independently and some of the menu choices leading to yet another menu. In this case, as you hold down the button, you'll see that a list of other menu choices is displayed. (If you don't have this part of your operating system mastered, you may want to crack open a manual and figure out what basics you'll need to master for future computer usage.)

Some of the menu choices here—and those throughout the course of this book, for that matter—are *context dependent*, which means that their behavior depends on the prevailing situation. For instance: Several pulldown-menu choices deal with frames, which you learned about in a previous section. If you're viewing a Web page with frames, then these menu choices will be displayed. If you're not viewing a Web page with frames, then these menu choices will be *grayed out*—that is, they'll be visible, but they'll appear to be shaded, and you can't access them.

The nice thing here is that the Netscape Communicator menus are pretty much the same no matter what operating system you use. (There are some small changes when you get down to the submenu level, which you'll see later in this chapter.) They're also fairly consistent from component to component—the way the pulldown menus work in Netscape Messenger is the same as in Netscape Navigator. We'll cover the pulldown menus in Netscape Navigator here.

The File Menu

The File menu has the following choices:

- New
- Open Page (**Ctrl-O**)
- Save As… (**Ctrl-S**)
- Save Frame As…
- Send Page
- Edit Page
- Edit Frame
- Upload File
- Go Offline
- Page Setup…
- Print Preview
- Print Page…
- Close (**Ctrl-W**)
- Exit (**Ctrl-Q**)

We'll cover each.

New

This selection is an access to a submenu of choices:

- New Navigator Window (**Ctrl-N**)
- New Message (**Ctrl-M**)
- New Blank Page (**Ctrl-Shift-N**)
- New Page from Template
- New Page from Wizard

Of the five choices here, your most-used options will be the first two, New Navigator Window and New Message. The second choice is fairly self-explanatory—a new message gives you the power to send a new electronic-mail message—but the first requires a little more explanation. Why would you want to open a new Web browser window? To directly compare Web pages, or if you're trying to get the content of two Web pages simultaneously (such as listening to a Web broadcast while looking at another Web page).

When you open a new browser, it inherits the same bookmarks and the same history list as your previous Web-browser windows. The Netscape folks did a little back-door promotion here: When you open the new window, it looks at the history of the old window and then goes to the top of the list to load the oldest window in your history list. Since this will usually be *http://home.netscape.com* (the page that Netscape Navigator is preconfigured to start with), Netscape is promoting itself in the new window.

New Blank Page opens a window in Netscape Composer, where you can begin a new Web page from scratch. You'll learn more about Netscape Composer in Chapter 7.

New Page from Template opens a new browser window and loads a Web page from the Netscape Communications Web site. This Web page includes templates that you can use to set up your own Web pages. Among possible template uses are Personal/Family, Company/Small Business, Departmental, and Product/Service pages. (You'll learn more about templates in Chapter 9's coverage of Netscape Composer.)

New Page from Wizard is a link to another Web page at the Netscape Communications Web site, which lets you interactively design a Web page and see the results in your browser. Again, you'll learn more about wizards and page design in Chapter 7's coverage of Netscape Composer.

Open Page

If you don't want to type in a Web address in the URL input field, you can do it manually with this selection. It brings up a window with an entry field where you can type in the full URL, and it also gives you the choice of bringing the page into the Web browser or Netscape Composer. This selection is shown in Figure 2.21.

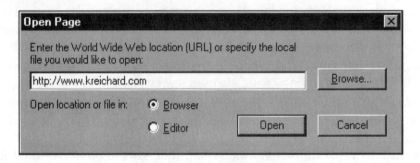

Figure 2.21 *Opening a page.*

Netscape Navigator doesn't care whether the page is somewhere on the World Wide Web or on a local filesystem. As you can see in Figure 2.21, you have the option of selecting the **Browse...** button, which opens a file-selection mechanism specific to the operating system that Netscape Navigator is running on. (For instance, Windows 95/NT users would have an Open dialog box, while Windows 3.1 users would have an Open File... dialog box.) The thing to remember here is that Netscape Navigator is opening a file on *your* local computer, not on the Internet. You can use this menu choice at any time—even when you're not connected to the Internet—as you're only making use of your local system and not the Internet.

Netscape Navigator actually opens several types of files. The most familiar will be the HTML page, which is a simply a Web page that's been stored on your hard drive. (Why would you do this? You may be creating Web pages from scratch and want to see how they look under a Web browser, or you may have saved a Web page for future reference while not connected to the Internet. Later in this section you'll see how to save this file to your hard drive.) Netscape Navigator also reads in straight text files, as well as executable files (in other words, you can use Netscape Navigator to run another program).

Save As and Save Frame

As you might expect, the Save As selection saves the current Web page to your hard drive, your floppy drive, or somewhere on your local network. The default is to save the document formatted in the HTML language, although you can also save the page as straight text.

Linux and UNIX users can save the page in the PostScript language.

If you're perusing a Web page with multiple frames, the Save Frame As line becomes active, and the Save As line becomes inactive. As you might expect, this saves only the information in the active frame, not in the total Web page.

Send Page

This menu choice opens a message-composition box for electronic mail. The difference between this electronic-mail message and a normal electronic-mail message (which you'll learn more about in Chapter 7) is that this electronic-mail message contains the contents of the Web page.

Let's go through an example. You've already connected to *http://www.kreichard.com.* You're obviously dazzled by this Web page, and you want to share it with your friends. With *http://www.kreichard.com* as your current Web page, you select **Send Page** from the File menu. A new message-composition window appears, as shown in Figure 2.22.

Figure 2.22 *Sending http://www.kreichard.com to a friend.*

The title of the page appears in the subject line of the message, and the URL of the page appears in the body of your outgoing mail message. However— and here's a crucial point that you won't realize because there's no way to know this by looking at the outgoing mail—but the actual contents of the Web page (including graphics and formatting—the complete HTML code) are also contained within the mail message. You can also add your own comments to the page, and niceties like signatures are also included. When the mail is sent to another Netscape Communicator user or to someone using an electronic-mail package capable of displaying HTML code within mail messages (a capability that is lacking in Microsoft Internet Explorer, for example, as well as industry-leading packages like Eudora), the Web page will be displayed with all formatting intact, as shown in Figure 2.23. (There's much more to addressing electronic mail, but that's a subject we'll save for the electronic-mail coverage in Chapter 7.)

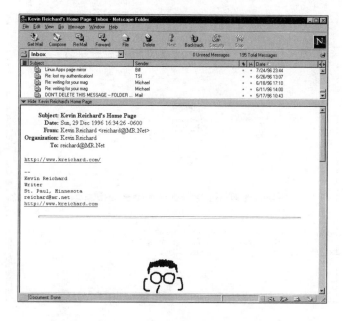

Figure 2.23 *The mail message with http://www.kreichard.com.*

Edit Page and Edit Frame

The Edit Page menu choice opens Netscape Composer for editing the page currently displayed by the Web browser. Netscape Composer is used for editing HTML code. Selecting this choice when *http://www.kreichard.com* is the current Web page will yield a window like the one shown in Figure 2.24.

However, there's one major drawback to this command: You're actually editing the HTML page that's been copied to your local computer, not the one that's on the server. This means, of course, that you can't really edit the home page at *http://www.kreichard.com*; all you can do is edit a local copy and save it to a local file system. To send a Web page to a Web server, you'll need to use the **Upload File** command, which will be covered the next section.

Figure 2.24 *Editing http://www.kreichard.com.*

If you're working on a page divided into frames, then the Edit Frames menu choice is visible, and the Edit Page menu choice is grayed out.

Upload File

This menu choice is used when connecting via FTP to an FTP site. Let's say you want to upload the file *cigars.html* to *ftp://ftp.kreichard.com.* You'd first connect to the FTP site by entering the following URL:

```
ftp://ftp.kreichard.com
```

You would then use the **Upload File** command to upload the file, in which case a dialog box (the exact form depending on the operating system) would appear, prompting you to specify a file to upload. However, this command works only under some specific circumstances. First, you need permission from the FTP server to upload the file, and you'll need to include the username and password as part of the URL (these commands differ according to FTP server). Second, you need to be in a directory that allows file uploads.

You could also drag and drop a file from the desktop onto the Netscape Navigator window. However, this is true only for the Windows 95/NT versions of Netscape Navigator.

Go Offline

This command will disconnect your computer from a dialup connection to the Internet via phone line and modem. If you're not connected to the Internet, this command appears as **Go Online**, and it launches a dialup process via the operating system.

This command wasn't actually implemented in the beta versions of Netscape Navigator used to prepare this book. Check the documentation for more information about this command.

N O T E

Page Setup

This selection is for information Netscape Navigator uses when printing Web pages. (The following selection actually handles the printing; this selection handles the page setup.) It's shown in Figure 2.25.

This menu choice is not available on Linux and UNIX versions of Netscape Communicator.

UNIX

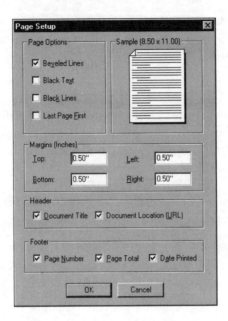

Figure 2.25 *The Page Setup window.*

When you select **Page Setup**, a dialog box appears (as shown in Figure 2.25), with the following sections:

- The Page Options section sets whether or not lines are beveled, text is printed black no matter how it's formatted (those of you with color printers would have all-black text anyway if this box is selected; remember, in Netscape Communicator text often is printed in various colors), lines are printed black no matter how they are formatted (again, lines can be formatted in many different colors), and whether the last page is to printed first (a handy setting for those who despair of collating their printouts).

- The Sample shows how a page setup with the designated margins would look. This does *not* show how a specific page would be printed; you'll need to select **Page Preview** (covered later in this chapter) for that.

- The Margins section sets the page margins. These are set in inches. Unless you have some odd printing needs, you won't need to change the margins.

- The Header section specifies what information is printed on the top of each page. The default is to print both the document's title and the document location (URL).

- The Footer section sets what information is printed at the bottom of the page, including the page number, how many pages are included in the document, and the date the page was printed.

Print Preview

This menu selection shows you how the page will look when printed. Our example page of *http://www.kreichard.com* is shown in print preview in Figure 2.26.

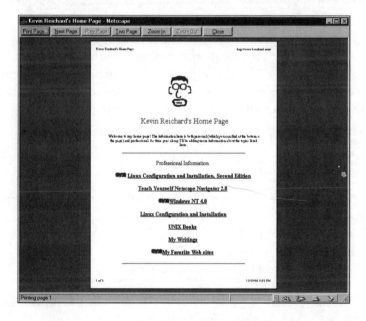

Figure 2.26 *Viewing our page in print preview.*

There are some dramatic drawbacks to this menu choice, as you can see in Figure 2.26. For starters, print preview can't display all the fonts as they appear in the Web browser, although these fonts will be correctly rendered when the Web page is actually printed. If you need to know precisely how something will print, then you had best not count on this feature.

However, the rest of the print-preview function works as it should. There is a series of buttons on the top of the window that control further activities:

- Print Page... brings up the printing mechanism specific to your operating system.

- Next Page will display the next page in a multipart Web page. Since there's no set length for Web pages, they can pretty much be any length. A long Web page can end up taking five or six pages when printed on paper.

- Previous Page displays the previous page in a multipart Web page.

- Two Page displays two pages in a multipart Web page side by side. This is good for comparisons.

- Zoom In displays the page in a larger form. The default is to show the page as it will fit on a single sheet of paper. When you zoom in, scrollbars will appear, since the entire page layout can't appear in the Netscape Navigator window. There are three size settings, and you use **Zoom In/Zoom Out** to move between them.

- Zoom Out displays the page in a smaller form.

- Close closes the print preview and then returns you to the Netscape Navigator Web browser.

You'll notice the cursor turns into a magnifying glass as you're displaying a page. If you click with the left mouse button, then the portion of the page you selected will be magnified, which is essentially the same thing as selecting the Zoom In button at the top of the window. If you can't magnify the page any more, then the cursor will be the normal arrow.

This menu choice is available only in the Windows 3.1 and Windows 95/NT version of Netscape Navigator.

N O T E

Print Page

This selection, obviously enough, prints the current Web document. When you start to print something, you'll see the print mechanism specific to your operating system. Basically, you'll be asked to select a printer, to confirm some information specific to your printer (for instance, you may have multiple paper trays available), and so on. This is the same as the Print button found on the toolbar.

When you are viewing a window made up of multiple frames, the Print command becomes the Print Frame command. As you might expect, Netscape Communicator prints only the active frame and not the total Web page.

N O T E

Close

This menu selection closes the entire Web browser window. (As opposed to the Exit selection from the File menu, which shuts down all Netscape Communicator windows.)

Exit

This selection closes the current Web browser window and all other Netscape Communicator windows.

Following operating-system guidelines, the Macintosh version of Netscape Communicator uses **Quit** instead of **Exit**.

MACINTOSH

The Edit Menu

This menu is pretty straightforward; anyone who has spent any time with a graphical interface will recognize almost all the selections, except the **Preferences** choice. This menu choice is where modifications to Netscape Navigator and Netscape Communicator are made, and as such it's perhaps the most important menu choice here. This menu has the following choices:

- Cut (**Ctrl-X**)
- Copy (**Ctrl-C**)
- Paste (**Ctrl-V**)
- Clear
- Select All (**Ctrl-A**)

- Find in Page (**Ctrl-F**)
- Find Again (**F3**)
- Search Internet
- Search Directory
- Preferences

We'll cover each selection here, except for Preferences. Since making changes via Preferences is so involving—and generally undertaken after you've used Netscape Communicator for a while and know what you need and want—we're devoting an entire chapter to the topic, Chapter 3.

NOTE   Most of the menu choices here have to do with cutting and pasting text. If you've experimented with your operating system, you'll know that the convention in a graphical interface is to use various tools to cut and copy to, and paste from, your operating system's *clipboard*. A clipboard is a section of your computer's memory that's set aside for temporary storage of text. When you cut text using the Cut menu choice, you're really not cutting the text—you're removing the text from the current document and then storing it in the clipboard, where it will stay until it's pushed aside by the next cut or copied text, or pasted by you. The difference between cutting and pasting text is that cut text disappears from the current document, while copied text will remain in the current document; both operations move text to the clipboard.

Cut

Choosing this cuts the highlighted text and pastes it to your operating system's clipboard.

Copy

Choosing this copies the highlighted text to your operating system's clipboard.

Paste

This selection copies the text stored in your operating system's clipboard to where the mouse cursor is located.

Clear

This deletes the selected text.

This menu item is available only on the Macintosh version of Netscape Communicator.

Select All

This highlights all of the text on your screen, preparing it for cutting and copying to another application, such as a text editor or a word processor. After you select all the text on a Web page with this menu choice, select **Copy** from the Edit menu, which copies the selected text to your operating-system clipboard. From there it can be pasted into any other application. This is convenient because only the text is copied; if you were to save the Web page to file, you'd have all the HTML formatting in addition to the text.

Find in Page

This simple dialog box allows you to search through the current document for a specific word or phrase. There are two settings: You can tell Netscape Navigator to match the case (if you don't, Netscape Navigator will return both **Go** and **go** if you specify **go** as your search term), and you can tell Netscape Navigator to look either before or after the current point of the document.

The selections in this dialog box differ by operating system. The Macintosh, Linux, and UNIX versions don't have a Match Case selection; instead, the term Case Sensitive is used (although both do the same thing). In addition, the Macintosh, Linux, and UNIX versions don't have Up and Down radio buttons; they have a Find Backwards check box to search backward, instead of forward (the default).

Find Again

This selection repeats the search specified in the Find menu selection.

Search Internet

This menu selection loads a page stored at the Netscape Communications Web site, linking you with search engines for the Internet. (We'll cover search engines in more detail in Chapter 4.)

Search Directory

This menu selection brings up a dialog box that searches through various Internet personal-information directories for listings. We'll cover these directories in more detail in Chapter 4.

The View Menu

The View menu features the following selections:

- Hide Navigation Toolbar
- Hide Location Toolbar
- Hide Personal Toolbar
- Show Menubar
- Increase Font (**Ctrl-]**)
- Decrease Font (**Ctrl-[**)
- Reload (**Ctrl-R**)
- Show Images
- Refresh
- Stop Page Loading
- Stop Animations
- Page Info
- Page Source
- Page Services
- Encodings

We'll cover each selection here.

Hide Toolbars

The first three selections, **Hide Navigation Toolbar, Hide Location Toolbar,** and **Hide Personal Toolbar**, control whether or not the three toolbars are visible on the screen. These three toolbars were covered earlier in this chapter, during your guided tour of the Netscape Navigator interface. Basically, these three toolbars are at the top of the screen and control various aspects of Netscape Navigator: the Navigation Toolbar is used to store buttons that are shortcuts to specific commands, the Location Toolbar governs the Bookmarks button and the URL location field, and the Personal Toolbar is for personal items; the default is to have them visible.

Show Menubar

This menu choice displays the menubar.

This menu choice is available only on Linux and UNIX versions of Netscape Communicator.

Increase Font

As you might expect, this makes the variable-width and fixed-width screen fonts one size larger. This new size will be sent along to the Preferences menu and stored in the fonts section. (In Chapter 3 you'll learn how to change font information in this manner.)

Decrease Font

As you might expect, this makes the variable-width and fixed-width screen fonts one size smaller. This new size will be sent along to the Preferences menu and stored in the fonts section. (In Chapter 3 you'll learn how to change font information in this manner.)

Reload

This selection reloads the current document. Netscape Navigator checks the Web server to see if the document has changed and will reload the document either from your cached memory (if there's been no change in the document) or from the Web server (if there has been a change in the document). This menu choice does the same thing as the Reload button found on the toolbar.

You might want to reload documents for a number of reasons. Many Web sites are becoming more interactive, which means that they may change every few minutes or so—there may be sports-score updates regularly, news or weather items that may be changed, chat threads where several folks are contributing—and, quite honestly, the World Wide Web isn't really set up for regular interactivity. There are also Web pages that give random output, and you may want to amuse yourself by seeing this output more than once.

You can tell Netscape Navigator to bring up a page from a server, instead of from the cached memory, by pressing the **Reload** button while holding down the **Shift** key.

MACINTOSH

Macintosh users will need to use the **Option** key, rather than the Shift key, to reload an image from the server.

Reload Frame

Instead of reloading the entire page, Netscape Navigator allows you to reload only a frame by selecting **Reload Frame**. Of course, the option is available only when your displayed Web page is making use of frames.

Show Images

You can set up Netscape Navigator to load Web pages without any images—this is handy when you have a balky network connection and don't want to sit there and twiddle your thumbs while too many images are transferred to your computer. In these cases, a small icon will appear on your screen in the place of an image, informing you that an image would have appeared there. However, there are some Web sites where images play an important role, such as large maps that allow you to move on the Web after clicking on a portion of a map. (To stop images from being automatically loaded, deselect **Automatically Load Images** from the Advanced submenu under the Preferences submenu.) After you select **Show Images**, the images will be downloaded from the Web server, but the page itself will not be reloaded.

Refresh

This summons the current Web page from memory. You may make changes to a Web page—by filling in some fields and checkboxes, for instance—and then decide you want to start over again.

MACINTOSH

This menu choice is not available to Macintosh users. However, Mac users can use **Control-Option-S** to refresh all Navigator windows.

Stop Page Loading

This stops the current page from being loaded into Netscape Navigator. This is the same as selecting the **Stop** button from the toolbar.

Stop Animations

Some Web pages use animations as a way to get your attention. These animations can come in several different forms, and if they are elaborate enough, they can drag down the performance of your system. This menu choice stops all animations that are running in the current Web page.

Page Source

This selection brings up the Web page formatted in the HTML source. You learned about HTML in Chapter 1; you'll also learn more about it later in this book. Basically, this menu selection brings up the current Web page in a deconstructed form, showing both the HTML tags along with the text.

The default HTML viewer in Netscape Navigator doesn't allow any interactivity: You can highlight text and copy it to the clipboard, and that's about it. It also doesn't have any commands, other than closing the window. (The HTML viewer in Netscape Navigator is shown in Figure 2.27.) If you're planning to work extensively with the HTML language, you may want to think about getting another editing and viewing tool, or else using Netscape Composer as your HTML viewer. Netscape Navigator allows you to specify another editor to view HTML source; this topic is covered in Chapter 3.

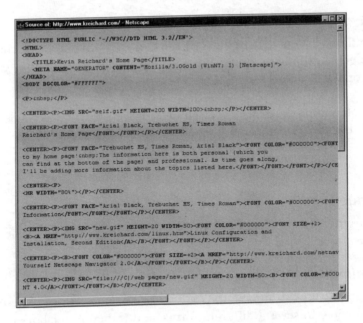

Figure 2.27 *The HTML viewer in Netscape Navigator.*

Linux and UNIX users of Netscape Communicator cannot specify another HTML viewer.

Page Source is the same as the Page Source menu option available when you select the hidden mouse menu, which you'll learn about later in this chapter.

You can also tell Netscape Navigator to display the source directly from the location field. Simply combine *view-source:* with the URL, such as *view-source:http://www.kreichard.com*. This opens the default HTML viewer with the URL loaded.

Page Info

This menu selection brings up an informational window that provides information about the current Web page. You can learn a lot from looking at this page, which is why we'll cover it some depth here.

The window is divided into two frames, as shown in Figure 2.28. The top frame lists the URL location of the page, followed by the images contained therein. The URL, as well as the images, are treated as hypertext links themselves.

The meatier information is contained in the bottom frame, beginning with the URL location of the document. When a document—in the form of a file—is sent over the Web, additional information is also sent before it ever appears on your screen. This information includes:

- Location or Netsite: The physical location of the page on the Web. If you click on this, the Web page will be displayed on the bottom frame instead of the document information. To get back the document information, click on the link specified in the top frame.

- File MIME type: Files are encoded in *MIME* formats, and this information is used by Netscape Navigator to properly display the file. Almost all Web pages are stored in the *text/html* format, which is basically text that includes HTML formatting.

- Source: The location of the document source. Most of the time the location will be stored on your hard drive, in the form of a disk cache, although intranet and corporate Internet users may find that a file is stored somewhere on a proxy server.

- Local cache file: This is the file where the source is stored. Netscape Navigator uses its own file-naming scheme when caching Web pages. If you look at your computer's hard drive in the directory Netscape Navigator uses for cache storage (the location will depend on your operating system; basically, there will be a subdirectory of the main Netscape directory that will be called **cache**), you'll see a lot of strangely named documents ending with the *HTM* suffix. These are the cached documents. There's nothing you need to do with these files: Netscape Navigator manages them and deletes them at the appropriate time. There are things you can do to limit the number of files stored, as you'll see in Chapter 3.

- Last Modified: There are two listings for when a file was last modified, in local time and in Greenwich Mean Time (GMT).

- Content length: The size of the file.

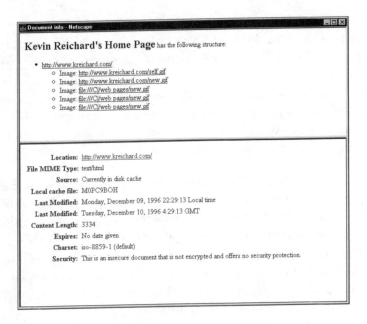

Figure 2.28 The Page Info window.

- Expires: This is when the document expires. Virtually all the documents you'll find on the Web have no expiration date.

- Charset: This is the *character set* the document is formatted in. All Web documents are encoded in a character set that corresponds to a language. The default in most Web pages is iso-8859-1, which corresponds to English.

- Security: If there's no security associated with a document, you'll be told that no security protection is available. If there is security involved, you'll be told the type of encryption used when sending the page, as well as the certificate information. All Web documents now have the potential of supporting some level of security. Most don't support security, because there's little need for security for the vast majority of Web documents—who needs to have a secure Web document from *www.suck.com*? However, as the Web grows as a commercial medium and supports financial transactions, there will be the need for secure Web documents. In fact, there's already been a lot of work done in this field, and to some degree you can be reasonably sure of security on the World Wide Web. Because this is such an important subject, we're saving it for extended coverage in Chapter 18.

Go back to the top of the screen shown in Figure 2.28. If you click on an image link, it becomes the active document, and you'll get a picture of the image on the bottom on the screen, along with information about the image: Its size in bytes and physical dimensions, its color and colormap, and whether it supports any transparency. Unless you're heavily into HTML coding, this information probably won't mean anything to you.

This is the same as the View Info menu option available when you select the hidden mouse menu, which you'll learn about later in this chapter.

NOTE

Page Services

If you're connected to a Netscape Enterprise Server, you have access to specialized services. This menu choice won't work if you're not connected to an Enterprise Server.

Encoding

Despite the Internet's status as a global phenomenon, the *lingua franca* on the Web is definitely English, and most Web pages are encoded as iso-8859-1 or Latin-1, which translate to English. When Netscape Navigator runs into a Web page where the encoding isn't specified, it assumes that the encoding is iso-8859-1. However, you may run into situations where the encoding is different. You may be doing research into Japanese history and want to make sure that the pages are displayed using the correct Japanese fonts. (You must have these fonts already loaded onto your system, however.) In such situations, you'll want to change the encoding. Netscape Navigator gives you the choice of the following encodings:

- Central European (Win1250)
- Central European (ISO 8859-2)
- Japanese (Auto-detect)
- Japanese (Shift JIS)

- Japanese (EUC-JP)
- Traditional Chinese (Big 5)
- Traditional Chinese (EUC)
- Simplified Chinese
- Korean
- Cyrillic (Windows-1251)
- Cyrillic (ISO 8859-5)
- Cyrillic (KO18-R)
- Greek (ISO-8859-7)
- Greek (Win-1253)
- Turkish (ISO 8859-9)
- Unicode (UTF8)
- Unicode (UTF7)
- User Defined
- Set Default

Frame Info

This menu choice launches a window that displays information about a frame, similar to the Info menu choice explained earlier in this chapter.

This menu choice is available only on Linux and UNIX versions of Netscape Communicator.

Older versions of Netscape Navigator contained a menu selection called **View Frame Source**. This menu choice is now obsolete; the new method for viewing the source of a frame is to click on the right mouse button when the pointer is over the desired frame and then select **View Frame Source** from the resulting pop-up menu.

The Go Menu

The Go menu has the following choices:

- Back (Alt-←)
- Forward (Alt-→)
- Home
- History

These are pretty simplistic choices that have to do with the loading and unloading of documents. For all the talk of the World Wide Web being some mystical, freeform, hypertext experience, using it is remarkably linear. You move from Web page to Web page in a straight line. Your route isn't necessarily predetermined, and there may be dozens and dozens of ways to get where you want to go. Don't let this fool you or intimidate you: Basically, all you can do is move forward or backward. The choices in this menu allow you to do so.

Back

This selection takes you to the page you just viewed, or the frame you were previously viewing. If you continue to choose **Back**, you'll keep moving backwards through the list of Web pages you have already visited. This is the same as the Back button on the toolbar.

MACINTOSH

Pressing the right mouse button (or merely the button on the Macintosh) brings up a pop-up menu, and Back is one of the selections on that menu.

Forward

If you've moved backwards through your previously visited Web pages, you can use the **Forward** selection to get back to the front of the history line. This is the same as the Forward button on the toolbar.

N O T E

Pressing the right mouse button (or merely the button on the Macintosh) brings up a pop-up menu, and Forward is one of the selections on that menu.

Home

This takes you to your designated home page (which you'll learn more about in Chapter 3). The default in Netscape Navigator is to use *http://home.netscape.com* as a home page. This is the same as the Home button on the toolbar.

History

Through they're not labeled as such, the remaining entries in this menu list the Web pages you've previously visited, in the order that you visited them (most recent at the top of the list). You can select any Web site on the list and it appears, either from a cached copy or (if you've been perusing a lot of sites and have run out of RAM) directly from the Web site.

The sites are listed here by title, not by address. You can summon a more complete listing of the sites you've visited by pulling down the **Window** and selecting **History**, which brings up a window that lists both titles and URL addresses. (More on this window later in this chapter.)

The Communicator Menu

This selections in this menu open other resources within Netscape Communicator. Some of the resources are tied to Netscape Navigator, such as the Bookmarks and History windows, while others are independent of Netscape Navigator. The menu selections are:

- Navigator (**Ctrl-1**)
- Messenger Mailbox (**Ctrl-2**)
- Collabra Discussion Groups (**Ctrl-3**)
- Page Composer (**Ctrl-4**)
- Conference (**Ctrl-5**)
- Calendar (**Ctrl-6**)
- IBM Host On-Demand (**Ctrl-7**)
- Show Component Bar
- Message Center (**Ctrl-Shift-1**)
- Address Book (**Ctrl-Shift-2**)
- Bookmarks

- History
- Java Console
- Security Info

We'll cover each.

Navigator

This menu selection opens another Web browser window. It's functionally the same as the **New Navigator Window** command under the File menu.

Messenger Mailbox

This opens the inbox for electronic mail. You'll learn more about electronic mail in Chapter 8.

Collabra Discussion Groups

This opens the Collabra discussions window, for intranet discussions or Usenet discussions. You'll learn more about discussions in Chapter 13.

Page Composer

This opens a Netscape Composer window. You'll learn more about Netscape Composer in Chapter 7.

Conference

This opens Netscape Conference, which can be use for Internet telephony and whiteboard collaborations. You'll learn more about Conference in Chapter 11.

Calendar

This open Netscape Calendar, which can be used to store personal and net-worked meeting information. You'll learn more about Calendar in Chapter 16.

Netcaster

This push technology will be introduced in Chapter 12.

Show Component Bar

You covered this menu choice earlier in this chapter. The component bar is used to provide shortcuts to the other Netscape Communicator components. The default is to have the component bar as a freestanding tool. If you select **Dock Component Bar**, the component bar ceases operation as a freestanding palette and is instead connected to the bottom of the Netscape Navigator window. To place the taskbar on the desktop again, select **Show Component Bar**.

Message Center

This opens up the Netscape Message Center, which organizes all your mail and discussion folders. You'll be introduced to this tool in Chapter 8.

Address Book

An address book is used by Netscape Mail to stored frequently used addresses. We'll cover the Netscape address book in Chapter 8.

Bookmarks

A bookmark is a tool for saving information about a specific Web resource for further use. This topic will be covered in Chapter 4.

History

This brings up a fuller listing of the Web pages you've visited, as shown in Figure 2.29. This list shows both the titles of the Web pages as well as the full URL.

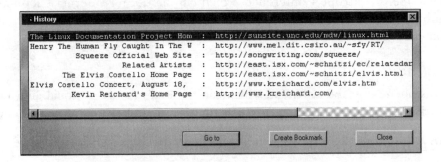

Figure 2.29 *The History window.*

As you can see in Figure 2.29, one of the items in the History list is high-lighted, which means that you can do two things with the item: You can go directly to that Web page (either by double-clicking on the item or pressing the **Go to** button), or you can incorporate this Web page into your bookmarks list by pressing the **Create Bookmarks** button. (Again, you'll learn more about bookmarks in Chapter 4.)

The History feature has been changed in the newest versions of Netscape Navigator. Previously, a History window showed only those items that had been visited in the current session. Now, the History feature shows all sites visited in the last day.

HOT LINK

You can change this setting through the Preferences menu, as you'll see in Chapter 3.

Show Java Console

This menu selection displays a Java console. Some Java applets create their own console, which is then used to run separately from the main browser. If you open this console and don't have a Java applet running, all it does is sit empty and eat up processing power. If you've been running a Java applet, you can use this menu selection to redisplay the Java applet.

Security Info

This menu choice displays information about the security measures associated with a window. Because this is an important subject, we're devoting Chapter 18 to the topic of security.

The Current Window

Finally, the last line on the Communicator menu lists the title of the current Web page, marked with a checkmark. If you open up multiple Web browsers, all the open Web browsers will be listed here.

The Help Menu

This menu brings you more information about Netscape Navigator. Unlike past versions of Netscape Navigator, the current versions has much Help information stored locally, which means that you can peruse it without being physically connected to the Internet. (In the past, you needed to be connected to the Internet to access the Help pages.) We note whether pages are local or stored on a Netscape Communications server on the Internet.

 Macintosh users don't have a Help menu. They can use either Balloon Help or access the Apple menu and look for Help selections.

MACINTOSH

The following items are included under the Help menu:

- Help Contents (F1)
- Release Notes
- Product Information and Support
- Software Updates
- Register Now
- Member Services
- International Users
- Security
- Net Etiquette
- About Plug-Ins
- About Font Displayers
- About Communicator...

We'll cover each.

Help Contents

This local page is the main window into the various subwindows that contain Netscape Navigator and Netscape Communicator Help. The Help is organized by component, as shown in Figure 2.30.

Figure 2.30 *The Help Contents window.*

To peruse the Help files for a specific component, just click on the component's image. This component replaces the old Handbook function in previous versions of Netscape Navigator.

Release Notes

This Netscape Communications page provides up-to-the-minute information about Netscape Navigator, including a listing of known bugs and new features.

Product Information and Support

This is the menu choice if you're having problems with Netscape Communicator. It contains links to important resources that will aid you in troubleshooting, such as release notes (which detail known problems with Netscape Communicator), discussion groups (which can be accessed with the Collabra Discussion Groups component), and the Frequently Asked Questions (FAQ) list.

Software Updates

This Netscape Communications screen details how to update your version of Netscape Communicator.

Register Now

This Netscape Communications screen tells you how to register your software and fork over some money to Netscape Communications, which you really should do if you're an honest person. If you have already registered, it will display your registration information and ask for your digital verification.

Member Services

This Netscape Communications screen details how to update your version of Netscape Communicator. It's the same screen as displayed under Software Updates.

International Users

This Netscape Communications page touts the advantages of Netscape Communicator for international users.

Security

This Netscape Communications page details the security measures used in Netscape Communicator. We'll cover these topics in Chapter 18.

Net Etiquette

This Netscape Communications page details how to get along with other Internet users. Some of it is useful, such as the location of Help resources, and other portions are condescending, especially when you're lectured about solving your own problems before asking others for help.

About Plug-ins

This local listing shows what Netscape Navigator plug-ins that you have installed. The default Netscape Communicator installation comes with several plug-ins, including media players, a virtual-reality (VRML) modeler, and a QuickTime player. This window is shown in Figure 2.31.

Figure 2.31 *A listing of plug-ins.*

You'll learn more about plug-ins in Chapters 10 and 11.

About Font Displayers

This local page shows what tools Netscape Communicator is using to display fonts. You'll learn more about this in Chapter 4.

About Communicator

This menu selection opens a local Web page that tells you what version of Netscape Communicator you're using, as well as any other tools that might be included as part of your package (such as Java or RSA encryption).

N O T E

You can get the same information by typing **About:** in the URL field.

THE HIDDEN POP-UP MENU

You can do a lot of work with just the mouse in Netscape Navigator. In fact, pressing the right button yields a pop-up menu of frequently used commands, if you're running Windows, Linux, or UNIX. These menus are context-sensitive, meaning that they change depending on where the mouse pointer is positioned. If the mouse pointer is over straight text, then all you can do is move back or forward, in the equivalents of the Back and Forward commands under the Go menu.

MACINTOSH

If you're using the Macintosh, you need to press and hold down the mouse button to do the same thing.

There is a long list of commands that may be part of a pop-up menu. Only two will be present at all times: Back and Forward, and the Forward command may be grayed out if you have no Web pages to go forward to.

In the rest of this section, we'll mention the commands you may see in your pop-up menu, other than the Back and Forward commands.

Open in New Window

This option opens a new Netscape Navigator window with the linked page loaded.

Open Link in Composer

This option opens Netscape Composer with the linked page loaded.

Save Link As...

This option actually has the possibility of being useful. This menu selection will save the linked page directly to disk, without being displayed in the Web-browser window. This can be useful if you want to do a lot of research without spending much time online; you can just grab the Web pages and then view them later when you're not connected to the Internet.

Copy Link Location

This selection takes the link information—the URL, basically—and copies it to your operating system's clipboard, where it can be pasted into another application. Only the actual link URL is copied, not the actual verbiage that represents the link in the Web page.

Add Bookmark

This menu selection adds the current Web page to your list of bookmarks. If the cursor is positioned over a URL, then that URL and not the current Web page will be added to your list of bookmarks.

Create Shortcut

This menu selection creates an Internet shortcut from the current Web page. A *shortcut* is an icon on your desktop that's a shortcut to a resource. If you were to click on a shortcut created for *http://www.kreichard.com*, the resulting action would be that a Web browser would be launched (if there was not running) with the URL loaded.

Win95

This menu option is available only in the Windows 95/NT version of Netscape Communicator.

View Source

This menu choice displays the document source of the current Web page. It's the same as Source from the View menu.

View Info

This menu choice displays information about the current Web page—the same information that's displayed when you select **Info** from the View menu.

Show Menubar

This menu choice displays the menu bar.

This menu selection is available only to Linux and UNIX users.

Working with Images

If the pointer is positioned over an image, a number of pop-up menu items will appear in addition to the previously explained menu selections.

View Image filename

This opens a new window with just the image on view. Use the **Back** button to move back to the full Web page.

Save Image as...

This saves the image to disk. Netscape Navigator will prompt you for a location on your hard disk to save the image to, keeping the image's original filename and format (in other words, you can't save a GIF file from the Web to a JPEG-formatted file on your hard drive).

Add Bookmark

This saves the location of the image to your list of bookmarks.

Set as Wallpaper

This converts the image into a wallpaper file, which will be displayed on the background of your desktop.

This menu selection is available only for Windows 3.1 and Windows 95/NT users.

Copy Image

This copies the image to the clipboard.

MACINTOSH

This menu selection is available only for Macintosh users.

Copy Image Location

This copies the image location—the URL, essentially—to your operating-system clipboard, where it can be copied to another window or application.

Load This Image

This loads the image from a Web server, if it doesn't appear on the screen, in those cases where you've grabbed Web pages and not their accompanying images.

View Source

This menu choice displays the document source of the current Web page. It's the same as **Source** from the View menu.

View Info

This menu choice displays information about the current Web page—the same information that's displayed when you select **Info** from the View menu.

ABOUT: YOUR SETUP

You can get more information about your current Netscape Navigator usage by using *about:* in the URL line, either by itself or in combination with other parameters. The following combinations are possible:

- *about:* returns generic information about your Netscape Communicator installation, including the version number and a link to your license. It's the same as About Communicator from the Communicator pulldown menu.

- *about:global* returns the contents of the global history file. This file contains the URL of every Web site you've visited recently, but it's amazingly detailed—it lists the URL and the date it was visited for every element on a Web page, as well as URLs that might have been contained with an electronic-mail message. For example, you might subscribe to one of the many e-mail services of Mercury Mail (*http://www.merc.com*). When you receive e-mail from Mercury Mail, there is usually advertising at the top of the message (after all, nothing is free!), and that advertising banner is actually a URL that's loaded every time you view the mail. When you're viewing the mail, you aren't actually told that the banner is a URL, but it is listed in the global history, appearing as something like this:

```
URL: http://images.merc.com/mail/sw/mlb/MLBGeneric.gif
Date: Tue Jun 03 07:42:50 1997
```

- *about:plugins* lists the plug-ins you have installed on your system. We'll cover this in more detail in Chapter 10.
- *about:cache* lists information about the status and contents of your disk cache. You'll learn more about your disk cache in the next two chapters, but for now all you need to know is that Netscape Navigator saves copies of Web pages to your hard drive in order to speed up Web-surfing time, and that this is the way for you to see the contents of this cache. The information looks like the following:

```
Disk Cache statistics
Maximum size: 7864320
Current size: 5603855
Number of files in cache: 960
Average cache file size: 5837

URL: http://home.netscape.com/escapes/images/navigation_bar.gif
Content Length: 1561
Content type: image/gif
Local filename: MVN6F36U.GIF
Last Modified: Wed Sep 18 17:54:17 1996
Expires: No expiration date sent
```

- *about:memory-cache* returns information about the cached Web pages in your system's RAM.

- *about:image-cache* returns information about the cached Web images in your system's RAM. This information looks something like this:

```
Image Cache statistics
Maximum size: 733856
Current size: 661820
Number of images in cache: 45
Average cached image size: 14707

URL: http://www.pcworld.com/home/graphics/by_icon30.gif
Decoded size (bytes): 28304
Image dimensions: 468 x 60
```

SUMMARY

This long chapter covers the steps needed to install and use Netscape Communicator, focusing on the initial usage of Netscape Navigator, the Web browser. This process is actually pretty simple, once you get a grasp on what's going on. Several important steps were covered in this chapter:

- How to acquire Netscape Navigator
- Setting up your computer to connect to the Internet
- Installing Netscape Communicator on Windows 95, Windows 3.1, Macintosh, and UNIX platforms
- Running down the elements of a Netscape window
- Reviewing the contents of all the pulldown menus

In the next chapter, you'll learn about configuring Netscape Navigator to make it do what you want it to.

## CHAPTER 3

Customizing Netscape Communicator and Netscape Navigator

You have a lot of control over how Netscape Navigator and Netscape Communicator look and act. In this chapter, we'll focus on the many customization options found under the Edit menu. Topics covered in this chapter include:

- Setting general preferences
- Changing fonts and colors
- Determining where Netscape Navigator connects when it first loads
- Adding other applications
- Setting the cache

CONFIGURING NETSCAPE NAVIGATOR

In theory, Netscape Communicator should work immediately when you start it, as long as you're running on a vanilla computer with a vanilla network connection. Indeed, most of you won't be interested in the topics covered in this chapter—not at first, anyway.

However, some of you may need to do some additional work on Netscape Communicator (especially with Netscape Navigator and the electronic-mail functions) before you can begin cruising the World Wide Web. Others will want to fine-tune Netscape Navigator after they've been using it a while. Because some of you may need to do some additional configuration work before actually using Netscape Navigator, we're putting this coverage of Navigator and Communicator configuration here, before many of you do any serious work with Netscape Navigator and the other Netscape Communicator components.

What exactly do we mean by *configuration*? Basically, this is a catch-all term that applies to anything that affects how Netscape Communicator works. This ranges from the languages supported by Netscape Navigator and how efficiently it grabs Web pages, to the electronic-mail addresses used in Messenger and other components. The creators of Communicator lumped these configuration options in Netscape Navigator under the Edit menu's Preferences menu choice, which brings up the Preferences panel (as shown in Figure 3.1). In this panel you see the following headings:

- Appearance
- Navigator
- Mail & Groups
- Composer
- Offline
- Advanced

In this chapter we'll cover all of the topics except for Mail & Groups, which will be covered separately in Chapter 8, and Composer, which will be covered separately in Chapter 7.

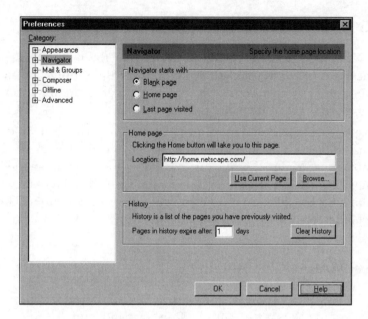

Figure 3.1 *The Preferences panel.*

N O T E

Windows 3.x users may get the following error message when they open the Preferences menu choice:

```
Call to undefined dynalink
```

This has to do with differing versions of a Microsoft Windows dynamic-link file, **CTL3DV2.DLL**, which is stored in your **windows** directory and your **windows/system** directory. Usually the file in the **windows** directory is older than the one in the **windows/system** directory. Because both directories are searched by Windows 3.x, you can rename the older file as **CTL3DV2.OLD** and restart Windows 3.x, which should clear up the problem.

Using Preferences

Veteran Netscape Navigator users will notice that the method of changing preferences has been overhauled. While most of the settings are similar to those found in earlier versions of Netscape Navigator, the ways you choose them and move between them are different.

Basically, Netscape Communicator uses items on the left side of the panel to organize subjects. Plus and minus boxes tell you whether there are additional submenus. A plus sign means that there are other submenus, and a minus sign means that there are no other submenus. You can open and close these submenus by clicking on the box with your mouse pointer. This is the same sort of interface that Microsoft uses with Windows 95/NT.

The Appearance Panel

The Appearance panel controls how Netscape Communicator appears, as well as how fonts and colors are organized. It's shown in Figure 3.2.

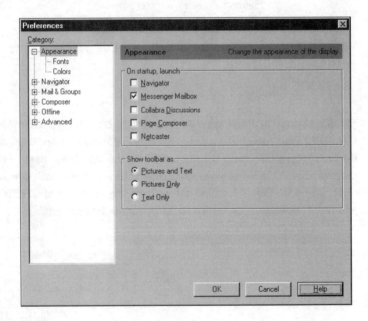

Figure 3.2 The Appearance panel.

The first section, **On startup, launch**, is something you'll probably want to look over. It indicates which parts of Netscape Communicator start when you launch it. The default is to have only the browser (Netscape Navigator) begin; you can change this to include the mailbox, discussion, page-composer, and Netcaster components. If you rely on Netscape Mail for all of your mail needs (which will be covered in Chapter 8), you may want to launch it immediately when Netscape Navigator loads. You can launch more than one component when you begin Netscape Navigator, so you can select any combination.

The **Show toolbar** as section determines how Netscape Navigator initially appears on the screen. Like all good graphical applications, Netscape Navigator uses a toolbar underneath the menubar. (You learned about the toolbar and what it does in Chapter 2.) The **Show Toolbar as:** radio buttons allow you to show both text and pictures on the toolbar, or only pictures, or only text. None of these choices affect how Netscape Navigator actually works, only how it appears on the screen. These changes are a matter of personal preference and, quite honestly, aren't very important. Also, you can't get rid of the toolbar through this dialog box—all you can do is change its appearance.

You can get rid of the toolbar altogether through a separate choice on the Edit menu, as you'll learn later in this chapter.

NOTE

The UNIX/X versions of Netscape Communicator have an additional setting: whether or not to underline text links. Other Netscape users can find this setting under the Colors panel.

UNIX

The Fonts Panel

This panel (as seen in Figure 3.3) sets the font choices. Because this area directly affects how much of Netscape Navigator looks, each choice will be explained.

The first pull down menu, For the Encoding, determines how Netscape Navigator deals with language. As the Internet becomes more of an international phenomenon, support for different languages becomes more important. The default choice of Western (or, as more properly known outside of Netscape Navigator usage, Latin-1) is for English-speaking users; it is the basic ASCII character set.

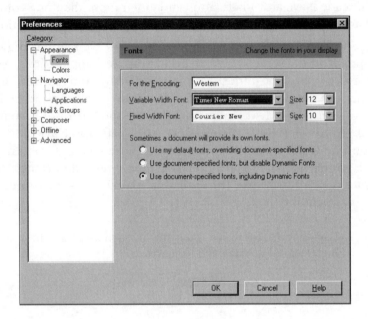

Figure 3.3 *The Fonts panel.*

However, not everyone in the world uses English, and Netscape Navigator is truly an international browser. Netscape Navigator uses *encodings* to support other languages in terms of fonts and characters. The For the Encoding pull-down menu supports a number of languages, including:

- Western
- Central European
- Japanese
- Traditional Chinese
- Simplified Chinese
- Korean

- Cyrillic
- Greek
- Turkish
- Unicode
- User defined

Basically, this part of the dialog box lets you link a font to a character encoding. When Netscape Navigator runs across characters encoded in Japanese, it needs to know what font to use to display those characters. Netscape Navigator does not include the necessary fonts, however, so you'll need to go out and grab those *kanji* fonts on your own, install them in your operating system, and then tell Netscape Navigator to use them by using this panel.

You might think that this dialog box is used to determine whether Netscape Navigator accepts a foreign language, but it's not. Later in this chapter you'll learn how to set the languages that Netscape Navigator accepts.

HOT LINK

This panel is also where you can specify which fonts are used with your system. Although it isn't explained very well, specific fonts are associated with encodings; when you change a font here, you're associating it with an encoding. To wit: Almost every reader of this book will be using Western (formerly known as Latin-1) as their encoding (i.e., everyone using English as their main language). This is where you specify the fonts to be used with Western encoding. (Why Netscape doesn't have a simple font-selection mechanism for the Latin-1 users is puzzling.)

To change your fonts, you need to change fonts for the Latin-1 encoding. Web pages generally use two different types of fonts: proportional and fixed. (They can also specify specific fonts for Web pages, which is a topic we'll cover later.) *Proportional fonts* treat the measurement of each letter individually:

This is a proportional font—Times New Roman

For instance, an *m* would be wider than an *i*, because that's how the letters are treated in the real world. (The text you are reading right now is in a proportional font.) Most popular computer fonts are proportional.

In *fixed fonts* all characters are the same width, no matter if the letter is an *i* or an *m*:

```
This is a fixed font—Courier New
```

In many Web pages, fixed fonts are used to denote file locations either within text or as part of an FTP directory tree. The default for the fixed font (in the Windows, Windows 95, and Macintosh versions of Netscape Navigator) is Courier New because it is found on virtually every system.

Why are these fonts important? Because when a Web server sends a Web page to your machine, the page itself doesn't necessarily contain specific font information. In some situations—like the case of *http://www.kreichard.com*, which you viewed repeatedly in Chapter 2—the Web-page designer will specify a font to be used in a headline or text. However, in most situations (at least when this book was written), the Web page will contain tags that say whether a font is proportional or fixed, as well as what size it is. If a proportional font is used in the place of the fixed font, the spacing of the page will appear to be incorrect. Conversely, a fixed font is more difficult to read than a proportional font, so if you use a fixed font for text, you'll probably get a headache from trying to read the text.

Unless you think you have a very good reason for doing so, don't mess with the proportional font *or* the fixed font. Some Web-page layouts rely on a specific spacings for fonts, and the proportional font relies mostly on specific spacings. (Indeed, this reliance on specific spacings is why the proportional font is used on a Web page.) If you do want to change your font, select **Choose Font...**. Netscape Navigator will display a dialog box specific to your operating system that lets you choose from a list of installed fonts.

Microsoft makes available new fonts designed for the World Wide Web. These fonts are installed as part of your operating system and can be used by any application, including Netscape Communicator. Some of the fonts shown in the screen illustrations for *http://www.kreichard.com* come from Microsoft. Check out *http://www.microsoft.com/truetype/* for more information and downloads.

Dynamic Fonts

There's a setting on the Fonts panel that covers the use of dynamic fonts. Basically, this has to do with the advent of Dynamic HTML, which enables Web pages to look exactly the same no matter where they are displayed.

To that end, Web designers can include dynamic fonts with their Web pages. If they do, Netscape Communicator will use the downloaded dynamic font in a page display instead of a locally stored font. These dynamic fonts don't take long to download or be rendered on your local machine, so there's no reason not to use them.

Using Fonts with UNIX and Linux

UNIX and Linux users will find that even if they use the correct settings for fonts on Netscape Navigator, they'll still have problems viewing fonts. That's because of the way the X Window System—the arbiter of the graphical interface on UNIX and Linux—deals with fonts.

Basically, X Window deals with two types of fonts: 75dpi (short for 75 dots per inch) and 100dpi (short for 100 dots per inch). The 75dpi fonts are for use on smaller (i.e., 13-inch) monitors, while the 100dpi fonts are used on larger (17-inch and larger) monitors. When you (or your system administrator) installs X, they choose between the font sizes (assuming that you're not using a font server, of course).

You can use the X command **xlsfonts** to see which fonts are installed on your system. You'll see a really long list of fonts, and somewhere in there you'll see either 75 or 100 in the line. Check your system documentation for an explanation of how to change your font set from 75dpi to 100dpi.

The Colors Panel

The Colors panel deals with the colors of Web pages and Netscape Communicator, and is shown in Figure 3.4. Four colors are to be specified:

- Text, which specifies the color of text (the default is black). Unless you have an aversion to readable text, you'll want to keep the default.
- Background, which specifies the color or pattern on the screen background (the default is gray).
- Unvisited Links, which specifies the color of hypertext links to pages you haven't seen (the default is blue). The only reason to make changes here is for aesthetic reasons.
- Visited Links, which specifies the colors of hypertext links you've already followed (the default is purple).

UNIX users do not have this panel choice. To play with color on a UNIX/X Window system, you'll need to edit the **.Xdefaults** file and change the colors from the global red-green-blue database.

UNIX

The color settings here will apply to all Netscape Communicator components, not just Netscape Navigator.

N O T E

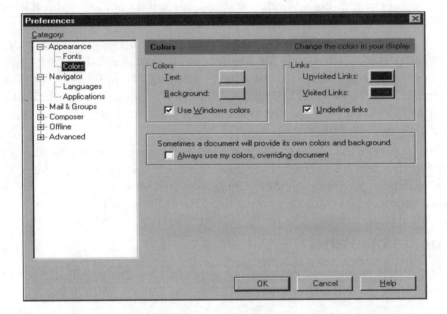

Figure 3.4 *The Colors panel.*

If you're a Windows/Windows 95/Windows NT user, you probably won't be changing the colors for the text and the background. The default setting here is to use the defaults Windows colors for text (black) and background (gray). If you do want to change the text and background colors, you'll need to deselect the **Use Windows color** box. At that point, you can select from a palette of system colors or create your own custom color.

Be warned that changing the text and background colors is not an absolute. Most larger commercial Web sites specify their own text and background colors, and these choices will always be implemented unless you check the **Always use my colors** box.

Obviously Macintosh and UNIX/Linux users won't have a choice entitled Use Windows colors. Instead, their menu choice is entitled **Use Default Colors**.

If you're a UNIX/X user, you may want to set absolutes for colors. Typically, X Window has a limited colormap, and you can run into problems with Web sites that eat up a large chunk of that colormap. If you find yourself running low on memory or having color-allocation problems, select the **Always use my colors** box.

You also have the option of underlining links. Generally speaking, you should do so, if only to make them easier to notice. If you're using a monochrome display, you'll definitely want to leave links underlined, since you'll have no other way to see them.

The setting for underlining links can be found under the Appearances panel.

The Navigator Panel

This panel—as shown in Figure 3.5—controls specific aspects of Netscape Navigator, as opposed to the rest of Netscape Communicator. There are basically two activities governed here: what Netscape Navigator loads with upon startup, and how history is managed.

Most of you will get rather tired of connecting directly to the Netscape home page every time you load Netscape Navigator; you'd rather connect directly to a site you want to check regularly. In this portion of the dialog box, you can change that. Note that the default HTTP address is:

http://home.netscape.com/

which, of course, is the Netscape home page. You can start with a blank page (the preferred method if you're often starting your Navigator sessions with a new Web site), your specified home page (which we'll get to a little later), or the last Web page that you visited.

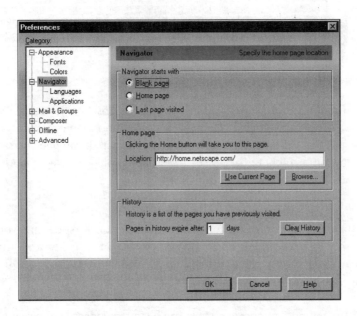

Figure 3.5 The Navigator panel.

Why would you want to begin with a blank page or a new URL? For many reasons. If you're working on an intranet, you don't want to be trying to connect to *http://home.netscape.com* and encountering error messages every time you launch Netscape Navigator. You may use Netscape Navigator for a specific reason that has nothing to do with Netscape Communications, and so you'll want to take Netscape out of the loop, as in the case of an accountant connecting every day to a tax-preparation site or a salesperson who connects to his firm's Web site every day to view product information. Or you may just find that your day begins on a much lighter note if you connect to *http://www.suck.com* rather than *http://home.netscape.com* in the morning.

If you do decide to start with a home page, you can use the default home page (which, not so coincidentally, is the Netscape home page) or specify your own in the Home page field. This home page can be on the World Wide Web, your local intranet, or your own hard drive. If it's a Web page, you can enter the URL in the Location text area (where the default is *http://home.netscape.com/*), select the current Web page with the **Use Current**

Page button, or browse your computer and/or intranet with the **Browse** button. This last button brings up the file-searching mechanism of your own operating system, which you should be familiar with.

Changing the home page also changes how Netscape Navigator reacts when you press on the Netscape logo on the main Navigator window. The default is to connect to the Netscape home page when that logo is selected with a mouse. However, if you enter a new home page in this panel, that new home page will be loaded whenever you select the logo.

Specifying History

As you jump from Web site to Web site, you'll amass entries in your history file, which keeps track of the Web sites you've recently visited. (You learned about the history function in Chapter 2 and will cover it more in Chapter 4.)

The setting here specifies how long history entries are archived before they are purged from the system. The default for history entries to expire is one day. If you rarely use Netscape Navigator, this may not be the best setting, as your history entries expire between sessions; in such a case, you'll want to increase the amount of time to around seven days. On the flip side, if you're an avid surfer and stoke up Netscape Navigator every day for some serious surfing, one day is your best setting.

  History visits are recorded only for the current session on the Macintosh and UNIX versions of Netscape Communicator.

MACINTOSH UNIX

The Clear History button does what you'd expect—clear the history listings.

 This setting is known as Expire Now on the Macintosh.

MACINTOSH

The Languages Panel

This panel, shown in Figure 3.6, controls the language Netscape Navigator uses to display Web pages. The World Wide Web is a worldwide phenomenon, and sometimes Web pages are available in more than one language. (Most of the time, however, English is the language of the Web.) You can choose that Web pages be displayed in these languages (if they are available):

- Afrikaans
- Albanian
- Basque
- Bulgarian
- Byelorussian
- Catalan
- Chinese (mainland or Taiwanese)
- Croatian
- Czech
- Danish
- Dutch (including Belgium)
- English (United States and the United Kingdom)
- Faeroese
- Finnish
- French (including Belgium, Canada, Switzerland, and France)
- Galician
- German (including Austria, Germany, and Switzerland)
- Greek
- Hungarian
- Icelandic
- Indonesian
- Irish
- Italian
- Japanese
- Korean
- Macedonian
- Norwegian
- Polish

- Portuguese (including Brazil)
- Romanian
- Russian
- Scots Gaelic
- Serbian
- Slovak
- Slovenian
- Spanish (including Argentina, Colombia, and Spain)
- Swedish
- Turkish
- Ukrainian

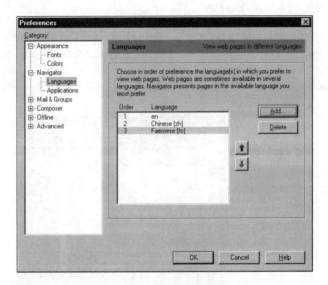

Figure 3.6 *The Languages panel.*

There's more to displaying a Web page in another language, however. If you want to display pages in Japanese, for instance, you'll need Japanese fonts. Generally speaking, these fonts are part of the operating system and can be installed when you install your operating system. However, if you want to add foreign-language support to an existing installation, then you'll need to check your operating-system documentation for directions.

You can also set up priorities; as you can see from Figure 3.6, there are three languages selected: the default English, as well as Chinese and Faeroese. (You never know when you need crucial information about sailing and fishing off the coast of Scotland or need data from the Faeroese College of Education in Torshavn!) You can use the buttons on the left of the language list to change the order, after highlighting the language. To use Faeroese as your preferred language, for example, you'd highlight it and then use the arrow to move it up in the pecking order.

There is no Language panel in the UNIX versions of Netscape Communicator.

The Applications Panel

The Applications panel, shown in Figure 3.7, specifies other applications that Netscape Navigator will call under specific circumstances. You may do very well without these applications, but there may be times when Netscape Navigator and you'll need to summon the power of another application.

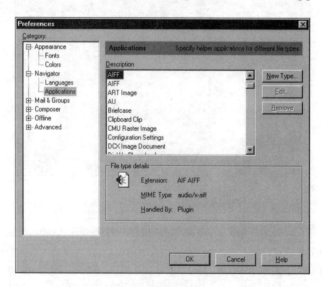

Figure 3.7 The Applications panel.

Netscape Communicator now uses *helpers* and *applications* interchangeably. Basically, applications perform tasks that Netscape Navigator cannot do. This includes playing audio and video files, as well as running programs written in the Java programming language. These aren't necessarily applications specifically written for use with Netscape Navigator. (These are not plug-ins, which we'll cover in Chapter 10.)

Some helper applications such as the naplayer application, are already included with Netscape Navigator. This application is written to play some simple audio files, but it can't handle the more robust RealAudio and DSP audio files currently more popular on the Internet.

When Netscape Navigator runs across *any* file, it looks to the information found in this tab to determine what action to take. Basically, Netscape Navigator can take three actions on a file:

- View in browser
- Save the file to disk
- Launch a specific application

How does Netscape Navigator know what kind of files it comes across? By the filename extension. The Internet tends to follow MS-DOS conventions—even though Windows and Macintosh users dominate the World Wide Web—and so files are sent over the WWW following the familiar eight-dot-three filename conventions: a main filename of eight or fewer characters, followed by a period (.) and then an extension of up to three characters. Specific extensions denote specific kinds of files: **.exe** extensions are for executable Windows or DOS programs, **.zip** is for files compressed using the PKZip method of compression, and so on. A good many of these extensions are codified as part of the MIME extensions widely supported in the Internet world.

And, since the Internet world is pretty good about sticking to these extensions, Netscape Navigator can assume that when it runs a specific file extension, it will figure out what to do with that file. Remember that Netscape Navigator is used to request files from the Internet and then present those files to you. In the vast majority of these cases, the requested files will be formatted in HTML. However, in other cases where the requested files may not be in HTML, you'll need to tell Netscape Navigator how to handle these files. Some extensions tell Netscape Navigator to save the file to disk. Some tell

Netscape Navigator to display the file. Other extensions tell Netscape Navigator to summon another program on your computer—the aforementioned helper application—to handle the file.

When Netscape Navigator can't handle a file, it reports one of the following error messages:

Unknown file type

No viewer configured for file type

Unable to launch external viewer

It's in this menu that you view the installed helper applications, as well as add some more of your own. Netscape Communicator recognizes the file formats listed in Table 3.1, but doesn't necessarily support them; the same table offers advice about how to extend this recognition.

Table 3.1   *Netscape Communicator File Types and Their Extensions.*

FILE TYPE	EXTENSION	ACTIONS
application/ms-tnef	*none*	Proprietary mail protocol used by Microsoft Exchange; support for it is why Exchange can be used for electronic mail instead of Messenger when other Communicator components are installed.
application/x-conference	nsc	Launches Netscape Conference.
application/x-gzip	gz	This is a file compressed with the gzip utility, popular in the UNIX freeware world (it's GNU software). Software that will uncompress files compressed with gzip can be found at *ftp://prep.ai.mit.edu/pub/gnu/*. At the time this book was written, the most recent version for MS-DOS (Windows or Macintosh versions are not available) was **gzip-1.2.4.msdos.exe**. The default is to ask the user what action to take on the file.

FILE TYPE	EXTENSION	ACTIONS
application/x-compress	Z	This is a file compressed with the UNIX compress command. The gzip utility mentioned previously can uncompress files compressed with this command. The default is to ask the user what action to take on the file.
application/x-pkcs7-signature	p7s	This has to do with security certificates issued by RSA Data Security and how the certificates should be handled. The default is to ask the user what action to take on the file. Security will be covered in greater detail in Chapter 19.
application/x-pkcs-7-mime	p7m, p7c	This has to do with security certificates issued by RSA Data Security and how the certificates should be handled. The default is to ask the user what action to take on the file. Security will be covered in greater detail in Chapter 19.
application/x-ns-proxy-autoconfig	pac	This program configures Netscape Navigator for use with a proxy server. The default is to let Netscape Navigator handle this file without any intervention from you.
application/x-javascript	js, mocha	This is a script written in the JavaScript programming language. The default is to ask you what to do with this file.
application/x-perl	pl	This is a script written in the Perl scripting language. Generally, these are programs that are run on a Web server, not on a local machine (indeed, Perl scripts won't run on your computer unless you have Perl installed). The default is to ask the user what action to take on the file.

FILE TYPE	EXTENSION	ACTIONS
application/x-tcl	tcl	This is a script written in the Tcl scripting language. Generally, these are programs that are run on a Web server, not on a local machine (indeed, Tcl scripts won't run on your computer unless you have Tcl installed). The default is to ask the user what action to take on the file.
application/x-sh	sh	This is a shell script for the UNIX **sh** shell. Generally, this is a program that should be run on a UNIX server, not on your local machine. The default is to ask the user what action to take on the file.
application/x-csh	csh	This is a shell script for the UNIX **csh** shell. Generally, this is a program that should be run on a UNIX server, not on your local machine. The default is to ask the user what action to take on the file.
application/postscript	ai, eps, ps	This is a file that's formatted with the Postscript page-description language. If you have a Postscript viewer on your system, you can configure it to view these files. In addition, the GNU Ghostscript utility (found at *ftp://prep.ai.mit.edu/pub/gnu/*) can be used to view and print these files. You may run into these files, as much UNIX system documentation is formatted in the Postscript language. The default is to ask you what to do with this file.
application/octet-stream	exe, bin	This is an MS-DOS or Windows executable program. The default is to save this file to disk.

FILE TYPE	EXTENSION	ACTIONS
application/x-cpio	cpio	This is a set of files archived with the UNIX cpio command. The default is to ask you what to do with the file; as there's no easy way to unarchive these files in the MS-DOS or Macintosh worlds, you'll want to save these files to disk. UNIX users, of course, will want to save these files to disk and then unarchive them with the cpio command.
application/x-gtar	gtar	This is a set of files archived with the UNIX **tar** command. The default is to ask you what to do with the file; as there's no easy way to unarchive these files in the MS-DOS or Macintosh worlds, you'll want to save these files to disk. UNIX users, of course, will want to save these files to disk and then unarchive them with the tar command.
application/x-tar	tar	This is a set of files archived with the UNIX **tar** command. The default is to ask you what to do with the file; as there's no easy way to unarchive these files in the MS-DOS or Macintosh worlds, you'll want to save these files to disk. UNIX users, of course, will want to save these files to disk and then unarchive them with the tar command.
application/x-shar	shar	This is a shell archive file. The default is to ask you what to do with the file.

FILE TYPE	EXTENSION	ACTIONS
application/x-zip-compressed	zip	This is a file compressed with the PKWare pkzip utility or the WinZip utility. The default is to ask you what to do with the file, but you could easily change Netscape Communicator to save this file directly to disk. You'll need PKZip (found at *http://www/pkware.com*) or WinZip (found at *http://www.winzip.com* to uncompress this file; MS-DOS, Windows, OS/2, and Macintosh versions of PKZip are available.
application/x-stuffit	sit	This is a file compressed with the Macintosh StuffIt utility. The default is to ask you what to do with the file, but you could easily change Netscape Navigator to save this file directly to disk.
application/mac-binhex40	hqx	This is a file formatted with the BinHex format, popular in the Macintosh world. The default is to let the browser handle this file.
video/x-msvideo	avi	This is a video formatted using the Microsoft Video format. The default asks you what to do with the file, but you could easily change Netscape Navigator to save this file directly to disk or invoke a player if you have Microsoft Video on your system.
video/quicktime	qt, mov	This is a video formatted using the Apple QuickTime format. The default asks you what to do with the file, but the final version of Netscape Communicator was slated to include a QuickTime player as a plug-in.

File Type	Extension	Actions
video/x-mpeg2	mpv2, mp2v	This is a video formatted using the MPEG-2 format. The default is to ask the user what to do with the file.
video/mpeg	mpeg, mpg, mpe, mpv, vbs, mpegvmpg	This is a video formatted using the MPEG format. The default ask you what to do with the file but you could easily change Netscape Navigator to save this file directly to disk or invoke a player if you have a MPEG player on your system.
audio/x-pn-realaudio	ra, ram	This is an audio clip formatted with the RealAudio encoding. This launches the raplayer application, which was installed as part of Netscape Communicator.
audio/x-mpeg	mp2, mpa, abs, mpega	This is an MPEG audio file. The default is to ask you what you want to do with the file.
audio/x-wav	wav	This is an audio clip formatted with the Windows audio format. The default is to ask the user what to do with the file, but you could invoke the Windows sound facility to play this file. (Macintosh and Linux users don't have this option, of course.)
audio/x-aiff	aif, aiff, aifc	This is an audio clip formatted with the AIFF audio format. The default is to ask you what to do with the file.
audio/basic	au, snd	This is an audio clip formatted in the basic audio format. The default is to ask you what to do with the file.
application/fractals	fif	This is a application used to create fractal images. The default is to ask you what to do with the file.

FILE TYPE	EXTENSION	ACTIONS
image/ief	ief	This is a graphics file formatted in the ief format. The default is to ask you what to do with the file.
image/x-png	png	The Portable Network Graphic (PNG) is a newer format for high-resolution graphics. It's not supported natively in Netscape Communicator, so the default is to ask the user what to do with the file. There are plug-ins for reading these files.
image/x-photo-cd	pcd	The Photo CD format from Kodak is used to archive high-resolution photo files. The format is not supported natively in Netscape Communicator, so the default is to ask the user what to do with the file. Many third-party graphics applications, such as Paint Shop Pro, read these files.
image/x-MS-bmp	bmp	This is a graphics file formatted in the Microsoft bitmap file format. The default (with the Windows versions of Netscape Communicator) is to launch the Windows Paintbrush application to view this file.
image/x-rgb	rgb	This is a graphics file formatted in the basic red-green-blue file format. The default is to ask you what to do with this file.
image/x-portable-pixmap	ppm	This is a graphics file formatted using the X Window ppm portable file format. The default is to ask you what to do with this file. Unless you have the PBM utilities, you won't be able to do much with this file.

FILE TYPE	EXTENSION	ACTIONS
image/x-portable-graymap	pgm	This is a graphics file formatted using the X Window pgm portable file format. The default is to ask you what to do with this file. Unless you have the PBM utilities, you won't be able to do much with this file.
image/x-portable-bitmap	pbm	This is a graphics file formatted using the X Window pbm portable file format. The default is to ask you what to do with this file. Unless you have the PBM utilities, you won't be able to do much with this file.
image/x-portable-anymap	pnm	This is a graphics file formatted using the X Window pnm portable file format. The default is to ask you what to do with this file. Unless you have the PBM utilities, you won't be able to do much with this file.
mage/x-xwindowdump	xwd	This is a graphics file formatted using the X Window screen-capture utility. The default is to ask you what to do with this file. Unless you're running X Window or have the PBM utilities, you won't be able to do much with this file.
image/x-xpixmap	xpm	This is a graphics file formatted in the X Window pixmap format. The default is to ask you what to do with this file. Unless you're running X Window or have the PBM utilities, you won't be able to do much with this file.
image/x-xbitmap	xbm	This is a graphics file formatted in the X Window bitmap format. The default is to use Netscape Navigator to view the file. Many smaller graphics on Web pages are stored in the xbm format.

FILE TYPE	EXTENSION	ACTIONS
image/x-cmu-raster	ras	This is a graphics file formatted in the CMU raster file format. The default is to ask you what to do with this file.
image/tiff	tiff, tif	This is a graphics file formatted in the Tagged Image File Format (TIFF). The default is to ask you what to do with the file, but you could configure a graphics program, such as Paint Shop Pro, to display this file.
image/jpeg	jpeg, jpg, jpe	This is a graphics file formatted in the JPEG file format, most often used for photo-quality files. The default is to use Netscape Navigator to view these files.
image/gif	gif	This is a graphics file formatted using the CompuServe graphics file format. The default is to use Netscape Navigator to view these files.
application/x-texinfo	texi, texinfo	This is a text file formatted using the GNU texinfo file format, which creates hypertext documentation. The default is to ask you what to do with this file, but Linux users can view these files using the built-in texinfo command.
application/x-dvi	dvi	This is an animation file. The default is to ask you what to do with this file.
application/x-latex	latex	This is a file formatted with the GNU LaTeX formatting language. The default is to ask you what to do with the file, but you'll need a LaTeX application (again, see *ftp://prep.ai.mit. edu/pub/gnu/*) to view or print the file.

FILE TYPE	EXTENSION	ACTIONS
application/x-tex	tex	This is a file formatted with the TeX publishing language. The default is to ask you what to do with the file. You'll need a TeX implementation (such as the aforementioned LaTeX) to view or print this file.
application/pdf	pdf	This is a file formatted with the Adobe Acrobat page-description language. The default is to ask the user what to do with this file, but you can download Acrobat readers from Adobe (*http://www.adobe.com*) to view the file. After downloading the Acrobat reader, Netscape will automatically launch the reader when it runs across a PDF file.
application/rtf	rtf	This is a file formatted using Microsoft's Rich Text Format, found most often in word-processing situations. The default is to ask you what to do with the file, but you can configure Microsoft Word, WordPerfect, or any number of word processors to display and/or print these files.
ext/html	html, htm	This is a file formatted in the HyperText Markup Language—in other words, a Web page. The default is to use Netscape Navigator to view this page, as you might expect.
text/plain	txt, txt	This is an unformatted text file. The default is to use Netscape Navigator to view this file.

Looking through Table 3.1, you'll see a lot of file formats you're unfamiliar with. And to be totally honest, you're not likely to see any of these formats on the Web any time soon, unless you go looking for a lot of files via FTP. And even then, you're not very likely to run across files in the PPM or PBM file formats.

You can always save the file to disk when Netscape Navigator runs across an unfamiliar file type, and in most cases this is all you need to do. However, if you're frequently running across the same file formats and want to configure Netscape Navigator to handle them, you'll need to create a new MIME type.

UNIX—and Solaris in particular—deals with helpers in a slightly different fashion. Check out *http://home1.swipnet.se/%7Ew-10694/helpers.html* for more information.

Macintosh and UNIX users have an additional choice to make within this panel: where to store downloaded applications.

Creating a New MIME Type

You will probably never have to do this, but Netscape Navigator allows you to create new MIME types to handle files not covered in Netscape Navigator. This might include some exotic file types, or it may be a document type that you regularly run across but that isn't widely supported elsewhere. For instance, intranet users might do a lot of work with files created with WordPerfect (the example we'll use here), and you may want to have Netscape Navigator launch WordPerfect every time it runs across a file ending in **.wp**.

To do this, you'll want to select the **New Type** button. This brings up a dialog box titled Configure New Mime Type, shown in Figure 3.8.

You can pretty much enter anything you want here, although you should enter application if you're planning to associate a program with a file type. Here, we'll use WordPerfect as the subtype. The Helpers tab has a new entry, shown in Figure 3.9.

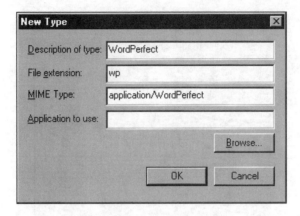

Figure 3.8 *The New Type dialog box.*

Changing Applications Settings

You can use the Edit function to change settings for applications, as shown in Figure 3.10.

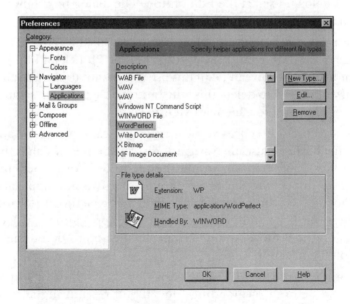

Figure 3.9 *The new MIME type, highlighted and installed.*

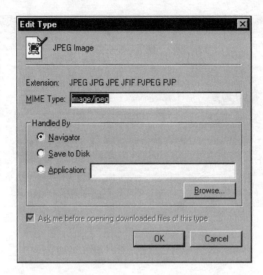

Figure 3.10 *Editing an application setting.*

Let's say that you want to change the tool for viewing JPEG images to an external viewer like Paint Shop Pro. You'd highlight the **JPEG** listing in the Description field and select the **Edit** button. The dialog box shown in Figure 3.10 would appear.

MIME types are organized by extensions, so all the file extensions that match the JPEG MIME type (JPEG, JPG, JPE, JFIF, PJPEG, and PJP) are listed here. (Unfortunately, you can't edit this list; if you want to include another file extension, you'd need to delete this entry and start again from scratch, or else create a new entry just for the new extension.)

There are three directives you can give Netscape Navigator about handling the file: having Netscape Navigator display the file (which is the default with JPEG files), automatically saving the file to disk, or launching another application to display the file. If we were to specify a new application, we'd click on the radio button next to Application and type the file location of the new application. If we didn't know where the application was located, we could click on the **Browse** button and specify the application using the operating-system file-selection tools.

One other setting needs to be considered: whether or not you want to be warned before downloading files. If you're running across a lot of files and want to store them in different places, then you'll probably want to be warned so you can specify a new file location. If you don't care where the downloaded files are stored, then you can leave this setting unselected.

After you're through, we can click on the **OK** button to save the changes. As always, you can use the **Cancel** button to negate the changes.

Editing Helper Applications Manually

If you're more comfortable editing configuration files in order to configure helper applications, you can do so by editing the following text files:

- Windows 3.x users can edit the **netscape.ini** file.
- Windows 95/NT users can edit the Registry.
- Macintosh users can edit **System Folder:Preferences:Netscape**.
- UNIX users can edit the **.mailcap** and **.mime.types** files in their home directories.

NOTE

Editing these configuration files is generally considered to be appropriate only for advanced users, especially editing the Registry file.

Netscape Communicator and Graphics

The World Wide Web is built on the assumption that all good Web pages have a slew of graphics. This reliance means that the Web can be entertaining, but it also means that the Web can be quite slow.

Graphics files come in a variety of formats, but most are formatted in one of the following:

- GIF (Graphics Interchange Format), popularized by the CompuServe online service
- JPEG (Joint Professional Experts Group), created by photographers and other graphics professionals
- XBM (X BitMap), an X Window-based file format that dates back to when the Internet was almost totally made up of UNIX users

If a graphic in one of these formats is part of a Web page, Netscape Navigator will be able to display the graphic as part of the page. Images in these formats require little work on your part.

However, there will be times when there's a reference to a Web page graphic that's not in one of these formats. Generally, this reference will be a link to another file, saying something like "Click here to see a picture of X." These images are not automatically loaded into Netscape Navigator, as they're merely references to a file and not part of the Web page. (There are situations when a reference is actually to a file format supported by Netscape Navigator. In these cases, a graphic will appear in smaller format on a Web page, in the form of a *thumbnail*. This thumbnail gives you an idea of what the graphic looks like, while cutting down on the time needed to send the file to you. If you want to see the image in a larger format, you can select the link and have the larger file sent to you.)

To view these images, you'll need a helper application to view the file. Generally speaking, if someone is passing along graphics files on the Web that can't be read by Netscape Navigator, they have a link to a helper application that can read the file. Follow this link to grab the application, which (in theory) should automatically install on your computer and Netscape Navigator.

The Offline Panel

We won't cover the panels devoted to other Communicator components (Mail, News, Composer) here; instead, we'll move to the two final panels.

The Offline panel is shown in Figure 3.11. It really only controls how Netscape Communicator launches, and how downloaded messages are handled. (We'll cover downloaded messages in Chapter 13.) The default is to assume that you're always connected to a network—surely the case of corporate users—but two other settings may be more appropriate for dial-up users.

This panel is available only to Windows 3.x/95/NT users.

Win95

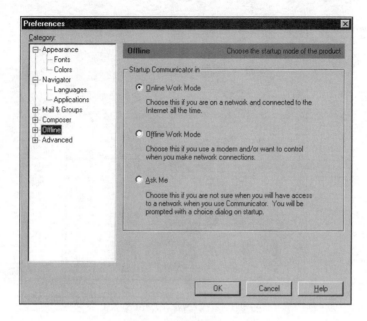

Figure 3.11 The Offline panel.

Selecting **Offline Work Mode** means that Netscape Communicator doesn't assume that you're connected to a network. It will inform you that you're not connected to the Internet when you launch Netscape Communicator, but it won't take any action toward connecting via modem. (This setting is of limited usefulness, actually.)

The more useful setting is **Ask Me**, where Netscape Communicator questions if you want to be connected to the Internet as you work with Communicator. (The dialog box is shown in Figure 3.12.) If you choose to work online, the dial up mechanism used by your operating system will be launched. If you choose to work offline, Netscape Communicator launches with no connection. If you're sure that you always want Netscape Communicator to connect to the Internet every time you launch it, then you can set that as the default.

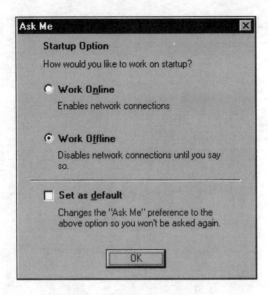

Figure 3.12 The Ask Me dialog box.

The Download Panel

This panel controls how discussion messages are downloaded from the server to your computer. It's shown in Figure 3.13.

This panel is available only to Windows 3.x/95/NT users.

This panel controls how discussion messages should be downloaded—only the unread messages, or according to their age.

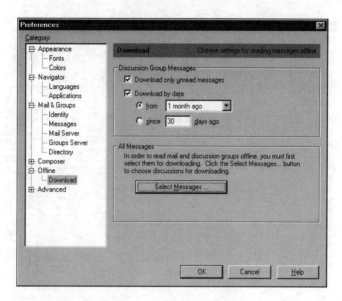

Figure 3.13 *The Download panel.*

THE ADVANCED PANEL

The other major configuration tool that we'll cover here is the Advanced panel. Even if you're a Netscape Communicator beginner, you'll find it worthwhile to pay close attention to these settings, particularly those having to do with memory management. We'll cover this panel in some detail through the rest of this chapter.

Advanced Settings

The main-level Advanced panel (shown in Figure 3.14) controls how Netscape Navigator deals with your system's basic settings. These settings were formerly shown on the main Netscape pulldown menus, but moved to this panel. We'll look at each of the settings.

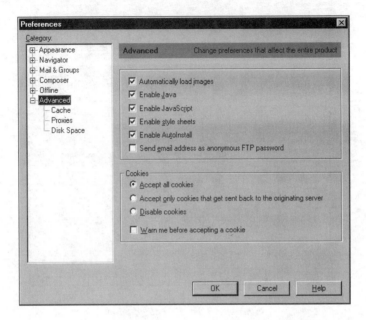

Figure 3.14 *The Advanced panel.*

Automatically Load Images

As you grow in your Netscape Communicator and Navigator usage, you'll find that some Web sites are so cluttered with images (graphics files) that they take many minutes to be downloaded to your computer. Of course, you could do other things with those minutes, like run to the dry cleaners or bake bread from scratch, but generally speaking it's wasted time.

If you find yourself waiting a lot for images to load, you may want to disable this setting. Images will be represented as small icons; if you want to view an image, you can click on the icon to load the image.

Enable Java

Java is the programming language promoted by Sun Microsystems and Netscape Communicator as the best tool for programming via the Internet. And if you're a programmer, you'll certainly want to look at using Java for your programming needs.

As a user, however, you need to approach Java a little more skeptically. Basically, Java sends a program to your hard drive, and the program is run on your computer. (By comparison, most Internet use involves your running a program on a remote server.) There are always security risks when you run a program on your machine, particularly one that you've not personally checked out in some manner. While there's not much chance that the average Java applet will maul your hard drive, that possibility does exist. And there's a performance issue: a poorly coded Java applet can crash Netscape Communicator or drag down performance.

If you're concerned about security, you'll want to disable Java.

Enable JavaScript

JavaScript is a Netscape Communications scripting tool that has some similarities to Sun's Java language (discussed in the previous section). It's not quite the same thing, but it can do the same sort of damage to your computer. Again, if you're concerned about security, you'll want to disable JavaScript.

Enable Style Sheets

Style sheets are formatting tools that allow Web pages to be displayed on your page exactly as the authors intended. Enabling style sheets is a rather low-risk proposition, so you can leave this choice enabled.

Enable Autoinstall

New to Netscape Communicator is the ability for a system administrator to automatically install and configure Netscape Communicator over the network. This setting enables the autoinstallation. Disabling this setting will probably alienate your system administrator—and you don't want to do that.

Send Email Address...

When you log on an FTP server on the Internet, you need to supply a password and a username. Most FTP servers that allow public access on the Internet accept a password of **anonymous** and a username of your e-mail address. With this setting enabled, your e-mail address will automatically be sent along to the FTP server. If you don't want your e-mail address sent to FTP server (which may be the case if you don't want anyone else to know about the FTP servers you're visiting), then leave this disabled.

The Cookie Monster

The rest of the Advanced panel concerns cookies, which have turned into quite contentious issues on the World Wide Web. Before you decide about these settings, you need a little background.

A *cookie* is a piece of information generated by a Web site that's stored on your system, in a file called **\ProgramFiles\Netscape\Navigator\Program\cookies.txt**. Having a server store information in the form of a cookie on a local machine is a long-standing practice in the network world (in the past, they were referred to as *magic cookies* in other authentication schemes; apparently they've lost some of their magic on the Internet). You can see a typical **cookies.txt** file in Table 3.2.

Table 3.2   *A Typical cookies.txt File.*

```
# Netscape HTTP Cookie File

# http://www.netscape.com/newsref/std/cookie_spec.html

# This is a generated file!  Do not edit.

.nytimes.com     TRUE      /auth/     FALSE      946684799      PW      xxxxxxxxx

ad.doubleclick.net     FALSE      /      FALSE      942191940      IAF      10e093c.netscape.com      TRUE      /

FALSE      1609372800      MOZILLA      MOZ_ID=CJKMKFKMOJLPPNO[-]MOZ_VERS=1.2[-]MOZ_FLAG=2[-]MOZ_TYPE=5[-

]MOZ_CK=cMzrdh7^#lil\Ec{[-]


.netscape.com     TRUE      /      FALSE      1609372800      NS_IBD

IBD_SUBSCRIPTIONS=XXXXXX|XXXXXX|XXXXXX|XXXXXX|XXXXXX|XXXXXX|XXXXXX|XXXXXX|XXXXXX|XXXXXX.nytimes.com

TRUE      /      FALSE      946684799      ID      XXXXXXXXXXXXXwww.hyperstand.com      FALSE      /      FALSE

915148800      Am_UserId      XXXXXXXXXXXXXXXXwww.newmedia.com      FALSE      /      FALSE      915148800

Am_UserId      XXXXXXXXXXXXXXXXX

.wcco.com     TRUE      /      FALSE      946684799      INTERSE

137.192.19.125214128471337256688www.apacheweek.com      FALSE      /      FALSE      878792659      Apache

msp7-137478847256659531.hotwired.com      TRUE      /      FALSE      946684799      p_uniqid

XXXXXXXXXXXXXXXXXX.webmonkey.com      TRUE      /      FALSE      946684799      p_uniqid

XXXXXXXXXXXXXXXXXX .netizen.com      TRUE      /      FALSE      946684799      p_uniqid      XXXXXXXXXXXXXXXXX

.packet.com     TRUE      /      FALSE      946684799      p_uniqid      XXXXXXXXXXXXXXXXX
```

```
.excite.com      TRUE    /    FALSE    946641600    UID       XXXXXXXXXXXXXXXXXX

.infoseek.com    TRUE    /    FALSE    879530715    InfoseekUserId   XXXXXXXXXXXXXXXXXX

www.sun.com      FALSE   /    FALSE    915148800    Am_UserId    XXXXXXXXXXXXXXXXXX

.wired.com       TRUE    /    FALSE    946684799    p_uniqid     XXXXXXXXXXXXXXXXXX

.netscape.com    TRUE    /    FALSE    946684799    NETSCAPE_ID   XXXXXXXXXXXXXXXXXX

www.netguide.com   FALSE   /   FALSE    915192000    AccessorID   XXXXXXXXXXXXXXXXXX
```

In this example file, different Web sites (*netscape.com, wcco.com, sun.com,* and a host of Wired-related sites) stored information in the user's **cookies.txt** file. Netscape Navigator is set up to transmit this file upon demand to a Web site. The Web site will request this file and use the information within. For instance, *The New York Times* site uses the **cookies.txt** file to store a username and a password (which is indicated by the xxxxxxxxx in the **cookies.txt** file). This is meant as a convenience measure—you don't need to enter a username and a password every time you log on to *The New York Times* Web site.

Not all the information in the **cookies.txt** file relates to usernames and passwords. Some of the information merely logs if you've ever visited the Web site before and exactly what you perused; a Web site can be programmed to store anything in a **cookies.txt** file, and this may range from demographics to past viewing habits.

For the most part, **cookies.txt** files are of more use to the Web site than to you (except in the case of convenience, when you don't need to pass along a username and password). But there's a downside to cookies, which is why they are such a source of controversy in the Internet world. When your username and password are sent to *The New York Times* Web site, they are sent as straight text, without any scrambling or encryption. If someone sitting on the Internet between you and the Web site were to intercept the cookie—and this can actually be done quite easily—they could steal your username and password to log on to *The New York Times* Web site.

In addition, there are privacy issues involved. Some Internet users are drawn to the Net because of the total anonymity that's possible—no one else needs to know that you're logging onto a Web site, for whatever reason. When a Web site grabs a **cookies.txt** file, they grab the *entire* file. Therefore, the entrepreneurial Webmaster could see what Web sites you visit regularly and perhaps program something in response. In the example **cookies.txt** file, there are references to *The New York Times, NetGuide* magazine, WCCO television, and various Wired and HotWired Web sites. The reasonable conclusion would be that the owner of the **cookies.txt** file is somewhat of a news junkie, and the enterprising Webmaster could rig a program that reads the **cookies.txt** file and sends a tailored response—in this case, perhaps sending Web pages with banners offering free access to other news-oriented Web sites, such as the *Wall Street Journal* or *News.Com*. Tailoring such responses, of course, is the backbone of direct mail, and some people dislike having demographic information like this available to any Web site requesting it.

There are four levels of cookie control in Netscape Communicator:

The default is to accept all cookies, which is of course the way all direct marketers and Web firms would like it. (This in and of itself is a good reason to change the setting.)

The second setting accepts only cookies that are sent back to the originating server. That is, if **wcco.com** places a cookie in your **cookies.txt** file, that cookie is sent back only to **wcco.com**. You may not want other Web sites to know the contents of your file, and this setting prevents some unauthorized snooping.

The third setting disables cookies altogether. If you enable this control and never allow a Web site to write to your **cookies.txt** file, you'll still have a **cookies.txt** file, since Netscape Communicator writes one upon installation. You could always delete this file or move it to another directory if you don't want the world to find it.

The final control warns you when a Web site is writing something to your **cookies.txt** file; it doesn't prevent cookies from being sent to Web sites.

The Cache Panel

The first subpanel under the Advanced category (shown in Figure 3.15) controls how Netscape Communicator interacts with your computer's memory, both on the hard drive and in your system RAM.

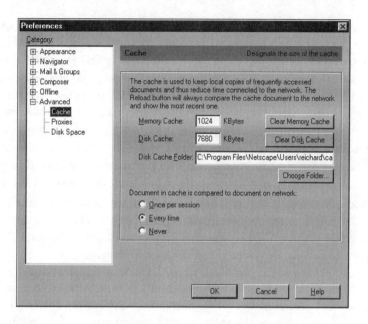

Figure 3.15 *The Cache panel.*

First, an explanation of how all this works. When you grab a Web page from the Internet, the image is stored in your computer's RAM. This section of RAM is called the *memory cache*, and its contents are controlled solely by Netscape Communicator. When you move from one page or another, the previous page is stored in the cache. When, using the History function in Netscape Navigator, you move to a previously viewed page, Netscape Navigator doesn't actually grab the previously viewed page from a Web server. Instead, it pulls that Web page from your RAM and compares it to a summary of the actual page. If there's a difference between the new page and the page on your hard disk, the new page is downloaded. If there's no difference, then the version in your system memory is used. This is a lot faster and more efficient than grabbing the page from the Web server each time you wanted to look at it again. It also makes you a good Internet citizen, because you cut down on network traffic.

The Netscape Navigator is called a *persistent* cache, which means that there's no session limit on what's stored on disk; a page you downloaded a week ago may still be stored in the cache.

When the memory cache is full, Netscape Navigator then stores Web pages to a *disk cache*, a section of your hard disk set aside for such storage. (You set the actual location of this directory in the **Disk Cache Directory:** section of the tab menu; the default is **C:\Program Files\Netscape\Users*user*\cache** on a Windows 95/NT system, where you are the *user* on a multiuser system.) Again, the space in this disk cache is limited, so Netscape Navigator keeps track of which pages were stored the longest, as these will be purged when disk space necessitates some pruning. This ensures that the most recently accessed pages are still in your system's memory, and which is why they are read in so fast— they're actually coming from your computer's hard disk and not the network.

This also leads to an unintended side effect: the reliance on cached pages instead of new pages when looking at previously accessed pages. Unfortunately, you can lose new content of some pages if Netscape Navigator uses the cached Web page instead of the new Web pages.

N O T E   You can override Netscape Navigator's default behavior in bringing up a cached document. Use the **Reload** button to reload the document, but make sure that you press the **Shift** key (the **Option** key for Macintosh users) while doing so. This summons a copy of the Web page from the server, no matter what is stored in the cache.

Running Down the Cache Settings

Armed with this information, you can make some informed decisions about how you want to set your cache settings—or whether you want to change these settings at all.

Memory Cache

The first field, Memory Cache, determines how much RAM is dedicated to storing documents in memory. The default for the Windows and Windows 95 versions is 1024K (a megabyte), and the default for the UNIX versions is 3000K (a little under three megabytes). Do you want to change this? Probably not. You may see some better performance if you specify a larger amount, but you may see worse performance in other applications if you devote such a large chunk of RAM to a single application. If you're really sharp, you can monitor how much leftover memory your computer typically has (each operating system has a tool for showing how much of the computer's resources are being used) and see if there's enough to add some to the Netscape Navigator cache.

To immediately clear the RAM cache, select **Clear Memory Cache**.

Disk Cache

The second field, Disk Cache (known as Cache Size on the Macintosh version of Netscape Navigator), determines how much hard-disk storage space is dedicated to storing documents. The default is 7690K. Why would you want to change this cache size? If you're running low on disk space, you may want to reduce the size of the cache. As a result, you'll find that it takes a little longer to meander the Web, since documents loaded from a remote server take longer to get to your screen than do documents on your hard drive. If Netscape Navigator has filled up all five megabytes with cached documents, it could take a while for Netscape Navigator to look through these documents for the information it needs (hence, you may want to clear the disk cache manually every once in a while, if only to speed performance). If Netscape Navigator is extremely slow to give up control of your computer after you quit, it's because the program is taking a long time to deal with cache management. In fact, you'll find that performance generally increases if you place a smaller number in this field—say, 1000K—to make sure that Netscape Navigator doesn't become mired in your hard drive looking for data, when it doesn't really matter if you have a cached copy of a document or not.

On the Macintosh side, the default is 1000K (a little under 1 megabyte). In addition, the Macintosh version of Netscape Communicator shows you how much memory is unused at all times.

The Macintosh version of Netscape Communicator doesn't allow you to set the memory cache in this menu. Instead, you need to use the **Get Info** box, found elsewhere (you need to go outside of Netscape Navigator to the Finder and choose **Get Info** from the File menu).

Disk Cache Folder

The Disk Cache Folder specifies the directory on your computer used for the temporary storage of cached documents. This directory is set up automatically when you install Netscape Communicator. If you change it—only if you're running low on disk space and want to move the cache to a different hard drive on your computer—you must make sure that the new directory already exists.

The final field determines how often Netscape Communicator checks a Web server to make sure that the document in your cache matches the document on the server. Netscape Navigator doesn't actually check the entire document—only the size of the documents in both locations are compared. The default is to check the document once in a session. You could tell Netscape Navigator to check the original every time a Web page is summoned from cache, but this will slow down your performance dramatically. Going to the other extreme, you could tell Netscape Navigator never to check the server to verify a document, but then you might miss out on an updated page.

Netscape Navigator doesn't check a server when you use **Back** to view a previously viewed page.

The Proxies Panel

Security—and the lack thereof—on the Internet sometimes makes setup and configuration more difficult than it should be. This is especially true if you're using Netscape Communicator in a corporate setting. This tab controls how Netscape Communicator deals with *proxy* servers, which put a level of security between you and the Internet. The Proxies panel is shown in Figure 3.16.

Since this is a security issue, Chapter 19 will cover the Proxies tab and how to set it up as part of a larger secure-computing environment.

The Disk Space Panel

The final Preferences panel governs disk space and file sizes and is shown in Figure 3.17.

These settings have more to do with mail and news, but we'll cover them here.

The first portion of this panel covers the size of messages. The default in Netscape Communicator is not to download any mail and news messages that are over 50K in size. There are many reasons to limit this size, but the most common is if you are on the road and using a relatively slow dial-up connection, you'll want to wait for a more convenient time to download a large message.

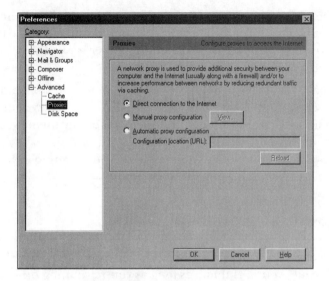

Figure 3.16 The Proxies panel.

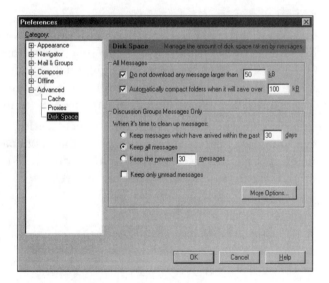

Figure 3.17 The Disk Space panel.

The second portion covers the compression of mail and news folders when they reach a certain size. There's really no reason to change this setting, since compressing these folders will ultimately save on disk space without affecting performance.

The remainder of this panel has to do with news and Collabra messages. Basically, discussion messages can be deleted from your system after they reach a certain age, or else you can choose to keep only the newest messages on your system. If you're continually running out of disk space and see that your discussion folders are of an immense size, you'll want to either purge all older messages or keep only unread messages.

SUMMARY

In theory, Netscape Communicator and Netscape Navigator should work immediately when you start them, as long as you're running on a vanilla computer with a vanilla network connection. And indeed, this will be true of most of you.

But what's the fun in software you can't tweak? This chapter covers the various tools for changing the way Netscape Navigator works and looks. Some of the changes, such as showing the toolbar, are relatively cosmetic. Other, such as fonts and colors, are both cosmetic and functional, as some Web pages expect you to adhere to certain conventions. Still others, like the cache settings, can affect performance to a great degree one way or another.

In this chapter, you learned about the wide variety of settings available in Netscape Navigator and Netscape Communicator. In the next chapter, you'll put this knowledge to good use, as you further customize Netscape Communicator and take an extended journey on the Web.

## CHAPTER 4

Cruising the Web with Navigator

The World Wide Web is the part of the Internet that has garnered the most attention from users and the media. It also served as the original rationale for Netscape Navigator usage, so it's appropriate that we begin our discussion of Navigator usage with a discussion of the Web. In this chapter, we'll cover the following topics:

- Using maps and forms
- Setting up your own bookmarks
- Searching for Elvis on the Web
- Using Internet directories and search engines
- Opening local files

JUMPING ON THE ON RAMP OF THE INFORMATION SUPERHIGHWAY

Now that Netscape Communicator up and running, it's time to start connecting to Web pages, using the Navigator Web-browser component of Netscape Communicator. First, you'll need to know how content is organized on the Internet and the World Wide Web.

As you've been told repeatedly through this book, the World Wide Web is merely one portion of the worldwide Internet. It's designed as a *hypertext* medium, where a link on one page will lead to another web resource. The World Wide Web supports transfers of files using the HyperText Transfer Protocol (or HTTP; that's why hypertext transfers begin with *http*).

All of this is a really fancy way of saying that documents, whether graphics or text, can be linked as part of the World Wide Web, and that when you point and click on a highlighted portion of a Web document, you'll jump to the Web address specified on that highlight.

Let's use the opening screen to Netscape Navigator as an example. By default, Netscape Navigator is set up to connect directly to the Netscape Home Page. (On the World Wide Web, a *home page* is an entry point to someone's resources. Think of a home page as a listing of occupants in the main lobby of an office building; by reading through the home page, you can see where you want to go.) While the content of the Netscape Home Page changes regularly (as do most major home pages), the basic layout usually doesn't. The top of the Netscape Home Page is anchored by a *map* of the Netscape offerings, followed by a listing of what's new and noteworthy, as shown in Figure 4.1.

What's noteworthy here isn't the content of the Netscape Home Page; the noteworthy aspect is how Netscape Navigator specifies this page. Look near the top of Figure 4.1, where you see a field called Netsite:. This is where you enter Web addresses, which are known more prosaically as *Uniform Resource Locators*, or *URLs*. In Figure 4.1, the URL is *http://home.netscape.com/*.

N O T E   In Figure 4.1, the URL field is preceded by *Netsite:*. In other examples in this book, the URL field was preceded by *Location:*. What's the difference? When you connect to a Web site running on a Netscape Communications Web server, you'll see Netsite:. When you connect to a Web site that's not running on a Netscape Communications Web server, you'll see Location:. Most of the time it won't matter to you whether or not you're connecting to a Netscape Communications server.

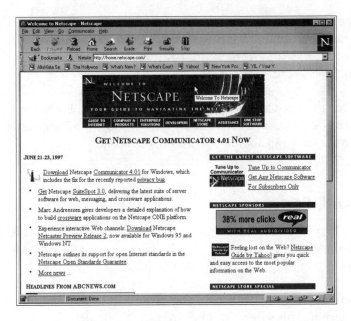

Figure 4.1 *The Netscape Home Page.*

Most Web addresses or URLs follow the same format. You can identify a hypertext page, because it begins with *http:*. This tells Netscape Navigator to use the HyperText Transfer Protocol to transfer a document from the Web site to your computer. (There are other protocols to use for transferring information, as you'll see in the section entitled "Other URL Formats.") The two slashes separate the transfer protocol from the actual address (in this case, *home.netscape.com*). When Netscape Navigator sees that URL, it knows to transfer the Web page at *home.netscape.com* using the HyperText Transfer Protocol.

Actually, a URL of *http://home.netscape.com* is somewhat unorthodox in the World Wide Web, as most sites have adopted the practice of placing *www* at the beginning of the actual address (as you'll see later in this chapter when we discuss some cool Web sites). For instance, the CBS Television Network has a URL of *http://www.cbs.com*, while Toyota has a URL of *http://www.toyota.com*. The same goes for *http://www.kreichard.com*.

Knowing this, you can make some pretty educated guesses regarding URLs, even if you're not sure about the actual address. You already know that most addresses begin with *www*. Commercial addresses—that is, companies and for-profit organizations—end in *com* (short for *com*mercial). Educational institutions end in *edu*, while nonprofit organizations end with *org*. Therefore, you can guess that Apple Computer's URL is *http://www.apple.com*, that PBS's URL is *http://www.pbs.org*, and that Hamline University's URL is *http://www.hamline.edu*.

You don't actually need to be that fussy with URLs. For instance, you could enter *apple.com*—as opposed to the unwieldy *http://www.apple.com*—and Netscape Navigator will fill in the rest of the URL.

N O T E

Other URL Formats

The HyperText Transfer Protocol isn't the only protocol for transferring data via the World Wide Web, although it's certainly the major one. Other protocols supported on the World Wide Web include:

- **Gopher** is a way to access text from older Gopher servers on the Internet. This subject will be covered in Chapter 6.

- **News** is a link to a Usenet newsgroup. This subject will be covered in Chapter 13.

- **FTP** is a connection to a Web server supporting File Transfer Protocol. This topic will be covered in Chapter 5.

- The **mailto** URL is for sending electronic mail to an address specified on a Web page. This subject will be covered in Chapter 8.

Browsing the Netscape Home Page

If you look closely, you'll see that Figure 4.1 incorporates almost everything you need to know about navigating the Web, as we'll explain here.

Figure 4.1 shows the Netscape Home Page when this book was being written. However, you're guaranteed to have a different home page when you run Netscape Navigator because the home page changed several times during the course of writing this book, and given Netscape's commitment to following the fast pace of the Internet, it's a virtual certainty that the home page will change again.

N O T E

You've already learned about the elements of Netscape Navigator itself—the toolbar, the menubar, etc. Figure 4.1 gives you a look at some elements of a Web page that you've not run into before. We'll run through a few of them.

Maps

The big trend in Web-page design is to use maps to head a page. A *map* is a set of images and words presented in a graphically pleasing manner. In Figure 4.1, Netscape Communications uses a map to distinguish the various parts of its Internet offerings—Guide to Internet, Company & Products, Enterprise Solutions, and so on.

The most noteworthy feature of a map for you as a user is that it's both attractive and functional. When you put the mouse over a section of the map—say, **Netscape Store**—you'll see a URL appear at the bottom of the screen. (You'll also notice that the pointer turns into a hand, indicating that a hypertext jump can be made.) This is no accident: A map can be used to navigate the wares of a Web site. If you want to go to the General Store, all you need to do is move the pointer over that section of the map and click away.

Be warned that navigating around a map isn't always as straightforward as it looks. For starters, the URL at the bottom of the screen will probably be gibberish to you—it's an internal notation used by the Web site, not an explicit statement of the location of the information on the server. (The URL will look something like *http://merchant.netscape.com/netstore/index.html*. Other maps use an even odder notation for positioning, with URLs ending with something like *?678*. The numbers are the coordinates of the pointer position on the map, and this information is used by the server to reconcile the coordinates to specific offerings on the map.)

Maps are used in a wide variety of circumstances on the Web, ranging from maps as maps (such as a world map or a regional map) to maps as navigation aids. Basically, all you need to remember is that a map is merely another way to get around a Web site.

Annotations

If you look closely at Figure 4.1, you'll see a little bit of text, **Welcome to Netscape**, in the middle of the map. This is where the cursor was positioned when the screen was captured. Web pages now have the ability to attach annotations or summaries to a position of the screen (usually a map or a graphic), with the short text description displayed when the cursor is left over that portion of the screen. These annotations don't affect how either the Web page or Netscape Navigator works; they're merely another tool for general enlightenment.

Shortcuts

Many Web sites are using buttons as shortcuts to popular offerings. In the case of Figure 4.1, on the right side of the content area there's a button entitled **Netscape Now!**. This button is merely a shortcut to the Web page that facilitates the download of the most recent version of Netscape Navigator.

Again, there's nothing too magical or confusing about these shortcuts. When you put the mouse pointer over a shortcut button, the pointer will change to a hand and a URL will be displayed at the bottom of the screen. To activate the shortcut, you click on it.

These shortcuts come in a wide variety of shapes and colors. Some of the more popular Internet services, such as the Point ratings for Web sites, give away their shortcut buttons to Web-page developers and encourage them to place it in a Web page. Netscape does the same thing with the Netscape Now button.

Pulldown Menus

Figure 4.2 has been scrolled down to show the bottom of the Netscape home page. In the middle of the figure is a pulldown menu, entitled **Visit a Netscape International Site**. When you put your cursor over the arrow at the right side of this menu, a set of menu selections appear. In this case, the menu lists international Netscape sites, which are designed for non–English-speakers across the globe.

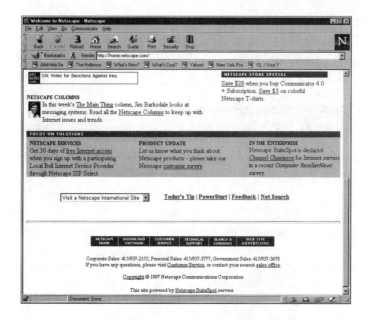

Figure 4.2 Pulldown menus.

As you can tell, navigating around a Web site isn't very complicated. Take a few minutes and poke around the various aspects of a few Web sites, then come back here to get some information on other Netscape features, including bookmarks and history.

BOOKMARKS

As you've already learned, a *bookmark* is a handy way for you to keep information about frequently used Web sites and resources. When you first install Netscape Navigator, you have no bookmarks installed. Although bookmarks are installed in chronological order (in other words, the most recent bookmark ends the list of bookmarks), you can edit this list to create any order of bookmarks you want, as well as placing bookmarks in folders and subfolders.

You can see your bookmarks by pressing on the Bookmarks icon, as shown in Figure 4.3.

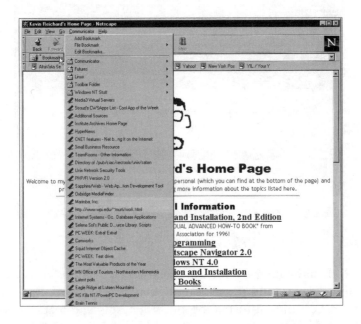

Figure 4.3 *Viewing bookmarks from the Bookmarks icon.*

You can also see your bookmarks by selecting **Bookmarks** from the Communicator menu, as shown in Figure 4.4.

You could also view your bookmarks by opening them as a Web page. Your Bookmarks file, **bookmark.html**, is nothing more than a HTML document. To view your bookmarks as a Web page, select **Open Page** from the File menu and then find your **bookmark.html** file using the **Browse** function. If you intend to do this regularly, you can drag the URL Page Proxy over to the Bookmarks icon.

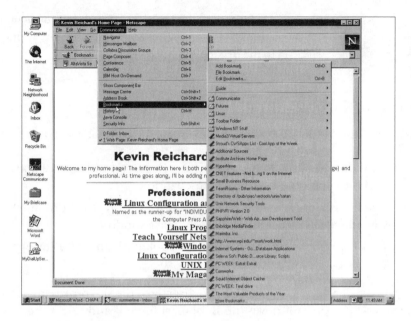

Figure 4.4 *Bookmarks selected from the Communicator menu.*

But we're getting ahead of ourselves here, as it's important for you to learn how to initially add a bookmark. You can add the current Web page to your list of bookmarks by using one of these methods:

- Dragging the Page Proxy icon (located next to the URL field) to the Bookmark icon. The icon changes to either a small link (as in a chain) or to a circle with a line through it (the international symbol for an unallowed action). The bookmarks menu will appear, and you can place the new bookmark in a folder, or you can just add it to the list of bookmarks.

- Pull down the Windows menu, select **Bookmarks**, and then select **Add Bookmark** (**Ctrl-D**) from the resulting cascading menu.

You can use the first method to place a link directly on your desktop if you're a Windows 95/NT or Macintosh user; simply drag the link icon to the desktop.

Win95   MACINTOSH

Keyboard Equivalents

You can also use keyboard equivalents to create a new bookmark:

- Windows 3.x/95/NT users can use **Ctrl-D** to add a bookmark and **Ctrl-B** to open the Edit Bookmark window.
- Macintosh users can use **Command-D** to add a bookmark and **Command-B** to open the Edit Bookmark window.
- UNIX users can use **Alt-A** to add a bookmark and **Alt-B** to open the Edit Bookmark window.

After you install a bookmark, you can go directly to the site represented by the bookmark when you pull down the Bookmarks menu and select the desired title. You don't need to enter a URL or do anything but select the title; Netscape Navigator does the rest. That's why bookmarks are so handy.

But there's more. When you add a bookmark, there's more information stored by Netscape Navigator than merely the title and URL of the bookmark. A complete listing of bookmarks can be found by selecting **Bookmarks** and then **Edit Bookmarks** from the subsequent menu. This brings up a window that lists the current bookmarks in an outline format, and it's this dialog box that we'll examine further.

THE BOOKMARKS WINDOW

The Bookmarks window yields an editing window like the one shown in Figure 4.5. You'll see that the basic bookmarks are listed as Bookmarks. There's nothing remarkable about this list, but there is some organization to the entries, as you can see from the folders entitled Communicator, Futures, and Linux.

As mentioned, Netscape Navigator keeps more information about bookmarks than is displayed in the Bookmarks menu. You can get at this information by highlighting a bookmark and then selecting **Bookmark Properties** from the Edit menu in the Bookmarks window, as shown in Figure 4.6.

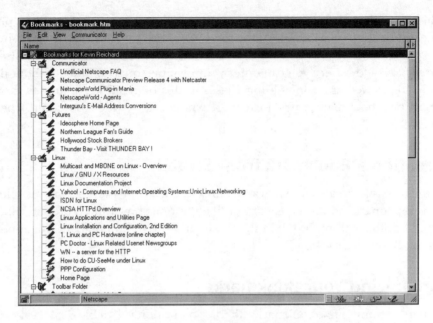

Figure 4.5 A Bookmarks window.

Figure 4.6 Properties for the Northern League Fan's Guide page.

This menu shows you the title of the page (which is the same information provided in the Bookmarks menu), the full URL of the page, when you last visited the site, and when you added the site to your list of bookmarks. There's also a *Description* field, where you can enter your own personal comments about the Web site, as well as a tool adding aliases to this bookmark. An alias is shorthand for a bookmark entry: instead of typing a long title, you could type a short alias.

Creating a Bookmark from Scratch

You can easily create bookmarks from scratch. From the File menu, select **New Bookmark**. You'll see a window like the one shown in Figure 4.6, albeit with no information yet. Fill in the fields, and the new bookmark will appear on the Bookmarks listing.

Organizing Your Bookmarks

If there are only a few bookmarks, then organization isn't a big deal. However, if you're dealing with a lot of bookmarks, then you may want to organize. In the case of the bookmarks shown in Figure 4.5, there's a file folder entitled Linux, and it contains Linux-specific bookmarks. Bookmarks and folders can be stored in outline form, with bookmarks and folders contained within other folders. (If you've used the Windows 95 Explorer or the Windows NT Explorer, you know how these folders are organized.) The little minus sign to the left of the folder (as shown in Figure 4.5) indicates that the contents of the folder are visible. When the minus sign is clicked, the contents of the folder disappear, as shown in Figure 4.7.

Netscape Navigator allows you to drag and drop bookmarks into folders, as well as moving folders into different places in the bookmarks list. In addition, you can insert separators between bookmarks.

In the case of the list shown in Figure 4.7, the best way to organize the list of bookmarks would be to create a few more folders and create lists based by theme. To create a folder, select **New Folder** from the File menu. A Properties window appears, set up like the one discussed and shown in Figure 4.5. However, in this case, the Name field merely says New Folder and is highlighted, which means that it's up to you to enter some new information. We'll call this one **NetComm**, and then select the **OK** button. A new folder appears right below the highlighted bookmark item, not at the end of the list of the bookmarks. If you want, you can place folders within folders to extend the hierarchy.

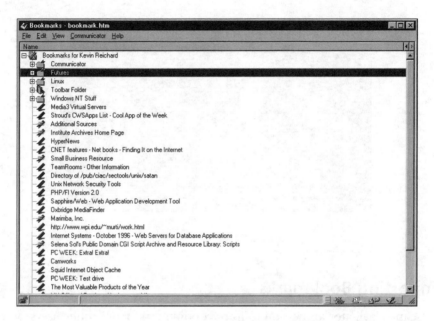

Figure 4.7 *A shrunken list of bookmarks.*

With this bookmark on the screen, we can merely drag and drop Linux-related Web sites into the NetComm folder.

Adding Separators

For purely aesthetic reasons, you could add separators between portions of the Bookmark window, which would carry forward into the Bookmarks pull-down menu. To insert a separator, pull down the Edit menu and select **New Separator**. In the Bookmark window, all you will see is an item tagged **<separator>**. But when you go back to the Web browser and pull down the Bookmarks menu, however, you will see a separator in the menu.

Searching Through Bookmarks

Finding something just by looking at the huge list of bookmarks in Figure 4.7 is difficult at best. Under the Edit menu, Netscape Navigator has a tool, **Find in Bookmarks** (shown in Figure 4.8), which searches through titles for a text string (either matching the case or not). This can be a sophisticated tool, as it allows you to search in three different fields (Name, Location, and

Description), as well as specifying a case for the search and whether or not to search only for whole words.

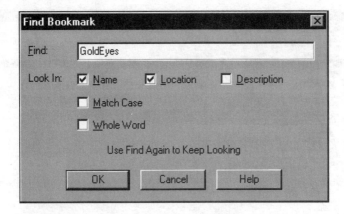

Figure 4.8 *Finding a bookmark.*

Importing Bookmarks

Netscape Navigator allows you to import bookmarks from other users. These bookmarks are stored in an HTML file, which can be shared with anyone— even those who use a Web browser like Microsoft Internet Explorer or Quarterdeck Mosaic.

To open another bookmark file, select **Open Bookmarks File** from the File menu. A dialog box asking you to select a file will appear; this dialog box will vary depending on your operating system. Your bookmarks file won't be changed or disappear; it will only be replaced by the new bookmarks file as the *current* set of bookmarks.

You can also import a set of bookmarks into your current bookmark file. To do so, select **Import Bookmarks File** from the File menu. A dialog box asking you to select a file will appear; this dialog box will differ depending on your operating system. The contents of the HTML page will be imported into your current bookmarks file.

The UNIX versions of Netscape Navigator include a shell script called **hot-convert.sh** that converts Mosaic hotlists to Netscape Navigator bookmarks.

The import functions only work if the bookmarks are stored in the HTML format. Some commercial browsers, such as Quarterdeck Mosaic, store hotlists in this format. Other Web browsers, such as NCSA Mosaic for Windows, do not. If you're trying to get a hotlist from NCSA Mosaic into Netscape Navigator as a bookmark file, use a utility called **WinH2htm** (which you can download from *http://www.envmed.rochester.edu/wwwrlp/html/WINH2HTM.HTM*; you'll also need to download Perl, which is explained at the same site) to convert the information.

To covert hotlists from the NCSA Mosaic for Macintosh and MacWeb Web browsers to Netscape Navigator booklinks, use the **HHConv** HyperCard stack (which you can download from *http://www.users.interport.net/ ~laronson/HHConv.html*).

Moving Bookmarks Between Platforms

Your bookmarks are stored in the file **bookmarks.html**, which is an HTML file just like every other Web page. So, in theory, you can move this file between platforms (PC, Macintosh, and UNIX), right?

Well… yes. However, you will need to massage the file a little before you can actually use it. Each operating system has a different way of ending lines—a combination of line feeds, carriage returns, and newlines. If you're moving your **bookmarks.html** file to UNIX, you'll see that it looks fine in a browser window, but is unreadable by Navigator itself.

You'll need to do some simple editing of the **bookmarks.html** file after you move it to a new platform. For example, if you want to use a Windows 95 **bookmarks.html** file on a Linux platform, you'll need to copy the file to the Linux machine and then manually insert end-of-line characters using the **vi** or **emacs** editors.

Deleting Bookmarks

To delete a bookmark, simply highlight it and then press the Delete key on your keyboard.

Updating Bookmarks

If you're a pack rat when it comes to bookmarks—and most of you will be after you spend some time cruising through the World Wide Web—you may find that you amass a large list of bookmarks. The size of your list may make it so that you don't check your bookmarks daily or even regularly.

Netscape Navigator contains a tool for updating bookmarks and telling you which Web sites have changed since the last time you viewed them. The checking mechanism is rather crude—it checks the date of the Web page—but it works. Select **Update Bookmarks** from the View menu. You'll be asked whether or not you want to update all the bookmarks or only the highlighted bookmarks. Netscape Navigator will run down the list of bookmarks, although the Web pages won't be loaded into the Web browser. (If you want to check on a specific bookmark, highlight it and then select **Update Bookmarks**. You can highlight a set of bookmarks or an entire folder and then have Netscape Navigator check the selected bookmarks.) Netscape Navigator gives you a running tally of how many Web pages have been checked and how long the rest of the process will take.

If a page has been updated, the icon next to the bookmark in the Bookmarks window will be changed, as well as the folders containing updated Web pages (as shown in Figure 4.9). If a page has not been updated, then the icon remains the same. If Netscape Navigator couldn't check on a Web page, a question mark appears next to the bookmark.

Other Bookmark Functions

There's a host of functions associated with bookmarks. We'll cover them here.

Editing Bookmarks

The Edit menu helps you edit your bookmarks. Supported are the typical Windows/Macintosh/X Window conventions in an Edit pulldown menu—i.e., cutting bookmarks, copying bookmarks, and pasting bookmarks. These menu selections work pretty much the way you'd expect: You can cut or copy a bookmark, move the highlight bar to another location on your Bookmark window, and then paste the bookmark into the new location.

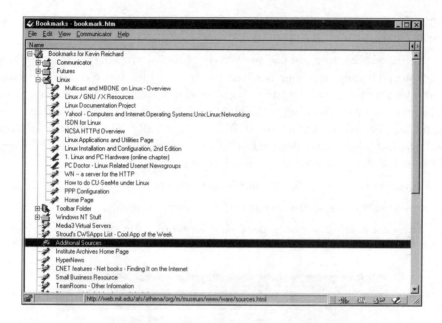

Figure 4.9 *Updating bookmarks.*

Similarly, you can use this menu to delete bookmarks and to select all bookmarks. If you find that you accidentally cut or delete a bookmark, the Edit menu also features an Undo function.

Sorting Bookmarks

The View menu gives you four different ways to sort your bookmarks: by name, location, creation date, last-visited date. It also allows you to choose if the bookmarks should be displayed in ascending or descending order.

The thing to remember when sorting bookmarks is that folders have their own attributes, and when you're sorting, these attributes are included in the order. So the date-creation information in a folder is included when sorting folders by creation date; the contents of the folder are secondary.

Starting with Bookmarks

If you need to begin the day with a site entered as a bookmark, you may want to use your bookmarks file as your startup page. Remember Chapter 3, when you learned how to change your startup page in a setting under **Preferences**, in the Navigator panel? You can combine that knowledge with what you've learned here.

Netscape Navigator can use any Web page as a startup page, including Web pages stored locally. And your Bookmarks file is nothing more than a Web page stored locally in the HTML format. So, instead of having *http://home.netscape.com* as your startup page, you can specify your own bookmarks entry. The Navigator panel allows you to browse for a Web page locally. The location of your Bookmarks file will differ depending on your operating system. For a Windows NT user, the Bookmark-file location will be something like this:

C:\Program Files\Netscape\Users\reichard\bookmark.htm

where you substitute your username for *reichard*, obviously.

The end result is a home page that looks like the one shown in Figure 4.10.

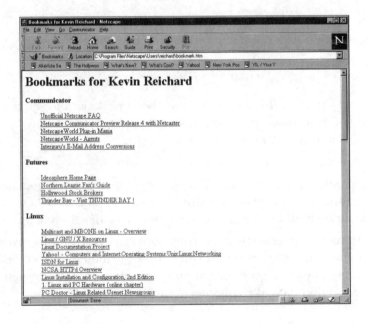

Figure 4.10 *Using your Bookmarks file as a home page.*

Going Back in History

Netscape Navigator users who also used older versions will notice that the History functions in Navigator are now much expanded. While the basic principle is the same—Netscape Navigator keeps track of the Web sites you've visited—you'll now find that your user tools are much more powerful.

History is tracked in its own application, which can be loaded from the Communicator menu. The History application is shown in Figure 4.11.

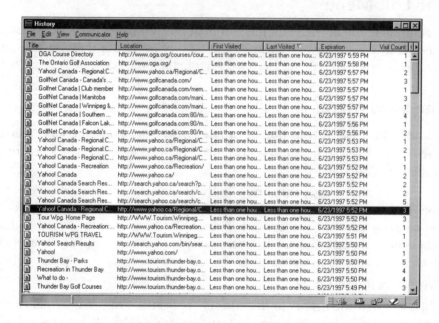

Figure 4.11 *The History application.*

There's a wealth of information here about the Web sites you've visited—their URLs, how long ago you visited them, and when their listing in the History file expires. In addition, you have a few unique options available to you via the File, Edit, and View menus.

The File Menu

In addition to the normal File menu functions, you have the ability to save your current History listing as an HTML file (via the **Save As** choice), as well as adding a page to your list of bookmarks or toolbar listings. Finally, this menu gives you the power to jump to a selected listing, although you can do the same thing by double-clicking on the listing.

The Edit Menu

In addition to the normal Edit menu functions (cutting, copying, and pasting selections), you can search through the History listing for a text string, and you can search through an external directory for a phrase.

The View Menu

The View menu sorts your listings by any field (Title, Location, First Visited, Last Visited, Expiration, and Visit Count). The default is to sort these listings by the Last Visited field.

You can also change the sort order by selecting a header. As you can tell from the arrow in Figure 4.11, the Last Visited field is the key to the order. If you click on another header—say, Title—the listings will be sorted by that field in descending order. Click on that same header again and the listings will be sorted in ascending order.

Viewing the History Cache

When you view the history in the History application, you're essentially viewing a summary of your browsing history. Remember that Web pages are usually made up of several elements—text is one file, a banner is another file, and graphics are other separate files.

If you want to view a very detailed description of the Web sites you've visited, listing all the elements of Web pages, then you can use the about: URL in the Netscape Navigator URL field, as in:

about:global

You'll see a listing like the one in Figure 4.12.

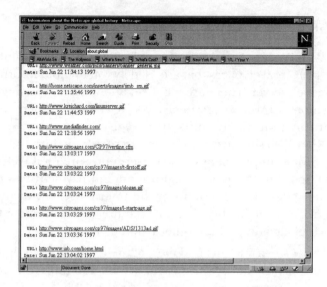

Figure 4.12 *Information from the about:global URL.*

WORKING IN KIOSK MODE

There may be times when you want to run Netscape Navigator with no distractions—no toolbars, scrollbars, or other screen elements—if you want to display a Web page as a demonstration or just want to view documents on your fullest screen possible. In these situations, you'll want to run Netscape Navigator in *kiosk mode*, where the only thing displayed is the Web page.

To do this under Windows 95/NT, you'll need to use the Start menu and manually enter a command line of:

```
Netscape -k
```

assuming that the Netscape executable is somewhere on the command path; if not, you'll need to enter an absolute pathname. Windows 3.x users can use the following command line:

```
C:> netscape -k
```

FORMS AND NETSCAPE NAVIGATOR

The World Wide Web has evolved into a place where you can interact with Web pages. *Forms* are Web pages that are used by you to input information and send it to the Web server. There are many situations where you might need to send information to a Web server; in fact, you've already run across one where you sent information about yourself to register your copy of Netscape Navigator. Other Web sites may require you to register before you gain access to their wares; for example, many of the newer sports-oriented Web sites (such as ESPN and Sportline) require a registration and payment before you can peruse all their offerings. Also, most of the Internet search engines (which you'll learn about later in this chapter) require that you enter the search terms you're seeking and perhaps other parameters.

Forms are rather easy to use, and most of them are set up in the same fashion. Let's use for an example the login screen for the Hollywood Stock Exchange (*http://www.hsx.com*), as shown in Figure 4.13.

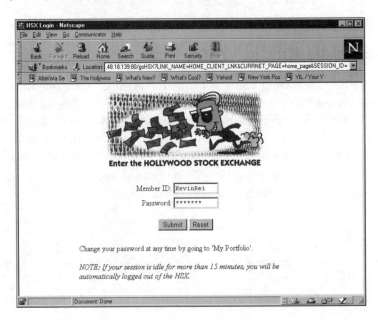

Figure 4.13 *The login screen for the Hollywood Stock Exchange.*

The Hollywood Stock Exchange is a virtual exchange based on the performance of movies. To buy and sell HSX stocks and bonds, you must first be a registered user. After you register, you're assigned a username and a password, and it's at this stage in the process where you enter the username and password. In most cases, a form is merely a front end to a program (called a *CGI* in Web parlance) that takes the information you enter and places it in a database. Then your username and password are passed along to the HSX database. After the database determines that you've entered the correct username and password, you're allowed entry to the Hollywood Stock Exchange.

Entering information into a form is fairly simple. Use the mouse to place the pointer over the beginning of the field, and type in the relevant information. To move forward between data-entry fields, use the **Tab** key (*not* the Enter key). To move backward between fields, press the **Shift** key and the **Tab** key. Data-entry fields come in a wide variety of formats; some fields, such as those for names and addresses, are on the longish side, while others, such as those for states and phone numbers, are of a specific length and don't take input past a certain point.

Some forms also feature *radio buttons* and *check boxes*. Radio buttons, shown in Figure 4.14, are mostly used to choose between two or more options, only one of which can be active, as in this informal poll asking you to vote for your favorite Batman.

Figure 4.14 A radio button.

Check boxes, on the other hand, are usually used in situations when more than one selection can be active. A set of check boxes is shown in Figure 4.15.

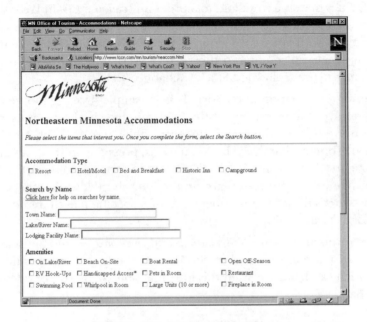

Figure 4.15 *A set of check boxes.*

Finally, a form can also have anything else that can appear on a Web page, such as a map and other pulldown menus.

When you've finished entering information, you can press a button that's usually at the bottom of the form. This button will say something like **Submit this information** or **Register to become a new member now**. Use the mouse pointer to click on this button to send the information in the form to the server. Most forms also feature a button called **Undo Changes** or **Start Again** that wipes out the information in the form's entry fields, allowing you to begin again.

HOT LINK

Not all information sent in a form is secure. When you send information that's not secure, Netscape Navigator will warn you that an insecure transaction is taking place. You'll learn more about this in Chapter 19.

SOME COOL WEB SITES

Now that you've mastered the mechanics of Netscape Navigator and the World Wide Web, it's time to spend some time surfing the Net and browse some of the truly fun and useful sites on the Web. This highly arbitrary list of Web sites was current as of July 1997, and for the most part they should still be active when you start on your Web surfing. (*Highly arbitrary* is an understatement. Some of the sites were included because we went to college with their Webmasters, while others are included because they're located close to our homes. Still others are listed because they made us laugh.)

You can also get a list of what the Netscape folks consider cool by clicking on the **What's Cool** button, which automatically loads a URL of *http://www.home.netscape.com/home/whats-cool.html.*

N O T E

If you're too tired to type in some of these long URLs, you can connect to *http://www.kreichard.com/netcomm.html* and go directly to these sites from there.

HotAIR

http://www.improb.com

The Annals of Improbable Research is one of the funniest Web sites—at least for us intelligent types who know a good, highbrow joke when we see one—known as the MAD Magazine of science. Each year the Annals of Improbable Research award the Ig Nobel Prizes to scientists who perform, well, interesting research; the winners in 1994 included four researchers whose work included "The Constipated Serviceman: Prevalence Among Deployed US Troops" (from the journal *Military Medicine*—really!).

Epicurious

http://www.epicurious.com/

From the company that brings us *Bon Appetit* and *Gourmet* magazines, Epicurious is a Web site devoted to fine dining and upscale traveling. And the dining is definitely finer than the average NetHead experiences (in other words, there are discussions of food that isn't stored in a can or delivered in 30 minutes or less). Epicurious is shown in Figure 4.16.

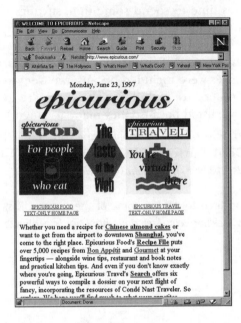

Figure 4.16 *The Epicurious Web site.*

Other notable food-related sites include:

- Chile-Heads home page (*http://neptune.netimages.com/~chile/*)
- Electronic Gourmet Guide (*http://www.foodwine.com*)
- Hot Hot Hot (*http://www.hot.presence.com/g/p/H3*), a mail-order vendor of hot sauces
- Godiva Chocolates (*http://www.godiva.com*)

Over the Coffee

http://www.cappuccino.com

Coffee was a very important ingredient in the creation of this book, especially some of the more frenzied passages. Over the Coffee is maintained by Tim

Nemec, a real coffee lover, and it's a great guide to all things coffee-related, including a listing of coffee vendors, coffee and tea books, brewing-equipment manufacturers, a glossary of coffee terms, and recipes for specialty drinks. (You probably were not aware of the furor surrounding the exact composition of an espresso macchiato.) Some other coffee-related sites include:

- Hawaii's Best Espresso Company (*http://hoohana.aloha.net/~bec*)
- *Coffee Journal Magazine* (*http://www.tigeroak.com/coffeejournal/index.htm*)
- *Coffee Talk Magazine* (*http://www.coffeetalk.com/*)
- The Coffee Companion (*http://www.bid.com/bid/coffeezine/*)
- Yahoo's List of Cybercafes (*http://www.yahoo.com/Society_and_Culture/ Cyberculture/Internet_Cafes*)

Beer & Brewing

There's only one thing that approaches coffee and delivered pizza in the hearts of NetHeads: beer. (Well, for these NetHeads, anyway.) Accordingly, there are a slew of beer-related resources on the World Wide Web, including:

- The Real Beer Page (*http://realbeer.com*)
- The Beer Info Source (*http://www.beerinfo.com/*)
- Golden Prairie Brewing Company (*http://www.mcs.com/~nr706/gp.html*)
- The Great American Beer Festival (*http://www.aob.org/gabfframeset.htm*)
- Redhook Ale Brewery (*http://www.redhook.com/*)
- Spencer's Beer Page (*http://realbeer.com/spencer//*)

Dining Out on the Web

http://www.ird.net/diningout.html

Ever been stuck in a new or strange city and didn't know where to find the really good restaurants? This site lists several Web resources that can help you find good restaurants across the United States. It includes a link to a frozen-custard flavor forecast in Milwaukee, including the noteworthy Kopp's—and if you haven't eaten Kopp's frozen custard in Milwaukee, you haven't lived.

Computer Magazines

There are many excellent print computer magazines that have electronic equivalents on the Internet, including:

- *NetGuide, Communications Week, Network Computing, Windows Magazine,* and *Home PC* (*http://techweb.cmp.com*)
- *PC Magazine, PC Week, PC Computing, Computer Shopper, MacUser, MacWeek, Windows Sources, Internet Life* (*http://www.zdnet.com*)
- *UNIX Review, Dr. Dobb's Journal, Keyboard* (*http://www.mfi.com*)
- *Web Developer, Internet World, Web Week* (*http://www.internet.com*)
- *PC World* (*http://www.pcworld.com*), *InfoWorld* (*http://www.infoworld.com*), *Macworld* (*http://www.macworld.com*), and *Multimedia World* (*http://www.mmworld.com*)
- *Byte* (*http://www.byte.com*)
- *Wired* (*http://www.hotwired.com*)
- *Boardwatch* (*http://www.boardwatch.com*)

Internet-Only Magazines

The World Wide Web has spawned some new "magazines" that are distributed only on the Internet. Some of these are clearly experiments, while some are the equivalent (quality-wise) of older, more established magazines. Some of the noteworthy titles include:

- *Addicted to Noise* (*http://www.addict.com/ATN*)
- *C\NET* (*http://www.cnet.com*)
- *Feed* (*http://www.feedmag.com*)
- *geekgirl* (*http://www.next.com.au/spyfood/geekgirl/*)
- *Interactive Age* (*http://techweb.cmp.com*)
- *Mr. Showbiz* (*http://www.mrshowbiz.com*)

- *NetSurfer Digest* (*http://www.netsurf.com/nsd/index.html*)
- *Salon* (*http://www.salon1999.com/*; shown in Figure 4.17)
- *Suck* (*http://www.suck.com*)
- *Word* (*http://www.word.com*)

Figure 4.17 *The Salon Web site.*

ESPN Sports Zone

http://ESPN.SportsZone.com/

This is a rarity on the Web: A Web site affiliated with a major network that can actually stand on its own in terms of content. ESPN Sports Zone has the same irreverent tone of cable's ESPN, while at the same time adding cool Web-oriented content, outspoken columnists, and more. (It's shown in Figure 4.18.)

Figure 4.18 ESPN's Sports Zone.

The Ultimate TV List

http://www.ultimatetv.com/

Computer folks tend to spend far too much time in front of one monitor or another. Still, why fight the inevitable? The Ultimate TV List gives you a searchable database of television shows both good and bad, recent and old. This list wins kudos because it managed to contain information about *The Goodies*, a rather obscure little British comedy. Also, here are some home pages (official and unofficial) for some popular television shows:

- *4616 Melrose Place* (*http://www.melroseplacetv.com*)
- *Mad About You* (*http://www.alumni.caltech.edu/~witelski/may.html*)
- *Mystery Science Theater 3000* (*http://www.scifi.com/mst3000/*)
- *Pathfinder* (*http://pathfinder.com*), a Time Warner service that includes information about Warner Bros. shows such as *Animaniacs* and *Pinky and the Brain*

- *Seinfeld* (*http://www.geocities.com/Hollywood/Lot/2756/seinfeld.html*)
- *The Simpsons* (*http://www.shaggynok.com/simpsons.htm*)
- *The X-Files* (*http://www.kersplat.com/x/*)

Other Media

It's really trendy for other media companies to establish a presence on the Web. Most of these sites are obnoxiously geared toward promotion and marketing, unfortunately. Still, most are worth checking out:

- ABC (*http://www.abctelevision.com*)
- CBS (*http://www.cbs.com*)
- *City Pages* (*http://www.citypages.com*), the alternative weekly in Minneapolis-St. Paul
- Isthmus (*http://www.thedailypage.com*), the alternative weekly in Madison, Wis.
- MTV (*http://www.mtv.com*)
- NBC (*http://www.nbc.com*)
- Pathminder (*http://pathfinder.com*), a Time Warner service that includes *Time, People, National Review,* and *Sports Illustrated*
- PBS Online (*http://www.pbs.org*)
- Sci-Fi Channel (*http://www.scifi.com*)
- USA Today (*http://web.usatoday.com/usafront.htm*)
- The Vibe (*http://www.vibe.com*)

Shareware

http://www.shareware.com

This C|NET-sponsored service (as shown in Figure 4.19) aims to be the complete guide to shareware on the Internet, and from the looks of things, it will succeed.

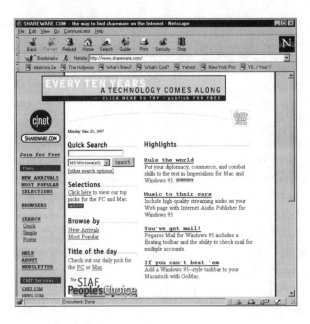

Figure 4.19 Shareware.com.

The Internet is a vast pool of shareware and freeware, and sometimes there are no easy ways to find what you want or need. The Virtual Software Library is a good place to start. Other interesting shareware sites on the Internet include:

- Stroud's Consummate Winsock Applications (*http://cws.internet.com/index.html*)

- Tucows (*http://www.tucows.com*)

- The Association of Shareware Professionals (*http://www.asp-share-ware.org/*)

- DoomGate (*http://www.gamers.org*), devoted to the popular *DOOM* game and other computer games

- The Father of Shareware Home Page (*http://www.halcyon.com/knopf/jim*)

- The Internet Pearls Index (*http://www.execpc.com/~wmhogg/share.html*)

- SunSITE (*http://sunsite.unc.edu/sunsite/sunsitehome.html*)

U.S. Government Sites

The truly cynical among us would note that while the United States Government is one of the largest data and information producers in the world, precious little of this data actually makes its way to users via the Internet; instead, we need to put up with vapid, image-enhancing government Web sites that may or may not include a nugget of useful information.

The trouble is, the less cynical among us would probably agree that—after viewing the vast wasteland that passes for government Internet sites—once you get past Library of Congress and the SEC, these sites are a lot like Oakland: there's no there there. See for yourself:

- Library of Congress (*http://www.loc.gov*) is one of the more useful sites on the Web, if only for the listings of holdings and upcoming exhibits.
- EDGAR (*http://www.sec.gov/edgarhp.htm*), a U.S. Securities & Exchange Commission (SEC) database of corporate information.
- Thomas (*http://thomas.loc.gov*), which lists pending legislation before Congress as well as the full Congressional Record.
- U.S. Senate (*http://www.senate.gov*) lists senators, committees, and historical information about the august institution.
- U.S. House (*http://www.house.gov*) lists representatives, schedules, and laws.
- The White House (*http://www.whitehouse.gov*) includes speeches, press releases, historical information about the building, and an audio file that features Socks.
- The Smithsonian Institution (*http://www.si.edu*)

Jack's Joint

http://www.primenet.com/~jkurtz

The personal home page of a very fine photographer and all-around nice guy.

The Capt. James T. Kirk Sing-a-long Page

http://www.loskene.com/singalong/kirk.html

This is where you can download clips from William Shatner's only recorded music ("The Transformed Man," released in 1968), featuring Shatnerian interpretations of such classics as "Mr. Tambourine Man," "Lucy in the Sky with Diamonds," and "It Was a Very Good Year." (The page is shown in Figure 4.20.) The site also contains sound clips from "Star Trek" regulars Leonard Nimoy (who released 10 albums!), Brent Spiner (who really should have know better), and Nichelle Nichols.

Figure 4.20 *The Capt. James T. Kirk Sing-a-long Page.*

Hubble Pictures

http://oposite.stsci.edu/pubinfo/Pictures.html

One of the best reasons to invest in a really good graphics card: High-quality photographs returned by the Hubble Space Telescope (as shown in Figure 4.21). You could spend hours and hours going through these gorgeous images.

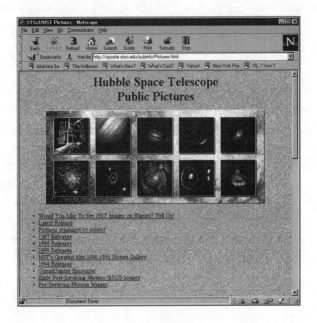

Figure 4.21 The home page for Hubble Space Telescope Public Pictures.

Ulysses for Dummies

http://www.bway.net/~hunger/ulysses.html

This is why we are on the Internet.

Teen Movie Critic

http://www.dreamagic.com/roger/teencritic.html

Roger Davidson is this precocious movie critic from Minneapolis who looks both at new movies and video releases. While some of his reviews are unintentionally hilarious (in a review of *The Doors*, he writes that "Oliver Stone recreates the sites [sic] and sounds of the sixties quite well"—quite a statement for a lad who is only 17 years old), most of his movie reviews are accessible, readable, and on the mark.

Internet Underground Music Archive

http://www.iuma.com/IUMA/index_graphic.html

There is a huge underground-music movement facilitated by the Internet and the World Wide Web. The Internet Underground Music Archive brings you information about hundreds of musicians, including many not signed to music labels who choose to distribute their music via the Internet. (These samples are distributed in various audio formats.) The IUMA also includes information on other artists who may be obscure and signed to smaller labels but still worth checking out. You can search through these musicians by name or by genre.

 You'll learn more about working with sound and Netscape Navigator in Chapter 12.

NOTE

The Duluth-Superior Dukes

http://www.dsdukes.com

OK, so it's not major-league baseball—but it's the way baseball was meant to be played.

The Duluth Shipping News

http://www.duluthshippingnews.com/

Duluth in the summer is as close to paradise as we'll get in the lower 48. This Web site details the activities around the harbor, as well as other interesting happenings in Duluth. It's shown in Figure 4.22.

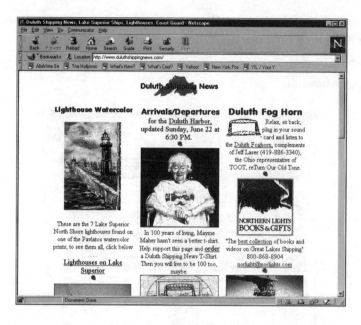

Figure 4.22 *The Duluth Shipping News.*

Felix the Cat

http://www.felixthecat.com

Felix the Cat—the wonderful, wonderful cat.

USING INTERNET SEARCH ENGINES

The Web sites covered so far in this chapter represent a mere drop in a huge ocean of sites. There are hundreds of thousands of Web pages out there, with more added every hour.

With so many Web pages, finding what you need can be a very daunting task—much more daunting than you can ever imagine. Luckily, there have been many attempts to index and organize the many offerings of the World Wide Web, in the form of Internet *search engines*. Basically, a search engine indexes the content of the Internet in such a way that you can easily retrieve it, either by searching an index of Web pages or by scrolling down a list of subjects and the Web pages devoted to them. Netscape Navigator includes a link to various popular search engines on its own Web site; you can access this link by selecting **Search Internet** from the Edit menu or entering a URL of:

http://home.netscape.com/escapes/search/ntsrchrnd-1.html

This page is shown in Figure 4.23.

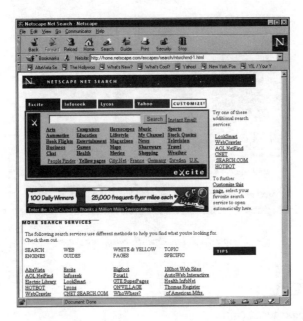

Figure 4.23 *The Internet Search page.*

 Be warned that the firms listed on the Internet Search page pay Netscape for the privilege. This is not a listing of what the Netscape folks think are the best search engines—this is a listing of the firms that pay Netscape the most money. The next time you think the Internet is populated by altruistic souls who want to create a huge, counter-cultural revolution, remember that firms pay for placement on a page like this.

To get what you need out of a search engine, however, you do need to know a little bit about Boolean logic, even though the search engines themselves rarely use this term. There's no reason to be intimidated by Boolean logic, especially after you read this short primer.

Basically, Boolean logic is used to define a search. Let's say you wanted information about the singer Elvis Costello. You use **Elvis** as your query. You're then connected to the Excite search engine and given pages that contain the term *Elvis*. You'll end up with output as shown in Figure 4.24.

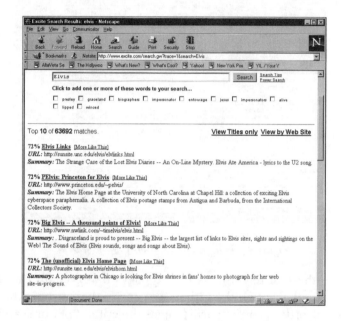

Figure 4.24 *Output for an Elvis search.*

Of course, since there's more than one famous performing Elvis, the results here are skewed toward the famous dead Elvis. You ended up with a limited number of Web pages that contained the term *Elvis* without really even scratching the surface. As a matter of fact, the Excite engine didn't even suggest that you combine *Elvis* with *Costello*. So there's obviously a need to narrow our search.

To do so, we can use **Elvis Costello** as a search term, the results of which are shown in Figure 4.25. (Excite assumes that two capitalized words together form part of a name, so there's no need to use quotation marks around the terms of the search, as is the case with other search engines and database applications.)

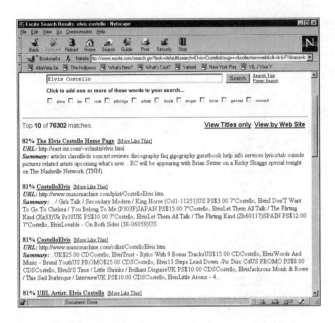

Figure 4.25 Output for an Elvis Costello search.

Here, we see the first few listings of the pages that contain the term *Elvis Costello*. As we look through the listings we can see that anyone who lists Elvis Costello as a favorite recording artist meets the criteria of our search. Now, if you're a real fan, you may want to look through every one of these pages, but that can be a huge chore for anyone—even those who think Elvis is God. Let's say you want more information about Elvis Costello in the form of Frequently Asked Questions, or FAQs.

You'll learn more about FAQs in Chapter 13. For now, all you need to know is that a list of FAQs is merely a list of frequently asked questions of a newsgroup. Such a list eliminates the need to ask routine questions regularly of the entire group.

HOT LINK

In this case, we'll want to narrow down the search to look for all Web pages containing the name *Elvis Costello* and the term *FAQ*. Every search engine handles this a little differently, although all make use of Boolean logic to modify a search term. With Excite, you begin with a search term and then add the word or phrase that is essential to the search. In Boolean terms, you're using the word *and* to string together a search. The search criteria then look like this: *Elvis Costello and FAQ*.

The Excite search engine returns 100 more pages that contain the name *Elvis Costello* and the term *FAQ*, as shown in Figure 4.26.

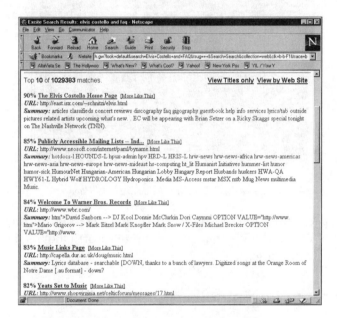

Figure 4.26 *Output for a refined Elvis Costello search.*

Excite uses a weighed system when returning Web pages, so the first listing returned is the one that most closely matches the search criteria. And sure enough, the first listing returned here is entitled Elvis Costello Home Page, as shown in Figure 4.27.

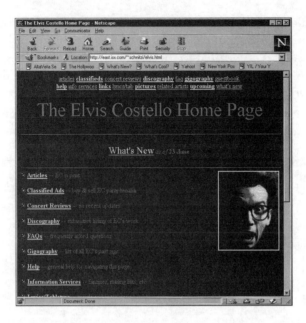

Figure 4.27 *The Elvis Costello Home Page.*

The FAQ is part of the larger Elvis Costello home page. (By the way, this is one of the coolest sites of the Web, and one definitely worth looking into if you're interested at all in music.)

Other Search Engines

There are more Web search engines than Excite, of course. By selecting the **Search Internet** menu choice, you're presented with a set of Internet search engines. Some of these search engines are much more sophisticated than the Excite search engine (at least when this book was written); the Open Text search engine, for example, allows for rather sophisticated searches based on a high number of criteria, included weighted searches and power searches. Table 4.1 lists the major search engines. All of these Web sites feature both indices of Web sites as well as subject-oriented lists of URLs.

Table 4.1   *The Major Internet Search Engines*

ENGINE	URL	DESCRIPTION
Alta Vista	*http://altavista.digital.com*	This is the most complete index to the vast wares of the Internet. If you're contemplating any search, you would do well to begin here.
DejaNews	*http://www.dejanews.com*	This is a searchable catalog of Usenet news archives. (You'll learn more about the Usenet in Chapter 13.)
Lycos	*http://www.lycos.com*	Lycos began as a project at Carnegie-Mellon University and is regarded as one of the most complete indices of the Web.
Open Text Index	*http://www.opentext.com:8080/*	Perhaps the most sophisticated search engine, the Open Text Index allows for elaborate searches based on a great number of criteria.
Yahoo	http://www.yahoo.com	This is the most usable search tool available, as it features editors that classify subjects and pages.

Internet Directories

In finding the Elvis Costello Home Page, we've made use of Excite's ability to search through its indices of URLs. Other search engines—most notably Yahoo and Lycos—also contain lists of Web sites organized by subject. These can useful for browsing. For example, the listings for independent baseball leagues are shown in Figure 4.28.

Figure 4.28 *The Yahoo independent baseball listings.*

While these listings aren't perfect—indeed, the Real Baseball site (*http://www.realbaseball.com*) has a much better set of links to independent baseball leagues—it's still a good start.

These listings (which can also be found on Lycos and the other major search engines) are organized around various topics; in the case of InfoSeek, the listings include Business & Finance, News, and Arts & Entertainment.

USING NETSCAPE NAVIGATOR LOCALLY

So far in this book we've discussed how to use Netscape Navigator in the larger Internet. However, you don't need to be connected to the Internet to use Netscape Navigator. Many companies are now using Netscape Navigator on their internal networks to distribute information to employees. For example, a company could set up its own home page and configure Netscape Navigator to automatically connect to that home page at startup. Company news can be posted to that home page, with links to home pages maintained by employees. This information would be limited to those on the company network, and thus unavailable to the world at large. In the networking world, this sort of network is called an *intranet*.

When you use Netscape Navigator locally, you'll need to learn a slightly different set of conventions when loading Web pages. None of these conventions are especially difficult, and you'll find that Netscape Navigator protects you somewhat from some of the messier details.

Opening a Local File

There are two ways to open a file on your computer or your network. You can either specify the file using its long URL, or else you can use the Open Page... dialog box (summoned by the **Ctrl-O** shortcut) on the File menu. It's easier to use the dialog box, of course, as it allows you to browse through your options (see Figure 4.29).

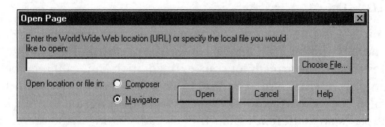

Figure 4.29 *The Open Page dialog box.*

At this point, Netscape Navigator doesn't really distinguish between a page on the Internet and a page on your local computer. However, if you select **Choose File**, you'll be presented with a file-opening dialog box specific to your operating system (the Windows 95 dialog box is different from the Macintosh dialog box, and they are both different from the UNIX/Linux dialog box).

By default, you'll be looking for a page with an extension of *HTM*, which means that (ostensibly) the file is formatted in the HyperText Markup Language. (Many Web sites leave the *L* off of the filename, knowing that DOS—and Windows 3.1—cannot handle the extra character in the suffix of the filename.) You have the choice of opening other kinds of files: Netscape Navigator can be used to read text files, and it supports a wide variety of other file types.

When you open the file, you'll notice the URL looks just like the path used on a command line.

Network Drives

If you're running Netscape Navigator on a local network, you'll have the option of looking for the file in your network drives. If you're running Windows 3.1 or Windows 95, you'll have to use the DOS drive conventions (like E:, N:, P:, etc.) to specify the drive on the network server. If you're using the Macintosh, you'll need to look on the folders on the server. Our intention here isn't to educate you about using your local-area network, but rather to point out that Netscape Navigator uses network drives the same way as any other application.

Link to Link

When you're browsing pages on your own internal network or file system, you should have no problems jumping between hypertext links—provided that the pages are set up correctly, of course. In addition, you can jump between pages on your internal system and pages on the external Internet, provided that you're connected to the Internet. Netscape Navigator doesn't handle internal pages any differently than it does pages sitting somewhere on the Internet. The mechanism for selecting the internal page differs, but that's the only difference.

SUMMARY

This chapter is perhaps the most fun chapter in the book—you finally get a chance to peruse the Web and see what cool sites are out there. The chapter focused on the tools you'll use everyday when working with Netscape Navigator, ranging from bookmarks and forms to local files and Internet search engines. In the next chapter, you'll make the leap to using FTP to download files in Navigator.

## CHAPTER 5

FTP and Navigator

The Internet is the world's largest repository of software, and you're welcome to browse around in search of something useful. To do so, though, you may need to have some knowledge of File Transfer Protocol (FTP) and Netscape Navigator. In this chapter, you'll learn about

- The history of FTP
- Shareware, freeware, and more
- Connecting to an FTP server
- Anonymous access and FTP
- Passwords and FTP
- Downloading software
- Uploading software
- Compressed files
- Using Archie to search FTP sites
- Why Archie is rapidly becoming outdated

GRABBING FILES THE OLD-FASHIONED WAY WITH FTP

As you use the Internet more and more, you'll realize how *new* the World Wide Web is when compared to most of the other Internet tools. One of older Internet tools available is FTP (short for File Transfer Protocol), but it is a useful way to get what you need from the Internet.

How old? Well, let's just say that before there was an entity recognized as the "Internet," there was a predecessor that was limited to electronic mail, FTP, and telnet. While electronic mail was the most popular offering at the time (it still is the most popular offering of the Internet, by the way), FTP was also a very popular tool—so popular that the Internet evolved into the largest software repository in the world.

This is partly because of the ethos shared by those early Internauts: software should be freely available and shared without charge. (It helped that many of these Internauts worked at universities and research institutions, where they tended to be shielded from the pressures of capitalism.) The other big reason is that FTP is fairly easy to use and is standardized between operating systems. Therefore, a PC or Macintosh can easily connect to a UNIX server via the Internet and transfer files without a hitch.

How easy is it? Let's go through a typical FTP transfer and see.

NOTE   There will be times when you use FTP and don't even know it until you're waist-deep in it. How can this be? A Web-page designer can place a link to an FTP site directly in a Web page. For instance, you probably used such a link if you downloaded Netscape Navigator directly from Netscape Communications. When you click on a link that appears as **Click here to download Netscape Navigator,** *ftp://ftp.netscape.com* will be loaded automatically as your URL. In this case, Netscape Navigator will prompt you to save the file. If this happens to you, you can skip ahead to the section entitled "Saving the File."

NOTE   Software available on the Internet comes under several different categories:

- Shareware is software distributed free of charge on the Internet and other alternative distribution sources (such as CD-ROMs). The software is distributed with the expectation that if you find the software useful, you'll send a contribution to the author; it's really a form of "try before you buy," rather than software given away for free. (The author also retains copyright to the software.) Shareware will contain text files as part of the distribution that explains this and asks for a registration fee on your part. To be a good Internet citizen, you should pay for the software that you use.

- *Freeware* is software freely given away to the world, with no expectation of registration fees. (The author does retains copyright to the software, however.)

- *Patches* are upgrades to specific portions of a commercial software release that address specific bugs or shortcomings in the original software. Without the original software, a patch is usually pretty useless.

- *Upgrades* are new releases of a product that may be available to users of an older version of the software. Generally, if a commercial vendor makes an upgrade of a software package available on the Internet, the upgrade won't do a lot of good if the original software isn't already installed.

How Do I Grab a File?

When you connect to an FTP site, you're basically logging on a computer with access to its file contents. These files are organized like your hard drive: There's a main directory, with subdirectories that contain files and perhaps other directories. Like MS-DOS, UNIX uses slashes to distinguish between levels on the directory tree.

There's one big difference, however—UNIX uses forward slashes, while MS-DOS uses backslashes. (That's why there are so many forward slashes in HTTP calls—you're actually calling files from a file directory.) Even though many Web servers run on Windows NT and Macintosh platforms, the Internet convention is to use the forward slashes everywhere, to maintain compatibility with the UNIX world that spawned the Internet.

FTP sites are also like World Wide Web sites—they exist on an Internet-connected computer and can be accessed via Netscape Navigator. When you connect to a Web site, you're grabbing a page with the HyperText Transfer Protocol (HTTP) that's formatted in the HyperText Markup Language

(HTML). When you connect to an FTP site, you're using the World Wide Web to download a file using the File Transfer Protocol.

The difference lies in how you tell Netscape Navigator that you're connecting to an FTP site. Instead of beginning the URL with *http*, in this case you'll begin it with *ftp*. You'll keep the colon (:) and the slashes (//) to separate the protocol and the address. So, to connect to an FTP site named *ftp.coast.net*, you'd use the following URL:

> *ftp://ftp.coast.net*

The results are shown in Figure 5.1.

NOTE   Actually, we're being rather formal here. Most of the time you can get by without using *ftp://* at the beginning of a connection to an FTP server. If you were to enter just *ftp.coast.net*, Netscape Navigator will be smart enough to insert the *ftp://* at the beginning of the URL. This will only work when the name of the FTP server actually begins with *ftp*; obviously, Netscape Navigator can't figure out that a name like *software.net* refers to an FTP server or some other type of server.

Figure 5.1 *Connecting to the software archive at ftp.coast.net.*

NOTE

If you've used other FTP tools, you'll recall that you need to enter a username and a password when connecting to an FTP server. If the FTP server supports *anonymous FTP*, it means that you enter *anonymous* as your username and your electronic-mail address as your password. Netscape Navigator automatically sends along a username of *anonymous* and your electronic-mail address when connecting to any FTP site.

If you're not connecting to an FTP site that doesn't support anonymous FTP (in other words, a private site—such as one maintained by a college or a business), then you'll need to pass along the username and the password in the URL. The syntax is kinda weird, so you'll need to watch it closely. Let's say you want to connect to an FTP site named *ftp.reichard.com* (no, this FTP site doesn't exist, so don't bother), where your username is *kevin* and your password is *geisha*. In this case, you'd enter the following URL:

```
ftp://kevin:geisha@ftp.kreichard.com
```

This breaks down to a format of:

```
ftp://username:password@ftpsite
```

You can also pass along an FTP formatted like the following:

```
ftp:username@ftpsite
```

In this case, Netscape Navigator will prompt you for a password after the initial connection is made to the FTP server.

You'll notice one thing in Figure 5.1: The absence of any graphics. Basically, FTP is a text-only medium (on a UNIX machine, it's run as a command-line application), and to make your way around FTP in the rawest form, you'd need to learn a series of FTP commands. However, Netscape Navigator hides you from these messy details. (It also hides you from some handy features, as you'll see later.) As we scroll down the screen first shown in Figure 5.1, we see that the contents of *ftp.coast.net* are organized in folders and documents, as shown in Figure 5.2.

Figure 5.2 *The contents of ftp.coast.net.*

The current directory is shown at the top of the page, in the large type. (On a UNIX system, the uppermost directory is the *root* directory, and it's designated with a single slash [/].) All of the documents (which are indicated by a page with a corner folded down; if you were to select a document, it would be displayed on your Navigator screen like any other Web text document) and folders are marked with underlined text, which means that you can access them from within Netscape Navigator. The parent directory of the current directory is denoted by the first file of the listings—the two periods (..) and the arrow. (This is better shown in Figure 5.3—after all, the root directory has no parent directory on any file system, so there's no indication of a parent directory in Figure 5.2.) The time and date when the file is also listed, the same as it would be if you viewed the contents of a directory on your own local computer, as well as the size of the document (when appropriate; again, this is better illustrated in Figure 5.3, which contains many document for download). When you move the cursor over a link, it turns into a little hand. To open a folder or view a file, you place the cursor over the link and click with the left mouse button. (Macintosh users would click with the only mouse button, of course.)

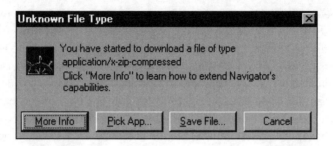

Figure 5.3 *The Unknown File Type dialog box.*

All things happen for a reason, and in this case we're using *ftp.coast.net* as an example because it's the home of the Coast to Coast software repository, which is possibly the largest single collection of PC shareware and freeware in the world. At the bottom of the screen shown in Figure 5.2 are directories. By clicking on the underlined SimTel folder, you'd move to the next directory down.

Let's move down two more levels, to **win3/internet**. This directory contains Internet tools for Windows 3.1 users. (OS/2, Macintosh, and Windows 95 users can browse through their own directories. This is used merely as an example.) Here, we'll grab the file named **alp16.zip**. This software is a chat client for the World Wide Web. We cover chat in Chapter 8; the purpose here isn't to use Netscape Navigator as a chat tool, but rather to show how to grab a file via FTP. Which is, after all, ridiculously easy. Simply position the cursor over the **alp16.zip** line, and press on the left mouse button. You'll get a dialog box like the one shown in Figure 5.3.

You'll note that there's a file beginning with **readme** in this directory. Generally speaking, most good FTP sites will have a file called **readme** or **index** that lists the contents of the directory in some expanded form. If you select this file, Netscape Navigator will ask you what you want to do with it; in these cases, you want to display the file in Notepad or another text editor.

N O T E

Generally speaking, you'll find that most filenames conform to the operating system they're meant for. DOS and Windows 3.x files follow the eight-dot-three file-naming convention (that is, a main filename of up to eight characters, followed by a period (**.**) and then a suffix. Since the Macintosh OS, Windows NT, and Windows 3.1 allow long filenames, you'll find that the files meant for these operating systems feature filenames longer than the eight-dot-three limit. Now, having said that, it's important that we note that these other operating systems will conform to some parts of the eight-dot-three limitation, especially when it comes to suffixes: Macintosh compressed files will end with **.sit**, even there's no need for the period and the suffix.

If you're grabbing some sort of documentation file, you may find that it exceeds the eight-dot-three limitation, even if you're using it under Windows 3.1. In these cases, Windows 3.1 will truncate the filename when you save it to disk. Sometimes this truncation is harmless, but there are other times when you'll want to maintain some vestige of the original filename (such as the extension). In these cases, manually change the filename in the **Save** dialog box.

N O T E

An FTP server also describes the contents of the file in a generic sense. Some of the filenames are rather self-explanatory (files ending in **.zip** would denote a MS-DOS file compressed with PKZip, while files ending in **.sit** would denote a Macintosh file connected with StuffIt), while others aren't. For those that aren't, the FTP server has a column in the directory listing (which you can see in Figure 5.3) that has a generic description of what *type* of file is listed (not a description of the specific contents of the file). Some of the more popular file types are listed in Table 5.1.

Table 5.1 *Common File Types on an FTP Server.*

DESCRIPTION	MEANING
Binary executable	A program file for any operating system.
Directory	A directory, which contains other files and (possibly) directories.
GNU zip data	A file compressed using the GNU **gzip** utility.
Macintosh archive	A file compressed using the Macintosh StuffIt compression utility.
Plain text	ASCII text, which can be read by any operating system.

Description	Meaning
UNIX archive	A file created using the UNIX **tar** utility.
Zip compressed data	An MS-DOS file compressed using the PKZip compression utility.

Saving the File

When Netscape Navigator is presented with an unknown file type, you're shown the dialog box shown in Figure 5.4. If you plan to download a lot of files, you'll want to configure Netscape Navigator to automatically store ZIPped files to your hard drive. In this case, Netscape Navigator hasn't been configured to do so, so you'll need to tell it to save the file to disk. Another dialog box will appear, asking you where you want to save the file. In the case of Figure 5.4, the **Save As...** dialog box is the familiar Windows 95 **Save As...** dialog box. If you're using another operating system, that operating system's saving mechanism will appear. In this case, Netscape Navigator defaults to saving the file in the same directory where Netscape Navigator is stored. You can use the tools found in your operating system to denote the correct directory. In most cases, it really doesn't matter where you store these files, although it's most convenient to store them all in one directory. (It's amazing how soon you can lose track of files and forget where you've stored them.)

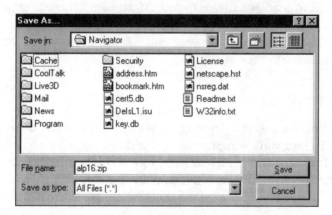

Figure 5.4 Saving the file.

There. You have mastered the fine art of FTP.

How Do I Uncompress/Unpack/Unzip/Unstuff Files?

Most files on the Internet are stored in a compressed format, where an original set of files has been shrunk and stored in a single archive. This allows the files to take up less room on an Internet server, while at the same time cutting down on the transmission time needed to transfer the files between the Internet server and your computer.

However, to make use of these compressed files, you'll need a tool to uncompress them. (The exception is a file compressed using Central Point's compression utility, which creates a compressed file that can be uncompressed from the DOS command line. As a matter of fact, you've already been exposed to this format: the version of Netscape Navigator on the Internet is compressed using this format.) There are several software packages that can do this; the most popular are PKZip (from PKWare) for MS-DOS and StuffIt (from Aladdin) for Macintosh. (A good alternative to PKZip for Windows users is WinZIP, widely available on the Internet.) Many of the archives listed later in this chapter will have uncompression tools available. In addition, those interested in PKZip can check out *http://www.pkware.com* for the most recent version and a Windows version of PKZip, which was not yet released when this book was prepared.

Basically, the compression utilities are used on the file after it's downloaded. The exact mechanism depends on the tool and the operating system; PKZip is run from a MS-DOS command line, while StuffIt automatically runs after you've downloaded a file onto your Macintosh. These are rather simple utilities, actually, but because they differ so much, the advice here is to grab the compression software and then spend a few minutes checking the documentation to see how they work.

Hitting the Wall

Most FTP sites have a limit as to the number of users that can be logged in at a single time. In fact, you'll run into these limits fairly often if you try to login to popular FTP sites. If you do try to login to a FTP site and it's running at full capacity, you'll receive a message that (usually) politely informs you that the site is full, and that you should try again later. An example is shown in Figure 5.5.

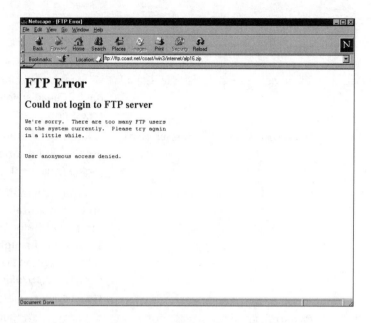

Figure 5.5 A denied connection to an FTP site.

When this happens, you'll just need to keep trying until you're connected. A simple way to avoid this problem is to try transfers at nonpeak times, i.e., early in the morning or late at night.

Major FTP Sites

There are several major FTP sites on the Internet, and they are described in Table 5.2. These sites allow access free of charge. In addition, many of these sites mirror the SimTel archives. Many of these are connectable via World Wide Web also (as noted).

Table 5.2 *Major FTP Sites on the Internet*

SITE	URL	LOCATION	NOTES
AGT Planet	*ftp.agt.net*	Alberta, Canada	General-interest archive run by Canadian Internet-access firm.
DEC FTP	*gatekeeper.dec.com*	Massachusetts	A large general-interest archive maintained by Digital Equipment Corp.
U of Illinois	*uiarchive.cso.uiuc.edu*	Illinois	A large general-interest archive maintained by the University of Illinois. To search through this archive, you can first connect to *http://uiarchive/ cso.uiuc.edu/*.
Microsoft	*ftp.microsoft.com*	Washington	A large archive of Microsoft patches, drivers, and free software.
MIT	*rtfm.mit.edu*	Massachusetts	This MIT site, named for the common Internet/computer phrase "read the f____g manual," is an archive dedicated to documentation.
Oak Software	*oak.oakland.edu*	Michigan	One of the largest archives and one of the most popular. A search engine can be reached at *http:// www.acs.oakland.edu/oak/*.
Oregon State U.	*ftp.orst.edu*	Oregon	A general-interest archive of freeware and shareware.

SITE	URL	LOCATION	NOTES
Pacific Hitech	*ftp.pht.com*	Utah	This archive features more Macintosh software than does the average FTP site; in addition, there are many game and utility software files available for Windows, DOS, Macintosh, and Linux.
THEnet	*ftp.the.net*	Texas	Educational archive run by the Texas Higher Educational Network.
Walnut Creek	*ftp.cdrom.com*	California	Large archive that specializes in UNIX, Linux, and programming tools.
Washington U.	*wuarchive.wustl.edu*	Missouri	A large general-interest archive maintained by Washington University in St. Louis.
Winsite	*ftp.winsite.com*	Indiana	This is the former *ftp.cica.indiana.edu* FTP site. As you might infer from the name, it's the place to look for Windows (NT, 3.x, 95, NT) shareware and some DOS software. Check out the README in the main directory.
UW-Parkside	*ftp.uwp.edu*	Wisconsin	This educational site features a slew of music archives, ranging from liner notes and reviews of works to FAQs about specific artists.

Uploading Files

Generally speaking, you won't need to upload files to public FTP sites; as a matter of fact, unless you're a programmer or a systems administrator of some standing in the IS community, you should have no reason to be transferring files to FTP sites.

In case you do, however, you can easily upload a file using the **Upload File...** from the File menu. When you choose this command, Netscape Navigator will pop up a dialog box asking you to specify a file (the dialog box will depend on the operating system, but generally all you're asked to do is specify a file and given the tools to browse for it).

Of course, you need to make sure that the current directory is the one you want to upload the file to. And, more importantly, you need permission to upload a file to an FTP server. Generally speaking, only one portion of an FTP server is set aside for uploads, and that directory is called **public** or **pub**. More important directories, like **bin** (short for *bin*ary), usually are controlled strictly by the person overseeing the FTP directory. And don't forget that many major FTP sites don't allow any public uploads at all.

Netscape Navigator and Archie

If you've been around the Internet a while, you may have used an Archie server to search for the contents of FTP sites. Basically, an Archie server allows you to plug in a filename or a partial filename (using wildcards to fill the rest of the filename), and Archie will return a list of FTP sites that contain a file by that name, along with the time and the date the file was created (useful for differentiating between different versions of software that may be posted to different sites).

Netscape Navigator as such doesn't support a direct connection to an Archie server. If you want to search Archie servers, you'll need to get an Archie client and use that, get a telnet client to plug directly into Navigator, or connect to a World Wide Web site that has a connection to an Archie server. There are a host of Web sites that interface with Archie servers and provide forms-based pages for input (remember, Netscape Navigator supports forms, so you can go this route); a master list of these servers is maintained at *http://web.nexor.co.uk/archie.html* (as shown in Figure 5.6).

Figure 5.6 *The master list of Archie servers.*

There are some large public Archie servers maintained by public institutions, and you'll want to check out one of these. As always, be a good Internet citizen and choose an Archie server close to you; even in the best of times, an Archie search takes a while (which is why Archie will never catch on in its present incarnation; it's too slow to rely upon for regular usage). If you're really interested in full-scale searches and aren't used to using Archie, you'll want to instead check out the search engines, as outlined in Chapter 4. If you're used to using Archie, you don't need a lesson here.

SUMMARY

FTP is one of the oldest parts of the Internet. As a matter of fact, FTP existed before the days of the Internet per se. Still, FTP is one of the more useful portions of the Internet. In this chapter, you learned how to connect to an FTP site, download software to your computer, and manage it once the software is stored on your hard drive.

In the next chapter, you'll learn about some other older Internet services that you may or may not find useful, such as Gopher and Veronica.

## CHAPTER 6

Gopher and Navigator

In terms of the Internet timeline, the World Wide Web is a relatively recent phenomenon. For years, many users were content with such older Internet tools as Gopher, Archie, Veronica, Jughead, and WAIS. In this chapter, you'll learn about the following topics:

- Introducing Gopher menus
- Making your way through Gopherspace
- Some notable Gopherspace sites
- The Mother of all Gophers
- A master list of Gopher sites
- Introducing indexing tools like Archie, Jughead, and Veronica
- Searching Gopherspace with Veronica
- Jumping from a Veronica search
- WAIS support in Netscape Navigator
- The future of WAIS

Living History: Gopher, the Archie Crew, and Older Utilities

Obligatory history lesson: Before the World Wide Web became a widespread phenomenon, there was a thriving Internet community that made do with such tools as Gopher, Archie, Veronica, and Jughead.

These tools didn't use graphics or flashy links to attract users; instead, these were text-based services that were meant for serious information miners. And, for the most part, they worked exactly as they were meant to work.

Today, with the WWW and Internet search engines becoming popular and sophisticated, the idea of using these text-based services may seem antiquated at best. And indeed, to be honest, you won't spend a lot of time using these tools. However, there are still a lot of useful resources in the pre-WWW world, and it doesn't hurt to know of their existence.

What Is Gopher?

In this case, Gopher isn't a reference to the diminutive rodent—it's a reference to the mascot for the University of Minnesota, where Gopher was originally developed before there was a World Wide Web or graphical computing on the Internet.

Gopher was an attempt to make the Internet a little more interactive; it presented menus that guide a user through menus. The process was simple: You would connect to a Gopher server (yes, there are Gopher servers, just like there are Web and mail servers), which would treat your screen as a full-page display, providing a set of numbered menus and an area for entering the number of a menu. (Later versions of Gopher added the ability to scroll through menu choices with cursor keys or use your mouse to click on a menu to select it.) These menus might lead to another set of menus, a file to be displayed immediately (such as the famous Gopher weather reports), or a file to be saved to your disk. Because of the relative ease inherent in moving through menus, the world of Gopherspace became a very large component of the Internet architecture—so large that it's only been in the very recent past that the number of World Wide Web servers has exceeded the number of Gopher servers.

Now, in these days of the World Wide Web and graphical computing on the Internet, the idea of Gopher menus seem somewhat quaint, and to be honest the WWW has stolen a lot of Gopher's steam, because development of new Gopher sites has slowed to a trickle.

This doesn't mean that Gopher is totally outdated, however. There are still a lot of very useful Gopher sites out there, as many governments and universities committed to Gopher early and maintain a lot of information on Gopher servers. In addition, there are a lot of Web pages that have links to Gopher menus, and Gopher is one of the "official" URL formats supported as part of the World Wide Web. Hence we need to cover Gopher in a book on Netscape Communicator, since Netscape Navigator can be used to access Gopher information.

A Typical Gopher Session

As stated, Gopher is one of the "official" URL formats supported by Netscape Navigator. Gopher features its own format. It's quite simple, really:

gopher://gopher.server

As an example, let's connect to the Mother of all Gopher Servers, the original Gopher server at the University of Minnesota. To do so, just type in the following URL:

gopher://gopher.micro.umn.edu

You'll see a screen like the one shown in Figure 6.1.

NOTE   Again, Netscape Navigator is pretty smart at figuring out that an address like *gopher.micro.umn.edu* means that you want to connect to a Gopher server, so you don't necessarily need to include the *gopher://* in the URL field. (It wouldn't be so smart if you want to connect to a site named *micro.gopher.umn.edu*; make sure that the address begins with *gopher* if you want Netscape Navigator to anticipate your wishes. Then again, it can't hurt to enter the full URL address.

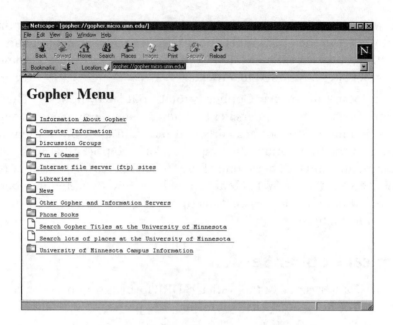

Figure 6.1 *The Mother of all Gopher Servers.*

The options in Figure 6.1 aren't difficult to figure out, really. You have a headline, **Gopher Menu**, that tells you that you're connected to a Gopher server (surprise!). You have a series of lines that begin with a little file folder and are both in a purple color and underlined—by now, you should know that these are links to other directories in the Gopher world. And there are two lines that begin.

What this all means is pretty simple, really. You should know enough about computing by now to know that a file folder means that there's something inside the folder, and that to see what's in the folder, you need to select it. In addition, binoculars indicate that the menu item leads to a search tool.

As mentioned before, there's not a lot to really do with Gopher sites: You can either view the information in a file, go to another directory, or download a file. If you do read a file, be warned that you're only displaying it on your screen. Because it's not a hypertext document with any links, there won't be any way to move through it with links, so you'll need to use the **Back** key to move to the previous screen or enter a new URL. However, the configuration work you've done with helper applications will also work on any file you run across in Gopherspace—for instance, if you run across a graphics file (like a **.GIF** or **.JPEG** file), Netscape Navigator will be able to display it.

Places to Go in Gopherspace

There are some very useful Gopher sites worth checking out. However, be warned that the majority of Gopher servers are *very* specialized. For instance, there are dozens of Gopher servers maintained by the state of Minnesota, but they are all tightly focused, maintained by department and state agencies; as a matter of fact, Minnesota (as well as many other states) maintain a list of currently pending bills only via Gopher server. A fuller list of major Gopher sites can be found at *gopher.tc.umn.edu:70/11/Other%20Gopher%20and%20Information%20Servers/al l* (yes, this *is* the URL, believe it or not). This list is 359K and contains pretty much every useful Gopher server in the world. Figure 6.2 shows an excerpt from this list, and as you can see the listings are very specific. The best approach is to either load the entire list (which, at 28.8Kbps, doesn't take that long, really) or search through Gopherspace using Veronica (which is the third option in the list). (We'll cover Veronica later in this chapter.) A more useful list—at least, more manageable, any-way—is the Gopher Jewels list found at *gopher://cwis.usc.edu/11/ Other_Gophers_and_Information_Resources/Gophers_by_Subject/Gopher_Jewels.*

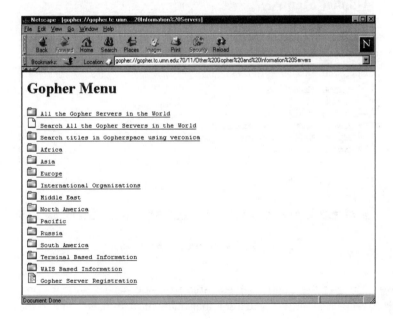

Figure 6.2 *A list of all the Gophers in the world.*

Here are some other Gopher sites that you may want to check out:

- **The EcoGopher** (*gopher://ecosys.drdr.virginia.edu*) is devoted to ecology and environmental issues, both with local information and with links to other related resources.

- **The Global Democracy Network** Gopher (*gopher://gopher.gdn.org*) is a clearinghouse for Gopher resources relating to human rights across the world.

- **The Internet Wiretap** Gopher (*gopher://wiretap.spies.com*) is a collection of text information concerning government documents of all sorts. It's shown in Figure 6.3.

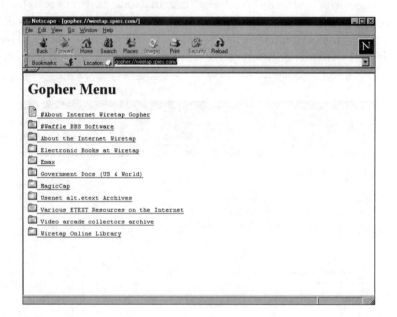

Figure 6.3 *The Internet Wiretap Gopher.*

Many of the Gopher servers listed here also have a presence on the World Wide Web. In fact, you'll see that many of them have a link in their Gopher menus to a WWW site.

N O T E

Searching through Gopherspace

Though the idea of searching through Gopherspace has been made somewhat redundant by Internet search engines (which you learned about in Chapter 4), there's the chance that something you need may be found only in Gopherspace and not found in the World Wide Web world that dominates the search engines.

That's why you may want to visit the world of Archie, Veronica, and Jughead—older attempts to index the Internet world in a searchable form. To be totally honest, these tools haven't always served as a reliable guide to the Internet world, and they're positively ancient when compared to the powerhouse Internet search engines. Here, we'll run through a session using Veronica, using Gopher as the entrance point. Veronica is the front end to a list of Gopher sites, while Archie is used mainly to index files (and is mainly accessed via telnet, which you learned about in Chapter 4) and Jughead is a variant of Veronica, although not as widely implemented.

Looking into the Glass, Darkly

As you saw in Figure 6.2, the Gopher server at the University of Minnesota provides a Veronica search engine. Like the search engines covered in Chapter 4, this search engine goes through an index of Gopher pages and matches your terms to the various entries in the Gopher pages.

When you choose the line entitled *Search Gopherspace using Veronica,* you see a Web page that presents a slew of options regarding how and what to search (as shown in Figure 6.4).

Basically, the task isn't as complex as this menu makes it appear. Because all you want to do is search through the titles of Gopher pages, you can choose to *Find GOPHER DIRECTORIES by Title word(s) (via NYSERNet).* This brings up a menu as shown in Figure 6.5, which features a text-entry area where you can provide the list of terms you're searching for. We'll use the terms "plant pathology" as an example.

Figure 6.4 *Searching Gopherspace with Veronica.*

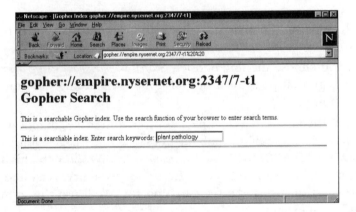

Figure 6.5 *Submitting search terms to Veronica.*

Veronica returns a list of Gopher servers related to plant pathology. The results are shown in Figure 6.6.

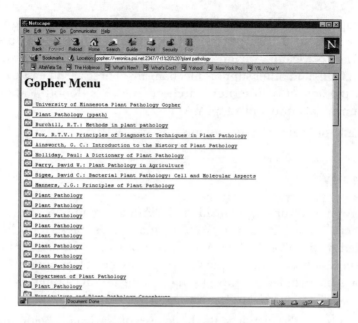

Figure 6.6 *The result of our Veronica search.*

We can then scroll through the list of the search results and connect to a Gopher server that looks as though it meets our needs. And that, friends, is about all there is to searching through Gopherspace with a Veronica search engine.

USING A WAIS SERVER

When it comes to raw power, Veronica is a relatively specialized search tool meant for Gopherspace. The original indexer for power users was the Wide Area Information Server, or WAIS. You can set up an index of any text- or HTML-based document with relative ease; a WAIS server then uses brute force to search through that index and return the results to you. Due to the power of indexing software, WAIS has lost a little of its luster.

And, quite honestly, there's a larger reason why WAIS's value has diminished in the Internet world: It's a pain to set up and use. First of all, you need to have a WAIS proxy to connect to a WAIS server. Even corporations with a serious commitment won't have a WAIS proxy server installed, so don't assume you have one available (although a check with your system administrator wouldn't hurt).

Netscape Navigator doesn't natively support WAIS, even though WAIS is one of the "official" URL types, as defined by Internet governing bodies. To use WAIS and Navigator, you must go through a WAIS server that provides you with input fields and other support mechanisms. These aren't easy to come by, and with the advent of Internet search engines, it's doubtful whether any large commercial entity will adopt WAIS.

Basically, only older legacy systems now use WAIS.

SUMMARY

Gopher, Archie, Veronica, Jughead, and WAIS are remnants of the Internet before there was a World Wide Web. In most cases, these tools have been superseded by the World Wide Web. However, Gopher is still an important tool in cyberspace, and this chapter covers the usage of Gopher with Netscape Navigator. Also included is a short listing of some useful Gopher sites and how they can be accessed via Netscape Navigator.

This ends our discussion of the basic uses of Navigator. Beginning in the next chapter, we'll cover some advanced topics in Netscape Communicator, including with a discussion of security and Netscape Communicator.

Netscape Composer

Don't be an Internet potato—get out there and create some Web content of your own! Netscape Communicator includes an excellent tool for creating your own Web pages called Netscape Composer. In this section—comprising Chapter 7—you'll learn how to create your own Web pages.

Creating Your Own HTML Documents

If you've worked your way through the first six chapters of this book, you're now surfing the Web and finding your way around the Internet. But so far, you've looked only at other people's (or company's) Web pages. In this chapter, we'll delve into the wonderful world of Web authoring using Netscape Communicator's Composer module. We'll learn about:

- HTML and tags
- Creating frames and tables
- Dynamic fonts
- Using Page Wizards and templates
- Publishing to the Web

NETSCAPE COMPOSER

Composer is an HTML authoring package that lets you create and style text and tables, add images, scripts, and multimedia objects by drag-and-drop, work with columns and frames, and publish the results to the Internet (or a local Web or intranet) with the click of a button. It may not be the tool you'd choose to do professional-level Web authoring, but it has the power needed to generate personal Web pages, résumés, and small to moderate size sites for businesses of many kinds.

Before we examine what Composer can do and how it does it, however, we'll take a look at the basics of HTML (Hypertext Markup Language), the simple programming language that made the World Wide Web possible.

AN HTML OVERVIEW

It's now time to learn what HTML is all about. Much of what moves over the World Wide Web is text, one way or another. But if it's well formatted, as much of the text in Web documents is (such as headlines and italicized phrases), the formatting was done by your browser (Netscape Navigator in this case), according to instructions that came with the text—also in the form of text.

This might seem to be a fine distinction, but it's important when learning about HTML. Look at Figure 7.1, which shows a Web page displayed under Netscape Composer.

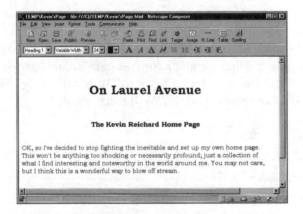

Figure 7.1 A Web page under Netscape Composer.

If we were to look at the text that actually came over the Internet leading to this page, we'd see something like the following:

```
<body>
<center><h1>On Laurel Avenue</h1></center>
<center><h3>The Kevin Reichard Home Page</h3></center>
<p>OK, so I've decided to stop fighting the inevitable and set
up my own home page. This won't be anything too shocking or
necessarily profound; just a collection of what I find inter-
esting and noteworthy in the world around me. You may not
care, but I think this is a wonderful way to blow off
stream.</p>
```

The words and other text enclosed in pointed brackets (< >) are HTML *tags*: formatting instructions that tell Netscape Navigator (or any other Web browser) how to *render* (display) the material enclosed by the tags on your computer.

 If you're a personal computer old-timer, you'll recognize this kind of tagging as the way that many popular word processing and desktop publishing pro-grams—WordPerfect for DOS, and early versions of Ventura Publisher, for example—formatted their pages.

NOTE

Tags work in pairs that say, in effect, "turn on this kind of formatting" where that formatting begins, and "turn it off now" where it ends. Taking our exam-ple, when Navigator sees <center> and <h1>, it knows that the text following should be centered and is a headline; when it sees </h1> and </center>, it knows to stop treating the line as a headline and to end the centering.

In the early days of the Web, there were just a few HTML tags. Now there are hundreds—some for styling and aligning text, some for inserting graph-ics, some for formatting touches like frames, some for forms.

The original method of creating HTML pages was to work in a simple text processor such as DOS Editor or Windows Notepad and enter text and tags together. Some professional HTML coders still work this way, because they know the language, and it's "easier" to work in pure HTML. For most of us, who don't spend the bulk of every day writing HTML code, some automation of the process is very welcome.

HTML Editing and Netscape Composer

Luckily, you don't need to know much about HTML or tags to create your own Web pages, since Netscape Composer features page-creation tools that hide the details of HTML from you. While the Web-page creation features in Netscape Composer aren't quite as extensive as those found in dedicated HTML editors (such as SoftQuad's HoTMetaL Pro), you can still create some very attractive pages on your own.

Composer simplifies HTML editing by creating a WYSIWYG (what-you-see-is-what-you-get) environment, similar to those of current word-processing or desktop publishing tools. You see the finished result as you work (or pretty close to the finished result) while the software takes care of inserting the proper HTML tags in the proper places.

Your First Web Page

Let's jump right in and get a feel for Composer by building a simple Web page. Once you've seen how easy it is, we'll go back and zero in on the details. We'll begin with a quick tour of the Composer screen. To launch Composer, either click the **Composer** icon on the Component bar or select **Page Composer** from the Communicator menu in any Communicator module (or use the keyboard shortcut **Ctrl-4**). Any of these methods brings up the Composer screen shown in Figure 7.2.

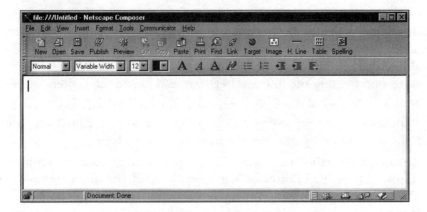

Figure 7.2 The Page Composer screen.

When you launch Netscape Composer, it becomes an independent application. You can close your Web browser and Composer will remain active.

N O T E

There are four areas of the Netscape Mail screen:

- A group of pull-down menus, where all of the program's commands can be accessed
- A Composition Toolbar with tool icons for frequently used functions and page elements
- A Formatting Toolbar with drop-down lists and icons for styling and aligning text
- A blank Edit window

We'll cover each of these areas as we review Netscape Composer by building a simple page.

If you ever need more screen space, you can hide either the Composition toolbar or the Formatting toolbar, or both, by clicking the small vertical bar with the pebbled texture at the left-hand end of either bar. When the windows are hidden, the bar is oriented horizontally. To redisplay either component, just click the appropriate bar.

N O T E

Launching Netscape Composer

To launch Netscape Composer, select **Page Composer** from the Communicator menu in the Navigator window (or use one of the other methods mentioned above). The Composer window should appear immediately with the text cursor blinking in the upper left-hand corner of a bright new blank page, just waiting for you to begin work.

The simplest way to begin is to type in an appropriate heading or two and a few sentences of text. Something like:

```
My First Page


Home Sweet Home
```

As the top Heading suggests, this is my first Web page.
Welcome. Here's where I plan to put all the latest pictures
of the kids, my favorite recipes, and links to my favorite
Web sites.

This should produce a page that looks like the one shown in Figure 7.3.

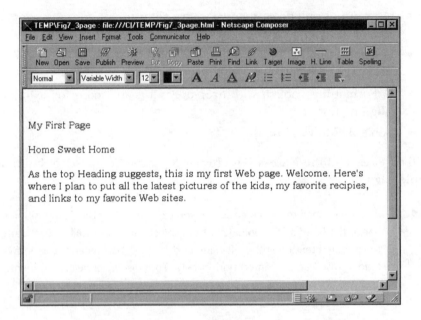

Figure 7.3 *Some text typed into Composer's Edit window.*

So far, so good. Now, let's apply some HTML formatting. (No, we're not going to type in HTML tags, we're going to let Composer do that behind the scenes.) Select (highlight) the top line of text, then click the arrow on the **Paragraph Style** window (the window at the left-hand side of the Formatting Toolbar). You'll see a list of 12 paragraph styles, headed by the default setting, Normal, used for the "body" of a document.

We're going to format this line as a heading. Let's select **Heading 2** by mousing down to that selection and releasing the mouse button. Immediately, the text is made larger and boldfaced.

That was pretty easy; now let's center the line on the page: Click the **Alignment** icon (the one at the right-hand end of the Formatting Toolbar with the lines and the downward arrow). This displays a drop-down selection of icons for the three available HTML text alignments: Flush left, Centered, and Flush right. Mouse down to the **Centered** icon and release. Your text line is instantly displayed in the center of the column.

Let's next take the Home Sweet Home line, center it, and apply the Heading 1 style. (You'll notice that the order in which you apply style choices makes no difference to Composer.) Not bad, but maybe the type could be bigger. Let's go to the **Font Size** window (the small one that now displays the number 24) and select a bigger size. Click the window or the **drop-down arrow** and you get a list of the available font sizes. Yes, there's one larger size: 36 (that's 36 "points"—a typesetter's measure). Perhaps making the type italic would be the perfect touch? No problem: With the text selected, just click the **Italic** icon on the Formatting Toolbar (or press the **Ctrl-I** key combination). That looks about right.

N O T E If it doesn't, in fact, look right to you, and you want to go back to square one and start formatting this text over again, just click the **Remove all Styles** icon. This will strip away all the style attributes, such as size and italics, that you've added from the toolbar.

N O T E If you're not sure what the icons and windows on the two toolbars stand for, just rest your mouse cursor over an icon and a text tool-tip will reveal its name or function.

These are nice headings, but page could use a little dressing up, don't you think? How about adding a decorative horizontal line (graphic designers call this a "rule) below the main page heading? Make sure there's a blank line there, click to put your text cursor on the blank line, then click the **H. Line** icon on the Composition Toolbar. Instantly, a rule is in place. Your heading should now look something like the one in Figure 7.4.

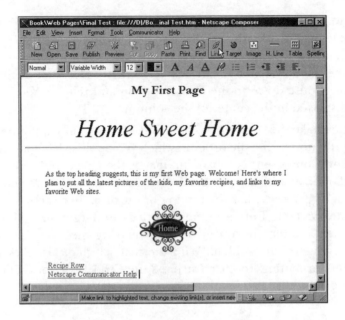

Figure 7.4 *Formatted page with graphic and links.*

ADDING MORE SPICE TO YOUR PAGE

Pretty easy, so far, right? But what about the links we talked about in our text? And plain text pages are pretty boring to look at: how about adding a graphic? Both are easily incorporated into the page.

Inserting a Link

To insert a link to another Web page, click the **Link** icon on the Composition Toolbar. This brings up a Character Properties dialog box containing three windows. In the top window, type the text you want to appear on your page, such as: **My Sister's Dance Page**. In the window below, type the URL (Web address) of the page. Click **OK**, and the link appears in colored, underlined type right there in the Edit window. There are other ways to insert links, too. We'll look at these later on in this chapter.

Inserting an Image

Web browsers can display graphics (images) in either the GIF or JPEG format. To insert a graphic, click the **Image** icon on the Composition Toolbar to bring up the Image Properties dialog box. In the box labeled **Image location**, type the path to an image file stored on your hard disk or the URL to an image located on the Web. Alternatively, click the **Choose** button and navigate to your image file. That's all there is to it.

We could go on adding to this page and tweaking it in various ways, but this was intended as a short, simple exercise. Let's save the file and be done. But wait! We don't really know how the page will look in a browser.

Previewing Your Page

To preview a page, just click the **Preview** icon on the Composition Toolbar. If Netscape Navigator is running, a new session will be launched, displaying your page. If it's not running, Navigator will be launched. And there's your Web page.

To save your page, select **Save** from the File menu, give your page a name, navigate to the directory where you want to store it, click **OK**, and you're through.

HELP FROM THE WEB

There are a couple of other quick ways to start your Web pages with Netscape Composer: the Netscape Page Wizard and Netscape Web Page Templates. These solutions aren't contained in Netscape Composer; they're Java-based applications that run from the Netscape Web site, so you need to be connected to the Internet to use them. Fire up your Internet connection and we'll check them out.

NOTE   Since these aren't contained in the Communicator program, they are subject to change without notice. That's one of the strengths of Internet-based applications: They can be updated in one location and the update works for everyone. On the other hand, details of operation may differ from what we describe here.

The Netscape Page Wizard

Perhaps you've used *wizards* in your other computing activities. They are automated routines—little programs, really—that guide you through the process of doing something fairly complicated, such as building a spreadsheet formula or creating a Web page.

To access the Netscape Page Wizard (again, you must be connected to the Internet), click the **New** icon on the main Composer toolbar. This brings up the Create New Page dialog box, which contains five buttons. One of these reads **From Page Wizard**. When you click this button, a new session of Netscape Navigator is launched—containing a text introduction to the Page Wizard. Read through the text if you like. In any case, you'll have to scroll to the bottom to click the **Start** button that takes you to the wizard proper.

You'll see instructions in the upper left pane; your evolving page is to the right. The first instruction is contained in a link: <u>give your page a title</u>. Click the link and the bottom pane comes to life with a text window, into which you type your page title, and a button that lets you **Apply** what you've typed to the real page. You can try out a variety of titles. When you've got a title you like, scroll down to the next link.

NOTE You may wonder how the Page Wizard is choosing the type font it's using for your title (and will later use for the rest of your page). To find out, select **Preferences** from the Edit menu on the main Composer window, click the **plus** sign next to Appearance, and click **Font**. The font displayed in the **Variable Width Font** window is the one your system is using. To change it, click the arrow to activate the drop-down list and choose another font.

Choosing the **type an introduction** link brings up a larger text box and an invitation to **Type your introduction here**. The instructions tell you that you can write up to 1,000 characters, but in fact, the program will limit you to something well under 300 characters. (You can, however, add to this section in the Composer editor, once you've saved this page.)

The next paragraph and link invite you to add links to other pages. Boxes are provided into which you can type titles and URLs to as many links as you care to add. There's also a Delete hot links link, in case you change your mind about any or all the links you added.

You get an opportunity to add a conclusion, and then, in a nice touch, the Page Wizard lets you include an e-mail link. If you opt for this, you'll type your e-mail address into a text box and the Wizard places it on the page as a live link with the following preamble: **If you have comments or suggestions, email me at [yourname@youraddress.com].**

With the exception of the mail link, this isn't much different from what we did in our little introductory exercise above, but the Page Wizard has a few more colorful moves, which we'll examine now.

Colors

First, you can choose among 16 prearranged color combinations that style the background, text, links, and visited links in reasonably coordinated colors. Optionally, you can create your own color scheme by selecting colors for each of those elements yourself. Mixed in with these color choices is one for **Background pattern**, which gives you 16 textures and graphic patterns to pick from. (Some are less distracting than others.)

Bullets and Rules

The final two links in the wizard present some style choices for bullets (should you decide to add bulleted lists to you page later on; there's no facility for doing it in the wizard) and rules (what the Composer program calls *horizontal lines*). These provide some nice decorative touches and can add a bit of extra fun in that two of the six bullet styles and one of the 16 rule designs are animated Java applets.

Finishing Up

You can move around the wizard as you like, adding, changing, deleting. When you're satisfied, scroll to the bottom of the instructions pane and click the **Build** button. A new Navigator window is launched, and your page is displayed as a real HTML page, complete with a little link to the Netscape software download page and the legend "This page created with Netscape Navigator Gold." If you don't like the legend—or anything else about the page—you can save your page (select **Edit Page** from Navigator's File menu, whereupon the page is transferred to Composer, then select **Save** or **Save As**) and edit it in Composer, as we'll discuss throughout this chapter.

The Netscape Web Page Templates

This is a collection of 14 precrafted Web pages provided by Netscape, grouped into the following categories:

- Personal / Family
- Company / Small Business
- Department
- Product / Service
- Special Interest Group
- Interesting and Fun

To check them out, click the **New** icon on the main Composer toolbar, then click the button labeled **From Template**. The button brings up a dialog box that will let you begin a new page from a locally stored template or go to the Web and review Netscape's Templates. To do the latter, click the button labeled **Netscape Templates;** you're whisked to the Netscape Web Page Template page, which contains the list of 14 templates plus full instructions for their use.

If you find a template that's similar in function or design to the page you've envisioned, you can bring it into Composer and save it (select **Edit Page** from Navigator's File menu, then select **Save** or **Save As** from Composer's File menu). You then transform the template into *your* Web page by substituting your text for the text in the original and removing elements that you don't want or need. Note that sample links in the templates are not live, but you can add your own live links, as discussed above.

N O T E   At the bottom of the Netscape Web Page Template page is a link to a wonderful Web publishing resource, the *Netscape Gold Rush Tool Chest*. From the Tool Chest you can access nicely crafted buttons, rules, clip art images—even animated GIF images—design tips and tutorials, information on Java and JavaScript, and more.

THE COMPOSER TOOLBARS

Netscape Composer's user interface is designed so that you can access most of the program's functions and features by mouse from the two toolbars, the main Composition Toolbar and the Formatting Toolbar, below it. These two toolbars are shown in Figure 7.5. We've covered some of the icons already, but we'll go over them all here.

Figure 7.5 *Netscape's Composition and Formatting Toolbars.*

The Composition Toolbar

There are no fewer than 16 icons populating this toolbar. Some are familiar, generic editing functions; some are quite specific to the purpose of Composer, that is, editing HTML pages. We'll touch on them all, but go into detail on the HTML-specific tools.

New brings up the Create New Page dialog box, which has the following five buttons:

- Blank Page, which starts a fresh, build-it-from-scratch document.

- From Template, which takes you to the Netscape Web Page Templates (on the Internet), as discussed above.

- From Page Wizard, which takes you to the Netscape Page Wizard (on the Internet), as discussed in depth above.

- Open Local File, which, oddly, duplicates the function of the adjacent toolbar icon.

- Cancel, which, as you'd expect, cancels the dialog box.

Open invokes a standard File Open dialog box, allowing you to edit an existing page stored locally on your system.

Save, like the equivalent icon on any editing toolbar, saves the current file to disk.

Publish is one of the Web-page–specific tools. It brings up the Publish dialog box, the function of which is move all the elements of your Web page from your local system to a Web server. We'll look at publishing in more detail later on in this chapter.

Preview launches a new Navigator session and shows your page as it would be seen over the Web.

Cut, **Copy**, **Paste**, and **Print** are generic editing commands that do exactly what you'd expect.

Find brings up a little text-search dialog box with which you can locate a specific word, phrase, or character string in your document. You have the option of searching either up or down from your current location and the option to "match case" (that is, search for the exact combination of upper- and lowercase characters you type in).

This Find dialog box lacks a whole-words-only option. Thus, if you search for *not,* it will stop when it finds *not*ation or a*not*her.

N O T E

Link brings up the Character Properties dialog box with the **Link** tab selected. As you'd expect, it lets you insert a hypertext link into your document. We'll examine this procedure in more detail below.

Target creates a target for a hypertext link at the position of the text cursor. This lets you place easy navigation tools in your Web pages by placing links to this (or any other) part of the document. The technique is of particular value in longer documents.

Image brings up the Image Properties dialog box with the Image tab selected. The purpose is to let you select and insert an image in your document, as well as to control its placement and presentation on the page. We'll examine this procedure in more detail below.

H. Line places a simple horizontal rule at the position of your text cursor.

Table brings up the New Table Properties dialog box, which inserts a table consisting of the numbers of rows and columns you specify. You can control other aspects of table appearance from this dialog box. We'll investigate Tables in more detail below.

Spelling summons the Netscape Communicator Check Spelling dialog box, which also appears in the Messenger e-mail module.

The Formatting Toolbar

For the most part, the elements that make up Composer's Formatting Toolbar are similar to those of an up-to-date word processor. Any experience you have in this regard will apply here. The Formatting Toolbar contains the following elements:

- Paragraph Style window
- Font window
- Font-Size window
- Font-Color window
- Four Character Style icons
- Two List icons
- Three Text-Alignment icons

We'll look at each component briefly:

The **Paragraph Style window** is a drop-down list, shown in Figure 7.6, that lets you select among 12 standard HTML paragraph styles.

Heading 1 through Heading 6 are standard boldface HTML heading styles; the higher the number, the smaller the type. Normal is the default for body text. Address is the italicized version of Normal. It's typically applied to Web or e-mail addresses, but can be used to italicize any text. Formatted renders the text in the fixed-space font and preserves any unusual spacing, such as tabs or extra spaces, that the browser normally suppresses. It's useful for program code and other applications where accurate spacing is important. List item, Desc. Title (Description Title), and Desc. Text (Description Text) are special paragraph styles not often used.

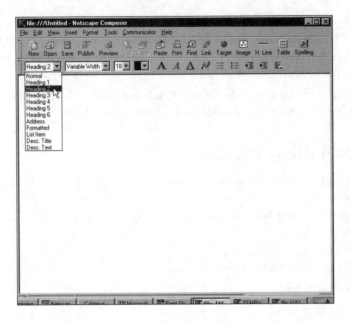

Figure 7.6 *The Paragraph Styles window offers 12 HTML styles.*

To apply these styles—and all the other formatting attributes we'll be discussing in the next few paragraphs—either select your style and then type your text, or highlight existing text and select the style to apply.

NOTE

The **Font window** is a drop-down list that lets you select among the typefaces available on your system. Default Fixed Width and Variable Width fonts are supplied with Netscape Communicator. Any Windows or Macintosh fonts on your system will also be available here. If the viewer of your page does not have the same system fonts, Netscape Navigator (and most other browsers) will substitute the available font most like the one your document specifies.

The **Font Size window** is another drop-down list. The available type sizes are 8, 10, 12, 18, 24, and 36 points. No in-between sizes are available.

The **Font Color window** is a graphical selector that lets you add color to your typography. Just click the **Down Arrow** key and mouse to the color of your choice.

Character Style icons provide four style choices. The first three, Bold, Italic, and Underline don't need to be explained here. The fourth, Remove all Styles strips off any style attributes you've added. This means that all style attributes other than those imposed by the Paragraph Style, if any, will be deleted.

List Style icons provide two kinds of formatted lists: Bullet Lists and Numbered Lists. As with the other formatting commands here, you can apply these either by clicking the icon, then typing in the requisite text, or by typing the text first, highlighting it, then clicking the icon. You can choose among three simple styles of bullets; we'll give details on how to do this later in the chapter.

N O T E   The automation of Composer's Numbered List function is a bit less sophisticated than the corresponding feature found in an up-to-date word processor: Composer only places the number sign (#) at the beginning of each paragraph; it doesn't attempt to keep track of the actual numbering.

Alignment icons provide three text-alignment options. The first two of these, Decrease and Increase Indent, do just what you'd expect. The third, Alignment, is a drop-down choice that lets you choose Left, Center, or Right alignment for text. The Left or Right alignments have a "ragged" other margin; there is no justified type in HTML.

THE COMPOSER MENUS

The pull-down menus for Netscape Composer largely duplicate the commands on the toolbars, but some of the program's commands can be issued only from the menus. We'll run through the menu commands noting where they are the equivalents of toolbar commands, and discussing the unique commands in greater detail.

The File Menu

The commands in the File menu are as follows:

- New
- Open Page
- Save
- Save As
- Publish
- Send Page
- Browse Page
- Page Setup
- Print Preview
- Print
- Close
- Exit

File-New contains a menu of subchoices. The first two, Navigator Window and Message, let you initiate a new browser session or send an e-mail message, in either case without necessarily having Navigator or Messenger running. The remaining three choices, Blank Page, Page From Template, and Page From Wizard, duplicate the functions of the New icon on the Composition Toolbar.

Open Page duplicates the function of the Open icon.

Save duplicates the function of the Save icon; Save As lets you save the current page under a new name or to a new location.

Send Page brings up the Messenger Composition window with a link to the current page in place. Thus, it sends not the page itself, but a hypertext pointer to the page.

Browse Page duplicates the function of the Preview icon.

Page Setup, **Print Preview**, and **Print** are the equivalents of those commands in any desktop application.

Close closes the current window.

Exit closes all Netscape Communicator sessions.

The Edit Menu

Many of the commands here are generic to all editing programs.

> **Undo / Redo**, for example, let you reverse the last editing command, and reverse that reversal, respectively. **Cut**, **Copy**, **Paste**, and **Delete** are standard commands.
>
> **Delete Table** and **Remove Link** are generic commands applied to these two special HTML constructs. Delete Table lets you delete the entire table or a Row, Column, or Cell of the currently highlighted table.
>
> **Select All** and **Select Table** let you select either the entire contents of your Web page or an entire table, presumably for a cutting or copying operation.
>
> **Find in Page** is the equivalent of the Find button on the toolbar; **Find Again** searches for the next occurrence of the string you've already entered in the Find dialog box. **Search Directory** is an e-mail related command with no relevant function here.
>
> **HTML Source** is an important command for Netscape Composer. It's how you get at the HTML code behind the WYSIWYG editor. If you haven't defined a default HTML editor, Composer asks you to specify one whenever you issue this command.

NOTE   To set up a default HTML editor for your Web page creation work, select **Preferences** from the Edit menu, then click **Composer**. In a panel in the middle of the screen headed External Editors, you can type the path to the third-party editor of your choice. It could be Windows Notepad or a professional level editing package like SoftQuad's HoTMetaL Pro. In the window below, you can specify an image editing program.

> **Preferences** is the same command that appears on the Edit menu of every Commander module.

The View Menu

There are several commands on this menu worth some discussion:

Show / Hide Composition Toolbar and Show / Hide Formatting Toolbar toggle the display of those interface elements. The commands are equivalent to clicking the pebble-textured bars on the left-hand ends of the toolbars.

Show / Hide Paragraph Marks toggle the display of carriage returns in your Web page.

The next group of commands—Reload, Show / Hide Images, Refresh, and Stop Loading are meant for Web browsing and have little relevance in this context.

Page Source shows you the plain text and HTML tags that Composer and Navigator are rendering as finished Web pages, but doesn't let you edit the code. To edit the HTML code, use the HTML Source command from the Edit menu.

The Insert Menu

This menu duplicates and expands upon the functions of the Link, Target, Image, and Horizontal Line toolbar icons. It duplicates the function of the Table icon as well, but also expands upon it, adding three subchoices—Row, Column, and Cell. These add the elements in question to an existing table.

The Insert-HTML Tag lets you place HTML tags in your documents. Although it lets you insert any HTML tag, its primary purpose is to insert tags not provided automatically by Composer. Little graphical tag icons mark the positions of tags inserted this way.

The first of the last three commands, Insert-New Line Break is the equivalent of pressing Enter.

The Insert-Break below Image(s) is also the equivalent of pressing Enter. It's a separate command because it's sometimes difficult to insert a text cursor after an image.

Insert-Nonbreaking Space places a space between words that acts like an alphabetic character: if it falls at the end of a line, the words surrounding it will never be separated by a line break.

The Format Menu

Like the Insert menu, the Format menu both duplicates and expands upon the toolbar elements.

>**Format-Font**, **Format-Size**, **Format-Color**, and **Format-Remove all Styles** are the exact equivalents of the corresponding windows and icons.
>
>**Format-Style** gives the Bold, Italic, and Underlined choices, but adds several others: Strikethrough, Subscript, Superscript, Blinking, and Nonbreaking. These are self-explanatory.
>
>**Format-Heading** gives the same range of choices as the numbered Heading types in the Paragraph Styles window.
>
>**Format-Paragraph** provides the remaining choices accessed via the Paragraph Styles window, and adds one more: Block Quote—which indents an entire paragraph.
>
>**Format-List** adds several list types to the Bullet and Numbered styles you can apply from the toolbar, but they aren't enabled in the current version. It also provides the command None, which removes list formatting previously applied. This is the equivalent of highlighting the text of a list that's already formatted and clicking the appropriate icon to remove that format.
>
>**Format-Align** provides the same Left, Right, and Center choices as the toolbar icon.
>
>The choices **Format-Increase** and **Format-Decrease Indent** function identically with the corresponding toolbar icons.
>
>The final three commands, **Format-Character Properties**, **Format-Table Properties**, and **Format-Page Colors and Properties** let you apply numerous style choices to individual characters and tables, and make basic design and color choices for entire pages. We'll look at them in detail very shortly.

The Tools Menu

The **Tools** menu has only one function; it brings up the Netscape spelling checker, and is thus the equivalent of the Spell icon on the toolbar.

The Communicator Menu

The **Communicator** menu offers the same choices in every Netscape Communicator module.

The Help Menu

The **Help** menu accesses the Communicator help files.

COMPOSER'S PROPERTIES DIALOG BOXES

As already mentioned, the Format menu provides three commands—**Format-Character Properties**, **Format-Table Properties**, and **Format-Page Colors and Properties**, that let you apply multiple formatting attributes in a single step, rather than piecemeal, through a series of toolbar or menu operations. We'll examine these dialog boxes one by one.

Character Properties

We've seen a number of ways that formatting can be applied to text—highlight it and change the type size or type face; highlight it and click the colors drop-down selection box; highlight it and click the Italics button; and so on. To make several formatting changes to a block of text—anything from a single character to your entire document—in a single operation, select **Character Properties** from the Format menu. This brings up the Character Properties dialog box, shown in Figure 7.7. (Incidentally, as you'll notice from the tabs, you can also access Link properties and Paragraph properties from this dialog box.)

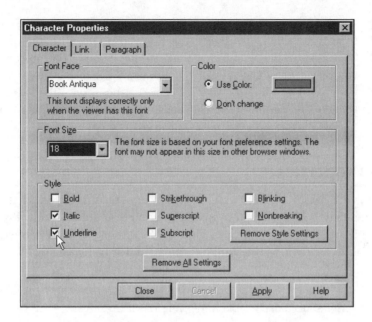

Figure 7.7 *Making multiple Character format changes.*

The two panels at the top of the Character Properties page, Font Face and Color, are equivalent to the Font and Color windows on the Formatting Toolbar. Font Face works exactly like the toolbar window, but Color works slightly differently here: click the color box to bring up the color-selection chart and mouse to the color you want to try. Once you've selected a color, a pair of radio buttons gives you the options Use Color or Don't Change.

The panel in the center of the Character page presents essentially the same Font Size drop-down that's on the toolbar. It works just the same way. In the bottom panel are eight check boxes for character styles—the same eight that are available via the Format-Style menu selection. The difference is that here you can make multiple choices. Do you want your text bold and underlined? Check the **Bold** and **Underline** boxes. Do you want it in italics with strikethroughs? Check those boxes. In fact, you can check all four if you want to.

To see the effect of your character-formatting choices, arrange the dialog box so as to be able to see the text you're working on, then click the button labeled **Apply** at the bottom of the Character Properties dialog box. This lets you preview any choice you've made while the dialog box is still open. Unfortunately, it doesn't work with color changes, since the selection highlighting obscures the color being applied. To view color changes, you'll have to close the Character Properties dialog box.

Table Properties

Tables have a lot of elements, all of which can be formatted in the Table Properties dialog box (which is invoked when you select Table Properties from the Format menu), shown in Figure 7.8. There are three tabbed pages; one for tables as a whole, one for rows, and one for individual cells.

The Table Properties menu item is unavailable (grayed out) unless your text cursor is located in a table within your HTML document.

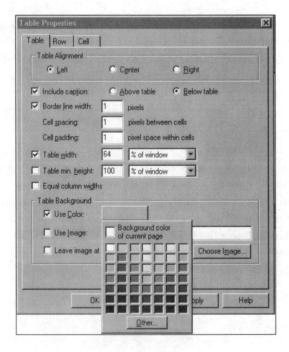

Figure 7.8 *The Table Properties dialog box.*

There are quite a few commands, and all are pretty straightforward, so we'll run through them briefly.

The Table Page

The top command group, Table Alignment, lets you orient your table to the left-hand side, center, or right-hand side of your document.

The middle area of the page is filled with commands mostly having to do with the dimensions and general appearance of the table, but the first check box lets you specify a caption to accompany the table, and the two radio buttons to its right place it above or below the table.

NOTE   If you've specified a caption for your table but can't seem to get the text cursor inside the caption box, it's helpful to know that the default alignment for captions is Centered. Click the center of the caption box and you'll be able to type your caption.

Border line width, Cell spacing, and Cell padding, all set by entering numbers in text boxes, refer respectively to the *outside* border for the table as a whole, the spacing between this border and the table cells themselves, and the distance between the edge of each cell and the cell contents.

You can specify an overall width for your table, expressed either in pixels or as a percentage of the window width. If you choose the latter, the width of the table changes when you resize the window. Similar specification can be made for the tables' minimum height. Finally, a check box lets you specify equal column width (although this can be overridden at the cell level).

The Table Background group lets you specify and pick a Color or an Image as a background for your table (again, this can be overridden at the cell level). If you opt for an image, there's a Choose Image button that brings up a navigation dialog box; alternatively, you can type in the path to the file you want. A check box lets you Leave image at the original location, rather than saving it with the rest of your page elements.

Finally, an Extra HTML button brings up the Extra HTML dialog box, a text window into which you can enter additional HTML attributes or JavaScript to be inserted into the <TABLE> tag. As with the Character Properties dialog box, there's an Apply button that lets you preview your setting without closing the dialog box.

The Row Page

Alignment is the first order of business on this page, as with the Table page, discussed above. In this case, however, there are both horizontal and vertical alignments to set. Choices are set with radio buttons and apply to the *contents* of the row. You can choose Default, Left, Center, or Right Horizontal Alignment. For Vertical Alignment, the choices are Default, Top, Center, Bottom, and Baselines (that is, the *type* baseline, a typesetter's term meaning one "*x*-height" above the bottom, so that there will be sufficient space for the descenders in the typeface).

Row Backgrounds are set exactly the same as Table Backgrounds. Again, there is an Extra HTML button that lets advanced users insert their own HTML code and an Apply button for previewing the effects you've chosen on the page.

Settings made from this page affect the row in which your text cursor is located when you select the Format-Table Properties command.

N O T E

The Cell Page

The commands here exactly duplicate those on the Row page, except for a group in the middle of the page. These let you create irregular tables and treat the text in special ways.

The first of these commands, which reads: Cell spans [X] row(s) and [Y] column(s), lets you merge or divide cells. The [X] and [Y] here are two text boxes into which you can enter numbers. If, for example, you have a two-column-by-four-row table and you want to run a heading across the top, you'd put your cursor in the upper left-hand cell and set this command to read **Cell spans 1 row(s) and 2 column(s)**.

The Text style command consists of two check boxes: Checking the Header style box renders the text in the cell as a header—bold and centered. Checking the Nonbreaking box prevents the text from turning a line and may cause the cell width to increase to accommodate the text.

The specifications for Cell width and Cell min. height adjust those dimensions, either in terms of a percentage of the table size, or in absolute pixels.

If you want irregular cell shapes within your table, the Cell page is where you create them. For example, if you have a row of three cells and you want the center cell twice as wide as the flanking cells, you'd set your cell widths—working from left to right—at 25 percent of table width, 50 percent, and 25 percent again.

Page Colors and Properties

Selecting Page Colors and Properties from the Format menu brings up the Page Properties dialog box with its three tabbed pages, General, Colors and Backgrounds, and META tags. We'll look at each.

The General Properties Page

This page is where you can enter—and review—descriptive information about your Web document. The information entered here all becomes part of the HTML contents. It's all pretty straightforward:

The Location (that is, the location of the files that make up the page) is filled in at the top of the page. Next is a field (text box) where you can enter a Title for the document; below that, a field for the name of the Author. The Description field holds, a prose description of the page, should you care to supply one.

The next grouping on the page, labeled Other attributes, contains fields for two other kinds of descriptive information: Keywords and Classification.

Here, as elsewhere in the computer world, Keywords are essentially targets for automatic searches—in this case Web search engines, local or Web-wide. If you were a blues fan living in Chicago, for example, and were creating a personal home page that contained information about the music scene in your city, you might enter keywords like *Chicago, music,* and *blues.* Classification is a field where you can enter a brief descriptive phrase like Personal Web page, Public directory or, in a more specialized context, something like Parts specification.

All of the information on this page will appear in the source code at the top of your HTML document, enclosed in <META> tags. We'll discuss the significance of these a bit later on.

The Colors and Backgrounds Page

On this page, you can set a color scheme for your document as a whole (as opposed to colored typography of document text and table backgrounds, covered above). There are several ways to go about this:

The default choice is a radio button at the top of the page that tells Composer to use the browser's default color scheme (those colors are displayed in a column of five color boxes, and again, in context, in a preview window). Below it is another radio button—Use custom colors (save colors with page)—that changes all that.

If you click **Use custom colors**, you can either pick a color for each standard page element—Background, Normal text, Link text, Active link text, and Followed link text (sometimes referred to as "visited link" text)—or you can choose one of the 12 prepackaged Color Schemes available via the dropdown pick list below the preview window. The preview window displays all color choices, both from the Color Scheme pick list and from the color boxes for individual page elements.

Choosing a Custom Color

To choose a custom color, click the **Color box** adjacent to the appropriate element; this brings up the familiar Color choice box with its 49 basic choices (including a scale of gray tones in the left-hand column). If any of these colors satisfies your need, mouse to that color and click. If not, click the **Other** button at the bottom of the selection box, and you'll see the Colors dialog box, shown in Figure 7.9 . Here you'll find a selection grid of 48 Basic colors along with another grid of 16 Custom colors. Any of these 64 colors can be selected in the manner just described: mouse and click.

Even if this selection gives you what you need, we suggest you take a moment to explore the do-it-yourself color selector on the right-hand half of the dialog box. In the main spectrum window, you'll find a little set of crosshairs. Drag them around the spectrum and the color in the cross hairs will be displayed in the Color Solid preview box below. On the right-hand side of the spectrum window is a slider that lets you adjust the luminance (essentially, mixing the color with white or black). Using the tools in this dialog box, you can select any of 16.8 million colors.

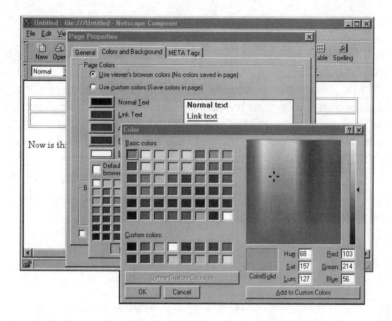

Figure 7.9 *The Colors dialog box lets you pick or create colors.*

If you're working with a standard color-specification system, you can type in numbers for Red, Green, and Blue, and/or for Hue, Saturation, and Luminance. You'll notice that these settings duplicate the make-up of the spectrum window, which is composed with hues going from left to right and saturations from top to bottom. Luminance, again, is selected by means of the slider on the right.

The Background Image selections work just like those for Table backgrounds, described above.

The check box at the bottom of this dialog box lets you Save these settings for new pages; that is, for new pages within this document.

The META Tags Page

If you entered information in the General properties page of this dialog box, take a moment to select **Page Source** from the View menu. You'll see the most of the items you entered enclosed in HTML tags that look something like this:

```
<META NAME="Author" CONTENT="Ted Stevenson">
```

The English prefix *meta* means "about," and HTML <META> tags let you insert information *about* your documents in an undisplayed portion of the header. While this information does not normally appear when your page is viewed in a browser, Web search engines read and index the contents, so one important reason for using META tags is to make your documents easy to locate, whether on the public Internet or a private intranet. Consider it the same as the library catalog card.

Assuming that the page you're working with has been saved, you'll always see at least one entry in the upper of the two main windows—the one headed **Netscape system variables**—that reads something like this:

```
Content-Type="text/html; charset=iso-8859-1
```

NOTE A "system variable" is a component of a Web document or program that carries identifying information provided by and for the system. The system variable that Composer includes automatically in a document header identifies, as you see, the type of content (text/html) and the character set used (charset=iso-8859-1). The system variable carried by a browser identifies the program itself (Netscape Navigator is identified by its pet name, Mozilla), the language it's for (such as French, Japanese, or English), and the platform it's running on (such as Mac, UNIX, or Windows).

If you click the entry, you'll notice that its two elements appear in the Name: and Value: text boxes below. If you wish to insert your own ("User") variables, click in the lower—(**User variables (META tag)**—window. Type a **Name** and a **Value** in the appropriate windows; then click the **Set** button. If you decide you don't want the tag inserted, highlight your entry and click the **Delete** button.

ADVANCED PAGE AUTHORING

In our discussion of the Composer menus, we've covered the program's capabilities methodically—following menu logic. Now, we'll rearrange the same information along a different axis, exploring the program in terms of its functions—using color, working with graphics, setting up tables, and the like.

Formatting Text

The text formatting capabilities of Composer have been covered quite thoroughly earlier in this chapter, but we'll quickly summarize the information again here.

Typefaces

Netscape Communicator specifies default typefaces for both a fixed-width and a variable-width font. You can select different defaults by going to the Fonts page under Appearance in the Preferences dialog box (which you find on the Communicator Edit menu). Of these, the variable width font is Composer's default; all text entered into Composer will be rendered in this typeface unless you specify another.

To change typeface within a Composer document, select from the Font window on the Formatting Toolbar or choose Font from the Formatting menu. The available choices (taken from your system fonts) will be displayed in either case.

To change the typeface of existing text, select the text, then choose the new typeface by either method. To change to a new face while typing in text, select the typeface and continue typing.

Type Size

Composer's default type size for Normal text is 12 points. You can change the default for either fixed or variable width fonts at the Fonts page in the Edit-Preferences dialog box.

Within your Composer document, you can choose among seven type sizes: 8, 10, 12, 14, 18, 24, and 36 points, using either the Font Size window on the Formatting Toolbar or the Size choice on the Formatting menu.

To change the size of existing text, select the text, then choose the new size by either method. To change to a new size while typing in text, select the size and continue typing.

Style

Both Paragraph styles and Character styles are available in Composer.

Paragraph styles—available either from the Paragraph Style window on the Formatting Toolbar or the Paragraph and Heading choices on the Formatting menu—combine two or more attributes in one setting. For example, the Paragraph styles, Heading 1 through Heading 6, render text in the default font, in boldface, in a variety of sizes. The Heading styles, obviously, are designed with document headings and subheadings in mind. Other Paragraph styles, such as Address, List item, and Description text, are designed for other standard document elements.

Character styles, such as boldface or italics, can be applied to any amount of text from a single character to the entire document. Three of the character styles—Bold, Italic, and Underline—can be specified from icons on the Formatting Toolbar; those plus five more—Strikethrough, Subscript, Superscript, Blinking, and Nonbreaking—can be applied via the Style choice on the Formatting menu.

To change the style of existing text, select the text, then choose the new style from either the toolbar or the menu. To change to a new style while typing in text, select the style and continue typing.

Dynamic Fonts

Early Web browsers could read and write only ASCII (plain vanilla) text, rendering it on-screen in DOS or other system characters. This was efficient, but not pretty. As the Web has evolved to include sophisticated documents, designers and users have constantly pushed the limits of Web-based font technology.

Until recently, however, the only way to ensure that your viewers would see exactly the typography you used in designing your page was to save your display type as a graphic bitmap. This was pretty but *not* efficient.

The latest development in Web typography is *dynamic fonts*. Anyone with a browser (such as Netscape Navigator) that supports this feature can see Web pages rendered with the same fonts the designer used, regardless of whether those fonts are initially available on the viewer's system. That's because dynamic fonts can download with the rest of the page elements, if not already present on the system. Once they've been downloaded, they're cached for future use.

The way it works is that the page header contains a URL for one or more font definition files. If the fonts are already available on the system, the font definition information is not downloaded. But if any or all the fonts specified are unavailable on the local system, they're downloaded and stored.

Specifying and using dynamic fonts in your HTML documents is beyond the scope of this book, but as a Netscape Communicator user, you have full support for any dynamic fonts in professionally designed Web pages.

Controlling Dynamic Font Use

Acknowledging that you may not always wish to add the overhead that dynamic fonts create (just one more thing for the browser to download and render), Netscape Communicator gives you some control over their use. This happens on the Fonts page under Edit-Preferences.

The default setting is for dynamic fonts fully *enabled*. That is, they will be used when specified in a page you view. To change the default, select **Preferences** from the Edit menu and click the **Fonts** page under **Appearance**. At the bottom of the command group are three radio buttons. The lowest of these, Use document-specified fonts, including Dynamic Fonts, is activated. As an alternative, you can either turn off all document-specified fonts and just go with the browser's default fonts (the topmost choice) or accept document-specified fonts *other* than dynamic fonts. Either choice should speed up your browsing to some degree.

Working with Colors

Netscape Composer lets you render both type and backgrounds in the colors of your choice. Selecting and applying colors is easy since Composer has a WYSIWYG color selection dialog box—rather, it has two color selection dialog boxes, a simple one and an advance color selector. These are described in detail above, in the sections on the Formatting Toolbar and, in particular, on the three Properties dialog boxes accessible from the Format menu.

To quickly recap here, clicking the **Font Color** window on the Formatting Toolbar or any color box in any of the formatting dialog boxes brings up the simpler color selection dialog box, where you can use the mouse to choose any of the 49 colors displayed there. In each case, the Other button at the bottom of this dialog box brings up the advanced Color dialog box. Here, you can choose from 48 Basic colors and/or 16 Custom colors.

To define any of the 16.8 million colors possible in the 24-bit/pixel system, you can either type in appropriate numbers in the six color-definition boxes in the lower right or use the mouse to drag the cross-hairs in the square hue/saturation window and the slider arrow in the Luminance bar on the right. To save a color to the custom-color table, select one of the 16 boxes, define the color by the method of your choice, then click **Add to Custom Colors**.

Document Color Schemes

By selecting **Page Colors and Properties** from the Format menu and clicking the **Colors and Background** tab, you can set a color scheme for the entire page (or document), either by selecting one of the 12 preset color schemes available from the Color Schemes window, or by specifying a custom color for any of the standard page elements: Background, Normal Text, Link Text, Active Link Text, and Followed Link Text. To do the latter, click the color box next to whatever element you want to set colors for. The color selection dialog box is displayed.

If you want to use your color selections for this page on other pages in the document, click the check box at the bottom of the dialog box: **Save these settings for new pages.**

Colored Text

To apply a color to any type in your document, select the text in question and either click the **Font Color** window or choose **Color** from the Format menu. Either option brings up the color selection dialog box, just mentioned. Mouse to the color you want, then release the button. The color is now applied.

You can apply a color to text as you type it by first making your color selection, then typing until another type color is called for.

Color in Tables

To select a color for the background of an entire table, select **Table Properties** from the Format menu and click the **Table** tab. In the **Table Background** group toward the bottom of the page, click the **Use Color** check box, then click the color box (which may be gray) to bring up the color selection dialog box.

You can select a color for any row in a table by clicking the **Row** tab and setting a color in the **Row Background** group, exactly as you would choose a color for the entire table. The Row Background color overrides the Table Background color specification. Similarly, by clicking the **Cell** tab and going to **Cell Background**, you can set a color that overrides both Row and Table background colors.

Making Lists

Netscape Composer currently automates the setting up of both bulleted and numbered lists. Actually, in the case of numbered lists, we'd have to say "sort of," since Composer doesn't supply actual numbers for the items, just the number sign (#).

If you've already typed your list (with a carriage return after each list item), simply select the list text and either click one of the two list icons on the Formatting Toolbar (one for bulleted, one for numbered lists) or select **List** from the Format menu and choose one of the five list styles. To remove list formatting from your text, select it, choose Format-List and choose the option **None**.

Working with Links

Links (formally, hyperlinks) are important to Web pages. You might go so far as to say they are what makes the difference between Web pages and traditional electronic documents: In effect, they create the "web."

While they are perhaps most often used to connect your page to remote pages on the Internet, they also can link to specific files—either local or remote—or to other locations (*targets*) within your site or document. Whatever the application, Netscape Composer makes it easy to create and otherwise work with links. We'll explore all types of links.

Linking to Remote Sites

Perhaps the easiest way to do this is to navigate to the site you want to link to using Netscape Navigator, adjust your on-screen windows so Composer and Navigator are on the screen together, then drag the current location icon (the one between the Bookmark icon and the Location Window) to the Composer Edit Window, and drop it into your document. You can drag and drop any Web URL stored in your History file or any Messenger or Collabra message in the same way. You can edit the descriptive text that's automatically inserted in your page to read the way you want.

A more traditional way to link to a remote site is through Composer's Link command: Either click the **Link** icon on the Composition Toolbar or select **Link** from the Insert menu. In either case, Composer displays the Link Properties dialog box, shown in Figure 7.10. In the **Link source** box, you type the text you want to appear on your Web page. If you were linking to Help files for Netscape Communicator, you might type **Netscape Communicator Help**. In the **Link to** box, you enter the URL for the site you're linking to. An easy way to do this is to navigate to the site and then copy the URL from the Location Window on the browser using your system Copy command and paste the text into the Link to box. Click **OK** and your link is done.

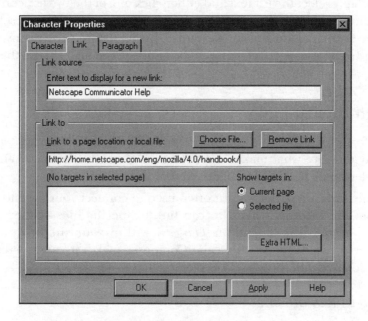

Figure 7.10 *Composer's Link Properties dialog box.*

Linking to Local Files

Creating hyperlinks to files on your local hard disk or network is often very useful. The procedure is exactly the same as for inserting links to remote Web pages, except that rather than entering the URL to a remote site, you enter the path and filename for an HTML document. Or, often easier yet, you navigate to the file in question by clicking the **Choose File** button.

Links for Document Navigation

If you publish long HTML documents, one of the best (and easiest) ways to make the contents accessible is to provide links to various portions of the document. You can do this in a Table of Contents style, by creating a series of links one after the other, along the lines of:

> Section One
>
> Section Two
>
> Section Three

Or, you can insert cross-reference links throughout, such as **See Section One**. And of course, there's nothing to prevent you from combining both approaches.

To link to *targets,* or *anchors* as they're also called, you begin by creating the targets (the place in the document your links will aim at). Click the **Target** icon or select **Target** from the Insert menu. This brings up the Target Properties dialog box. It's a simple text box that asks for a name for your target. This name won't appear on your document, but it is referenced by the link you'll build later. You can either create a series of targets, then go back and create the links, or do one pair at a time. Circumstances will dictate the better method.

NOTE It's a good idea to give your targets descriptive, easily remembered names that correspond logically to the link text you'll use. If you're careful at the naming stage, you'll have an easy time when it come to mapping your links to your targets.

To create the link that references a target, you follow the same procedure as making any other kind of link: Click the **Link** icon or select **Insert-Link**. However, instead of entering a URL or path and filename in the Link to box, you'll select one of the targets displayed in the window at the bottom.

NOTE

To save a bit of time when creating links, you can use link text that's already in your document. Select the text, then bring up the Link Properties box. The selected text will already be in the Link Source box.

Linking to Images

To add a bit of visual interest to your pages, use graphics as links. The graphic could be any of the many buttons or dingbats available free on the Internet or with graphics utilities, or any GIF or JPEG graphic that's appropriate. Here's how it works:

First insert your image, then select it. Next, bring up the Link Properties dialog box by whatever method you like. The graphic will already be entered as the Link Source. Then simply add a Link to location, click **OK**, and you're through. You'll probably want to add some text above, below or next to the graphic saying something to the effect of **Click here to see Bob's page**. That's all there is to it.

Working with Tables

Tables are useful in Web pages—as they are in other kinds of documents—for a variety of communications tasks, such as presenting numeric information systematically and arranging text in orderly configurations. In Web pages, tables often control the positioning of graphics in a page layout. (We'll discuss this special use in greater detail a bit later on.) Netscape Composer makes it easy to insert and work with tables.

To create a basic table, either click the **Table** icon on the Composition Toolbar or choose **Table** from the Insert menu. In either case, Composer will display the New Table Properties dialog box, shown in Figure 7.11.

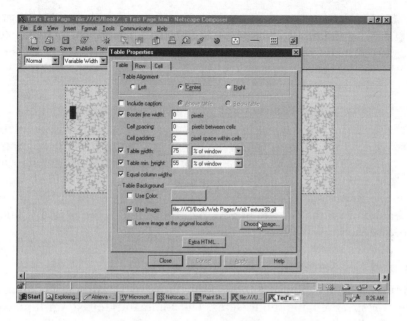

Figure 7.11 *Composer's Table Properties dialog box.*

Basic Table Specifications

Your first task is to specify the number of rows and columns for your table. In the upper left-hand corner the number of rows (defaulting to 1) is already highlighted, waiting for you to type in a number. Next, you'll tab over to the text box for the number of columns (unless the default, 2, is what you want).

Next, you'll want to choose an alignment for your table (within the overall page). The default is Left alignment (along the left-hand side of the page), but Center or Right alignment can be chosen by clicking the appropriate radio button in the Table Alignment group.

If you want a caption, click the **Include caption** box just below the alignment group. You'll then need to specify a position for your caption, either above or below the table by clicking one of the radio buttons to the right.

NOTE

To place a text cursor so you can type your caption in the box Composer provides, click in the center of the box: The default alignment for caption text is
centered. If you try to set your text cursor at the left-hand side of the box, you
won't be able to do it.

Sizing the table in terms of its overall height and width is easy, but not entirely
straightforward. First of all, either dimension can be expressed absolutely (in
pixels) or relatively (in terms of a percentage of the page window). Second,
the specification for height is actually for minimum height. If you enter more
text in the cell than will fit within the specified height, the cell will expand vertically to accommodate the overflow. Finally, there's a check box to select
Equal column widths (which, as you might imagine, is the default), but this
can be overridden by settings on the Row or Cell pages.

Row and Cell Settings

Both the Row and Cell pages under Table Properties have special commands
for their respective table subdivisions. The commands for background colors
have been discussed earlier; those for background images, we'll discuss below
in the section on "Working with Graphics." The Alignment settings for both
rows and cells apply not to those entities themselves, but to *text* within them.
The choices are self-explanatory with the exception of the **baselines** setting
for vertical alignment, which is similar to bottom alignment, but slightly
higher, leaving room for the descenders on letters like p and y.

Irregular Tables

On the Cell page of Table Properties are several settings that let you create a
variety of irregularities in your tables. Immediately under the Alignment
groups is a pair of text boxes into which you can enter a number of rows and
a number of columns for the cell to span. The defaults, of course, are 1 in
both cases, but by entering a larger number in either box—or both—you can
merge cells to form larger cells.

Suppose your table is three columns wide, but you want the top row to be
a single cell, so as to hold a heading. You'd create this effect by entering **Cell
spans 1 row(s) and 3 column(s)**.

To create columns or rows of unequal widths or heights, you'd use the
Cell width or **Cell min. height** settings. If, for instance, you wanted the left-
hand column of your three-column table to be only half the width of the other

two—to hold short row headings, say—you'd set the units for **Cell width** to the relative **% of table**, then enter **20** in the text box, telling Composer to make the cell 20 percent of the width of the entire table (and forcing the other cells in the column to the same width). This would leave the two remaining columns at 40 percent each of the overall table width.

There are many possibilities here. Having illustrated one, we leave it to you to work out others, if you so desire.

Editing Cells, Columns, and Rows

Composer lets you add or remove components of a table at any time. To add, place your text cursor in the appropriate spot, choose **Table** from the Insert menu, and then one of the subchoices: Table, Row, Column, or Cell. The most logical choices are Row and Column, but the others work too. Adding cells can give rather unpredictable results, but some special effects are possible.

To remove one of these elements, place your cursor in it, then choose **Delete Table** from the Edit menu, followed by the appropriate subchoice.

Nested Tables

If you opt for the Table subchoice mentioned above in connection with adding columns or rows, Netscape Composer will actually place a table within a table. In fact, you can do this by any of the methods we've looked at for creating tables: First create the primary (outer) table, then place your text cursor in the cell within which you want the secondary (inner) table and use any of the table creation commands, specifying the desired number of columns and rows. That's all there is to creating nested tables. Working out the design details will probably take much longer.

Working with Graphics

Using image graphics in either GIF or JPEG format is pretty simple with Composer. Probably the most common use of graphics is as illustrations interpolated into the text, but there are other ways, too. Images can be *tiled* as backgrounds to one or more pages, and they can be displayed within tables as well.

Inserting a Graphic

Netscape Composer gives you several ways to insert graphics into your Web pages:

To place an image using Composer's toolbar or menu commands, place your text cursor where you want the picture to go and either click the **Image** icon on the Composition Toolbar or select **Image** from the Insert menu. This brings up the Image Properties dialog box. Here you can specify a file to insert by typing the path to the file or clicking the Choose button to bring up a navigation dialog box.

Alternatively, you can drag and drop an image file from your Macintosh or Windows desktop or file manager. Just grab the icon, drag it to your Composer page and drop it; the image will appear at the position of your cursor. Yet another method is to use the system copy command to copy the image file to the clipboard, then paste it at the cursor position in your Web page.

Automatic File Conversion

GIF and JPEG are the file formats of the Web, but Composer lets you use other types of image files (such as those in PCX or BMP format) in your Web pages, by automatically converting the files when you add them. To do this, simply insert the file by any of the methods discussed above. This will bring up the Image Conversion dialog box with the full path to the chosen file displayed on top and the file format you're converting to (only JPEG was available at press time)

The Image Properties Dialog Box

If you used either the toolbar icon or the Insert-Image command to place your graphic, you've already used the Image Properties dialog box. Besides letting you insert graphics, it gives you a number of useful options for manipulating them.

For example, once you've inserted an image, you can bring up an image editor and alter the file—if you've specified a default image editor on the Composer page in Edit-Preferences.

If you don't want a copy of the image file saved with the rest of your page elements, click the **Leave image at original location** check box. If you want to use the image as a page background (a topic we'll discuss fully later on in this section), click that check box.

If you're going to add a caption, you can select one of five alignments between image and caption text. You can also elect to have text flow around the image, with the picture aligned either to the left or the right. (To see the wraparound effect, you must preview in Navigator.)

NOTE In working with graphics, you may need to bring up the Image Properties dialog box frequently. Fortunately, you can do this with a simple click of the right mouse button: **Image Properties** is the first selection on the function menu you get when you click the right mouse button over a graphic.

Sizing, Scaling, and Padding

If your image is the right size for your space, great; if not, you'll need to resize it. You can do this visually, by grabbing a corner of the graphic and dragging it diagonally to make the image larger or smaller. Or, you can bring up the Image Properties dialog box (try clicking the image with the right mouse button) and working with the Dimensions group toward the bottom of the page.

Here you can specify height and/or width, either relatively (as a percentage of the page dimension) or absolutely (in pixels). As long as the Constrain box is checked, entering a number into either the height or width text box will cause Composer to fill in the other dimension, since Constrain means "don't change the aspect ratio" or relative height to width. If you uncheck Constrain, you can change the aspect ratio and hence the appearance of your image.

To the right of the Dimensions group are some settings for Space around image. Here you can specify "padding" (the space between the image and any other page element, like text) in pixels. Vertical and horizontal space settings can be made independently of each other. You can also specify a solid border around your picture, again in pixels.

Image Alternates

At the bottom of the Image Properties dialog box are three buttons. Remove Image Map was not a functioning command at the time this book went to press. Alt. Text / LowRes brings up the Alternate Image Properties dialog box where you can enter a text caption that will be displayed while your image is loading into a viewing browser, or in text-only browsers, or where the browser user has turned off the loading of images. It's a very good idea to enter something here; whoever views your page will know what occupies this space regardless of whether they can or want to see the image. There's a second text box where you can type the path to a low-resolution version of your image, which will load quickly and serve as a placeholder while the high-res version loads. (There is a Choose file button that will let you navigate to the file rather than type in the path.)

Images as Backgrounds

Whenever you use a page background other than a plain color, you're using an image file. You can add a background image to your Web page in either of two ways:

- Click the **Image** icon (or select **Image** from the Insert menu), specify a file, and then click the **Use as background** check box below the Choose file button.

- Select **Page Colors and Properties** from the Format menu, go to the Background Image group, and specify a file to use—either by typing in the path or using the Choose file button.

N O T E   Images for backgrounds are generally (though not always) unobtrusive. Most of the time you choose them when you want something that adds a pleasing but subtle element of visual interest without distracting viewers' attention from the page contents. Textures are common choices for page backgrounds, and many can be found free on the Internet. A good place to start is the Netscape Gold Rush Tool Chest (`http://home.netscape.com/ assist/net_sites/starter/samples/index.html`) discussed above in connection with the Netscape Web Page Templates earlier in this chapter.

You can also add images as backgrounds to tables within your Web pages, and to individual rows and cells within a table. All of these options are available through the Table Properties dialog box (choose Table Properties from the Format menu). Backgrounds for the entire table are handled from the Table page, for rows from the Row page, for individual cells from the Cell page. The procedure is exactly the same as for adding page backgrounds.

N O T E   Adding images as "backgrounds" in table cells—and then not adding anything over the background—is a common way of displaying images (single or multiple) together with other material in a controlled layout. Using the various techniques of manipulating cell sizes and configurations discussed in the section on Table Properties above, you can create striking and effective layouts for your images. You basically size a cell to contain your whole image, add borders or space around the image if desired, place text or other images in adjacent cells—leave some cells blank if you wish. The details are up to you.

USING THE SPELL CHECKER

Before you publish your Web pages, you owe it to yourself—and the rest of the world—to eliminate as much random sloppiness as possible. Netscape Composer's spelling checker will help in this endeavor by finding misspelled or mistyped words.

N O T E If you've worked with word processors and used their spelling checkers, you've probably learned the big pitfall with these electronic aids: If you inadvertently typed a word that exists in the spell checkers's dictionary, the checker will not flag it, even if it is the wrong word for that context. A simple example is typing **form** when you intended to type **from.** You're on your own with this type of error. Only careful proofreading can spot it. All the spelling checker can do is point to words that it doesn't recognize, and suggest possible corrections.

To check the spelling in your HTML document, select the only command from the Tools menu: **Check Spelling**. This brings up the Check Spelling dialog box, shown in Figure 7.12, and flags each word in your document that might be incorrectly spelled with colored underlining. The elements and functions of the dialog are fairly self-explanatory, but we'll run them down briefly:

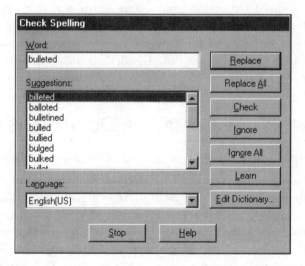

Figure 7.12 Composer's Spell Checker cleans up your act.

The Word window displays the first potentially misspelled word. The Suggestions window, beneath lists one or more possible correct spellings or says (no suggestions). The Language window below this lets you choose between U.S. English and U.K. English. Down the right-hand side of the dialog box is a series of action buttons:

- **Replace**, which replaces the word currently being checked with the suggestion that's highlighted in the Suggestions window.

- **Replace All** replaces every instance of the Word throughout the document.

- **Check** lets you check against the dictionary a word that you enter manually in the Word window.

- **Ignore** tells Composer not to change the Word, and to continue with the spell check.

- **Ignore All** tells the program to leave alone all instances of the Word that appear in the document.

- **Learn** adds the current Word to the Dictionary.

- **Edit Dictionary** lets you proactively enter words and strings so that Check Spelling won't flag them and/or remove or change words added this way or by using the Learn button.

When the spell check has run its course (gone through all the flagged words and disposed of them in one way or another), the Replace button changes to Done, which you click to exit the dialog box. Alternatively, you can interrupt the spell-checking process at any time by clicking the Stop button at the bottom of the dialog box.

PUBLISHING YOUR COMPOSER DOCUMENTS

Building Web pages is not merely an exercise: The object is to publish, and the time has come to explore that awesome topic. Actually, it's quite easy to do.

By now, presumably, you have one or more Web pages to publish; you may or may not have a place to publish them. What's needed? Some space on an HTTP server connected to the Internet (or to a private intranet). How do you get this? If you have an account with a commercial Internet Service Provider (ISP), hosting of your personal pages may be included in the deal. This also holds true for accounts with commercial online services like America Online and CompuServe. As an alternative, there are many commercial hosting services that will accommodate your pages for a small monthly charge. Finally, if your company has an intranet, you may be able to arrange for some space on its server.

N O T E   If you don't use an ISP or online service that provides space for personal Web pages, you'll have to find your own. This is not difficult: Use Netscape Navigator, surf on down to your favorite search engine or directory (such as Excite, Infoseek, Yahoo, etc.), and run a search. Our first search—on the phrase "web hosting"—pulled just shy of 17,000 hits. Another search—on the phrase "personal web pages"—pulled less than 1,000, but the first hit offered complete service for $60 per year (that's $5 a month) per megabyte of space, plus a setup charge.

Setting up Publishing Preferences

As with many other aspects of Netscape Communicator, there's a place where you can set defaults for Web publishing. Select **Preferences** from the Edit menu, then click the **Publishing** page under the **Composer** heading. Of primary interest here is the Default Publishing Location group. The first of the two boxes is where you type the URL of the site where you'll normally be sending your files. It may be either an FTP server or an HTTP server. This is information you'll get from your service provider or system administrator. If you'll be delivering to an FTP site, you'll then want to fill in the HTTP server location where your page(s) will be mounted, which is what the second text box is for.

In the **Links and images** group, above, are two check boxes. The first of these tells Communicator to adjust your links to work with the new location; the second dictates that copies of the page's images be stored with the rest of the page contents on the server. Both are selected by default. As the **Tip** at the bottom of the group suggests, unless you have a specific reason to change these defaults, leave them alone.

The Publish Dialog Box

When you and your pages are ready for the big step, open your page in Composer (if it isn't already open) and click the **Publish** icon on the Composition Toolbar or select **Publish** from the File menu. Either action displays the Publish dialog box.

Most of the information fields will already be filled in for you automatically, namely: Page Title, HTML Filename, HTTP or FTP Location to publish to (if you've set up a default publishing location on the Publishing preferences page, as described above), and a group of Other files to include.

N O T E

If you don't choose to open your page before publishing it, you can fill in the file-related fields yourself.

This leaves a **User name** and a **Password** field for you to fill in. Most of the items are fairly self-explanatory, but we'll discuss them all at least briefly:

- You may or may not have given your page a formal Title. If not, you may still add one here; it's not a bad idea.

- The Filename for the core HTML file that makes up your page is *not* optional; without it, you've got nothing to publish.

- You also must supply a publishing server Location. If you specified a default server on the Publishing page in Preferences, that location will always be available in the drop-down list attached to this field. You may also type in other server locations here. Composer will store them all, and you may select from the accumulated list at any time. A Use Default Location button quickly selects the default.

- Your User name is the log-on name or code that identifies you to the server where you'll be sending your files.

- The Password confirms your identity in the log-on process. If you want Composer to remember and supply your log-on password for future sessions, click the Save password check box.

- In the file-display window under Other files to include, Composer lists by default all the files associated with (linked to) your page. A radio button gives you the option of listing all the files in the page's folder. You can then choose to select all or none, or to select individual files.

Once you've filled out the Publish dialog, click **OK** and you've finished—a published author.

SUMMARY

The World Wide Web consists of tens of millions of HTML documents, or pages. Netscape Page Composer lets you quickly and easily build you very own Web pages (or mail or discussion postings), including such elements as graphic images, tables, and links to other documents and Web pages. To give you a quick start on the art of HTML authoring, Netscape provides an online Web page wizard and a variety of templates that you can save and modify.

Netscape Messenger

When it comes to applications that have fueled the incredible growth of the Internet, electronic mail leads the way. Netscape Communicator happens to feature one of the best electronic-mail packages on the market, Netscape Messenger. In this section, we cover Netscape Messenger in excruciating detail.

Chapter 8 begins with an overview of Messenger, detailing how to send and receive electronic mail and how to set up Messenger to work with different mail servers.

Chapter 9 covers advanced topics, including folders and mail-configuration options.

Electronic Mail: Your Interactive Link with the World

Though people assume that the World Wide Web has spurred the growth of the Internet, the tool that's actually stoking the Internet's tremendous growth is electronic mail, a truly ubiquitous Internet application. Topics in this chapter include:

- An e-mail primer
- Receiving electronic mail
- Creating electronic mail
- Searching mail
- Business cards

ELECTRONIC MAIL: REACH OUT AND TOUCH SOMEONE

More than any other, electronic mail is the tool fueling the enormous growth of the Internet. Although the World Wide Web tends to get star billing, the fact remains that at this time (mid-1997) the most popular service of the Internet is—and has always been—electronic mail, nor is this expected to change in the near future. Even the new name of Netscape's overall Internet tools-suite, *Communicator,* reflects the importance of electronic messaging.

This should be no surprise, as the Internet historically has been a tool for sending and receiving electronic mail, long before there was a World Wide Web. Since those early days, electronic mail has been the province of specialized software programs, such as PINE, ELM, Eudora, or Pegasus.

Netscape Communicator not only contains an electronic-mail module, Netscape Messenger, it's a flexible, full-featured program that holds its own with the best of the competition. Messenger sends and receives mail from an Internet POP3/IMAP mail server, stores the mail in folders, and threads these mail messages so you can easily browse their contents, reading responses to earlier messages. Messenger is an integral part of the whole Netscape Communicator package, so you don't need to go out and purchase another mail package. Its interface is shown in Figure 8.1.

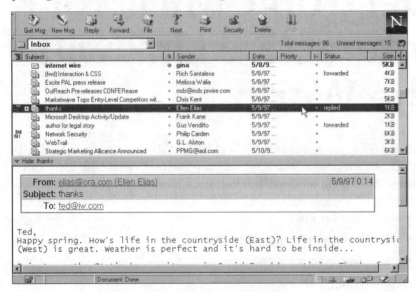

Figure 8.1 *The main Netscape Messenger screen.*

Whereas in previous versions of the Netscape Navigator suite the mail module was perhaps a bit underpowered for people who worked a lot with electronic mail, it's now able to deal with a high volume of messages and has most of the advanced features you'll find in the best desktop e-mail packages—such as searching, sorting, and organizing messages, and routing them automatically, based on text in the subject line of the message or other factors—along with some features you won't find elsewhere.

If you're using an older version of Netscape Navigator, you'll find that the Netscape Mail module contained in that product lacks some of the advanced features mentioned above and discussed later in this chapter.

Netscape Navigator actually lets you send electronic mail messages while you're browsing the Web, without recourse to the Netscape Messenger program. To send a message from the browser (but not receive messages), just select the **New-Message** option under the File menu and you're in business. Most of the time, though, you'll want to use the full-featured Netscape Messenger module, which allows you to send, receive, and manage electronic mail.

In this chapter, we'll cover how you set up electronic mail under Netscape Messenger and how you can use the module efficiently and to your best advantage.

HOW ELECTRONIC MAIL WORKS

Before you embark on your electronic-mail journey, you should know a little about how Internet electronic mail works.

Internet electronic mail moves messages on a *store-and-forward* model. Another user with a connection to the Internet—-a person with a personal Internet account, a user of an online service such as CompuServe or America Online, or possibly someone with an Internet connection at the office— addresses an e-mail message to you. This mail is sent to a mail server, which then forwards the mail to your mail server. When you log into the Internet and launch your mail software, it checks to see if you've got mail on the server; if so, the messages are downloaded to your computer where you can read them. You can respond to the mail, forward it to another e-mail user, or create new messages from scratch. In all cases, you send your outgoing mail to a *mail server.*

Note that the notion of a mail server is important in these transactions. If you want to send and receive electronic mail from Netscape Messenger, you'll need to give it the name of your mail server. (Or, rather, mail *servers*, as Netscape Communicator asks you to specify one server for outgoing mail and another server for incoming mail.) We'll cover mail servers in more depth in the discussion of mail configuration.

UNIX treats electronic mail a little differently than do Windows or Macintosh, since e-mail is built directly into the UNIX operating system. Setting up your e-mail on a UNIX system will call for slightly different procedures than those we'll describe here for Windows and Macintosh systems.

Addressing Electronic Mail

Like traditional hard-copy mail electronic mail, messages won't reach their intended recipients without a proper address. The Internet uses a special, easy-to-grasp formula for electronic-mail addresses. You'll need to understand this format to use electronic mail in Netscape Messenger.

Basically, Internet electronic mail addresses consists of two distinct parts: the name of the addressee and the addressee's location. The two parts are joined by the @ (at) symbol. Therefore, a user named Ted who uses the Panix dial-up service would have an Internet address of:

```
ted@panix.com
```

The same addressing logic can be applied to commercial online services such as America Online, CompuServe, MCI Mail, and Prodigy. A user named Ted on MCI Mail would have an Internet address of:

```
ted@mcimail.com
```

When you sign up with a commercial Internet provider, you'll be assigned (or allowed to choose) an Internet address.

N O T E

Generally speaking, you don't need to know the ins and outs of Internet addressing to actually use Netscape Messenger; all you need to have is an address.

You can send mail to a single individual, or to many Internet users at once; just supply an address for each recipient. Messenger supports both CC (carbon copy) and BCC (blind carbon copy) functions, which send copies of your message to people other than the main addressees of the letter. If you "copy" someone via CC, every other recipient will see this address notation. If you send a copy to someone via BCC, no other recipients will be aware of this recipient.

Netscape Communicator deals with electronic mail on three levels: sending messages from the browser (which we've covered above), with the mailto URL, and with the standalone mail program called Netscape Messenger. We'll cover each of the last two in depth below.

NETSCAPE MESSENGER

Netscape Messenger, new in Netscape Communicator version 4.0, is a full-featured mail program, substantially more robust than the Netscape Mail program that was part of earlier Netscape Navigator suites. Unless your electronic mail needs are unusually sophisticated, Netscape Messenger will probably more than satisfy them. It has a great many useful, time-saving features, so we'll spend a lot of space on these later in this chapter and in the chapter that follows. Before you can send and receive any electronic mail, however, you'll need to set up Netscape Communicator to handle your mail. (We've explored other aspects of setting up the Netscape Communicator Preferences earlier in this book.) Understanding how Internet electronic mail works makes this setup a lot easier.

TIP

You can configure Netscape Communicator to load Netscape Messenger every time you start the program. Simply check the Messenger Mailbox check box under the heading **On startup, launch:** on the **Appearance** page under **Edit–Preferences.**

SETTING UP MAIL PREFERENCES

When you sign up for Internet access from a service provider, you'll probably be given a lot of information about Domain Name Servers and the like.

From this, you'll need to get the names of your outgoing and incoming mail servers. These may be identified as your SMTP and POP3 or IMAP servers, respectively. The Simple Mail Transfer Protocol (SMTP) server is used to send mail; when you tell Netscape Messenger to send a letter to `reichard@mr.net`, you're telling the program to send the message to your service provider's outgoing (SMTP) mail server. This server in turn sends the message to an incoming Post Office Protocol (POP3) or Internet Mail Access Protocol (IMAP) mail server governed by `mr.net`. When `reichard` wants to retrieve his mail, he connects to the POP3/IMAP server at `mr.net`, provides a password, and collects his messages.

This is a somewhat simplified scenario. As a matter of fact, there are many things to set up when it comes to electronic mail and Netscape Communicator, as you'll see in this section. Here, we'll run down the setup screens that you'll need to work with before you can use Netscape Messenger; later in the chapter, and the chapter that follows, we'll discuss additional configuration options. You access these configuration options by selecting Mail Server under the Mail & Groups section in the Preferences dialog box, which you access from the Edit menu.

HOT LINK

You'll need to set similar "preferences" to be able to use the Collabra newsreader, which we'll cover in Chapter 10.

You'll need to complete these settings before you can send or receive mail. If you launch Netscape Messenger without entering essential information—such as the name of your mail server!—you'll get an error message that tells you to go through the Preferences choice under the Edit menu. You can do this either from within Netscape Messenger or from the Navigator (browser) screen. Our advice is to go through the settings before you even fire up Netscape Messenger, although this isn't written in stone.

Anyway, on to our task of configuring mail. Armed with our knowledge of the inner workings of Internet mail, we'll make short work of it.

The Mail Server Configuration Screen

This screen is where you specify the locations (or, more correctly, the addresses) of your mail servers. When you signed up for an Internet service account, your service provider should have given you the name of an outgoing (SMTP) mail server and an incoming (POP or IMAP) mail server. (If you're configuring Messenger in a company setting, you should be able to get this information from the administrator of your company's mail system.) This dialog box is shown in Figure 8.2.

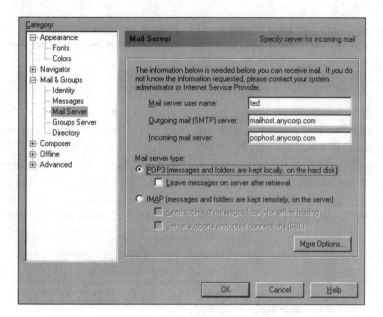

Figure 8.2 *The Mail Server configuration screen.*

Often, the name of the outgoing and incoming mail servers will be the same, but since they have different functions, the two types of servers use different protocols. As mentioned above, the server that forwards your mail to the Internet uses SMTP (or Simple Mail Transport Protocol); the server that receives and stores your mail, forwarding it to you at your request—a more complex set of tasks—uses either POP (short for Post Office Protocol) or IMAP (Internet Mail Access Protocol). IMAP is the latest thing in electronic mail protocols, a more advanced solution than POP. Netscape Messenger takes full advantage of the features of either type of incoming mail server.

In practical terms, IMAP differs from POP mainly in that it stores your mail on the server rather than automatically downloading it to your local computer system every time you log on. This means you won't have to take up lots of space on your local hard disk storing your mail. More significant, if you log into an IMAP server from different computers at different times, you'll always be able to access your entire mail "store" (your accumulation of messages). With a POP mail server, the default is for messages to be downloaded to your computer and cleared from the server.

NOTE   Just to make things more confusing, most IMAP servers give you the option of downloading local copies of your messages, and some POP servers let you leave messages on the server.

The first line of the Mail Server configuration screen asks you for your mail server "user name." Generally speaking, this is the beginning of your Internet address; in our example in Figure 8.2, the user with an Internet address of ted@anycorp.com has a user name of . (Some mail servers are configured to allow as a username on the mail server, rather than . The documentation you received from your Internet service provider should make this clear; if it doesn't, try both your username and your Internet address and use whichever works.)

The second and third line let you specify the names of your outgoing and incoming mail servers, respectively. Again, these servers may have the same name or different names, depending on how your service provider (or your company) has set things up.

Below the box where you provide the name of your incoming mail server, you'll notice radio buttons and check boxes. These let you set some options for how the incoming server should handle your mail. If your incoming server is a POP3 server, you *may* have the option of storing copies of your messages on the server. Unless your service provider (or system administrator) tells you that this option is available, the only way to find out (if you do want to leave your messages on the server) is to check the box and test it out. If the server isn't capable of storing copies, you'll get an error message from Messenger, at which point it's a good idea to return immediately to this screen and uncheck the box. (Those error messages will become very annoying after a while.)

If your server is running IMAP and you want to keep local copies of your messages on your computer, check the first box following the IMAP radio button. If your server supports encrypted connections using Secure Sockets Layer technology, check the second box.

By clicking the **More Options** button in the lower right-hand corner of the screen you'll get an opportunity to make some additional settings, as we show in Figure 8.3.

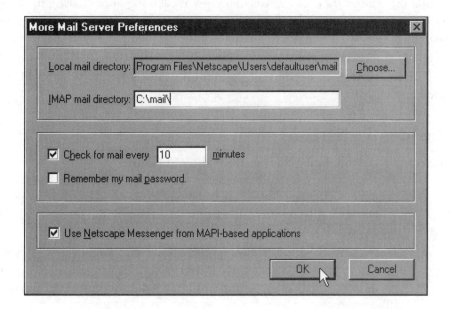

Figure 8.3 *More mail server configuration options...*

The box at the top of this screen contains the name of the directory or folder where local copies of your messages will be stored. You'll notice that a directory is already listed there when you moved to this screen. Unless you have an excellent reason to change the location of this default mail directory, we suggest that you simply accept it. If you do have a compelling reason, just type in the full path to the directory you want to use for local mail storage.

In the next section of the screen, you can set Messenger to check your incoming mail server for messages automatically, at intervals you specify. Handy as it is, this option doesn't actually download your mail, though; it merely alerts you to the fact that mail is waiting on the server. It does this by placing a green arrow next to the Mailbox icon in the Component Bar. Once you've collected your messages, the arrow disappears.

The check box below this tells the program to keep your password and enter it for you automatically every time you log on to get your mail. This is convenient, of course, but in most office situations, system administrators prefer that users enter their passwords manually at each log-on, as having the program enter them automatically pretty much defeats the security purpose of having a password. If you are in such a situation—or if you simply don't wish to have your password entered automatically, leave this box unchecked.

The final check box gives you the option of using Netscape from MAPI based applications.

The Identity Screen

The contents of this dialog box are fairly straightforward:

- **Your name**: That is, your full, normal name, as you'd like it to appear on messages. Of course, you can insert here any name you wish to have as part of your mail; it doesn't have to be your real name.

- **Email address**: As with your name, above, the e-mail address you enter here doesn't necessarily need to be accurate; it will appear only as part of the message and not be acted upon by other Internet software.

- **Reply-to address:** Normally this is the same as your e-mail address. If it's different (or you've chosen to enter an inaccurate e-mail address and you actually want to receive replies), enter it here. This is the address that other mail packages will use to route return mail should someone respond to your messages.

- **Organization**: This is entirely up to you; leave it blank if you wish.

- **Signature file**: This field lets you optionally point to a file that can be attached to your outgoing mail and news messages as a *signature.*

It's an Internet tradition to attach some lines of text to your outgoing mail. This serves to fully identify you (most people include their company names, titles, phone numbers, and electronic-mail addresses) and also to distinguish you from the rest of the Internet world (many place a witty phrase or quotation within their signature file).

Netscape Messenger lets you specify a file as your signature, but doesn't provide the tools for creating the file itself. Thus, you'll need to create the file elsewhere, either using a Windows text editor such as Notepad or a Macintosh text editor such as TeachText. To specify a signature (or "sig") file, type the path to the file of your choice. By selecting **Choose**, you'll summon the tool in your operating system that allows you to browse through your disk and specify a file. When you create a new outgoing mail message, Messenger will automatically insert the contents of your signature file into the message, as shown in Figure 8.4.

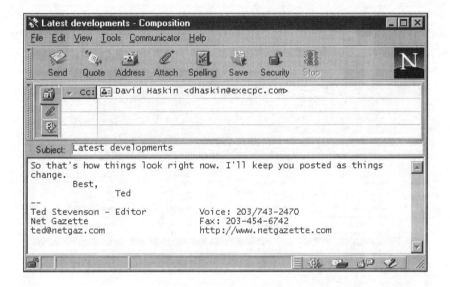

Figure 8.4 *A sample signature.*

If you create (or choose) a sig file longer than four lines, Netscape Messenger will warn you of this. Unless your file is ridiculously long, you can ignore this warning, since the file will probably work fine. To test it, simply send yourself a message.

When you receive an electronic-mail message that contains a URL, Netscape Messenger (like many other e-mail packages) is smart enough to recognize it as a URL and turn it into a hot link that you can jump to directly (assuming your browser is running) by double-clicking. When you include a URL in your signature, others will probably be able to link to the address in question.

The final item on the Identity screen is a check box that tells Messenger to attach information from your personal Address Book card to the ends of outgoing messages. This is an easy alternative to a signature file. This address book information is referred to elsewhere in Messenger as the *vCard* or *business card*. We'll discuss vCards more fully later on in this chapter.

SENDING AND RECEIVING MAIL

Now you're ready to plunge into Internet e-mail with Netscape Communicator! Let's take a tour of the Messenger screen (as shown in Figure 8.5), then run through a typical Internet mail session.

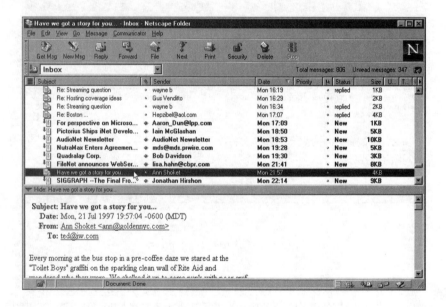

Figure 8.5 *The Netscape Messenger screen explained.*

There are several ways to launch Netscape Messenger from the main Communicator screen:

- You can select **Messenger Mailbox** from the Communicator menu.
- Alternatively, you can click the **Mailbox** icon in the **Component Bar**, which may either be floating on your browser screen or docked in the lower right-hand corner.

- If you prefer keyboard-shortcuts, the key combination **Ctrl-2** will also take you to the Messenger screen.

Go ahead and begin Netscape Messenger by any of these methods. The Messenger window will appear, and a dialog box will ask you for your password. This password is provided by your service provider and tells the mail server that it's OK to send you any waiting mail messages. If this is the first time you've connected to your Internet mail server, you'll probably receive a message telling you that there are no new messages. If there are mail messages waiting, they will be sent to you.

When you launch Netscape Messenger, it becomes an independent application that doesn't rely on the Web browser. You can close your Web browser and Netscape Messenger will remain active.

NOTE

The Netscape Messenger screen consists of six main areas:

- **Pull-down menus** where commands can be accessed.
- A **Navigation Toolbar** where frequently used Netscape Messenger functions can be accessed via mouse click.
- A **Location Toolbar** containing a Current Folder window, which lets you navigate among your various mailboxes and mail folders.
- A **Message Headers pane**, which contains the headers of mail messages found in the selected folder.
- A **Message pane**, immediately beneath the Message Headers pane, where the contents of a highlighted message are displayed.
- A **Component Bar** that contains icons to move you to Netscape Communicator's four main modules: Navigator, Messenger, Collabra, and Composer.

We'll cover each of these areas as needed as we review Netscape Messenger through a sample session.

To get more screen space, you can hide either the Navigation Toolbar or the Location Toolbar, or both, by clicking the small vertical bar with the pebbled texture at the left-hand end of either bar. When the windows are hidden, the bar turns magenta for easy visibility and is oriented horizontally. To redisplay either component, just click the appropriate bar.

NOTE

Launching Netscape Messenger

To launch Netscape Messenger, select **Netscape Messenger** from the Communicator menu on the main browser screen (or use one of the three methods listed earlier). Netscape Messenger loads and immediately connects to your mail server (hence the need to configure the incoming mail server before using Netscape Messenger). If there is mail waiting for you on the server, Messenger displays the number of waiting messages in a small dialog box, along with an indication of which of these messages is currently being retrieved (for instance, you'll see **Receiving: message 1 of 3** on the bottom of the screen) and a "thermometer" bar that shows the progress of the download.

After your mail is retrieved, the new messages will appear in Message Headers pane. Normally, they are placed at the end of the accumulated list of messages, in the order in which they arrived. The contents of the first unread message will appear in the Message pane.

To the right of the Current Folder window on the Location Toolbar, you'll see a notation telling you how many messages are in the folder and how many of those are unread.

You can adjust the size of the message pane relative to the headers pane (or vice versa): Simply drag the separator bar with your mouse until the panes are adjusted to your liking.

NOTE

To read through your messages, you can manually select the message from the Message Headers pane via mouse or cursor keys; the scrollbar on the right side of the pane moves the list of messages up and down. In addition, the **PgUp** and **PgDn** keys (for Windows and Windows 95 users) allow movement through the Message Headers pane. Other methods of moving from message to message are the **Next** button on the toolbar, a series of commands accessed under the Go menu—Next message, Next Unread message, Previous message, etc.—and the keyboard shortcuts **Shift-N** for Next message and **Shift-P** for Previous message.

To select a different folder (such as Outbox, Drafts, Samples, or Trash), click the **down arrow** at the right side of the Current Folder selection window and mouse to the folder you want.

A small icon is displayed to the left of the Current Folder selection window that indicates which of the mailbox folders is currently in use. There are special icons for Inbox, Outbox, Drafts, Sent, and Trash, plus a generic folder icon for user-created folders.

The Message pane displays the contents of the message highlighted in the Message headers pane. The scrollbar on the right side of the window lets you scroll through the message text.

Working without the Message Pane

If you prefer, you can hide the Message pane by clicking the small blue triangle at the left-hand side of the bar that separates the Message Headers pane from the Message pane. The combined area will now be devoted to the Headers list, as shown in Figure 8.6.

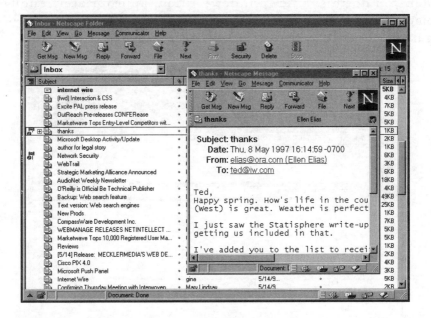

Figure 8.6 *The Message pane hidden.*

To display messages in this configuration, highlight a header and press **Enter** or double-click the header; this will bring up the Netscape Message window with the message displayed in it.

To redisplay the Message panel, click the blue triangle at the very bottom right-hand corner of the screen.

CREATING AND SENDING AN E-MAIL MESSAGE

To begin a new e-mail message, you need to call up the message Composition window, which you can do by any of the following methods:

- Click the **New Msg** button on the main toolbar
- Select **New Message** from the Message menu
- Use the keyboard shortcut **Ctrl-M**

When you do this, a new window—titled, appropriately enough, Composition—will appear on your screen. (This screen is shown in Figure 8.7.)

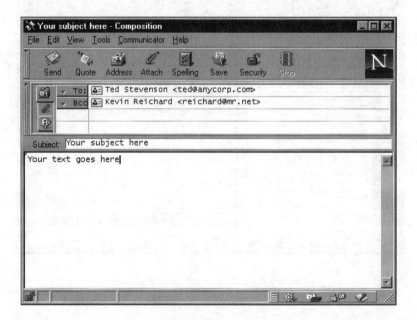

Figure 8.7 *The Composition window.*

The text cursor will be blinking in the field next to a button labeled **To:**, waiting for you to enter the recipient's address. Once you've entered an address or nick-name, you'll notice that Messenger creates another **To:** on the line below. Click the button and you'll see a list of addressing options that include Cc: (carbon copy), Bcc: (blind carbon copy) and others. To select one of these, mouse down to the appropriate line and click. Then enter the appropriate address in the field to the right. Enter as many To: or other addresses as you like.

The Attach tab (with a paper clip icon) below the addressing tab lets you attach a file or document to your message. To do this, you click the tab, then click the blank space to the right. This brings up a dialog box that lets you choose a file to attach to the message. Alternatively, you can click the **Attach** button on the tool bar, and this gives you an additional option: You can attach a Web page by entering its URL. You'll learn more about attachments throughout this chapter, but basically you can choose any file on your hard disk or a floppy drive and incorporate it as part of a mail message. A Message Sending Options tab below the Attach tab gives you some advanced choices, which we'll explore a bit later.

The **Subject** field is for entering the subject of the message, such as **Meeting: 3:15 today**. Like the initial address, this is something you'll use most of the time.

To move between the fields, use the mouse or the **Tab** key or press the **Enter** key.

If you don't remember the address of an intended recipient, click the **Address** button on the toolbar. This brings up the Netscape Messenger Address Book, the place where you store a list of electronic-mail addresses and other contact information for people you correspond with via e-mail.

You'll learn more about the Address Book in Chapter 9. For now, just type in an address in the field.

HOT LINK

You'll learn about all of your various options when composing mail later in this chapter.

HOT LINK

Go ahead and type in an Internet e-mail address (say, ann@anycorp.com), or perhaps your own e-mail address, a subject (Quick meeting?) and then type your message. When you're done writing your letter, send your message by means one of the following actions:

- Click the **Send** button on the toolbar.
- Press the key combination **Ctrl-Enter.**
- Select **Send Now** from the **File** menu.

The window will close, and your electronic message is on its way. Once the mail is sent to a mail server, there's no retrieving it, so don't send a message in haste or anger and expect to be able to get it back. Similarly, there's no certain way to make sure that the mail was received. You can click the Messaging Sending Options tab and then the Return Receipt check box, but not all mail servers support this feature. If you've addressed your message incorrectly, or the recipient's server is not functioning when the message is routed to it, you'll very likely get an error message telling you the e-mail address you entered is invalid.

Responding to Mail

Responding to an incoming e-mail is very simple. Just click the **Reply** button on the toolbar and choose **Reply to Sender** or press **Ctrl-R**. If there are multiple recipients and you want to include them all, choose **Reply to Sender and All Recipients** or press **Ctrl-Shift-R**. A new window will appear, as shown in Figure 8.8.

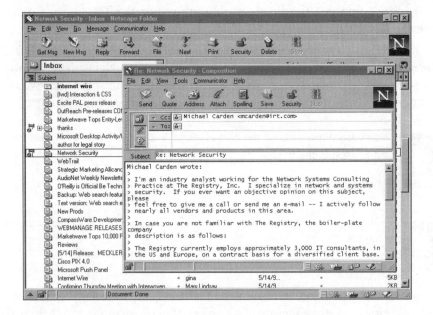

Figure 8.8 *A response to a mail message.*

You'll notice that Netscape Messenger does several things automatically: The name and the e-mail address of the sender of the original message are automatically entered as the recipient of the new mail. The subject of the original message becomes the subject of the response, with *Re:* (Latin for *With reference to:*) inserted at the beginning. And the text cursor jumps to the message area, waiting for you to type your reply. If you specified a signature file in setup (see above) your signature file is attached to the end of the message.

If you want your reply to quote the original message, there are two ways to do this. If you *always* want to quote the original, you can set things up to do so permanently by going to **Preferences** on the Edit menu, click **Messages** under Mail and Groups and check the box **Automatically quote original message when replying**. To quote sometimes, use the **Quote** button on the Composition window's toolbar.

In either case, the sender's name is affixed to the beginning of the response in the phrase **[Sender] wrote:,** and the original mail is inserted, each line marked with the greater-than symbol (>). And, although you can't tell this from Figure 8.8, the cursor is placed at the end of the original message, so you can begin typing your response right after the original.

You can make your response as long or short, simple or complicated, as you like. Once you're finished typing your message, you can send it by simply clicking the **Send** button on the toolbar or pressing **Ctrl-Enter**. Netscape Messenger will immediately pipe the message to SMTP server, and on out to the Internet.

That is, Messenger will send the message *if* you're actively connected to the Internet when you hit the Send button. If you aren't, you'll get an error message from Netscape Messenger that warns you about the lack of an Internet connection, and advising you to try again later. You can, however, create messages while you're off-line: Instead of clicking Send, select **Send Later** from the File menu. Messenger will store your outgoing mail in the Outbox folder. To send the mail stored in your Outbox once you do have a connection to the Internet, simply select **Send Unsent Messages** from the File menu; additionally, Netscape Messenger asks if you want to send mail in the Outbox when you attempt to close the Messenger program.

Forwarding E-Mail

Forwarding mail means sending a message you've received to another Internet mail user. There are three ways to forward mail: by clicking the **Forward** button on the Navigation Toolbar, by selecting **Forward** from the Message menu, by pressing **Ctrl-L**.

The procedure for forwarding mail is almost identical to responding, except for two crucial differences: The To: field is empty, which means you must supply a new electronic mail address; and the contents of the original message are stored as an attachment, rather than as part of the main message text. (If you'd prefer that the contents be included in the body of the forwarded message, select **Forward Quoted** from the Message menu or press **Ctrl-Shift-L**.) Otherwise, you can use the same steps to forward mail as you did to respond to mail.

SEARCHING THROUGH MAIL

Electronic mail can accumulate very rapidly. And whether they get a few messages a day, or dozens, or hundreds, most people want to keep much of their mail—just as people have always kept their letters—since it's a good record of ones life and activities. Fortunately, Netscape Messenger helps out not only in the organization and storage of mail, but also in searching through e-mail to find specific messages. Better yet, the same search "engine" that finds mail messages also hunts down Usenet articles and Collabra discussion postings.

The Search Messages Dialog Box

Many e-mail programs have search capability, but Netscape Messenger's **Search Messages** dialog box (shown in Figure 8.9) is one of the fastest and most flexible. It lets you search for a particular *string* (a name, word, phrase, or specific sequence of characters) in almost any part of a mail message. Not only that, it lets you set multiple search criteria (to look for messages sent by Jones before 6/17/1997, for example). The more precise you are in setting up your search criteria, of course, the more precisely you'll pinpoint what you're looking for.

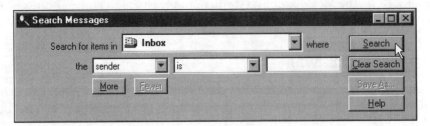

Figure 8.9 The Search Messages dialog box.

The Current Folder window (labeled **Search for items in:**)at the top of the Search Messages dialog box is identical to the one on the Location Toolbar in the main Netscape Messenger window. It's a drop-down list that lets you select a particular mail-storage folder—in this context, to search through. Narrowing the search down to a single folder, such as **Inbox**, helps to speed the process—if you're pretty sure which folder to look in. To search through all your messages, select **Local Mail**, at the top of the list.

Below the Current Folder window is a row of three windows that let you construct a search profile or query. The first lets you select a particular Field of the message to search (such as **sender**, **subject**, **date**, or **priority**); the second lets you apply a Logical Operator (such as **is**, **contains**, or **begins with**); the third lets you pick or specify a Search String (such as a word in the subject field, or the sender's name).

The Field window is a drop-down list containing the following choices:

- sender
- subject
- body
- date
- priority
- status
- to
- CC
- to or CC

All the choices correspond to fields in a message or header with which you are familiar, with the possible exception of **body;** this is nothing more than the main message text. The **to or CC** choice simply combines two criteria in one choice for convenience, just in case you can't remember if you were a principal addressee, or were merely copied on the message in question.

The Logical Operator window is also a drop-down list, but the choices change depending on which field you chose in the Field window. For most of the Field choices that involve names or other variable text, you can pick a logical operator from the following list:

- contains
- doesn't contain

- is
- isn't
- begins with
- ends with

Field choices with special Logical Operators include **date** (for which the operators are **is**, **isn't**, **is before**, and **is after**), **priority** (for which the operators are **is**, **is higher than**, and **is lower than**), and **status** (for which the operators are **is** and **isn't**).

In most cases you fill in the Search String window by typing in the word, phrase, name, or other string you're trying to locate. When you're searching the date, priority, or status fields, however, Messenger populates the Search String window with the appropriate choices.

For date, you get a month/day/year date display with spinner arrows to change the numbers. Click in the appropriate portion of the display to insert a text cursor, then either delete and retype the number you want or click the spinner arrows to increase or decrease the number currently displayed. You may need to alter any or all of the three parts—month, day, and year—to get the date you want to specify.

For priority, the drop-down choices are None, Lowest, Low, Normal, High, and Highest. For status, the drop-down choices are read, replied, and forwarded.

Running a Search

Once you've filled in all three windows, just click the **Search** button and Messenger blasts through the messages in the folder or folders you've specified and finds messages that match the profile you set up. As it finds "matches," it displays information about them in the Message Headers window below. When the search has run its course, a notation in a panel at the bottom of the dialog box tells you the total number of matches found.

The Header fields displayed include Subject, Sender, Date, Priority, and Location. The last of these displays the name of the folder in which the message is stored. This is important information (which the search facilities in many popular e-mail packages unfortunately don't supply), since you often want to manipulate the message in question—copy it or move it to a new folder, for example. To facilitate this kind of procedure, the Search Messages dialog box provides a Go to Message Folder button (immediately beneath the Message Header window), which takes you directly to the folder in which the currently highlighted message is stored.

To read a message that matches your search profile, highlight the header and press **Enter**, or double-click the header. This brings up the message in a Netscape Message window, so you can not only read it, but Reply, Forward, File, etc., as well.

Multiple Search Criteria

As mentioned above, if you know two or more things about something you're trying to find, you'll be able to locate it more quickly. For example if you know the car leaving the scene of the accident was blue, or that it was a four-door, or that it was probably a 1994 or newer model, you might be able to track down the car, but if you search by all three criteria, you've narrowed down your field of search quite a lot. It's the same with mail messages, and Messenger's Search Messages dialog box lets you set up as many as five criteria and run them against your mail database all at once.

If you were looking for a message about the "Widget merger" but couldn't remember the Subject line, you could certainly run a search on the body field, looking for the string **widget merger**. But suppose you had hundreds or thousands of such messages, stored in many different folders. If you knew this message was from your boss, was sent at highest priority, and was probably mailed before the board meeting last month, you can construct a more precise search profile using multiple criteria.

Using this example, you'd start by setting up one criterion that says **body / contains / widget merger**. You'd then click the **More** button below the three windows to display a second row of three. Into this you might enter **sender / contains / Jackson** (or whatever your boss's name is). Click **More** again and enter **date / is before / 4/12/97** (or whatever the date of the board meeting was). Finally, click **More** a third time and enter **priority / is / Highest**. Then run your search. Instead of dozens of messages that you'd have to review one by one, this search may return only one or two. The complete search query is shown in Figure 8.10.

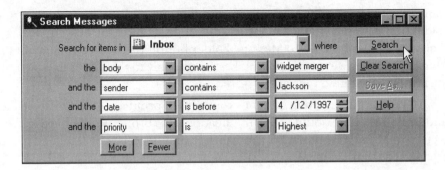

Figure 8.10 Searching by multiple criteria.

But suppose it returns none at all. Well, perhaps the priority wasn't Highest. You're not sure. You can eliminate that element from the search by clicking the **Fewer** button. Run the search again, and perhaps you get seven messages, and one of them has priority High. That's probably the item you were looking for.

Using the speedy and sophisticated searching capabilities of Netscape Messenger, you'll rarely be at a loss to find a message you really need. This feature is one of the program's greatest assets.

MESSAGE-COMPOSITION OPTIONS

Whenever you start a new e-mail message, you open Messenger's Composition window. No matter if the message is forwarded, responding to an incoming message, or created from scratch, you have a host of options when creating mail. This section covers those options by reviewing the contents of the pull-down menus. As we discuss the various commands, we'll point out the instances where they are replicated on the toolbar.

NOTE

The Composition window takes two forms, depending on whether or not you've elected to send messages in HTML format. If your default is HTML, the version of the Composition window you'll see and work with has an added toolbar, the Formatting Toolbar, and two additional drop-down menus, Insert and Format. Finally, several of the common menus have additional, HTML-related commands. We'll note where a menu or command is available for HTML only or Plain Text only.

The File Menu

This menu handles some basic file-management functions, including the following options:

- New
- Save Draft
- Save As
- Send Now
- Send Later
- Quote Original Text
- Select Addresses
- Attach
- Go Offline / Go Online
- Close
- Exit

Each menu item will be briefly described here.

- **New:** This lets you create several kinds of Communicator entities. As the small arrow to the right indicates, selecting New leads to a menu of subchoices: Navigator Window, Message, Blank Page, Page from Template, and Page from Wizard.

  - **New–Navigator Window** opens an additional session of Navigator, allowing you to connect to an additional Web page.

  - **New–Message** creates a new e-mail message; it is the equivalent of the New Msg button on the Messenger toolbar.

  - **New–Blank Page/Page from Template/Page from Wizard** are options for various ways of creating new Web pages in Netscape Composer, not e-mail messages. We explored this function of Netscape Composer in Chapter 7.

- **Save Draft, Save As**: These let you save the current message, either to the Drafts folder (a place for unfinished messages or those you're unsure about sending for any reason) or to disk as a text file. Save Draft is the equivalent of the Save button on the toolbar.

- **Send Now, Send Later**: These send the current message. If you're connected to the Internet, you'll be able to send the message immediately; if you're working off-line, you'll be able to send the message later. This whole procedure will be covered later in this chapter, in the section entitled "Working Offline." Send Now is the equivalent of the Send button on the toolbar.

- **Quote Original Text:** This inserts the text of a message you're replying to—if you haven't opted to do this automatically (on the Messages page in your Mail & Groups Preferences).

- **Select Addresses:** This brings up Communicator's Address Book, which we'll discuss in detail in Chapter 9.

- **Attach:** You can attach several types of items to your mail messages. As the arrow indicates, selecting Attach leads to a menu of subchoices: File, Web Page, Address book card, My address book card. (This group is the equivalent of the Attach button on the toolbar.)

  - **Attach–File** attaches a document or image file to the message. In the world of Internet electronic mail, you can attach files to messages; it's a good way to move documents around and is a feature you'll probably use a lot—once you get used to the idea. Attached files are encoded using MIME, or another system, before being sent. We'll discuss this shortly.

You can also attach files to mail messages via drag and drop. Just drag file icon or icons from Windows Explorer and drop them on the Attach tab in the address space.

N O T E

  - **Attach–Web page** brings up a dialog box into which you can type the URL of a Web page you want your recipient(s) to see.

You can also attach Web pages to mail messages via drag-and-drop. To attach the page you're currently viewing in Navigator, drag the **Current Page** icon (just to the left of the Location Window) and drop it on the Attachments tab in the address space. You can also drag URLs from the History window (which you access by selecting **History** from the Communicator menu).

N O T E

  - **Attach–Address book card** (grayed out on the menu) was not implemented by the time of the product release.

- **Attach–My address book card** tells Messenger to attach information from your personal Address Book card. You can opt to have Messenger *always* attach your card by clicking the **Always attach Address Book Card** check box on the Identity page under **Mail & Groups** in Edit–Preferences.

What Is MIME?

The Multipurpose Internet Mail Extension format, or MIME, governs how documents or other files are attached to your electronic mail messages. (No, MIME does not stand for *Multimedia* Internet Mail Extension.)

MIME is an encoding system that turns "binary" files (those containing both ASCII and non-ASCII characters) into pure ASCII so they can be sent via the Internet's SMTP (Simple Mail Transfer Protocol). A MIME-enabled mail program on the receiving end, de-encodes the attachment, transforming it back into a true binary file. When this system is working properly, neither sender nor receiver sees the binary, just the text of the accompanying message. However, if you were able to look at the raw text of the mail message (which you can do by selecting **Page Source** under the View menu), you'd see one long message, beginning with a header and followed with your text message and then a lot of gibberish. This gibberish is actually the MIME attachment to your mail. A mail message with a MIME attachment is shown in Figure 8.11.

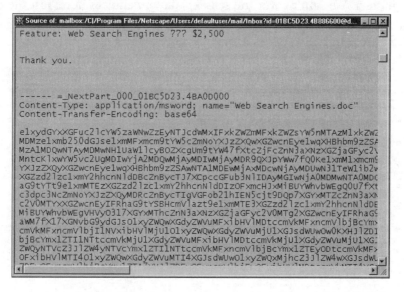

Figure 8.11 A MIME attachment to a mail message.

Go Offline / Go Online

If you're connected to the Internet and want to end that connection, select **Go Offline**. This choice brings up a dialog box that gives you the option of telling Messenger to download Mail and/or Discussion Groups, and of sending unsent messages and then logging off the server. If you're disconnected, the menu entry reads Go Online. Selecting it logs you back onto the server, once again giving you the option of downloading Mail and/or Discussion Groups, and of sending messages.

Close

This closes the message-composition window without affecting other Netscape Communicator windows.

Exit

This closes all active Netscape windows and exits Communicator.

The Edit Menu

These items are pretty straightforward for the most part and much the same as the commands found in any other Netscape Communicator Edit menu (or any other Edit menu in a Windows, Macintosh, or X Window application, for that matter). We won't cover the self-explanatory choices here; just the ones particular to Messenger. The choices in this menu are:

- Undo / Redo
- Cut
- Copy
- Paste
- Paste as Quotation
- Delete
- Delete Table (HTML only)
- Remove Link (HTML only)
- Select All
- Select Table (HTML only)
- Find in Message

- Find Again
- Search Directory
- Preferences

Paste as Quotation

A mail-specific choice that copies the contents of your operating system's clipboard (that is, material you've copied or "cut" to the clipboard) to the Composition window. Copied text is in a distinctive type face, with each line preceded by a vertical bar (|), very much as Messenger handles quoted e-mail message material.

Delete Table

A command that appears only in the HTML version of the Composition window. It deletes an HTML table, or, following the subchoices, a Cell, Row, or Column within a table.

Remove Link

Another HTML-only command. If you include links to Web pages in your mail messages (a subject we'll discuss later in this chapter), this command removes the HTML source code for the link, leaving only the link name in plain text.

Select All, Select Table

This highlights either the entire message contents (All) or a table (Table) within the current message for cutting or copying. Select Table is available only in the HTML version of the Composition window.

Find in Message, Find Again

Find searches for a word, phrase, or other string in the current message, flagging it when found. (The keyboard shortcut is **Ctrl-F**.) The Find dialog box gives you the option of searching up or down. Find Again (**Ctrl-G**), repeats this search, an option you can also select from the Find dialog box.

Preferences

This choice brings up Communicator's main configuration menu system. We've already worked with Edit–Preferences in configuring our mail server and account information.

The View Menu

This menu governs what items are shown as part of the message-composition window. The selections are:

- Show/Hide Message Toolbar
- Show/Hide Addressing Area
- Show/Hide Formatting Toolbar (HTML only)
- Address
- Attachments
- Options
- Show/Hide Paragraph Marks (HTML only)
- Page Source (HTML only)
- Page Info (HTML only)
- Wrap Long Lines on Send (Plain text only)
- Encoding

Many of these fields (the first six) merely let you control what portions of the Composition window interface are displayed; the rest control how the contents of your message are displayed.

Show / Hide Message Toolbar, Addressing Area, Formatting Toolbar

These commands control the display of the screen areas in question. The Message Toolbar and Addressing Area can also be controlled by clicking on the small pebbled bars at the left-hand edge of the respective screens areas, exactly as with the analogous areas on the main Messenger screen. The Formatting Toolbar is available only in the HTML version of the Composition window, so this menu choice is absent in the plain text version.

Address, Attachments, Options

You toggle among these three options by mousing down to the one you want. It is the equivalent of clicking one of the three tabs on the left-hand side of the Addressing Area.

Show / Hide Paragraph Marks

This feature, available only in the HTML version of the Composition window and similar to that found in many popular word processors, inserts a large vertical bar wherever you've hit the **Enter** key. This lets you see which line breaks Messenger is making automatically (via text-wrap), and which reflect deliberate paragraph terminations. Line feeds in ASCII text files are marked with a small bar at the line's end.

Page Source

This reveals the HTML code underlying the rendered (displayed) text—for Web pages or HTML-based messages. We'll discuss the use of HTML in mail later in this chapter.

Page Info

This reveals the "structure" of the document currently being viewed. For a Web page viewed in Navigator or edited in Composer, you'll learn information such as the location of the text and image components. In the e-mail context, the information is not generally very meaningful.

Wrap Long Lines on Send

This tells Messenger to wrap or "turn" long text lines at the number of characters you selected on the Messages page of Edit–Preferences. The default is 72 characters.

Encoding

This choice covers the language a message is encoded in, in case the information isn't contained within the message header. However, virtually always the encoding information will be contained within the message header.

The Insert Menu

This menu is available only in the HTML version of the Composition window. We'll discuss its commands in the section "Using HTML in Mail Messages," below.

The Format Menu

Like Insert, Format is available only in the HTML version of the Composition window. We'll discuss its commands in the section on HTML-based mail, below.

The Tools Menu

There is only one command under the Tools menu in the current version of Messenger: Check Spelling, which as you'd expect, launches the spell checker.

The Communicator Menu

The Communicator menu is the same for all Communicator modules. The first group of commands allows you to select among seven components of Netscape Communicator (and provides the keyboard shortcuts for these selections).

Below this is a group of options that include Messenger subcomponents (such as Address Book—the equivalent of clicking the Address icon on the toolbar—Bookmarks, and History) and some overall program functions, such as Security settings (the equivalent of clicking the Security icon on the toolbar).

A third section shows you all the message and folder windows currently in use within Messenger and lets you move among them.

USING HTML IN MAIL MESSAGES

One of the major departures from earlier Netscape e-mail products is that Messenger can read and write Hypertext Markup Language—HTML. This makes possible highly formatted messages that can contain images and other nontext objects (the sort of thing that's been available in LAN-based corporate mail systems such as cc:Mail and Microsoft Mail for several years). This elevates electronic mail from a simple but effective mode of communication to one in which presentation takes on an equal role with content. The price for this progress is increased message size and a slowdown in the display of messages in the mail reader.

Before you can create HTML-based mail messages you must set up Messenger to use the HTML version of the Composition window. Select

Preferences from the Edit menu in the main Communicator or Messenger screen. Go to the **Messages** page and click the check box at the top of the screen that reads **By default, send HTML messages**. Now, every time you begin a new message or reply to a message, Messenger will display the enhanced Composition window shown in Figure 8.12.

You'll notice that this window has a Formatting Toolbar and some additional pull-down menus. We'll examine the commands on the Formatting Toolbar and the pull-down menus that let you work with HTML in your mail messages. Then we'll discuss some tactical issues, such as how you can avoid sending HTML-based mail to those who can't read it.

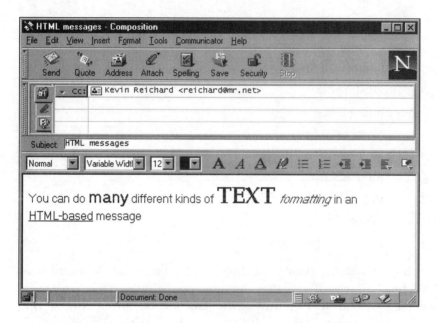

Figure 8.12 *The HTML version of the Composition window.*

The Formatting Toolbar

Formatting capability in an e-mail editor would have been meaningless window-dressing before the advent of HTML-enabled mail programs like Messenger, since without HTML, an Internet mail program can't transmit anything but ASCII characters. For the most part, the icons and menu commands that make up Messenger's formatting arsenal are very much like those of an up-to-date word processor. Any experience you have in this regard will apply here.

The elements of the Formatting Toolbar are:

- The Paragraph Style window
- The Font window
- The Font-Size window
- The Font-Color window
- Four Character Style icons:

    Bold

    Italic

    Underline

    Remove all Styles

- Two List icons:

    Bullet List

    Numbered List

- Three Text-Alignment icons:

    Increase Indent

    Decrease Indent

    Alignment

- The Insert Object icon

The Paragraph Styles, Heading 1 through Heading 6, are standard boldface HTML heading styles; the higher the number, the smaller the type. Normal is the default for body text. Address is the italicized version of normal, typically applied to addresses. Formatted, List item, Desc. Title (Description Title), and Desc. Text (Description Text) are character styles appropriate to Web pages, not mail messages.

To apply these styles—and all the other formatting attributes we'll be discussing in the next few paragraphs—either select your style and then type your text, or highlight existing text and select the style to apply.

Default Fixed Width and Variable Width fonts are supplied with Messenger. Any Windows TrueType (or Macintosh) fonts on your system will also be available here. The recipient of your message may not have the same system fonts, but Messenger will substitute the available font most like the one your document specifies.

The available Font Sizes—8, 10, 12, 18, 24, and 36 points—correspond to the Heading styles Heading 6 through Heading 1. No in-between sizes are available.

The Font Color selector lets you add color to your typography. Just click the down arrow and mouse to the color of your choice.

The Character Styles Bold, Italic, and Underline don't need to be explained here. The Remove all Styles icon strips off any style attributes you've added. That is, all style attributes other than those imposed by the Paragraph Style, if any.

Bullet List and Numbered List create or transform text items into these types of lists. Again, you can pick the style and then type your text or type first, highlight, then pick the style.

The Decrease and Increase Indent choices do just what you'd think. Alignment lets you choose Left, Center, or Right alignment for text. The Left and Right alignments have "ragged" opposite margins; there is no justified type in HTML.

Insert Object lets you place any of five types of nontext entities on your message page: Insert Link lets you add a hyperlink; Insert Target lets you add a link targets; Insert Image lets you add a GIF or JPG file; Insert Horizontal Line places a decorative rule; and Insert Table creates a text table. For details on how to use these tools, see Chapter 7 on Page Composer.

HTML Commands in the Composition Menus

The Page Source command on the View menu shows you the content of your message together with the HTML tags that Messenger has inserted. The Insert and Format menus each contain a number of commands specifically related to HTML formatting. We'll examine them briefly.

The Insert Menu

This menu duplicates and expands upon the functions of the Insert–Object toolbar icon. Insert–Link, Insert–Target, Insert–Image, and Insert–Horizontal Line are all exactly equivalent to the icon-based commands.

Insert–Table adds three sub-choices—Row, Column, Cell—to the basic table-creation function. These add the elements in question to an existing table. Insert–HTML Tag lets you place in your documents HTML tags not provided by Messenger. The last three commands, New Line Break, Break below Image(s), and Nonbreaking Space, are fairly self-explanatory.

The Format Menu

As with the Insert Menu, Format both duplicates and expands upon the toolbar icons. Font, Size, Color, and Remove all Styles are the exact equivalents of the corresponding windows and icons.

Style gives the Bold, Italic, and Underlined choices, but adds several others: Strikethrough, Subscript, Superscript, Blinking, and Nonbreaking. These are self-explanatory.

Heading gives the same range of choices as the numbered Heading types in the Paragraph Styles window. Paragraph provides the remaining choices accessed via the Paragraph Styles window, and adds one more: Block Quote—indented on both left and right.

List adds several list types to the Bullet and Numbered styles you can apply from the toolbar, but these have no role in e-mail messages. Align provides the same Left, Right, and Center choices as the icon, as do Increase and Decrease Indent.

The final three commands, Character Properties, Table Properties, and Page Colors and Properties, let you apply numerous style choices to individual characters, and tables, and make basic design and color choices for entire pages. They are really the province of HTML authoring with Page Composer.

Sending HTML-Based E-Mail

While HTML-enabling electronic mail certainly increases the potential impact of your messages, that potential drops back to zero unless your recipient's mail program can render HTML documents. An HTML message that turns up in a text-only mail client will look like total gibberish. That is, your message will be heavily encrusted with HTML tags that obscure the content.

Netscape Messenger addresses this problem in three ways:

- First, there's a check box on each address card in the Address Book that lets you record that person's preference for receiving mail in HTML format.

- Second, if you haven't checked that box, or you're mailing to someone who's not in the Address Book, or you're mailing a message to multiple recipients, when you issue the Send command, Messenger displays a dialog box that gives you the option of sending the message in HTML only, in text only, or in both formats. The Recipients button at the bottom lets you separate multiple recipients into two groups: one that prefers HTML and one that doesn't.

- Third, the HTML Domains command in the Edit menu of the Address Book brings up an editable list of domain names. You enter here the mail-server domains of organizations you know use Messenger or another HTML-capable mail program (**netscape.com** is already entered here, for example), and Messenger automatically send your messages in HTML format to all recipients in this domain.

LINKING TO WEB DOCUMENTS

Netscape Messenger makes it easy to place live links to Web sites in your messages. Why would you want to do this? Perhaps in order to show a particularly cool graphic or share some other interesting bit of cultural information with a friend; possibly to guide a business corespondent to some particular product information on your company's Web site. There are countless possible reasons.

Messenger is smart enough the recognize Web addresses (also known as Universal Resource Locators or URLs). If you simply type in a URL, such as **http://www.netscape.com**, if you send it to a user of Netscape Messenger, it will appear as a live hyperlink (highlighted in color and underlined). Obviously, whenever you receive messages from your correspondents that contain URLs, Messenger will display them as live links.

You can also drag and drop URLs from the Netscape Navigator window. To drop in a link to the page currently displayed in Navigator, simply drag the Bookmark icon (the one to the *right* of the word *Bookmark*) and drop it on your message page.

You'll notice when you do this that the mouse pointer changes from an arrow to a little hand. This indicates you're pointing to a draggable object. You'll also find that this happens when you mouse over any live link on the Web page. You guessed it! You can drag any of those links to your message, too. As a matter of fact, this works even for mail-to e-mail addresses.

Finally, you can bring up the History list (select **History** from the Communicator menu) and drag any entry or group of entries into your mail message.

LINKING TO DISCUSSION POSTINGS

Netscape Messenger also makes it easy to add live links to articles in Usenet News groups or postings in Collabra discussion groups—for users who can read HTML-based mail messages. The reasons for linking postings are similar to those for linking to Web pages. Essentially, it's a quick way to hook up your recipient to information that resides elsewhere but that has some significance to your correspondence in some way. In the case of group postings, you could, of course, copy and paste the relevant contents into a mail message, but linking to postings is both easier and more efficient: If you use a link, your server doesn't have to needlessly transport a lot of extra data.

The procedures for inserting links to groups are similar to those for linking to Web pages. To insert a link to an entire Usenet group or Collabra discussion group folder (as opposed to an individual posting), navigate to the group folder in the Current Folder window, then drag the Current Folder icon (which sits to the left of the Current Folder window on the Location Toolbar) into your message. To link to specific postings, navigate to the posting you want, then drag its icon into your message. For this to work—in either case—you *must* send the message in HTML format.

vCARD BUSINESS CARDS

One of Netscape Messenger's conveniences is the vCard Business Card, a rather demure, businesslike substitute for the Internet mail signature file so many people use. If you choose to use it, the vCard presents information contained in your personal Netscape Messenger address card, neatly formatted and boxed at the bottom of the messages you send out. The vCard is shown in Figure 8.13.

To attach the vCard to your outgoing messages, go to the **Identity** page under **Mail & Groups** in **Edit–Preferences** and click the check box at the bottom of the screen that reads **Always attach Address Book Card to messages.** The **Edit Card** button to the right brings up your card so you can add or change information.

At the recipient's discretion, Messenger displays the card either in condensed form—name, e-mail address, title, and organization—or in full form, which includes postal mailing address, phone numbers, Netscape Conference address and DLS Server location, and the contents of your address card Notes field.

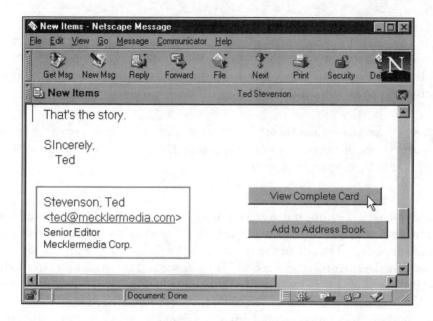

Figure 8.13 The Condensed vCard display.

If you opt to attach vCard to your messages, it's a good idea for you to think carefully about what information you record in your personal address card. Remember, this is for public consumption. The Notes field becomes, in effect, a little advertising banner for you or your business. You probably don't want it to say anything like "Don't forget Mom's birthday."

Messenger's default is to display the Condensed card. To display the Complete card, simply click the **View Complete Card** button to the right of the card itself. To add the card contents to your Address Book, click the **Add to Address Book** button.

Sender's names in vCards will be displayed either in Firstname Lastname mode ("Joan Smith") or Lastname, Firstname mode ("Smith, Joan"), depending on the setting you've chosen on the Directory page under **Mail & Groups** in **Edit–Preferences**. The choice is actually for display of names in the Address Book, but the vCard display reflects that preference.

SORTING THROUGH MESSAGES

By default, Netscape Messenger places all incoming messages in the Inbox folder, in the order in which they were sent, but the program provides many useful ways to sort your mail.

NOTE
Don't be surprised to get new messages and have them appear in the headers list before messages you've already seen. The order is based on the time stamp of the outgoing mail server.

First, you have the option to display message threads. (A message thread is an original message together with all the generations of replies that use the same Subject header.) That is, all the headers in the thread are displayed together so as to make clear the parent/child relationships. This makes it easier to follow the give and take in an extended e-mail discussion. With threading turned off, the messages are displayed in date order (or any other order you've chosen, as described below). To display messages as threads, click the small **Thread** icon in the upper left-hand corner of the message-headers window, as shown in Figure 8.14, below. To display messages in any other order, click the any of the fields to the right of the Thread icon.

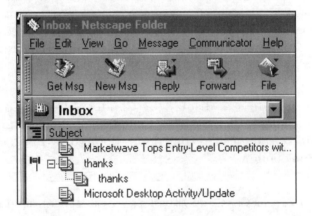

Figure 8.14 Messages displayed as indented threads.

Netscape Messenger gives you a number of other ways to organize your mail: You can sort the list of headers according to several of the fields at the top of the Message Headers pane, shown in Figure 8.15.

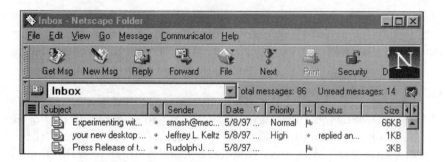

Figure 8.15 *The sort fields in the Message-Headers pane.*

There are eight fields in the header display (Figure 8.12):

- The Sender field tells who sent the message. If a message was received without a real name (remember at the beginning of this chapter, when you were asked to provide your real name to Netscape Messenger), then Netscape Messenger will use the electronic-mail address.

- The Read / Unread field (marked with a green diamond) indicates whether you've read the messages or not.

- The Subject field lists the subject of the message.

- The Date field tells when a message was sent. If there's no date and only a time, that means the message was sent today.

- The Priority field records the priority, if any, assigned by the sender.

- The Flag field is used to mark messages for future sorting (you'll learn about this later in this section).

- The Status field notes whether a message is New (was downloaded at your most recent log-on) or whether you've replied to or forwarded it.

You'll notice that there's a little downward-pointing arrow next to **Date**. This arrow indicates that the messages are sorted by date. However, you can sort the messages by Subject, Unread, Sender, or Size fields, as well. To sort the messages by sender, for example, simply click the box labeled **Sender**. Your messages are instantly displayed in order of the senders' names (alphabetized A to Z). To reverse the sort order (alphabetize Z to A), just click **Sender** again; the little arrow now points up for ascending order. To sort by Flag, just click the **Flag** field, clicking again to reverse the sort order if desired, and so forth.

These same sort settings can be made from the Sort submenu found under the View menu, including changing from Descending to Ascending order or vice versa.

Flagging Messages

The purpose of flagging messages isn't primarily to single them out for attention, rather it's to aggregate messages that share a common characteristic that *you* understand but Messenger doesn't, usually in order to move them into other folders. Let's say you want to move all the messages centered around a particular work project. There's no simple unifying criterion—no common sender, no common subject field—and so you must manually go through the list of messages, but instead of filing the messages one by one, you can click on the Flag field of each message (as opposed to the Flag-Sort field), to mark it.

When you're through flagging messages, choose **Select Message–Flagged** from the Edit menu. This highlights the flagged messages. You can then move these messages en masse to another folder (or delete them). When you're through moving them, the messages will no longer be flagged.

In addition, three menu selections from the Go menu allow you to scroll through flagged messages: First Flagged, Next Flagged, and Previous Flagged.

Dealing with Unread Messages

Being able to mark messages as unread is simply a handy way to go through a list of messages without having to look at every message. When you mark a message as unread by clicking in the **Read/Unread** field (marked by a small diamond), the message header will become bold and a green diamond will appear in the field. In addition, the Unread messages tally at the right-hand side of the Location toolbar will reflect one more unread message.

You can move down through unread messages by selecting **Next** from the toolbar. In addition, three menu selections from the Go menu allow you to scroll through unread messages: First Unread, Next Unread, and Previous Unread.

Summary

Electronic mail has always been the most popular use of the Internet, and that situation shows no signs of changing. As you—and your family, friends, and business associates—use it more, you'll discover how valuable e-mail can be as an adjunct to your daily work and/or play.

In this chapter we covered the basics of e-mail using Netscape Messenger, beginning with configuration issues such as giving Messenger the addresses of your mail servers, moving through the essential mail functions of creating, sending and receiving messages, as well as replying to and forwarding mail. We delved into some mail management topics, such as sorting and searching through mail, and touched on some enhancements, such as vCards and the use of HTML formatting.

In the next chapter, you'll become an e-mail expert, learning advanced topics such as organizing your mail using folders and creating "rules" for automatically "filtering" incoming mail.

CHAPTER 9

Advanced Messenger Topics

Did you ever dream that there was so much to know about electronic mail? The bad news: There's still quite a bit we haven't covered. The good news: You can handle an amazing variety of message-related tasks and work with enormous volumes of mail—all quite efficiently due to Netscape Messenger's rich set of features. In this chapter, we'll dig down into Messenger's toolbars and menus, looking at all the specialized commands that make for powerful mail processing and speed your work. Topics covered in this chapter include:

- The Messenger Toolbar and Menus
- Filing your messages
- Working with the Address Book

319

- Directory Searches on the Web
- Working with mailing lists

THE NETSCAPE MESSENGER TOOLBAR

In the course of learning to create, send, reply to, and forward messages in the previous chapter, you learned about some of the toolbar buttons in the main window. Now it's time to review the rest. (The toolbar is shown in Figure 9.1.) Most have to do with the Message Headers pane and whatever mail messages happen to be highlighted there. They also are rather easy to figure out, which is why we won't spend a great deal of time on them.

Figure 9.1 *The Main Messenger toolbar.*

The Delete Button

This button deletes the highlighted message in the message-headers pane. Actually, the message isn't *really* deleted: It's merely moved to the Trash folder. Only from that folder can you truly delete messages from your system. (In other words, if there's a message you really want to erase, make sure it's deleted from the Trash folder.)

The Next Button

The Next button moves you from the message currently highlighted in the message-header pane to the next *unread* message on the list, making that the active message.

The Print Button

This button does pretty much what you'd expect; it prints the current message.

The Stop Button

This button does the same thing as it does in the Web browser: It stops the transfer of mail messages. You'll notice it is available only when transfers are actually taking place. At other times, the icon is rendered as a ghost image only.

The File Button

This button lets you file the highlighted message in one of your storage folders. To file the message, click the button, mouse down to the folder in which you want to store the message, then release the mouse button. If you've selected multiple messages, all the selected messages will be placed in the chosen folder. There are other ways to file messages; we'll learn more about these, later in this chapter.

RUNNING THROUGH THE PULL-DOWN MENUS

The mail examples we worked with in Chapter 8 were rather simple—some plain text sent to a single recipient—and if that's all you ever got to know about e-mail using Messenger, you would certainly be able to function comfortably as a mail user. But there's a *lot* more to know about this program: The dozens of commands and options nestled in the pull-down menus of the main Netscape Message window can make you an e-mail power user. We'll now review each and every one.

The File Menu

This menu, shown in Figure 9.2, handles a lot of basic file-related functions provided by Messenger, as well as some functions (such as printing and opening files) that are really provided by your operating system.

Figure 9.2 *Displaying the File pull-down menu.*

The File menu items are:

- New
- New Folder
- Open Message
- Open Attachments
- Save As
- Edit Message
- Rename Folder
- Empty Trash Folder
- Compress Folders
- Get Messages
- Send Unsent Messages
- Subscribe to Discussion Groups
- Go Offline/Go Online

- Page Setup
- Print Preview
- Print
- Close
- Exit

We'll cover each option here.

New

This lets you create several kinds of Communicator entities. As the arrow to the right indicates, selecting New leads to a menu of subchoices: Navigator Window, Message, Blank Page, Page from Template, and Page from Wizard.

New–Navigator Window opens an additional session of Navigator, allowing you to connect to an additional Web page. This command is also a handy way to reopen Netscape Navigator (the browser portion) when you've closed it for any reason.

New–Message creates a new e-mail message; it is the equivalent of the New Msg button on the Messenger toolbar.

New–Blank Page/Page from Template/Page from Wizard create new Web pages in Netscape Communicator's HTML editing module, Page Composer.

New Folder

Netscape Messenger organizes mail in folders. As you saw when you launched Messenger, there is a window below the toolbar that displays the name of the folder you're currently working with. The contents of that folder are displayed in the message header window. When you install Communicator, six folders are created automatically: Inbox, Outbox, Drafts, Sent, Trash, and Samples. This command allows you to add folders of your own. You'll learn more about this command later in the chapter.

Open Message

This opens the highlighted message if you are not using the split-pane method of reviewing your mail. (Otherwise, the message is automatically displayed in the lower pane.) You can also open a message by double-clicking the message header.

Open Attachments

This opens any document files that may have been attached to the currently highlighted message. If there are multiple attachments, a branch menu lets you select which attachment to open. Attachments were discussed in depth in Chapter 8.

Save As

This stores the current message as a text file. The keyboard shortcut is **Ctrl-S.**

Edit Message

This opens the currently highlighted message in the Composition window, so you can modify or add to the contents. Typically, you'd use this command to continue work on messages you'd stored in the Drafts folder. To save your edits, use the **Save as Draft** command or **Send** the message.

Rename Folder

This command doesn't function in this context and is therefore grayed out. When you bring up the Message Center, however (the window that shows you the entire hierarchy of your mail and group message folders), it lets you change the name of the highlighted folder.

Empty Trash Folder

This deletes the contents of the Trash folder.

Compress Folders

To save on disk space, Netscape Messenger can compress the contents of mail folders. Depending on how many messages are in the folder and their sizes, you can save between 10 and 40 percent in the disk space occupied by mail messages.

Get Messages

This choice connects to your mail server and retrieves any new mail messages; it is equivalent to the Get Msg icon on the toolbar. As indicated by the arrow, there are some subchoices, but these don't apply to e-mail.

Send Unsent Messages

This choice sends any mail that's accumulated in your Outbox folder. Typically, these would be messages you've elected to Send Later (as discussed above under Message Composition Options) or that you've composed while offline (see below). You'll learn more about this later in this chapter, in the section entitled "Working Offline."

Subscribe to Discussion Groups

This lets you participate in threaded discussions carried on via Netscape Collabra. To find out more about Collabra, see Chapters 13 and 14.

Go Offline/Go Online

If you're connected to the Internet and want to end that connection, select **Go Offline**. This brings up a dialog box that gives you the option of telling Messenger to download Mail and/or Discussion Groups, and of sending unsent messages and then logging off the server. If you're disconnected, the menu entry reads **Go Online**. Selecting it logs you back onto the server, once again giving you the option of downloading Mail and/or Discussion Groups, and of sending messages. We discuss these commands in more detail in the "Working Offline" section later in this chapter.

Page Setup

This brings up the dialog box that sets the size and other particulars of a printed page. This dialog box is the same as if you selected Page Setup from the File menu in the Web browser.

Print Preview

This shows how the current message will appear when printed. This dialog box is the same as if you selected Print Preview from the File menu in the Web browser.

Print

This prints the current message. This dialog box is the same as if you selected Print from the File menu in the Web browser.

Close

This closes Netscape Mail, but leaves any other windows (such as a Web browser or the newsreader) open.

Exit

This exits Netscape Communicator completely.

The Edit Menu

This menu governs the editing and manipulation of mail messages. Items in the Edit menu are:

- Undo
- Cut
- Copy
- Paste
- Clear (Macintosh only)
- Delete Message
- Select Message
- Find in Message
- Find Again
- Search Messages
- Search Directory
- Manage Mail Account
- Manage Discussion Group
- Mail Filters
- Properties
- Preferences

Many of these commands work the same way as they do under the Web browser, so we won't waste time covering these menu choices in depth, unless they are unique to Netscape Mail.

Undo

This selection undoes the last action. Unlike some other applications with an Undo command, Messenger has no Redo command to reverse it. To reverse Undo, you simply issue Undo again. If the last action cannot be undone, this selection will be grayed out.

Cut

Choosing this cuts the highlighted text and stores it in your operating system's clipboard.

Copy

Choosing this copies the highlighted text to your operating system's clipboard.

Paste

This selection copies the text stored in your operating system's clipboard at the location of the text cursor.

The **Clear** menu selection deletes the selected text in the Macintosh version of Netscape Communicator only.

MACINTOSH

Delete Message

This menu selection deletes the current message—that is, it moves the message to the Trash folder. You must empty the trash folder separately to actually delete a mail message from your system. (You learned about this in the section entitled "The File Menu.") You can also delete highlighted messages by pressing the **Del** (Delete) key.

Select Message

This doesn't select a message (which you do by clicking one or more headers in the message header pane), rather it brings up the following sub-choices: **Thread, Flagged, All Messages**.

- **Select–Thread**—A message "thread" is a group consisting of a message and all the replies of all the recipients that use the same subject header. Threads may be many generations long; a thread continues as long as replies are generated. Netscape Messenger gives you the option of seeing message threads grouped together in a tree structure that shows "parent-child" relationships (which messages spawn which replies). This choice selects all the messages in a thread, which makes it easier to move them to another folder.

- **Select–Flagged**—This highlights messages you have manually flagged for attention. Flagging and the manipulation of flagged messages are covered in Chapter 8.

- **Select–All Messages**—This highlights all of the messages in a folder, making it easier to cut or move them.

Find in Message

This simple dialog box allows you to search through the current document for a specific word or phrase. The keyboard shortcut **Ctrl-F** accomplishes the same action. There are two settings: A check box lets you tell Netscape Messenger to match the case (if you don't, Netscape Messenger will return both *Go* and *go* if you specify *go* as your search term), and a pair of radio buttons tells Messenger to look either Up or Down (before or after the current location of the text cursor).

MACINTOSH

The selections in this dialog box differ by operating system. The Macintosh, Linux, and UNIX versions don't have a Match Case selection; instead, the term Case Sensitive is used (although it does the same thing). In addition, the Macintosh, Linux, and UNIX versions don't have Up and Down radio buttons; they have a Find Backwards check box to search backwards, instead of the default forward.

Find Again

This selection repeats the search specified in the **Find** menu selection. The keyboard shortcut is **Ctrl-G**.

Search Messages

This command brings up the Search Messages dialog box, which in turn lets you locate specific messages in your Messenger mail store (the contents of your entire collection of mail folders). We investigated the Search Messages dialog box in depth in Chapter 8.

Search Directory

This brings up the Search dialog box, which in turn lets you locate information in a number of online directories, such as the Four11 directory (e-mail addresses of individuals) and the Federal Express Package Trace Web site. You'll learn more about the Search dialog box later in this chapter.

Manage Mail Account

If you have an account on a Netscape Messaging Server version 3.0, this command lets you mange your own account services, such as changing your password, setting up a vacation message, or configuring the automatic forwarding of your mail.

Manage Discussion Group

This lets you manage account services on your Collabra server.

Mail Filters

This brings up the Mail Filters dialog box, which lets you create and manage procedures for organizing and manipulating your incoming messages. You'll learn more about filters and the rules that define them later in this chapter.

Properties

This lets you edit your folder or discussion group properties on a per-folder basis.

Preferences

This brings up the Preferences dialog box, the comprehensive configuration tool you used when first setting up your Messenger account.

The View Menu

This menu, shown in Figure 9.3, controls the display of many components of the Netscape Messenger interface, and determines many aspects of how messages are displayed.

Figure 9.3 *The View menu pulled down.*

Many of these choices will be covered in detail later in this chapter, but we'll briefly cover all the choices here:

- Show/Hide Navigation Toolbar
- Show/Hide Location Toolbar
- Show/Hide Categories
- Show/Hide Message
- Sort
- Messages
- Headers
- Attachments
- Increase Font
- Decrease Font
- Reload
- Show Images

- Refresh
- Stop Loading
- Unscramble (ROT-13)
- Wrap Long Lines
- Page Source
- Page Info
- Encoding

Show / Hide Navigation Toolbar

This toggles the display of the main icon toolbar. You can also accomplish this by clicking the vertical pebbled bar at the left-hand side of the toolbar.

Show / Hide Location Toolbar

This toggles the display of the Location toolbar (the bar that contains the Folder window). You can also accomplish this by clicking the vertical pebbled bar at the left-hand side of the toolbar.

Show / Hide Categories

Postings to Collabra discussion groups and Usenet news groups can be organized into categories for easier access. (These are analogous to mail folders.) This command toggles the display of that hierarchical scheme.

Show / Hide Message

This toggles the message display pane on and off. You can also do this by clicking the small blue triangle in the bottom left-hand corner of the screen to display the message pane, and clicking the blue triangle in the divider bar to hide the pane.

Sort

This menu choice brings up a list of secondary choices that govern how mail messages are listed in the Message-Header pane. We discussed this topic ("Sorting through Messages") in Chapter 8. You can select any of the eight header fields to sort on (though not all of these are meaningful) and toggle the sort order between ascending and descending.

Messages

This option brings up a list of secondary choices that filter the listing in the Message-Header pane to show only certain groups of messages. There are four primary choices, of which you can select one:

- New
- Threads with New
- Watched Threads with New
- All

Selecting New tells Messenger to display the headers of the unread messages only. Threads with New results in the display of threads that contain any new messages; Watched Threads with New does the same for threads you've tagged as watched (see Message Menu, below). All, the default choice, naturally displays all the messages in the folder. Or *may* display all headers. This depends on the final choice, Ignored, which you'll notice is available only when All is selected above. This is a toggle, which controls the display of threads that have been marked with Ignore Thread (see Message menu, below).

Headers

This option controls how headers appear *within* the displayed message. There are three subchoices: All, Normal, and Brief.

- **Headers–All** displays, in addition to the "normal" information (see below), all the information about how the message reached you.
- **Headers–Normal** displays Subject:, Date:, From:, Organization:, To:, and CC: fields.
- **Headers–Brief** displays From:, Subject:, To:, and CC: fields, formatted with some shading in a neat header box.

Attachments

- **Attachments–Inline** places attachments as part of the page, not treated separately (except for binary files and HTML pages, which are attached as icons to the end of a message). This is the default choice.

- **Attachments–As Links** treats attachments as links, which need to be explicitly selected before they appear on the screen.

Increase Font, Decrease Font

These commands (for which **Ctrl-]** and **Ctrl-[** are the keyboard shortcuts) change the type size for the entire message display when you're using the Message Display pane. Selecting the command multiple times multiplies the size change. The command works not on the currently displayed message but on subsequent messages you display.

Reload

This command reloads from the server the message currently highlighted in the Message Display pane or the Composer window.

Show/Hide Images

This toggles the display of any images that might be embedded in your messages.

Refresh

This reloads the mail message from your hard disk.

Stop Loading

This interrupts the loading of a message into the Message Display pane or Composition window. This is handy for canceling the loading of a large message component, such as an image file.

Unscramble (ROT-13)

Netscape Messenger lets you send information that could be offensive—such as a joke—in scrambled form. This scrambling, a relatively simple procedure using the ROT-13 scheme, is not to be confused with secure encryption (which we'll discuss both later in this chapter and in a chapter of its own), but it's good enough to ensure that your joke or other scrambled information can't be seen without some effort on the part of the user. This menu choice unscrambles data that's been scrambled.

If you wish to scramble your own messages using ROT-13, you'll find a scrambler/unscrambler at the ROT-13 Page on the Internet (*http://www.brookings.net/~darina/rot13.html*). To use it, type your text into the scrambler window (or paste it in using a system editing command) and click the **rot-13** button. The text is instantly scrambled. To use it in a message, use system editing commands to copy the text, then paste it into your mail message.

Load Images

This loads images that may be inserted as part of a mail message.

Page Source

This displays the mail message *exactly* as it was sent over the Internet, with no client-imposed formatting (such as quoted original message text italicized in a reply). The page source view shows all the routing information that accumulates as a message travels on its way; if the message has a binary file attached, it shows that file, encoded as a jumble of ASCII characters, as part of the message.

Page Info

This reveals the "structure" of the document currently being viewed. For a Web page viewed in Navigator or edited in Composer, you'll find out such information as the location of the text and image components. In the e-mail context, the information is not generally very meaningful.

Encoding

This covers the language a message is encoded in, just in case the information isn't contained within the message header. However, virtually all of the time the encoding information will be contained within the message header.

The Go Menu

No, this has nothing to do with the ancient Oriental board game, but rather with maneuvering through a list of messages. The options are relatively straightforward:

- Next Message
- Next Unread Message

- Next Flagged Message
- Next Unread Thread
- Next Category
- Next Unread Category
- Next Folder
- Next Unread Folder
- Previous Message
- Previous Unread Message
- Previous Flagged Message
- First Flagged Message
- Back
- Forward

Here are brief explanations of these menu options (not necessarily in menu order):

- **Next Message**: This moves focus to the next message in the headers list.
- **Previous Message**: This moves focus to the previous message in the headers list.
- **Next Unread Message, Previous Unread Message:** These menu choices let you make your way through unread messages. Unread messages will be covered later in this chapter.
- **First Flagged Message, Next Flagged Message, Previous Flagged Message:** These menu choices let you make your way through flagged messages. We covered Flagged messages in some detail in Chapter 8.
- **Next Category, Next Unread Category:** These commands apply to Collabra discussion groups, not e-mail messages.
- **Next Folder:** This takes you to the next folder in your Current Folder list.
- **Next Unread Folder:** This takes you to the next folder in the list that contains unread messages.
- **Back:** This takes you backward through a sequence of messages you've previously viewed (as opposed to moving you upward through the headers list).

- **Forward:** This reverses one or more **Back** commands.

The Message Menu

This menu determines how you respond to incoming messages. By and large, the selections in this menu have already been covered in this and the previous chapter, but we'll still (briefly, anyway) cover these choices:

- New Message
- Reply
- Forward
- Forward Quoted
- Add to Address Book
- File Message
- Copy Message
- Mark
- Flag
- Unflag
- Ignore Thread
- Watch Thread

New Message

Opens the Composition window and starts a new message, just like the New Msg toolbar button.

Reply

This selection summons the Composition window, with the subject and the appropriate address or addresses already inserted. There are four subchoices:

- **Reply–to Sender** (keyboard shortcut, **Ctrl-R**) addresses only the sender of the current message.
- **Reply–to Sender and All Recipients** (keyboard shortcut, **Ctrl-Shift-R**) addresses all recipients of the message being replied to, both To: and CC:.

- **Reply–to Group** and **–to Sender** and **Group** don't work in the e-mail context; they are used in Collabra discussion groups, which we'll cover in a later chapter.

Forward

This selection forwards the current message as an attachment, just like the **Forward** icon on the main toolbar. You must fill in the address of the recipient. The keyboard shortcut is **Ctrl-L**.

Forward Quoted

This selection forwards the current message with its contents displayed in the message body, rather than as an attachment, as above.

Add to Address Book

This selection places names and e-mail addresses in your Netscape Messenger Address Book.

- **Add to Address Book–Sender** brings up the Address Book Card for... dialog box with the sender's e-mail address in place. Messenger also tries to put the sender's name in the appropriate fields, if that information is in the header.
- **Add to Address Book–All** brings up the Card... dialog box for each addressee of the current message, as well as the sender.

File Message

This allows you to move the current message to any of your storage folders. When you make the selection, a menu of subchoices lets you pick any of your existing folders as the filing target. We'll discuss creating and using folders later in this chapter.

Copy Message

This allows you to place a copy of the current message in any of your storage folders, leaving the original where it is. When you make the selection, a menu of subchoices lets you pick the appropriate folder.

Mark

This changes the state of the Read/Unread marker (the field to the right of the Subject in the message header display) for the current message. There are a number of reasons you might want to change this status, including the possibility that a message was automatically displayed (and therefore marked as read) simply because you highlighted the header in passing. A menu of subchoices presents the following options:

- **Mark–as Unread**, **Mark–as Read** are the two basic options. Unread messaged are distinguished from those you've read (in reality, Messenger can only know if it has *displayed* the message, not if you've actually read it) in two ways: the header is rendered in bold, and the messages are marked with a bright green diamond in the header display. When you've read a message (that is, Messenger has displayed it), the header switches to normal type and the diamond gets smaller and paler. These commands toggles the state of the marking symbol. You can also do this by clicking the marker diamond in the header display.

- **Mark–Thread Read** changes the marking display for all messages contained in a thread.

- **Mark–Category Read** applies to Collabra discussion groups, not to e-mail messages. We'll cover that subject in a later chapter.

- **Mark–All Read** changes the marking display for a group of highlighted message headers.

- **Mark–by Date** arbitrarily marks as read all the messages in your folder up to a date you specify. Messenger presents a dialog box so you can enter a date.

- **Mark–for Later** keeps the message marked as **unread** and opens the next unread message.

Flag, Unflag

These flag or unflag the currently highlighted message or messages—not so much to call attention to them as to aggregate them for mass file operations. The subject of flagged messages was covered in Chapter 8.

Ignore Thread

This simply toggles on or off a small icon (the international TK (to come) symbol) next to any thread you don't want to bother checking in the long- or short-term future.

Watch Thread

This toggles on or off a small icon (a pair of eyeglasses) next to any thread you especially wish to check up on.

The Communicator Menu

With this menu, you can move to other components of Netscape Communicator 4.0 and access various ancillary functions of Messenger. This menu is the same in all Communicator windows.

The Help Menu

This menu is the same in all Netscape Communicator windows. Check in Chapter 2 for a more complete explanation of this window.

OTHER MAIL-CONFIGURATION OPTIONS

You've already done some mail configuration before you ever launched Netscape Mail. In this section, we cover the remaining configuration issues.

The Appearance Configuration Screen

This dialog box determines which Netscape Communicator modules are displayed when you start the program, and lets you decide whether to show toolbars with pictures (icons) only, text only, or icons with text captions.

N O T E

Choosing either **text only** or **pictures only** will significantly reduce the amount of screen space that your toolbar takes up. This action leaves more room for message content.

The Fonts Configuration Page

Here you have the opportunity to choose default styles and sizes for a variable-width and a fixed-width font for use in your outgoing messages. This is great, but you'll find that the selections work only if you have also elected to use HTML (to do so, check the box **By default, send HTML messages** at the top of the Messages page in Preferences).

NOTE   What's the difference between a fixed-length and a variable-length font? Netscape Communicator runs on a number of operating systems—Windows, Windows 95, Macintosh, and X Window/UNIX. These operating systems use different fonts, and Netscape Communicator (as well as the entire World Wide Web) can't assume that the same fonts are available to all users. So the entire issue of fonts is side-stepped by leaving fonts to the local system; the Internet merely designates something as having a fixed-length or a variable-length font.

Basically, a fixed-width font has characters that are all the same width, no matter the character. With a fixed-length font, the characters *a, i,* and *m* (and all the other characters, upper- or lower-case, numbers or letters) are all the same width. That is, they are allotted the same amount of lateral space in the type line.

```
This is a fixed-width font. Note the i and w.
```

Conversely, the characters in a variable-length font are spaced depending on their real width. This text is formatted with a variable-width font.

Chapter 2 covers how Netscape Communicator deals with fonts in other situations.

HOT LINK

Another choice on this screen is whether Communicator should display documents using the fonts specified therein, or use your chosen default styles and sizes, and whether to allow or disable the use of Dynamic Fonts. We'll discuss dynamic fonts later in this chapter.

The Colors Configuration Page

Here's where you can set up Messenger to display mail messages in yellow type on a maroon background, if that's how you like to see them. (There are some other color choices, of course.) You can also set the colors for visited and unvisited links.

NOTE The default for text and background colors is to use the Windows color scheme you've chosen. To override this, click the check box **Use Windows colors** and deselect that choice.

A check box at the bottom of this screen tells Communicator to override the color formatting that's native to a message or document and use your personal default colors.

WELCOME TO THE WORKING WEEK

While a review of menus and configuration issues is handy, it's perhaps more useful to cover practical mail matters in Netscape Messenger, independent of menus and such. In this part of the chapter, we'll focus on some specific day-in, day-out mail issues and explain how you can deal with them.

Folders and Filing

We've mentioned (and you'll quickly discover), that keeping track of the accumulation of messages is one of the big, ongoing tasks associated with electronic mail. Filing messages is a good way to deal with that problem—or an essential procedure, depending on how much mail you get. Netscape Messenger's folder-based filing system is one of its more highly touted new features. It is powerful—but only if you get in the habit of using it regularly. We'll investigate Messenger's filing features in some detail here.

When you install Netscape Messenger, six folders are set up for you: Inbox, Outbox, Drafts, Sent, Trash, and Samples. The contents of these folders are pretty self-explanatory: The Inbox is where Messenger automatically places incoming messages (both read and unread); the Outbox stores unsent outgoing messages; Drafts is the folder where you keep messages in progress; the Sent folder stores a copy of each message you actually mail out; Trash is used to store messages you've deleted, and the Samples folder contains one elaborate sample message that shows some of the fancy stuff you can do with messaging in Netscape Messenger. The Samples folder also serves as an example of the fact that you can create folders of your own devising that serve your personal mail storage needs.

NOTE   When you delete a message from the Inbox or any other mail folder, it's sent to the Trash folder, so you can in fact retrieve it. When you delete messages from the Trash folder, though, they're gone forever. Remember that if you want to truly erase a message from your system, you'll have to move it to Trash and then delete it.

Folders are a wonderful, flexible tool for organizing your mail. As with real (physical) file folders, you can name and organize them thematically in whatever way makes sense to you—for instance, you can have a folder entitled *Blather* for messages from your boss, a folder named *Love* for messages from your beloved, and so on.

To navigate among your folders, click the down arrow at the right side of the Current Folder window on the Location Toolbar, and mouse to the folder of your choice. The messages in that folder will now be displayed in the Message Header pane below.

When you receive a mail message, it's automatically delivered to the Inbox folder, where it stays until you move or delete it. Messenger's folders are simple to work with: You can create them, rename them, and delete them to your heart's content, and you can file messages—move them from one folder to another—by several methods, which we'll explore below. You can even organize folders hierarchically, that is, place folders within folders.

Moving Messages Among Folders

Filing mail mostly means moving messages from the Inbox to other folders where they're stored with other messages to which they're thematically related.

Again, to Messenger, moving messages is *Filing*. There are several ways to accomplish this (all of which begin with highlighting one or more headers in the main Message Header window):

- Click the **File** button on the Messenger toolbar. This displays a drop-down list of your mail folders. Simply mouse down to the folder of your choice and release the mouse button. This method is shown in Figure 9.4.

- Select **File Message** from the Message menu. A fly-out menu will appear, allowing you to mouse (or cursor) down to the folder of your choice.

- Click the header with the *right* mouse button. Mouse down to the **File Message** command on the menu that will automatically drop down, then mouse to the folder of your choice.

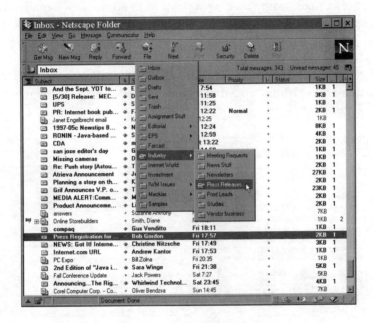

Figure 9.4 *Using the File Button to store a message.*

The **Copy Message** choice from the Message menu copies highlighted messages to another folder, leaving the originals intact. This can be a very handy option if a message relates to two or more of your folder categories.

Creating a New Folder

To create a new folder, go to the File menu and select **New Folder**. This brings up the New Folder dialog box. Type in a name for your new folder in the Name: field.

A drop-down list at the bottom of the dialog box lets you position your new folder within the existing hierarchy as a subfolder of any existing folder. Just mouse down to the appropriate choice. If you want your new folder to be on the same level as Inbox and Trash, mouse up to the top entry in the list, called Local Mail. Once you click **OK** on the New Folder dialog box, you're in business. That's all there is to it.

WORKING WITH THE ADDRESS BOOK

Most electronic mail programs have a place to keep track of e-mail addresses. Messenger's Address Book is quite a bit more than that, but that's its basic function. When you receive e-mail from someone, you can add their name and e-mail address to your address book by clicking the name or address in the message header or by selecting **Add to Address Book** from the Message menu. Either action brings up a dialog box headed Card for [the name of the person] as shown in Figure 9.5.

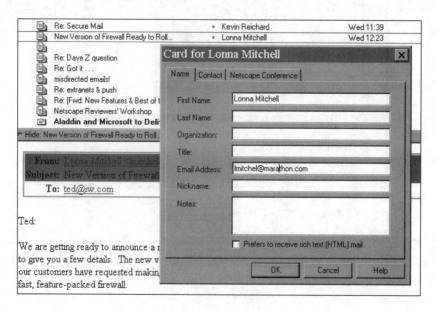

Figure 9.5 *Adding a card to the Address Book.*

Netscape Messenger fills in the fifth (Email Address:) field of the Card dialog box with the electronic-mail address of the sender. If the message contains the sender's real name, Messenger places the first and last name in the First Name: and Last Name: fields. You may fill in the other fields or not, as you wish: The Nickname: field is a good one to fill in. Type in a brief, easy-to-remember shortcut (or *alias* as some mail packages call it) for the user—it could be *mom, dks, lefty,* whatever—and you won't have to enter a full name or e-mail address when addressing a new message.

If you click the **Contact** tab, you'll be able to fill in postal address, fax, and phone information for your addressee. Click the **Netscape Conference** tab and you'll be able to enter server and address information for contacting the person via Netscape Conference. We'll learn more about Netscape Conference communications in Chapter 15. Once you click the **OK** button on the dialog box, the address card becomes part of your permanent Personal Address Book.

When you start a new message, you'll see an Address icon on the toolbar of the Composition window. Clicking this brings up the Select Addresses dialog box, as shown in Figure 9.6.

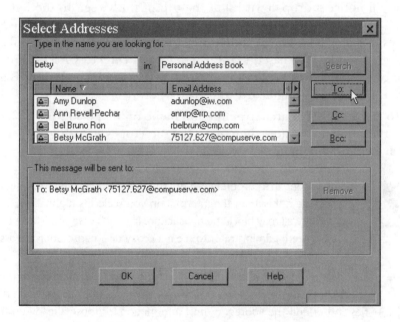

Figure 9.6 *The Select Addresses dialog box.*

At the top of the screen, there's a field where you can type in the name of the person whose address you want to locate. Or you can simply scroll through the list of addressees in the large window below. Once you find an addressee you want and have highlighted the name, you can click the **To:**, **CC:**, or **BCC:** buttons on the right. The name then appears in the large window at the bottom of the screen. You can add as many names in the various addressing categories as you like.

To remove a name from your list of addressees, highlight it and click the **Remove** button to the right of the window. When you're through entering addressees, click **OK** and the names and addresses will be entered in the appropriate address fields in your message.

Directory Searches on the Web

If you want to send an e-mail to someone for whom you don't have an electronic mail address, you may be able to locate the necessary address (and possibly a postal address and/or phone number as well) through one of the public directories on the Internet.

You'll notice a drop-down list at the top of the screen to the left of the Search button. This is a list of directories you can search from the Select Addresses dialog box. The default listing is your Personal Address Book, but a number of public Web-based LDAP (Lightweight Directory Access Protocol) directories and other services are listed here as well, including Bigfoot, Four11, Infospace, Switchboard, and WhoWhere.

To run an LDAP search, type the full name of the person you're looking for in the left-hand window, then select the directory you wish to target. Click **Search**, and Messenger goes to work.

If you're working in a corporate setting, running LDAP searches may get you an error message rather than the information you seek: It's highly likely that the company firewall may block the transaction. In which case you'll have to check with your system administrator to see if a proxy or other solution is possible.

NOTE

To edit the list of available LDAP directories, go to **Edit-Preferences** and select **Directory** under **Mail & Groups**. Here you can add or delete directories and/or edit the address or port information for those already on the list. Just click the **Edit** button and make your changes.

NOTE

Working with Mailing Lists

One of the beauties of electronic mail is that you can easily send one message to many recipients. Of course, you can do this by entering each address separately, but the feature called Mailing Lists (also called Mail Groups in some other mail packages) lets you compile permanent lists of addresses of groups you communicate with regularly, give them names, and store them ready to be used when needed. You might have a list for your e-mail–enabled family members, for members of your department at work, for your community organization, your political representatives, and so on.

With a mailing list in place, you use it like any other address, but Messenger sends the message to everyone on the list. If you had a Family mailing list, for example, you can insert it in the To:, CC:, or BCC: fields in a new mail message just like the address of an individual. Mailing lists can be created only through the main Address Book window, which we'll discuss below.

The Main Messenger Address Book

Selecting Address Book from the Communicator menu brings up the Address Book proper. It is similar to the Select Addresses dialog box: It has a type-in field, a directory selection list box, a Search button, and a large window containing an alphabetized list of your addressees. It lacks the To:, CC:, and BCC: buttons and the selected addresses window, but unlike Select Addresses, it has menus and an icon toolbar.

The Address Book Toolbar

The toolbar contains seven icons: **New Card**, **New List**, **Properties**, **New Msg**, **Directory**, **Call**, and **Delete**. In most cases, their functions are simple and straightforward, as follows:

- Clicking the **New Card** icon brings up the same dialog box that comes up when you click the sender's name or address in a mail message or select **Add to Address Book** from the Message menu in the main Messenger screen. Here, it's titled New Card, but once it's filled in, it changes to read Card for [name of person].

- Clicking **New List** brings up the Mailing List dialog box, with fields for a Name, a Nickname, and a Description for a new mailing list. We'll discuss the details of building a mailing list below.

- Clicking **Properties** brings up one or more highlighted cards for editing.

- **New Msg** displays the Composition window, just as the equivalent icon on the main Messenger toolbar does. However, if you highlight one or more addresses in the Address Book list before clicking **New Msg**, the Composition window will come up with the addresses in place.

- The **Directory** icon lets you look up an address an any of the address directories you're registered with, using the Search dialog box. Clicking the **Search** button on the Address Book or Select Addresses dialog boxes accomplishes the same thing.

- The **Call** icon brings up Netscape Conference and initiates a call with the addressee or addressees you've highlighted in the main list. We'll learn more about Netscape Conference in Chapter 15.

- The **Delete** icon deletes any addressees that are highlighted in the main list. You can also do this by pressing the **Del** key.

The Address Book Menus

Three of the five pull-down menus—File, Edit, and View—contain at least some commands unique to the Address Book. We'll examine them briefly. (The Communicator and Help menus are identical to those found elsewhere in Netscape Communicator.)

The File Menu

The Address Book File menu is not a miracle of logical consistency; nonetheless, we'll examine its options.

- **New** and its subchoices Navigator Window, Message, Blank Page, Page from Template, and Page from Wizard are found in main Messenger File menu.

- **New Card** and **New List** are the equivalents of the Address Book toolbar icons of the same names.

- **Import** displays the Import address book file dialog box, which lets you navigate to any Netscape address book file and select it for import into the current file.

- **Save As** lets you save the current address book file under a new name.

- **Call** is the equivalent of the Address Book toolbar icon of the same name.

- **Close** exits the Address Book only, not any other Communicator component.

The Edit Menu

An odd collection of commands drop down from the Edit menu: Undo and Redo are apparently not enabled. Delete deletes the currently highlighted entry. Search Directory is the equivalent of the Directory icon on the toolbar. HTML Domains calls up an editable list of domain names that can accept HTML mail. Card Properties, like the toolbar icon of the same name, lets you edit one or more highlighted entries. Preferences is the same core list of Netscape Communicator configuration screens you can access from any Edit menu within Communicator.

The View Menu

The first command on the View menu lets you toggle the display of the Address Book Toolbar on and off. The next six commands—By Type, By Name, By Email Address, By Company, By City, By Nickname—allow you to sort your Address Book entries by those factors respectively. With the exception of By Type, which sorts the mailing list names separately from the names of individual addressees, all of these sorting selections can be made by clicking the appropriate field header boxes, just as with mail messages. To reverse the sorting order, click the box a second time, or select Sort Ascending or Sort Descending from the View menu. The final View menu command, My Address Book Card, displays—you guessed it—your personal card.

Creating a Mailing List

As mentioned above, to build a new mailing list you can either click the **New List** button on the Address Book toolbar or select **New List** from the File menu. This brings up a dialog box with fields for a Name, a Nickname, and a Description for a new mailing list, as shown in Figure 9.7.

In the ruled window, you add names and e-mail addresses from the main Address Book. To do this, place your text cursor on the line next to the address icon and begin to type the name of the person you want to add. Messenger will type ahead and fill in the name. If it gets the wrong name, keep typing until the right name is inserted. Press **Enter** and your cursor is moved down and a new address icon is inserted. Continue adding names until you're through.

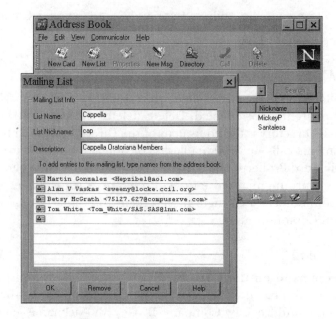

Figure 9.7 *Creating a mailing list.*

Making Changes in the Address Book

You can perform basic list management with the Address Book, as in the following:

- You can delete an e-mail address by highlighting the name and then pressing the **Del** key or selecting **Delete** from the Edit menu.
- You can add a new user by clicking the **New Card** toolbar button or selecting **New Card** from the File menu. The New Card dialog box will appear. Simply fill it in.

WORKING OFFLINE

You don't need to be connected to the Internet to compose or manage mail messages. In fact, doing all your e-mail work—at least everything short of sending and collecting messages—while disconnected from the Internet is a very attractive option to those on a metered Internet access plan where time is money, or where a long-distance call is needed to connect to the Internet.

Another important dimension of working offline relates to mobile e-mail users and the logistics of using mail on multiple computers (typically a desktop system at the office, and a laptop that travels with the user). Nowadays, travel time (in a plane or train) is often prime e-mail time—time to read and answer mail that was downloaded previously.

Messenger has an Offline work mode that contains number of features designed to make offline e-mail work easy and efficient—especially for those using IMAP servers—including commands to disconnect and reconnect you to your mail server. We'll take a look at these a bit later.

Whether your mail server uses IMAP or POP, you can compose messages (or forward or respond to already-received messages) without being connected to the Internet:

First, launch Netscape Communicator and then Messenger without initiating your Net connection. You may receive error messages when launching Communicator or Messenger, telling you that there's no network connection; just click **OK** and proceed: Go ahead and compose your messages. As you're through with each, select **Send Later** from the File menu; Messenger stores it in the Outbox folder. (Unless you've selected the Go Offline command or configured Messenger for Offline mode—both discussed below—if you click the Send icon, you'll get an error message from Messenger telling you you're not connected.) When you're ready to send your messages, connect to the Internet, select **Send Unsent Messages** from the File menu and off they go.

Configuring Messenger to Work Offline

To take advantage of Messenger's Offline mode—sometimes or all the time—you can make a setting in the Edit-Preferences dialog box. Select the Offline page and decide whether you want Offline mode to be your default, or whether you want Messenger to ask, each time you start the program, whether you want to be in Online or Offline mode.

Online assumes a continuous (typically networked) connection to the Internet. Offline lets you control your connection status using the Go Offline/Go Online commands discussed below.

The Download page (hierarchically below the Offline page) provides some settings for downloading mail from an IMAP server. Choices available are Download only unread messages and Download by date (you can choose both). If you select Download by date, you can specify some time parameters to control your downloads.

The Go Offline/Go Online Commands

As mentioned above, Netscape Messenger has a built-in toggle command designed to make it easy to work offline. This is designed primarily for users with accounts on Netscape Messenging Server version 3.0 or later, which supports IMAP (Internet Mail Access Protocol) and thus can store and manage mail. Select **Go Offline** from the File menu, and a dialog box containing several options pops up, as shown in Figure 9.8. The options, all quite straightforward, are:

- Download Mail
- Download Discussion Groups
- Send Messages

By default, all three options are enabled. To disable any of them, simply click the appropriate check box. Also click a button labeled **Select Items for Download**. This brings up a headers list for your e-mail and Usenet news and Collabra discussion groups, letting you pick headers from the list that you wish to have downloaded.

Once you've finished selecting the work options you want, just click the **Go Offline** button and Messenger disconnects you from the server. At this point, any messages you send are automatically moved to the Outbox folder and sent when you reconnect.

When you wish to resume your connection, you'll find that the **Go Offline** command on the File menu has toggled to **Go Online**. Select this and you'll get the same dialog box, with the same work options, but its function is now to reconnect you to the server.

Figure 9.8 Messenger's Go Offline dialog box.

Using the Right Mouse Button

Quite a few of the operations we've covered in these two chapters on Messenger can be accessed via the right-hand mouse button, which is often the simplest way to do what you need to do. When you've highlighted a header in the Message Headers pane, clicking with the right-hand mouse button gives you the following options, all of which are commands that we've covered in these pages:

- Open Message
- Open Message in New Window
- Reply to Sender
- Reply to Sender and All Recipients
- Forward
- Forward Quoted
- Add to Address Book
- Ignore Thread
- Watch Thread
- Change Priority to

- File Message
- Delete Message
- Save Message
- Print Message

When you're looking at a mail message (either in the display pane or the Netscape Message window) and select the right-hand button, you have the following options available:

- Reply to Sender
- Reply to Sender and All Recipients
- Forward
- Forward Quoted
- Add to Address Book
- File Message
- Delete Message
- Save Message
- Print Message

When you're selecting a folder in the Message Center window, the right-hand mouse button will give you the following menu options:

- Open Folder
- Open Folder in New Window
- New Folder
- Delete Folder
- Rename Folder
- Compress Folder
- New Message
- Search Messages
- Folder Properties

MACINTOSH

The options listed here are accessed with the Macintosh's only mouse button.

SECURITY AND E-MAIL

Keeping electronic mail private is a critical issue for many, many e-mail users, particularly in business situations. The reasons for this are basic and obvious.

Previous versions of Netscape mail products lacked serious security features, but Netscape Messenger has full, up-to-date security that encrypts messages based on the Secure Multipurpose Internet Mail Extensions or S/MIME. In this section, we'll delve into Messenger's native security provisions pretty thoroughly.

Netscape Messenger Security

A good clue to the importance that Netscape Communications attaches to security in Communicator is the Security icon on the Navigator and Messenger toolbars. It brings up the Security Advisor, a dialog box with lots of sophisticated settings. These may appear intimidating, but they add up to fairly iron-clad security. We'll sort them out, but first we need some background on the technology of encryption.

Public-Key/Private-Key Encryption

While there are many ways to encrypt text, the overwhelming choice for working in a public environment like the Internet is a scheme known as Public-Key/Private-Key encryption, invented by three MIT professors in the mid-1970s. We don't need to understand the technique in great detail, just capture the essentials.

Each user of this technology has two *encryption keys* (formulas or algorithms) that transform text into structured gibberish and back again into readable text. The key-holder actually distributes the Public key to his or her e-mail correspondents. When the correspondent wishes to send a secure communication to the key-holder, that public key is used to encrypt the message. But only the *private key*, the one the key-holder never gives out to anyone, can decrypt a message that was encrypted with the public key. In this way, it's impossible for anyone but the intended recipient to read a public/private-keyed message.

Certificates and Certification Authorities

So, how do you get your encryption keys? You go to a "trusted" certification authority or CA—an organization that the world has acknowledged as honest, incorruptible, and technologically sound—and apply for a digital certificate or digital ID.

The primary certification authority is VeriSign, Inc.; it issues certificates in four classes. Class 1 is for individuals, and you don't have to prove much of anything about who you are (aside from having an e-mail address) to get it. Higher certification classes, which are available for individuals and organizations, require increasing levels of verification (from third parties) of the certificate-holder's identity. VeriSign does, of course, charge fees for its services. We'll profile the process of getting a certificate a bit later on.

Digital IDs and Signatures

A VeriSign certificate is also known as a *digital ID*—pretty much what it sounds like. It contains some basic information about you—your name, e-mail address, what browser you use, and so forth—and comes with both a public and a private encryption key. You install the ID in your Netscape Communicator's Security module, which stores and manages it as well as sending your public key to e-mail correspondents whenever you attach your *digital signature* to your messages. The digital signature is an encrypted string created by your *private* key—and therefore capable of being decrypted only by your public key—that serves in the same quasi-legal capacity as your written signature, verifying that the communication is indeed from you.

The Netscape Communicator Security Advisor

Communicator 4 has a robust security module that stores and manages your encryption keys and those of others, and gives you some control over how Communicator's various security features are implemented.

To display the Security Advisor, use one of the following methods:

- Click the **Security** icon on the Communicator or Messenger toolbar.

- Select **Security Info** from the Communicator menu on any screen.

- Click the small icon in the lower left-hand corner of the Communicator or Messenger screen.

In all three cases, the Security dialog box will appear, showing the security information associated with the message (or Web page) you're currently viewing (see Figure 9.9). If there is no security information, it tells you that, too.

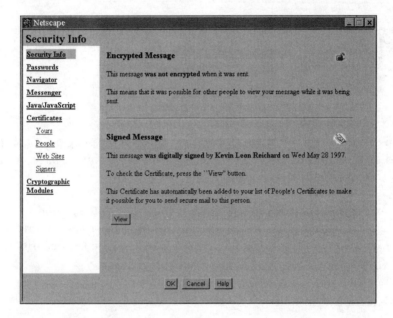

Figure 9.9 *Netscape Communicator's main Security screen.*

Of the seven subject tabs along the left-hand side of the main Security screen, only three are of interest to us here: Passwords, Messenger, and Certificates. We'll discuss the remainder in Chapter 18.

The Passwords Page

If you plan to use Messenger's security features, this page is where you go to set up and manage a password that verifies your right to use certificates stored in Communicator's Security module. Passwords aren't absolutely required (unless you share your computer system with another Messenger e-mail user), but they're an excellent idea.

Setting Up a Password

To establish a password, click the button labeled **Change Password**. This brings up a screen with fields for your old password, your new password, and a confirmation of your new password. If you're setting up a password for the first time, you can leave the Enter your old password field blank. Type in your password in the New Password field (the longer your password is and the less like any words obviously associated with you, the more secure it is); then retype it in the box below and click **OK**. That's all there is to it.

NOTE Don't forget your password. If you do, you'll lose access to all the digital certificates you've registered with Communicator. There's absolutely no way to get around this.

The Messenger Page

On this page you can make several settings that tell Messenger how you want your digital certificate used. The three options on the main page are pretty much self-explanatory:

- **Encrypt mail messages, when it is possible** (that is, when you have a certificate and you're corresponding with those whom you've entrusted with your public key *and* whose public key Security Advisor has on file)

- **Sign mail messages, when it is possible** (that is, when you have a valid certificate installed)

- **Sign discussion (news) messages, when it is possible** (that is, when you have a valid certificate installed)

To activate any of these choices, simply click the appropriate check box.

You also get to specify which of your certificates Messenger should use in signing and encrypting your messages (assuming you have more than one).

At the bottom of the page, under the heading **Advanced S/MIME Configuration**, is a button that lets you enable or disable two S/MIME ciphers. Unless you know you have an excellent reason to alter these settings, we suggest that you leave them alone.

The Certificates Page

Here you'll find a succinct explanation of certificates and their use, along with pointers to four subordinate pages: Yours, People, Web sites, and Signers. These pages list certificates belonging to you, certificates received from people and organizations you communicate with, certificates from secure Web sites, and certificates from entities that Netscape Communications has accepted as *valid signers* (that is, "trusted organizations") and *Certificate Authorities* (issuers of certificates). The Signers page is designed to become an editable list of Certificate Authorities *you* trust.

The Yours page is typical, and the one you'll be most concerned with. It contains a list of certificates you've installed and has buttons that let you **View, Verify, Delete,** or **Export** these certificates. These functions are fairly straightforward. Here are brief explanations:

- **View** lets you read the contents of your certificate, which includes information such as the issuer, the term of the certificate's validity, a serial number, and a certificate "fingerprint."

- **Verify** contacts the issuing authority to determine if the certificate is currently registered and valid.

- **Delete**, of course, lets you remove the certificate from your system—if it's expired, for example.

- **Export** lets you move a copy of the certificate to a backup directory for safekeeping, or to another system.

How to Get a Digital Certificate

At the bottom of the Yours page is a button labeled **Get a Certificate**. Click this button and (assuming you're connected to the Internet) you'll be taken to a Web page from which you can access several Certification Authorities (CAs). At the top of the list is VeriSign, Inc., the very first CA and the principal issuer of certificates for the United States and North America.

Navigate to VeriSign's Digital ID Center and apply for a Class 1 individual ID. You'll supply your name, address, e-mail address (optional but recommended), and a bit of other personal information, be asked to accept a user agreement, then submit your application. In a few minutes you'll receive an e-mail containing a personal identification number (PIN) and instructions for retrieving your certificate.

As mentioned above, it's a good idea to install a password in the Passwords page of Netscape's security module. It's an easier and more reliable way to identify yourself to the system during the certificate download and installation process than typing out the cryptic 16-character PIN.

Exchanging and Using Certificates

You may be wondering how certificates get distributed to those who want to carry on secure e-mail correspondence. It's simple, though not necessarily obvious. When you digitally sign a message, which you can do whenever you like assuming you have a valid certificate installed, your digital signature file carries a copy of your public key. When your correspondent receives your message, Messenger (or another S/MIME-compliant mail program) stores that key. For example, when correspondents digitally sign their messages to you, their keys are automatically stored in Security Advisor—on the People page— and you can view them there.

Once two parties have each other's certificates (and hence each other's public keys), they can exchange secure messages using S/MIME.

N O T E   To digitally sign a message, click the **Message Sending Options** tab in the addressing area of the Composition window and click the **Signed** check box. To encrypt a message, click the **Encrypted** check box. Alternatively, you can set signing and/or encryption as a default, as discussed above in the section on "The Messenger Page."

E-MAILING TO LINKS ON THE WEB

Many Web pages contain one or more links to the person administering the site, such as *webmaster@bigcompany.com,* or perhaps a more general invitation to correspondence like Send us your comments . When you click on one of these links, up pops the now-familiar Composition window with the e-mail address of the linked person or organization already in place in the To: field. We clicked the link on the page contained in the line If you like, you can send me mail, as shown in Figure 9.10.

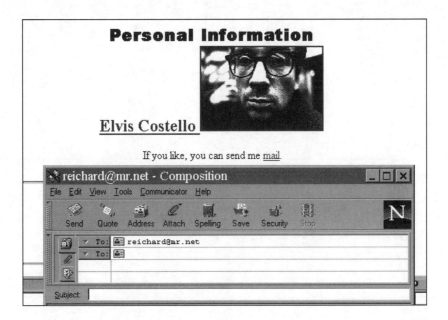

Figure 9.10 *Mailing to a link in Netscape Navigator.*

At this point the full power of Messenger's mailing capabilities are at your disposal. Just type your message as usual and click the **Send** button. That's all there is to it.

SUMMARY

This chapter covered the techniques for configuring your electronic mail, including address books and security tools.

In the next chapter, we'll shift our focus to multimedia and delve into the wonders of plug-ins.

SECTION 4

Multimedia

What's the fun of working on the Internet without having access to the whiz-bang features that make it so exciting? In this section, you'll learn about the bells and whistles that make the Web come alive.

Chapter 10 covers RealPlayer, the audio and video player from Progressive Networks that's becoming the standard for audio and video on the Internet. Although RealPlayer doesn't come with Netscape Communicator, we strongly recommend that you get down and download it—if you seek out only one plug-in, make it RealPlayer.

Chapter 11 lists other plug-ins, software programs that extend Communicator's capabilities and enhance your Internet experiences.

Chapter 12 covers Netcaster, Netscape's initial foray into the exciting world of push technology.

Audio and Video with RealPlayer

Audio and video are the sizzle that makes the World Wide Web so much fun. In this chapter, we'll cover RealPlayer, the plug-in from Progressive Networks that brings streaming audio and video to your desktop. Some of the topics include:

- Video and audio on the Web
- Downloading RealPlayer
- Playing audio
- Viewing video
- RealPlayer and the Macintosh

VIDEO AND AUDIO ON THE WEB

So far you've spent your time focusing on text-based Internet offerings, such as Web pages and FTP files. Now it's time to spend some time on the bells and whistles associated with the Internet and the World Wide Web. We'll begin with RealPlayer, the audio and video plug-in from Progressive Networks.

What's a plug-in? Basically, a plug-in is a piece of optional software that extends the capabilities of Netscape Communicator—and more specifically, Netscape Navigator. Remember that Netscape Communicator is really at its core a software tool for handling files; these files happen to be transmitted via the Internet in the form of Web pages, mail messages, and more.

Netscape Communicator isn't set up to handle every kind of file found on the Internet, however. So there exists a need for *plug-ins*, software programs designed to handle those files that Netscape can't. Some of these are audio and video files, while other are proprietary files used in very specific circumstances. (You'll learn about other plug-ins in Chapter 11.)

Netscape Communicator comes with some tools that handle audio and video files. However, you'll get the best results if you update to the newest version of RealPlayer software from Progressive Networks, a tool that plays RealAudio sound files and RealVideo video files. While you can use RealPlayer with a relatively slow Internet connection (i.e., 14.4Kbps), you're better off using RealPlayer with at least a 28.8Kbps connection. RealPlayer handles streaming audio and video, which means that the sound and video are played as they're received via the Internet. (By contrast, older sound systems needed to download an entire file before playing it.) The sound quality of RealPlayer keeps improving with each release, but the video is still choppy compared to broadcast-quality video. (The recommendation here is to avoid the video unless you have a faster connection to the Internet, such as a T1 or ISDN line.) Audio is transmitted either in mono or stereo.

NOTE   To use RealPlayer—as well as the other audio and video tools discussed in this chapter and the following chapter—you need to have a sound card installed on your computer and configured with your operating system. Installing and configuring a sound card is beyond the boundaries of this book; check your system documentation and your operating-system documentation for more information.

GETTING REALPLAYER

Grabbing RealPlayer is not complicated; simply enter the following address:

> *http://www.real.com*

and connect to the Progressive Networks home page. From there, you will be given directions on downloading and installing RealPlayer. We'll go through the installation step here for a Windows 95/Windows NT setup, although the steps for other operating systems (i.e., Macintosh, Linux) will be very similar.

When you request a download of RealPlayer, Netscape Navigator will prompt you for a location for the installation file, the default being your desktop. Go ahead and save the file to your desktop.

NOTE   At the time this book was written, Progressive Networks offered two versions of RealPlayer: a free version and a low-cost ($29.95) commercial version. We're going to cover the free version here, but that doesn't mean that you should buy the commercial version.

After downloading the RealPlayer software, you'll see a new icon and filename on your desktop (at the time this book was written, the file was **rp32_40.exe**). After closing down Netscape Communicator, click on this icon to begin the installation process.

There's nothing complicated about the installation; just follow the directions. You'll be asked if you want to delete the current RealAudio player that ships as part of Netscape Communicator; your answer should be yes.

Configuring RealPlayer

After you install RealPlayer, Netscape Communicator launches automatically, connecting you with a Progressive Networks Web site that lists destination sites, a procedure akin to setting the buttons on a car radio. (Though the site is bound to be a little different when you install RealPlayer, we're showing you in Figure 10.1 the page that was current when this book was written.) You can choose one Web site from each of the categories, and when RealPlayer is launched, their logos will appear in the interface (as shown in Figure 10.2). Audio sites are listed in the regular text, while video sites are highlighted in green.

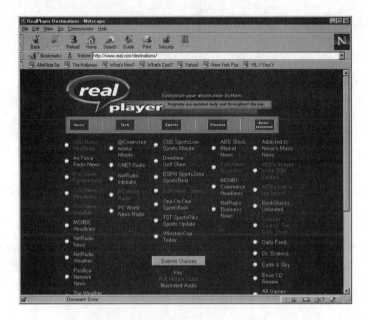

Figure 10.1 *Selecting destination sites for RealPlayer.*

Figure 10.2 *The RealPlayer interface.*

You can launch RealPlayer directly, but most of the time you'll let Netscape Navigator launch RealPlayer directly when it runs across a RealAudio or RealVideo file.

Where to Find Video and Audio

You may randomly come across RealAudio and RealVideo files as you meander through the Internet, but your bet best is to peruse one of the sites that specialize in RealAudio and RealVideo.

A good place to start is the Progressive Networks Web site at *http://www.real.com*, which contains links to other Web sites that feature RealAudio and RealVideo (like NBC, ABC, PBS, Pacifica News, and more). One of the more popular destinations is Daily Briefing (*http://www.dailybriefing.com/*), a service of Timecast that presents daily clips from popular news services (most of which you ran across when you configured the destination buttons on your RealPlayer software). One of the daily briefings involves a clip from the Weather Channel, as shown in Figure 10.3. The representation of the image in Figure 10.3 is actually fairly accurate, as the video quality on a 28.8Kbps line is less than stunning.

Figure 10.3 *The Weather Channel via RealVideo.*

The Timecast site itself (*http://www.timecast.com*) is also a valuable guide to live audio and video, including concerts and other events.

The first time you run across a RealAudio or RealVideo file, Netscape Navigator will ask you if you want to save the file to disk or play it. This is a security precaution that has nothing to do with the RealPlayer software; Netscape Navigator will ask you about this every time you run across a new file type. When prompted, tell Netscape Navigator that you always want to play the file, and not to ask you about whether or not to play it in the future.

Another good place to look for audio and video is the WebActive Web site (*http://www.webactive.com*), a politically ambitious "liberal" site created and managed by Progressive Networks. Among the unique offerings here are briefings from Pacifica Networks and commentaries by former Texas Agriculture Secretary Jim Hightower and comedian Will Durst.

Finally, there's AudioNet (*http://www.audionet.com*), which provides a central point to hundreds of radio stations across the world, ranging from zydeco music from New Orleans to Greek news from a Canadian radio station.

RealPlayer and Macintosh RAM

Sometimes you'll run out of memory when you use the RealPlayer software. Windows 95 and Windows NT are fairly reliable about telling you that you're running out of RAM and should close some applications, but the Macintosh OS isn't as good. Usually you will receive a message from MacOS that tells you you're out of RAM, but sometimes RealPlayer just refuses to play.

In these cases, you have a few choices in trying to solve the problem. The first obvious choice is to close down some applications before running RealPlayer. If this isn't possible, then you should launch RealPlayer *before* trying to play streaming audio.

If these suggestions don't work, you can do what Macintosh users have been doing for years: remove system extensions or INITs that eat up huge chunks of memory.

MACINTOSH

You do need a powerful Macintosh to use RealPlayer, unfortunately. If you have an older Mac, such as a Mac IIsi, Mac LC, or Mac II, you can't use RealPlayer.

Summary

This chapter covers downloading and installing RealPlayer, the audio and video software from Progressive Networks.

In the next chapter, you'll learn about other plug-ins that can extend your Netscape Communicator capabilities.

## CHAPTER 11

Other Netscape Plug-Ins

Many other computer-software manufacturers have released their own plug-ins to extend Netscape Communicator's capabilities. In this chapter, we'll cover these plug-ins, which fall into the following categories:

- Virtual reality
- Formatted pages
- Multimedia
- Audio
- Remote computing
- Miscellaneous

Plugging More into Netscape Communicator

RealAudio isn't the only plug-in available for Netscape Communicator. In this chapter we list other plug-ins available via the Internet, organized by type. In addition to the download site, we also list the operating-system platforms that the plug-ins run on. Since they tend to have different installation techniques, be sure to read the supporting documentation before downloading them. Not all of these plug-ins are free of charge; we note when they require a payment.

We list the plug-ins according to their different categories.

Virtual-Reality Plug-Ins

These plug-ins allow users to view Web pages formatted using the Virtual Reality Modeling Language (VRML) from within the Netscape Web browser. VRML was once the hot trend in the computer world (and still has its set of admirers), but interest has cooled somewhat. Still, as you surf the Web, you'll probably find some neat sites that use VRML formatting, and it's in these cases where you'll need a plug-in.

Flying Carpet

AccelGraphics

http://www.accelgraphics.com/prod06.htm

Windows 95, Windows NT 4.0 and 3.51

Cost: $49 (trial version available at no charge)

Flying Carpet uses OpenGL for reading VRML files, as well as supporting a proprietary data format called Real Time Binary (RTB).

Hotsauce

Apple Computer

http://mcf.research.apple.com/index.html

Windows 95, Windows NT, Macintosh

Cost: Free

Hotsauce is the Apple Computer version of virtual reality, using three-dimensional graphics to navigate through enabled Web sites (of which there are precious few).

Passport

Black Sun Interactive

http://ww3.blacksun.com/download/index.html

Windows 95, Windows NT

Cost: Free

Passport is a multiuser VRML plug-in that can be used with the Black Sun VRML server or other VRML tools.

Viscape

Superscape

http://www.superscape.com/download/viscape/index.htm

Windows 95, Windows NT, Windows 3.x

Cost: Free

Viscape displays Web pages formatted in virtual reality.

VR Scout

Chaco Communications

http://www.chaco.com/vrscout/index.html

Windows 95, Windows NT, Windows 3.x

Cost: Free

VR Scout is a VRML plug-in.

Wirl

VREAM

http://www.vream.com/3dl1.html

Windows 95, Windows NT

Cost: Free

Wirl displays files displayed using VRML technology.

WorldView

Intervista

http://www.intervista.com/download/index.html

Windows 95, Windows NT

Cost: Free

WorldView displays VRML files.

FORMATTED-PAGE PLUG-INS

There are a host of formats available for documents on the Internet; HTML is merely one of several. These plug-ins allow you to display these formatted pages from within Netscape Navigator.

Amber Acrobat Reader

Adobe Systems

http://www.adobe.com/prodindex/acrobat/readstep.html

Windows 95, Windows NT, Windows 3.x, Macintosh, Linux, UNIX (SunOS, Solaris, IRIX, HP-UX), DOS, and OS/2

Cost: Free

Adobe Acrobat Reader manages PDF files created with Adobe Acrobat and Acrobat Capture. PDF files are formatted with text, fonts, and images. Many larger media organizations, such as *The New York Times*, use PDF formatting for their Web content, and many other companies format their documentation in PDF format. As such, the Acrobat Reader might be the first plug-in you seek.

AnimaFlex

RubberFlex Software

http://www.rubberflex.com/getplug.htm

Windows 95, Windows NT, Windows 3.x, Macintosh

Cost: Free

The AnimaFlex plug-in displays graphic animations in the AnimaFlex and GIF formats.

ASAP WebShow

Software Publishing Corp.

http://www.spco.com

Windows 95, Windows NT

Cost: Free

The ASAP WebShow plug-in allows users to view, download, and print Web presentations created with WordPower presentation software.

Calendar Quick

Logic Pulse Software

http://www.logicpulse.com/dlcalplugin.htm

Windows 95, Windows NT, Windows 3.x

Cost: Free

The Calendar Quick Plugin displays files created with Calendar Quick embedded in a Web page.

Chemscape Chime

MDL Information Systems

http://www.mdli.com/chemscape/chime/download.html

Windows 95, Windows NT, Macintosh, Windows 3.x, IRIX

Cost: Free

Chemscape Chime displays chemical information directly on an HTML page, supporting the Molfile, Rxnfile, Brookhaven Protein Databank (PDB) formats, and more.

CMX Viewer

Corel

http://www.corel.com/corelcmx/INDEX.HTM

Windows 95, Windows NT

Cost: Free

The CMX viewer displays CMX-formatted files. This is a format used by Corel in its line of products.

CommonGround Viewer

Hummingbird Communications

http://www.hummingbird.com/cg/cgplugin.htm

Windows 95, Windows NT, Macintosh

Cost: Free

This viewer displays documents formatted with CommonGround, a format that maintains formatting no matter where the document is displayed.

Envoy

Tumbleweed Software

http://www.tumbleweed.com/plugin.htm

Windows 95, Windows NT, Windows 3.x, Macintosh

Cost: Free

The Envoy plug-in displays standalone Envoy documents as well as Envoy documents embedded in HTML pages.

Formula One/Net

Visual Components

http://www.visualcomp.com/f1net/download.htm

Windows 95, Windows NT, Windows 3.x

Cost: Free

Formula One/Net displays embedded spreadsheets.

Fractal Viewer

Iterated Systems

http://www.iterated.com/fractalviewer/

Windows 95, Windows NT, Macintosh

Cost: Free

The 32-bit Fractal Viewer displays fractal images from within Netscape Communicator.

Internet Plug-In

CE Engines

http://www.cengines.com/products/products.htm

Windows 95, Windows NT

Cost: Free

This plug-in displays WIF files directly from your browser. WIF files are high-quality, ultracompressed files.

IPIX Viewer

IPIX

http://www.ipix.com/home/home.htm

Windows 95, Windows NT

Cost: Free

The IPIX viewer displays IPIX pictures: interactive, spherical images, offering users a complete field of view, from earth to sky, floor to ceiling, horizon to horizon.

Jutvision

Visdyn

http://www.visdyn.com/tv/static/products.html

Windows 95, Windows NT

Cost: Free

The Jutvision plug-in displays Jutvision scenes on the Web.

Lightning Strike

Infinitop

http://www.infinop.com/nhtml/extvwr_pick.shtml

Cost: Free

Windows 3.1, Windows 95, Windows NT, Macintosh, Digital UNIX, Solaris

The Lightning Strike plug-in displays images that were encoded in the Lightning Strike format.

Navigate with Accent

Accent Software International

http://www.accentsoft.com/product/nwaaeng.htm

Windows 95, Windows NT, or Windows 3.x

Cost: $99 (trial version available)

Navigate with Accent displays pages created with Accent Global Author, software used to create multilanguage Web pages and other documents.

PowerBuilder Window Plug-In

Powersoft

http://www.powersoft.com/download/product.html

Windows 95, Windows NT

Cost: Free

This plug-in displays database information created with the PowerBuilder database-management system.

Quick View Plus

Inso Corp.

http://www.inso.com/frames/siteindx/sitepd1a.htm

Windows 3.1, Windows 95, Windows NT

Cost: $59

Quick View Plus displays files formatted in the following formats: Ami/Ami Professional, DEC WPS Plus, DisplayWrite 2-5, Enable, First Choice, Framework, HTML IBM FFT, IBM Revisable Form Text, IBM Writing Assistant, JustWrite, Legacy, MacWrite II, Manuscript, MASS11, Microsoft Rich Text Format, Microsoft Windows Write, Microsoft Word for DOS, Microsoft Word for Macintosh, Microsoft Word for Windows, Microsoft Works, MultiMate, Navy DIF, Nota Bene, Novell Perfect Works for Windows, Office Writer, PC-File, PFS:Write, Professional Write/Professional Write Plus, Q&A/Q&A Write for Windows, Samna Word, SmartWare II, Sprint, Total Word, Volkswriter 3 & 4, Wang PC, WordMARC, WordPerfect, WordPerfect for Macintosh, WordPerfect for Windows, WordStar, WordStar 2000, WordStar for Windows, XyWrite, Lotus 1-2-3, Lotus Symphony,

Microsoft Excel, Microsoft Multiplan, Mosaic Twin, PFS:Professional Plan, Quattro Pro, SmartWare II, SuperCalc 5, VP Planner 3D, Access, DataEase, dBASE, dBXL, FoxBase, Paradox, Personal R:Base, Q&A, R:Base, Reflex, SmartWare II, AutoCAD DXF, Binary Group 3 Fax, GIF, CGM, TIFF, DCX, HPGL, JPEG, Lotus PIC, Lotus Snapshot, PICT, MacPaint, Micrografx Designer and Draw (DRW), OS/2 Bitmap, PCX, TARGA, Windows Bitmap, WordPerfect Graphics (WPG and WPG2), Corel Presentations, Freelance, Harvard Graphics, PowerPoint, and Novell Presentations.

Real World Navigation

Infinite Pictures
http://www.smoothmove.com/free/mirror_downloads.html
Windows 95, Windows NT
Cost: Free
The Real World Navigation plug-in displays images formatted with the SmoothMove technology, used to create panoramic and fluid-motion graphics files and images.

Vdraft Internet Tools

SoftSource
http://www.softsource.com/plugins/plugins.html
Windows 95, Windows NT
Cost: Free
These plug-ins display AutoCAD drawing and DXF files, as well as SVF files.

VHSB Viewer

Paragraph International
http://www.paragraph.com/vhsb/viewer/viewerlicense.htm
Windows 95, Windows NT, Windows 3.x, Macintosh
Cost: Free
The VHSB viewer displays house plans created with the Virtual Home Space Builder design software.

Watermark Webseries Viewer

Filenet

http://www.filenet.com/watermark/plugin/

Windows 95, Windows NT

Cost: Free

The Webseries Viewer displays TIFF images as well as images and documents stored on a Watermark Enterprise Image Server.

MULTIMEDIA PLUG-INS

Many multimedia producers have formatted their Web pages using a combination of sound, text, animations, and more. These plug-ins are used to display these multimedia presentations.

Astound Web Player (AWP)

Astound

http://www.astoundinc.com/awp/awp.html

Windows 95, Windows NT

Cost: Free

The Astound Web Player (AWP) displays Astound and Studio M multimedia creations directly from a Web page. Astound is used to create multimedia presentations that typically include animation, sound, and graphics.

CineWeb

Digigami

http://www.digigami.com/cineweb/

Windows 3.x, Windows 95, Windows NT

Cost: $29.95

CineWeb displays QuickTime, Video for Windows, MPEG, and Autodesk AnimatorX animations.

ClearVideo

Iterated Systems

http://www.iterated.com/clearvideo/decoder/info/cp_fswin.htm

Windows 95, Windows NT

Cost: Free

ClearVideo displays video images—AVI, QuickTime, and more—in real time.

Crescendo

Live Update

http://www.liveupdate.com/dl.html

Windows 95, Windows NT, Macintosh

Cost: Free

Crescendo plays MIDI files from the World Wide Web.

Enliven Viewer

Narrative Communications

http://www.narrative.com/download.htm

Windows 95, Windows NT 4

Cost: Free

The Enliven Viewer displays multimedia presentations created with Enlighten Producer software.

mBED Plug-In

MBED

http://www.mbed.com/noembed/download.html

Windows 95, Windows NT, Macintosh, Windows 3.x

Cost: Free

The mBED plug-in displays multimedia presentations created with mBED Interactor.

NET TOOB Stream

Duplexx Software

http://www.duplexx.com/dl_nt.html

Windows 3.x, Windows 95, Windows NT

Cost: Free

The NET TOOB Stream plug-in plays streaming or downloaded MPEG, AVI, MOV, FLC/FLI, WAV, MID, and SND video and audio files.

NetMC Player

NetMC-NEC

http://netmc1.neclab.com/netmc/plugin/dnplug.html

Windows 95, Windows NT

Cost: Free

The NetMC Player displays multimedia files created with the NetMC Multimedia Authoring Tool.

Olivr Viewer

Olivr

http://www.olivr.com/download/

Windows 95, Windows NT, Macintosh

Cost: Free

The Olivr plug-in displays movies created in the streaming Interactive Image Format format.

PointPlus

Net-Scene

http://www.net-scene.com/

Windows 95, Windows NT, Windows 3.x

Cost: Free

The PointPlus plug-in plays PowerPoint 7.0 presentations and RealAudio files.

Roadster

Allegiant Technologies

http://www.allegiant.com/roadster

Windows 95, Windows NT, Macintosh

Cost: Free

Roadster displays presentations created in Supercard, a scripting hypertext language that combines various data formats—graphics, text, sound, animations and QuickTime movies—into presentations.

Shockwave

Macromedia

http://www.macromedia.com

Windows 95, Windows NT, Macintosh

Cost: Free

The Shockwave plays multimedia presentations created with three Macromedia products: Flash, Director, or Authorware. It supports streaming input.

Surround Video Plug-in for Netscape

Black Diamond

http://www.bdiamond.com/Support/netscape.htm

Windows 95, Windows NT, Macintosh

Cost: Free

The Surround Video Plug-in for Netscape displays high-resolution images created with Surround Video. These images usually are panoramic, displaying images in 360°.

VDOLive Player

VDOnet

http://www.vdolive.com/

Windows 95, Windows NT

Cost: Free

The VDOLive player plays VDOLive clips and movies.

VivoActive Player

Vivo Software Inc.

http://www.vivo.com/dldv2/cgi-bin/dldform.cgi

Windows 95, Windows NT, Windows 3.x, Macintosh

Cost: Free

The VivoActive Player plays streaming video from the Internet.

Web Theatre

VXtreme

http://www.vxtreme.com/plugin.html

Windows 95, Windows NT

Cost: Free

The Web Theatre player plays streaming video from the Web.

WebXpresso

DataViews Corp.

http://www.dvcorp.com/

Cost: Free

Windows 95, Windows NT, UNIX (Solaris 2.5, SGI 6.2, HP-UX 10.20)

WebXpresso is used to create two- and three-dimensional Web presentations, and this plug-in displays them.

AUDIO PLAYERS

RealAudio isn't the only plug-in that supports streaming audio broadcasts on the Web. Some alternatives follow.

Beatnik

Headspace

http://www.headspace.com/

Windows 95, Windows NT

Cost: Free

This plug-in plays RMF-formatted sound files that can be found on Web sites. The Beatnik plug-in supports many different music and audio file formats and can play RMF, MIDI, MOD, AIFF, WAV, and AU files.

EchoCast

Echo

http://www.echospeech.com/

Windows 3.x, Windows 95, Windows NT, Macintosh

Cost: Free

The EchoCast plug-in plays audio compressed using Echo encoding.

Koan

Sseyo

http://www.sseyo.com/browser.html

Windows 95, Windows NT, Macintosh

Cost: Free

The Koan plug-in plays music from the SSEYO Koan Music Engine (SKME).

MOD Plugin

Olivier Lapicque

http://www.castlex.com/modplug/modplug.html

Windows 95, Windows NT, Macintosh

Cost: Free

The MOD plug-in plays MOD files that have been embedded in Web pages as background music.

StreamWorks Player

Xing Technology

http://www.xingtech.com/products/sw_player.html

Windows 95, Windows NT, Windows 3.x, Macintosh, UNIX

Cost: Free

StreamWorks plays audio and video files encoded with the StreamWorks encoder.

True Speech Player

DSP Group

http://www.dspg.com/player/main.htm

Windows 3.x, Windows 95, Windows NT, Macintosh, Power Macintosh

Cost: Free

The True Speech Player plays audio files encoded using DSP's True Speech encoding technology.

ToolVox

Voxware

http://www.voxware.com/

Windows 95, Windows 3.1, Solaris 2.5, IRIX, Macintosh, HP-UX

Cost: Free

The ToolVox player plays audio files encoded using the ToolVox Encoder.

Webtracks

Wildcat Canyon Software

http://www.wildcat.com/Pages/WebTracksDownload.htm

Windows 95, Windows NT, Macintosh

Cost: Free

Webtracks plays music files embedded in Web pages.

REMOTE-COMPUTING PLUG-INS

The Internet allows you to grab documents from any site connected to the Internet. However, some tools allow you to perform tasks remotely across the Internet, just as though you were sitting down at the remote machine.

Carbon Copy/Net

Microcom

http://www.microcom.com/

Windows 95, Windows NT

Cost: Free

Carbon Copy/Net lets you remotely control another PC over the Internet, used for remote access, remote support, collaboration, remote software demonstrations and more.

Look@Me

Farrallon

http://www.farallon.com/www/look/ldownload.html

Windows 95, Windows NT, Macintosh

Cost: Free

Look@Me displays another user's screen anywhere in the world in real time, so long as both of you are running Look@Me.

WinFrame

Citrix Systems

http://www.citrix.com/plugin.htm

Windows NT, Windows 95, Windows 3.x

Cost: Free

WinFrame allows Netscape users to view remote computing sessions across the Internet.

MISCELLANEOUS PLUG-INS

Some of these plug-ins just don't fit in the preceding categories. They appear next.

AboutPeople

Now Software

http://www.nowsoft.com/plugins/plugins.html

Windows 95, Windows NT, Macintosh

Cost: Free

AboutPeople displays address books published by Now Up-to-Date Web Publisher, including synchronization with PalmPilot users.

AboutTime

Now Software

http://www.nowsoft.com/plugins/plugins.html

Windows 95, Windows NT, Macintosh

Cost: Free

AboutTime displays calendars published by Now Up-to-Date Web Publisher, including synchronization with PalmPilot users.

AnySearch

PrivNet

http://www.privnet.com/

Windows 95, Windows NT, Macintosh

Cost: Free

AnySearch adds a new button and text-entry field to Netscape's Directory bar, providing instant access to search engines on the Internet.

Earth Time

Starfish Software

http://starweb.starfishsoftware.com/products/et/get_earth.html

Windows 95, Windows NT

Cost: $19.95

EarthTime displays the local time in up to eight cities around the world.

Ichat Chat

Ichat

http://www.ichat.com/products/chat_client.html

Windows 3.1, Windows 95, Windows NT, Macintosh, Power Macintosh, UNIX

Cost: Free

Ichat is a plug-in that allows users to chat via chat rooms on the Internet.

Intermind Communicator

Intermind

http://www.intermind.com/prod_demo/imc.html

Windows 95, Windows NT, Macintosh, UNIX

Cost: Free

Intermind Communicator uses push technology that allows users to be notified of changes in subscription Web sites.

Plugsy

Digigami

http://www.digigami.com/plugsy/index.html

Windows 95, Windows NT

Cost: $29.95

Plugsy is a Netscape plug-in that manages other plug-ins.

Tcl Plugin

Sun Microsystems

http://sunscript.sun.com/products

Windows 95, Windows NT, Solaris for SPARC, Solaris for Intel, SunOS, Macintosh, Linux, IRIX, HP/UX 9.0, OSF/1 (Digital Unix)

Cost: Free

The Tcl Plugin runs embedded Tcl and Tk applications in a Web page and displays Tk user interfaces in windows on Web pages.

ViruSafe

EliaShim

http://www.eliashim.com/

Windows 95, Windows NT

Cost: Free

ViruSafe scans downloaded files for viruses.

## CHAPTER 12

Push Me, Pull You

Push technology has been one of the hottest topics surrounding the Internet in the last year. Netscape Communicator has an optional software add-on called *Netcaster* that adds push capabilities to Netscape Communicator. Some of the topics in this chapter include:

- Grabbing Netcaster
- Launching Netcaster
- Subscribing to channels
- Working with channels
- Looking for channels

PUSH TECHNOLOGY: DIRECT TO YOU

If you've followed the Internet at all in the last year, you've run across many references to *push technology*, where information is delivered directly to your desktop. Some say that it's the future of the Internet, while others say that it's a dangerous waste of bandwidth—so much so that some corporations are preventing push technology from coming into their corporate Internet connections.

Such debates are endemic to the Internet, of course, and won't be settled any time soon. In the meantime, you can sample the wares of push technology in Netscape Communicator, via Netcaster.

How does push technology work? Instead of your asking a Web site for a document (either a Web page or a mail message), you tell the Web site that your desktop is available to receive messages. At preordained times, your desktop is updated with messages from the push site.

To reconcile the preceding explanation to the prevailing terminology (lest you think that any aspect of the Internet might be jargon-free), Netcaster sets up subscriptions to *channels*. These channels broadcast content to your desktop, at intervals that you set. These channels are akin to cable channels in that they specialize in various topics (as we'll see later when we cover Netcaster installation). For example, Netscape Communications has its own channel covering Netscape-related topics (see Figure 12.1).

The desktop shown in Figure 12.1 takes up the full screen; in Netscape parlance, this is the *webtop*. It's always in the background. You can choose between making it visible or hidden.

Netcaster isn't a core part of Netscape Communicator's standard edition. You'll need to manually grab Netcaster from the Web, as you'll see as we begin the installation and configuration process.

WARNING

Netcaster eats up a lot of RAM—*a lot*. The version we tested in the course of writing this book drained our system RAM—all 32 MB worth—and frequently slowed our Pentium Pro processor to a crawl.

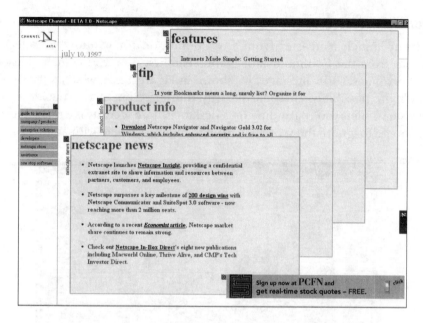

Figure 12.1 *The Netscape channel.*

Grabbing Netcaster

With the advent of Netscape Communicator, Netscape Communications instituted a "smart updates" program that updates specific portions of Netscape Communicator as needed. When this book was written, the URL for grabbing Netcaster was:

http://home.netscape.com/download/smart_update.html?

although it may not be the same when you get around to grabbing Netcaster. (In other words, you may have to poke around the Netscape Web site before you actually find Netcaster.)

The Smart Update program will list a set of programs that are available for instant download and installation. From this list choose Netcaster. You won't be prompted for any information, but you'll be informed when Netcaster has finished downloading.

Launching Netcaster

You can launch Netcaster from any Communicator window, by selecting *Netcaster* from the Communicator menu. The first time you launch Netcaster triggers some security messages (as shown in Figure 12.2), which tells you that there's the possibility for some security transgressions if you decide to run Netcaster. Unless you're running on a desktop where security is a real issue, you can choose to ignore the security warnings and plow ahead with an installation.

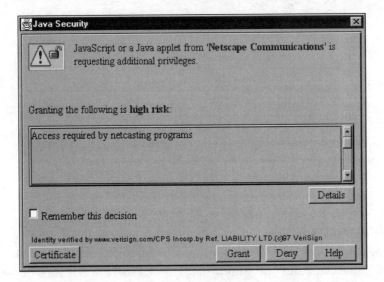

Figure 12.2 *Security messages and Netcaster.*

After the security rigmarole is finished, Netcaster is running on the right-hand side of the screen, as shown in Figure 12.3. (Your list of channels will undoubtedly be different, as more and more vendors are bringing forth channels.)

You can use the selections in the Channel Finder to check out new channels or channels that you've never sampled. In the bottom of the Channel Finder window is a listing of the channels that you've subscribed to. The gray areas of the Channel Finder window are those areas that can be clicked on to start new actions. For instance, you can click on **My Channels** to get a listing of the channels that you've subscribed to. If you have subscribed to the channel as a webtop, there will be a small blue indicator next to the site.

Of course, we're early enough in the process that you've not yet subscribed to any channels. To subscribe to a channel, select the listing from the top of the Channel Finder window. A new Netscape window will appear, showing the channel along with a button that subscribes you to the channel. The window that subscribes you to ABC News is shown in Figure 12.4.

Figure 12.3 *The Netcaster Channel Finder.*

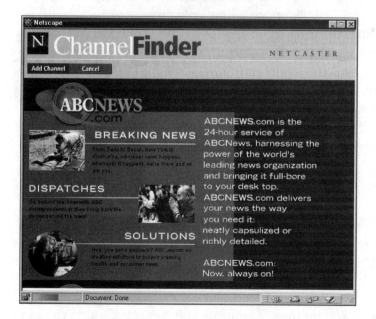

Figure 12.4 *Subscribing to ABCNEWS.com.*

After you've subscribed to the channel, a window appears that allows you to set channel properties, as shown in Figure 12.5.

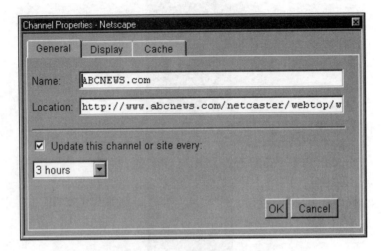

*Figure 12.5 Channel properties for **ABCNEWS.com**.*

There are three tabs in this window: General, Display, and Cache. You won't need to worry about these settings, for the most part. In the General tab—which is shown in Figure 12.5—the only thing to worry about is how often to update the channel. The default for this particular site is three hours, but the setting can be changed for as short a time as 30 minutes or as long a period as a week.

The Display tab toggles the settings between a desktop window and webtop window.

The Cache tab sets how much information associated with this channel to store on your hard disk (the default is 5000KB), and how many levels associated with the Web site (the default is 0).

After you've made your changes, you can select **OK** to save the changes.

Working with Netcaster

Unless you're working on a *really* large screen, you'll find that you don't want the Channel Finder on your screen all the time. To minimize the Channel Finder, click on the tab next to the Channel Finder. The tab will appear on the Channel Finder while Netcaster is minimized.

There are two rows of controls with Netcaster, which you can see at the bottom right of Figure 12.6. The first row has the following commands:

- **Add** is used to add a channel to your personal list of channels.

- **Options** is used to bring up the Properties dialog box associated with channels. This is the same dialog box that was discussed in the previous section and shown in Figure 12.5.

- **Help** opens a help window.

- **Exit** quits Netcaster, but not any open Netscape Communicator windows you might have.

The second row applies to an open webtop and is made up of icons, not words. (Obscure icons, at that.) If you look at Figure 12.6, we'll cover each, from left to right:

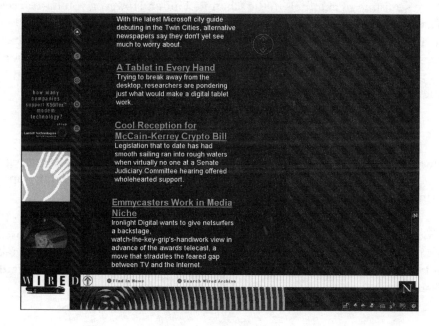

Figure 12.6 Netcaster controls.

- The padlock represents security functions. As mentioned earlier in this chapter, security can be an issue when dealing with Netcaster and push technology. An open padlock means that there are no security measures invoked.

- The left and right arrows take you to back and forward channels, respectively.

- The printer prints the webtop.
- The small screen switches between a webtop and a desktop.
- The up and down arrows brings the webtop to the front of all other windows. If it's already in front of other windows, then this button will bring up the desktop.
- The screen with an *x* closes a webtop.
- The Navigator icon open a Netscape Navigator window.

Looking for Channels

There's a listing of channels in the Channel Finder. However, you have access to a whole host of additional channels available via Marimba's Castanet-based channels. Netcaster is compatible with Castanet, which means you always have access to channels that use Castanet push technology. At the time this book was written, Netcaster could not connect to other push channels offered by other vendors, such as Pointcast.

Working with Channels

Once you've chosen your channels, you'll probably want to check them regularly. You can select a channel from the My Channels list, which will then open a window or display the channel on the webtop.

You'll also want to specify a default channel, unless you want to go through life with the Netscape channel as your default channel. To choose a default, select **Options** from the bottom of the screen, click on the **Layout** tab, and then pick a channel from the pulldown menu underneath **Default Channel**.

SUMMARY

Push technology has the potential to change the Internet, and Netcaster is Netscape's first foray into this trendy area.

In the next chapter, we'll shift gears and begin our coverage of Collabra.

Netscape Collabra

The Internet is rapidly becoming an environment for creating shared experiences, and Netscape Communicator features Netscape Collabra, a workgroup collaboration tool. This section covers Collabra, ranging from internal discussion groups to Usenet newsgroups.

Chapter 13 introduces Netscape Collabra in the context of Usenet newsgroups. The Usenet is the world's largest discussion group, and Collabra is a powerful way of reaching Usenet users around the globe.

Chapter 14 covers advanced Collabra functions, such as configuration and using Collabra for private discussions within an intranet.

Netscape Collabra

If the idea of conversing with people all over the world (or perhaps merely all over your organization) on every imaginable topic intrigues you, Netscape Collabra is a tool you'll want to get to know. It's your window to Usenet news— a global sharing of information, ideas, wisdom, colloquy, and hot air—and Collabra discussions, a scaled-down, private version of the same. In this chapter we'll learn a lot of what there is to know about discussion groups and most of what there is to know about Collabra. Topics include:

- An overview of the Usenet
- Configuring Netscape Collabra
- Reading the news
- Netiquette
- Just the FAQs
- The Usenet and pornography

- Internal Collabra discussions
- Creating new discussion groups

Using the Usenet

You don't hear as much about Internet newsgroups as you once did—they've been largely overshadowed by the Web—but this doesn't mean they're dying out. There are some 15,000 separate public newsgroups functioning over the Internet today. *(News* in this context refers not to the kind of daily information about politics and current events that we get from newspapers or radio or television, but to *postings* in ongoing, threaded public discussions on a bewildering variety of topics that take place over the Internet via the Usenet, also known as *Network News.*) Similar discussions can also take place inside an organization over an intranet using the Netscape Collabra server. In any case, Netscape Collabra is the tool you'll use to access and contribute to discussions. We'll spend a good deal of space in this chapter talking about the public—Usenet—aspect of discussion groups, then home in on the workings of internal Collabra discussions.

What Is the Usenet?

Whenever a lazy journalist needs to quickly poll what is perceived as public opinion (ignoring the fact that Internet users tend to be upper middle class, white, and richer than the average populace), they troll Usenet newsgroups for a sampling of opinions, comments, and postings.

Leaving aside the highly debatable question of how representative it is, the Usenet is unquestionably the biggest and most accessible collection of opinion anywhere in the world. The purpose of this chapter and the following one is to show how to use the news and discussion functionality in Netscape Communicator.

What Is a Newsgroup?

Basically, a *newsgroup* is a collection of *postings* (that is, messages from Internet users) centered around a specific topic. These topics are named in a unique format: the broad category of the topic, followed by a more specific description of the newsgroup. Periods or "dots" (.) separate the elements of the news-group name. The topic can be something as broad as:

```
alt.tennis
```

or something as specific as:

```
alt.barney.dinosaur.die.die.die
```

The *alt* in these newsgroup names is short for *alternative*. Table 13.1 lists the major newsgroup categories.

Table 13.1   *The Major Usenet Newsgroup Categories.*

CATEGORY	SHORT FOR	MEANING
alt	alternative	Topics that have a narrow appeal or fall out of the mainstream (5,666 of them as of this writing). **Alt** newsgroups are unusual in that as few as 10 users may request that an alt newsgroup be created, and that they cover virtually every subject under the sun, ranging from attractive Star Fleet captains (**alt.sex.bald.captains**) to discussions of cooking (**alt.creative-cooking**).
bionet	biology	Various biology-related topics, such as **bionet.chlamydononas** and **bionet.gly-cosci**.
biz	business	Business-related topics, most of which are rather irrelevant (such as discussions of Univel and Zeos, two companies that don't exist anymore).
comp	computer	Computer-related topics are discussed here, both broad (such as **comp.unix.ques-tions**) and specialized (such as **comp.os. linux.answers**). Some **comp** newsgroups are for beginners, but most are meant for advanced computer users. It's hard to envi-

CATEGORY	SHORT FOR	MEANING
		sion many beginning computer users flocking to **comp.os.plan9** or **comp.ivideodisc**. Still, the **comp** newsgroups are the ones most valuable when it comes to useful information, since the vast majority of Usenet users are also dedicated computer users with a vast amount of knowledge to share.
humanities	humanities	Topics for liberal-arts types, covering writers like William Shakespeare, composers like Richard Wagner, and languages like Sanskrit.
news	news	News about the news. These newsgroups range from a general discussion about the Usenet itself (**news.answers**) to a best-of newsgroup (**news.groups**) and a group meant specifically for new users (**news.newusers.questions**).
rec	recreation	This collection of 792 newsgroups covers a wide range of recreational topics, from **rec.arts.marching.drumcorps** to **rec.gardens**. Oddly enough, this is one of the few categories where you can find something approaching intellectual discussion (of a nonscientific kind, anyway) on the Usenet.
sci	science	Science-specific discussions, ranging from the general (such as **sci.agriculture**) to the specific **sci.energy.hydrogen**). Remember that most Usenet users tend to be from the academic and government worlds, so the discussions here can be highly technical. Don't expect a lot of sympathy if you ask the readers of the **sci.agriculture** newsgroup about getting rid of your Creeping Charlie.

CATEGORY	SHORT FOR	MEANING
talk	talk	The Usenet equivalent of talk radio. Be prepared for hordes of true believers in discussions like **talk.abortion** and **talk.atheism**. Be prepared for hordes of *flame wars* (which you'll learn about later in this chapter, in the section called "Netiquette").

In addition to the general range of newsgroups detailed in Table 13.1, there are a host of regional newsgroups, such as **bermuda.business.society** and **mn.politics**. Not all regional newsgroups are carried by all service providers; indeed, some service providers only carry a small portion of the newsgroups, since newsgroups tend to eat up a lot of disk-storage space and aren't read by most people. And if you're getting a news feed from an internal news server, don't be surprised if you have only a very small number of the potential newsgroups available.

What Do Usenet Groups Contain?

As mentioned, a newsgroup can contain just about anything. Take, for example, the entertaining newsgroup named **alt.buddha.short.fat.guy**, hosted by Alf the Poet. The discussion is ostensibly about Buddhism, but it's really a forum for Alf the Poet and others to muse about the vagaries of life and the meanings of spirituality—all done with a distinctly sardonic tone. As the FAQ for the **alt.buddha.short.fat.guy** newsgroup says:

```
Does this newsgroup have a FAQ list?
Yes.


How can I get it?
Apparently, you don't.


Does this newsgroup have a purpose?
Yes.
```

Which is?

See question 2.

Is this an actual newsgroup, or is my system being toyed with?

Yes, and yes.

What is the meaning of alt.buddha.short.fat.guy?

Well, since you asked:

Three lizards sit on a rock in the sun, in a clearing in the forest. A clown comes walking out of the woods wearing a name tag that says "Juan Hand." He stops, drops his baggy pants, and takes a dump. The lizards watch this and then turn to each other. "Dha-a-arma," croaks the first lizard. "Ka-a-arms," croaks the second. The third one opens a book titled "Traveling the Southwest on the Cheep" authored by E. Dupree. A ferret pops up from behind the rock and eats him. Suddenly a tree falls in the forest, making a sound like...

I forgot.

(Also, to meet any annoying legalistic criteria, you're welcome to peruse the legalese regarding the quotation of this material at *http://www.epix.net/~alf/copyrite.html.*)

HOT LINK

FAQ is short for Frequently Asked Questions. You'll learn more about FAQs later in this chapter.

This isn't to say that every newsgroup is full of light ruminations on spirituality. Some very intense discussions occur, as well as some genuine exchanges of information and wisdom. And there are honest requests for information, as this posting from the **rec.arts.wobegon** newsgroup:

```
Subject: Wobegon Q - please help
Date: 2 Mar 1996 19:31:50 GMT
From: susasil@utu.fi (Miia Maarit Susanna Silvennoinen)
Organization: University of Turku, Finland
Newsgroups: rec.arts.wobegon


Hi all,

I am finishing my thesis on translating of literature in
Finland and have as an example the Finnish version of
Keillor's "Lake Wobegon Days". After asking what the Finns
thought about the book, I am still puzzled about one thing
and would like an American perspective. Please answer the
short questions as soon as possible.


1. Do you think that the characters in Lake Wobegon are ordi-
nary Americans? It has been said that the book is "a comic
anatomy of what is small and ordinary and therefore poten-
tially profound and universal in American life."
```

A good rule of thumb for newsgroups is: The more focused and technical the newsgroup, the more valuable will be the information contained within. The Usenet is still most popular in the academic and government worlds, and these folks tend to have a lot of technical knowledge at hand. This knowledge isn't limited to computer-related subjects; indeed, anyone with an interest in gardening or agriculture will find a lot of useful information in related newsgroups, as the professionals who work in these fields tend to be clustered in the academic and government worlds.

HOW THE USENET WORKS

The news travels to you in a simple fashion. First, you connect to an NNTP news server via the Internet; most Internet service providers (and many corporations and other organizations) provide one.

This connection is governed by the Network News Transfer Protocol (NNTP), the standard Usenet protocol. You request information from the news server, and you send new newsgroup postings back to the same news server. Generally, you won't need to pass along any information, such as a username or a password.

UNIX

Normally, a UNIX newsreader (like **nn** or **rn**) will not go directly to a mail server for the news, but rather to a file located somewhere on the UNIX filesystem. However, Netscape Collabra uses its TCP/IP link to access the news server directly. If you're using Netscape Collabra in a corporate setting, you may want to check with your system administrator and make sure that you can access an NNTP news server directly.

Newsgroup postings are numbered, and this is how Collabra knows what newsgroup postings to request whenever you connect to a server.

Before we discuss newsgroups in any greater detail, you should set up the Netscape Collabra and take it for a first spin.

Setting Up Your Groups Server

In fact, there isn't a great deal to do before you can connect to the Usenet newsgroups. Like specifying the names of your mail servers before you could successfully launch Netscape Messenger, you need to specify the name of a news server before you can successfully launch Collabra.

And, as with Netscape Messenger, you do this by selecting **Mail & Groups** under **Preferences** on the Edit menu, then going to the **Groups Server** page. This brings up a dialog box, as shown in Figure 13.1.

There are only two fields that you need to pay attention to—really only one. The crucial one is the first, **Discussion groups (news) server:**, where you enter the name (URL) of your internal news server or public NNTP server. In this case, **nntp.noc.netcom.com** has been entered as the name of the news server, but you'll need to enter the name of the news server as provided by *your* Internet service provider or system administrator.

N O T E

What if I have both? If your organization uses the Collabra Server for in-house discussion groups, you may well also have an NNTP server. But there's only room for one server URL here. What to do? For now, enter the URL of your Collabra server here. You can communicate with multiple NNTP servers by entering their URLs in Collabra, a topic we'll take up later in this chapter.

The other field you might want to change is the one at the bottom that places a limit on the number of messages Collabra will download from any given newsgroup without asking you. If the default seems too large or too small to you, go ahead and change it. You can always go back and readjust later.

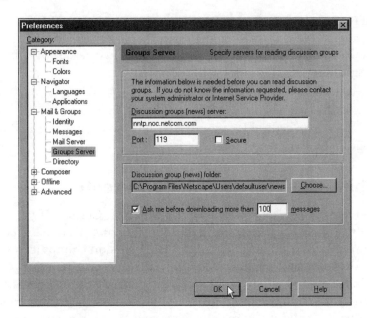

Figure 13.1 *Setting Groups Server Preferences.*

There are three other fields here, and it's conceivable that you might need to alter these also. If you are using an internal Collabra server, your system administrator may have set it up to work on a port other than the default—in which case he or she will tell you what port number to enter. If the server is being operated in secure mode, you'll need to click the Secure check box. The fact that the remaining field, Discussion group (news) folder: is grayed out is a good indication that you're not expected to alter the setting already entered here. When you install Netscape Communicator, a news/discussion group folder is set up for you. If you don't have an excellent reason to change this, we suggest that you leave it as is.

After you press the **OK** button to save these changes, you should be ready to roll with Netscape Collabra.

Since public Usenet groups and private Collabra discussion groups are, to some degree, separate subjects (because the Collabra server has some features and capabilities that public NNTP servers lack), we'll concentrate first on working with public newsgroups, then devote a separate section to the details of Collabra discussions.

AN INTRODUCTORY USENET NEWS SESSION

Now that Collabra knows where to find the news, you can start right in to work with newsgroups.

Groups live in the Netscape Message Center. (If you've already become familiar with Netscape Messenger, you're probably also familiar with the Message Center, the central location from which you can access and manage all messages, whether mail or discussions.)

Launching the Netscape Message Center

There's a variety of ways to invoke the Message Center. If you use the Component Bar, either floating or docked in the lower right-hand corner of any Communicator window, simply click the **Discussion Groups** icon (the one with the dueling dialog balloons). Alternatively, you can select **Collabra Discussion Groups** from the Communicator menu (present in all Communicator windows), or use the keyboard shortcut to this command, which is **Ctrl-3.** Finally, if you're using Netscape Messenger, you can click the **Message Center** icon—the looping green arrow, just beneath the animated Netscape logo on the right-hand side of the window.

There's one more, indirect, way to invoke Collabra: If you select a link to a newsgroup from a Web page or a mail message, Netscape Collabra will launch automatically.

N O T E

Go ahead and launch the Message Center by any of these methods. Again, if you've already worked with Netscape Messenger, the Message Center window, shown in Figure 13.2, should look familiar. In fact, Messenger and Collabra are very closely tied, and work quite similarly.

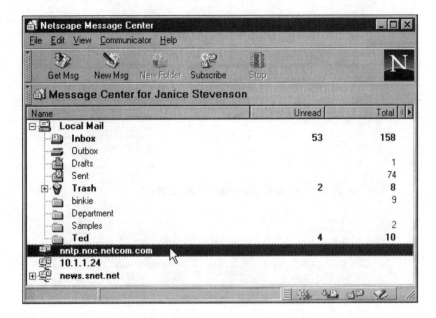

Figure 13.2 *The Netscape Message Center Window.*

Subscribing to Newsgroups

Before you can begin your active involvement with newsgroups, you'll need to subscribe to one or more groups. This will take a while, but it's really quite simple.

Below your mail folders in the Message Center window, you should see the Groups server you set up from Edit Preferences. Click that entry to select it (as shown in Figure 13.2, above), then click the **Subscribe** icon on the Navigation Toolbar or select **Subscribe to Discussion Groups** from the File menu. Either of these actions invokes the Subscribe to Discussion Groups dialog box. By default, the **All Groups** page is selected, and after a few moments, a list (which is actually just the beginning of a very long list) will appear in the window, as shown in Figure 13.3.

It will take some time to load all of the newsgroups from your news server (a progress bar in the lower left-hand corner of the window keeps you apprised of how the task is proceeding). Feel free to take a break and go make a cup of tea while the list is loading; it will take you lots more time to go through the list.

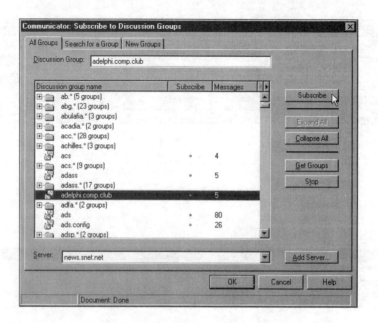

Figure 13.3 *The Complete Newsgroups listing.*

 Resist any temptation to noodle around while the newsgroup list is loading, or clicking tabs or buttons in order to see what will happen. Just about anything you do in this vein—including clicking the **Get Groups** button—will interrupt the loading process and you'll have to return to square one and start over.

WARNING

Like the Netscape Messenger window, the Subscribe dialog box displays headers for discussion groups. Where a header represents a single group, you'll see the number of messages currently posted displayed in the Messages column to the right. You'll notice, however, that many of the entries have a blue folder icon and a plus sign (+) in the left margin. These are groups of groups; the number of subgroups is displayed in parentheses to the right of the name heading. To see all the subgroups, either click the + icon or click the **Expand all** button on the right side of the dialog box.

You can work with the list as soon as Collabra begins to display it, scrolling down through the newsgroups and subscribing to any that appeal to you.

To subscribe to a group, either select it by clicking the name in the header list and pressing the **Subscribe** button on the right-hand side of the dialog box, or click the green dot in the **Subscribe** column next to the group name. A big blue check mark will appear in the Subscribe column.

If you change your mind and decide not to subscribe, just click the **Subscribe** button again (it will now be labeled Unsubscribe) or click again in the **Subscribe** column; the blue check mark will disappear, confirming that you are no longer subscribed for this group.

You may subscribe to as many newsgroups as you want, but we'd suggest you limit yourself to two or three until you get the hang of things. You don't necessarily want to load yourself down with a month's reading.

Searching for Newsgroups

If you have a topic in mind and you'd like to see if there's a newsgroup that deals with it, once you have the full newsgroup list loaded, click the **Search for a Group** tab. This brings up Collabra's search dialog box, shown in Figure 13.4. To find a newsgroup, type an entry in the **Search for:** text box.

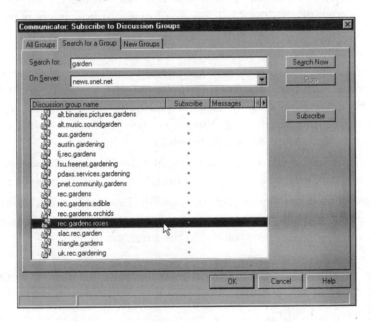

Figure 13.4 Searching for groups about gardens and gardening.

Keep in mind that this search engine does not recognize the wildcard characters that some computer applications use. Rather, it finds all the entries in which the characters you type appear, regardless of context. Thus, if you enter **dance**, the engine will find all the groups that contain those characters, such as *rec.dance.ballroom* or *alt.quebec.independance*, but it would not find *rec.folk-dancing*. If your objective is to find sites about dancing, your best tactic would be to enter **danc**, which would find all forms of the word *dance*.

There is another search function in Collabra. It lets you find specific postings within a news or discussion group. We'll discuss this type of searching in Chapter 14.

HOT LINK

Downloading Messages

Once you've made a few selections, click **OK** to close the Subscribe dialog box. At this point, Collabra will add your selections under the server heading and will automatically download information about how many messages are currently posted in each group.

To actually download message headers and messages themselves, highlight one of the group headers and either double-click it or select **Open Discussion Group** from the File menu (or use the keyboard short **Ctrl-O**). Collabra will open the Netscape Discussion window and download headers for the messages contained in the group—up to the limit you specified when you configured your Groups Server Preferences.

The Discussion window looks exactly like the Netscape Messenger Inbox (or another mail folder) window, and it functions in pretty much the same way.

As you'll see from Figure 13.5, the message headers contain a lot of information aside from the message content, such as the Subject, Sender, Date, and the number of Lines contained in the message.

To review the features and functions of the Messenger window, see Chapter 8.

HOT LINK

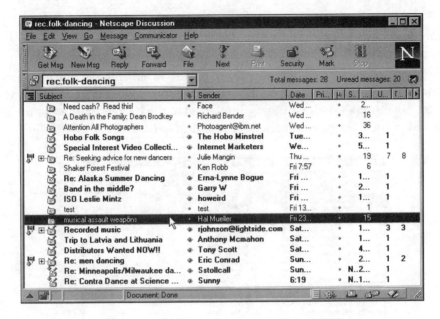

Figure 13.5 Message headers downloaded from rec.folk-dancing.

Display and Sort Options

The default in Netscape Collabra is to present the messages as part of a thread, so an original message and its responses appear next to each other. Collabra retrieves the most recent messages first. As with mail, you can sort on any of the header fields, just by clicking the appropriate header button. (That is, to sort by Sender, click the bar at the top of **Sender** column.) To reverse the sort order, click the button again.

As with mail messages, the Discussion window gives you the option to display message contents in a pane at the bottom of the window. To close the display pane and devote the entire window to headers, click the small blue triangle at its upper left-hand corner; to reopen it, click the upward-pointing blue triangle in the lower left-hand corner of the window. With the display pane open, as you click a header in the header pane, the contents of the corresponding message will be displayed in the contents pane. Collabra actually retrieves the message contents when you make the selection.

If you prefer a full message window, leave the message display closed and double-click the message header (or select **Open Message** from the File menu), and the Netscape Message window opens.

You can choose any message that appears in the message-header pane. Since the note on musical assault weapons seems interesting (or, at the very least, not mundane), that message is selected in the header pane and then displayed in the message-text pane, as shown in Figure 13.6.

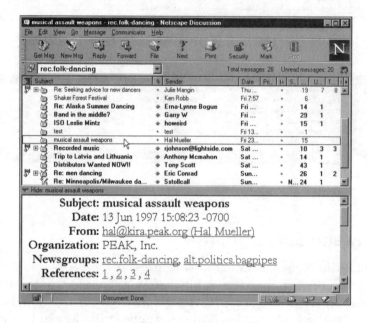

*Figure 13.6 A posting from the **rec.folk-dancing** newsgroup.*

There's a lot of information in this news posting, even aside from the text of the message (which we're not showing). The Subject and Date lines are self-explanatory. The From field tells who posted the message—both the name of the person (as they supply it; remember, there's no security mechanism to make sure that this name is genuine) and their electronic-mail address. The Organization uses information corresponding to what you entered on the Identity page in Edit-Preferences (if you didn't enter an organization, then your news posting won't contain an Organization entry). The final field lists the newsgroups the message was posted to. Sometimes messages will be posted to more than one newsgroup (this is known as *cross-posting*). Any newsgroup entry in this field is treated by Netscape Collabra as a hypertext link; you can click on the link to be taken directly to the newsgroup. (In this case, selecting the link would be a bit silly, since you're already perusing the offerings of the **rec.folk-dancing** group.)

Responding Directly to a News Posting

After you spend some time with the news, you'll feel emboldened enough to join in the discussion and respond directly to a posting.

Doing so is quite easy—simply select the **Reply** button from the toolbar or select **Reply** from the Message menu. In either case, you'll have four response choices to pick from:

- Reply to Sender
- Reply to Sender and All Recipients
- Reply to Group
- Reply to Sender and Group

The first two of these are for e-mail, the last two for news and discussion groups. We'll discuss replying directly to a message sender shortly. In most cases, you'll want to select **Reply to Group**.

This brings up Netscape's Composition window (which you'll remember from Netscape Messenger) with its own commands and toolbar. As with replies to mail messages, this newsgroup reply is already addressed (the group URL is listed in the first address field in the addressing area) and the subject is entered in the Subject field, preceded by *Re:* (Latin for "with regard to").

 Unless there's a good reason to change the subject line, leave it as it is; this allows messages to be threaded by other newsreaders, since threading mechanisms rely on the information in the Subject field to set up threads.

N O T E

If you want to quote the previous message contents in your reply, press the **Quote** icon on the toolbar. Then, just type your response, as shown in Figure 13.7.

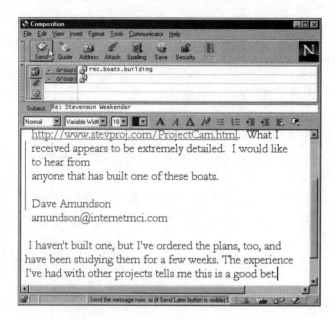

Figure 13.7 *Responding to a newsgroup posting.*

When you're through composing your response, press the **Send** button on the toolbar.

Responding via E-Mail

Sometimes you don't want your response to a posting to be seen by the entire newsgroup. In these cases, it's more appropriate to respond directly to the poster with an electronic-mail message.

In this case, select **Reply to Sender**, either from the choices under the **Reply** button on the toolbar or the **Reply** selection on the Message menu. This brings up a Message Composition box, with the electronic-mail address and subject already inserted, as shown in Figure 13.8. Again, if you want to quote the message you're replying to, just click the **Quote** button.

Responding via e-mail obviously requires some knowledge of electronic mail and having Netscape Messenger mail functions set up properly. If you skipped Chapter 8, which covered Netscape Messenger and electronic mail, it's time to go back to it and set up electronic mail.

HOT LINK

Figure 13.8 Responding to a posting via e-mail.

When you're through composing your response, select the **Send** button from the toolbar.

Originating News Postings

Of course, you don't need to be responding to a posting in order to contribute to a Usenet newsgroup. You may want to ask a general question of the group, or just contribute an observation.

In these cases, you just select **New Message** from the toolbar, bringing up a Composition window like the one shown in Figure 13.9. The name of the current newsgroup is already inserted in the Group: address field, but you don't need to stick with that name; you can post to any valid newsgroup without subscribing to it. You can also cross-post by entering the URL for one or more additional (presumably related) newsgroups in the address lines below. If you want to send a copy of the message to another user via e-mail, you can enter the address in the next address line (click the **Address** tab in the Addressing area and select **To:** or **Cc:**). You can even select an address from your address book.

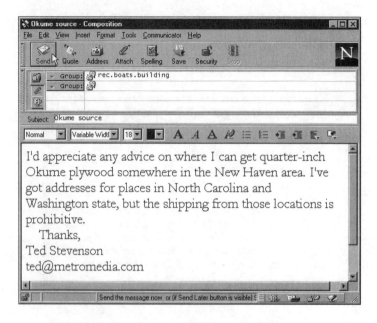

Figure 13.9 *Creating a news posting from scratch.*

Basically, the mechanics of creating a newsgroup posting from scratch are the same are creating an e-mail message from scratch. Of course, since you're not responding to a message, there's no message to quote, but if you want to include an excerpt from another posting, you can copy it and present it as a quotation in your post by choosing **Paste as quotation** from the Edit menu. You can also include binary file attachments to your message (by pressing the **Attach** button) and/or links (type in the URLs or drag and drop them from Navigator, Messenger, or Collabra).

NETSCAPE NEWS AND GRAPHICS

In the older, more primitive days of the Usenet, graphics in newsgroup postings were a hassle. Since only text travels over the Internet, a fact we've mentioned often in this book, sending a graphic required that the binary image code first be "encoded" into text, usually by separate software that used the **uuencode** format. To view the graphic you had to save the message, copy the uuencoded portion of the message to a **uudecode** program, then view the graphic.

For better or worse, things are considerably easier today: Netscape Collabra—along with most other newsreaders—can display graphic file types that Netscape Navigator can handle (such as JPEG or GIF), whether they are uuencoded or MIME encoded. No, this doesn't apply only to the many newsgroups devoted to pornography (which we'll discuss later), but also to newsgroups like **alt.binaries.clip-art**. A posting from **alt.binaries.clip-art** is shown in Figure 13.10.

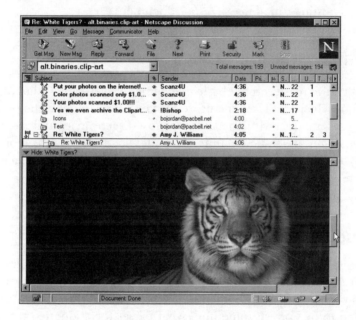

Figure 13.10 *A posting from the **alt.binaries.clip-art** newsgroup.*

Once a graphic is posted to a newsgroup, you can save it to your hard disk with relatively little fuss. Place your mouse pointer over the graphic and press on the right mouse button (Macintosh users will press their only mouse button and keep it pressed down). A menu will appear. There will be quite a few choices (most of which you covered earlier in this chapter), but only the two at the top of the list will be of interest here:

- Save Image As
- Copy Image Location

If you want to save the image, select **Save Image As**. A dialog box will pop up, asking you where you want to save the image. The name of the graphic, as contained in the body of the news posting, will already be inserted in the filename field. About the only choice you really need to make is the directory you want the image stored in.

The other selection, **Copy Image Location**, copies the location of the image to your operating system's clipboard, from where you can paste it into other news postings, mail messages, or documents.

SOME NEWSGROUP TOPICS

Now that you've mastered the basic mechanics of Netscape Collabra, it's time to look more deeply at Usenet culture. Because the Usenet is the place where Internet users interact with one another most directly in a public setting (basically, Web pages are static documents, while electronic mail is a one-on-one medium), it's also the place where passions run closest to the surface, and the place where the smallest slight can turn into a full-fledged *flame war* (Net jargon for an acrimonious exchange of insults).

Netiquette

The Usenet is a world unto itself. As with any other world that's self-contained and self-referential, the rules of acceptable conduct that apply in the Usenet world may seem hard to fathom at times. Indeed, they are classic "unwritten" rules—and to be honest, sometimes what passes for etiquette on the Usenet seems totally arbitrary and formulated on the spot.

Still, when in Rome. … In the case of the Usenet, this means trying to figure out what the rules are.

The first and foremost rule is that you should avoid attacking other users unnecessarily—an action known as *flaming* in Usenet parlance. Sure, there may be times when someone responds rather rudely to something you post— but that's their problem, not yours. If you pick up the gauntlet and respond in kind, you're into a flame war, and these always intrude on and detract from the main topic of a newsgroup and are almost always a waste of time.

Which brings up another prime rule—stick to the main topic.

Perhaps as important, you should take the time to read through an entire thread before jumping in with your response. The scenario is pretty familiar:

You're a new user, and you're all excited about being able to contribute to a discussion, so you jump right in and send a response to a posting. This is a very courteous thing to do, and your heart is in the right place—just as is the case with the 20 other new users who jump in with the same response. The entire group has to read your response, as well as the responses from the other 20 users. This can be a waste of time for everyone involved. So, again, read first; post afterwards—if the thought hasn't already been offered by another.

 As an alternative, you can send your responses via e-mail, instead of wasting everyone's time. If you're correcting someone about some arcane point or basically changing the subject in response to a posting, you're better off keeping the discussion in electronic mail, outside the public dialog.

N O T E

Just the FAQs

As you start to investigate Usenet newsgroups, you'll occasionally run across a large posting (or several postings) headed Frequently Asked Questions or FAQ. This is a well-established Internet tradition, rooted in Usenet culture. It's an efficient way to bring newcomers fairly quickly up to speed on the discussion by putting the ground rules, objectives, and any special traditions into a document that's permanently accessible to any visitor.

FAQs are set up in question-and-answer format, with a listing of questions at the beginning of the message. As you read through the FAQ, you'll probably find answers to questions you've been wondering about—especially if you've joined a newsgroup where you're a relative rookie in terms of expertise.

In fact, FAQs originated when veteran newsgroup participants grew tired of answering the same questions from new users over and over again. Instead of trotting out individual answers to repeated questions and wasting a lot of bandwidth, group elders typically direct new users to read through the FAQ. Think of a FAQ as the collected wisdom of the more active members of the newsgroup.

If you're really interested in a topic, you may want to save the FAQ to disk for offline reading. If a FAQ passes you by and you want to save it on your computer, you can connect to *http://rtfm.mit.edu* and grab the FAQ of your choice. An alternative is subscribing to the Usenet newsgroup **news.answers**, which collects FAQs from all the newsgroups and sends them around regularly. (In fact, this may be a great way to tap into the collective wisdom of the Internet—just subscribe to this newsgroup.)

On the flip side, don't spend a lot of money or compromise your honor based on anything you've read in a FAQ, much less a newsgroup. Collective wisdom can be wrong, and sometimes the opinions of the person maintaining the FAQ cloud the information contained within. Let's put it this way—a FAQ is likely to be more valid if it contains technical information not open to personal interpretation.

Newsgroups and Pornography

When the press focuses on pornography and the Internet, the discussion is really about pornography and the Usenet. There are some Web sites that feature pornography, but by and large the Usenet is the larger purveyor of pornography. There are literally hundreds of Usenet newsgroups specifically devoted to pornography.

If you have children, you'll need to put some thought into how you want to approach this issue. On the one hand, there's nothing inherently "dirty" about nude pictures of either sex, and one person's erotica is another person's smut. On the other hand, there is a good deal of disgusting stuff in newsgroups dedicated to bestiality, rape, incest, and S&M. (A personal note: You know you're growing old when you don't see the erotic possibilities found in newsgroups like **alt.sex.toupee**, **alt.sex.nasal-hair**, or **alt.sex.bondage.sco.unix**.) Ironically, Netscape Collabra gives you the power to view these pictures easily and directly. With older newsgroup software you had to download a picture, then load separate software to view it; with Collabra, all you need to do is read through a message, and the graphics file will be displayed directly. Most parents aren't thrilled that their 10-year-old child can browse the pictures in **alt.sex.bestiality.pictures**. And, of course, there are issues concerning the early sexualization of children and the objectification of women (make no mistake—almost all Internet pornography outside of the gay newsgroups involves women) that are way too involved for this discussion.

It used to be that much of what passed for pornography on the Usenet was in text, in the form of messages posted to newsgroups like **alt.sex** (a frank discussion of all things sexual), **alt.sex.first-time** (where virgins can ask questions in anticipation of, and former virgins discuss, their first experiences), **alt.sex.bondage** (the name is self-explanatory), and **alt.sex.wizards** (where "experts" offer some rather clinical advice about personal topics, most of which involve some sort of lubricant). The discussions here can get quite personal and explicit—but they're just words. Today, however, images are everywhere, and that's where you, as a parent, may be a little concerned.

Obviously there's a fine line here; the Usenet is built on the assumption that free speech is sacred, but there's also speech—in the form of some rather nasty pictures—that can be harmful to the innocent. It used to be that you had to put some work into finding these sites and newsgroups, but it's certainly easier to run across the smut than it once was. Still, even an involved user can spend a lot of hours on the Internet before running across even a reference to pornography.

In any case, if you're at all concerned about this issue, you may want to check out Internet guardians—software packages that restrict access to certain parts of the Internet. These packages include:

- NetNanny (*http://www.netnanny.com/netnanny/*)
- CyberSitter (*http://www.solidoak.com/*)
- SurfWatch (*http://www.surfwatch.com/*)

All of these programs work in basically the same way: They have a database of Web sites and Usenet newsgroups that are off-limits. If someone tries to access these sites, the browser or newsreader is automatically shut down. Some of the packages have a database of forbidden words (including the seven immortalized by George Carlin) and either warn the user or shut down the browser or newsreader if those words are received via the Internet. In addition, some of these packages can be used to "snoop" on unsuspecting users, keeping a log of the URLs and newsgroups visited.

In general, these packages work pretty well, and they can prevent access to the more egregious examples of Internet pornography. (They can also block access to material that's in no way sexual or erotic but that the program's developers consider unsavory for other reasons.) In any case, they're no substitute for parental involvement with children and their activities. If a child is regularly spending hours and hours a day on the Internet—which, despite the many millions of users, is a solitary endeavor—there may be something wrong at home.

INTERNAL DISCUSSION GROUPS

So far, we've focused this chapter more or less entirely on public newsgroups on the Usenet, but the Netscape Collabra client is designed as much, perhaps more, to work in tandem with the Netscape Collabra server to create organizational discussion groups.

Using the Collabra client/server team, companies and other organizations can set up groups to handle the dissemination of important information, foster workgroup collaboration, and generally promote organizational communication. With internally controlled Collabra servers, groups can be created quickly and easily to suit the needs of the organization and can include access controls, where appropriate, to maintain privacy. Also, discussion groups can employ the latest SSL 3.0 (Secure Sockets Layer Version 3) security, which makes them a safe venue even for potentially sensitive material.

A simple example of an organizational discussion group would be a press-clippings group. Here employees or members could post items about the organization culled from newspapers and Internet news sources. Naturally, some such items would spawn discussion, but in this case the main point would be getting the material into an easily accessible place for all to see.

A policy-review discussion group, on the other hand, would probably be quite different. First, it would probably be accessible only to members of a specific policy review group—management folks whose job it was to debate and establish organization policies. Using Collabra's HTML and binary attachment capabilities, drafts and finished documents could easily be circulated among the members for review and comment. Collabra's *categories* feature (which we'll discuss very shortly) could be used to keep each phase of the process separate.

Collabra Group Names

The names of groups on an NNTP server, which is what Usenet and Collabra servers are, are organized hierarchically. The Usenet newsgroup name **alt** is the hierarchical "parent" of **alt.pets**, which is, in turn the parent of **alt.pets.dogs**, and so on. Collabra discussion groups are not strictly bound by this hierarchical naming system; they can have more normal names with spaces and uppercase characters, like **Sports Cars** or **Gene Maps**.

Actually, to be strictly accurate, Collabra groups have split personalities. They stick with Usenet-style names behind the scenes, but can also have "display" names like the examples just given. This is not an earth-shattering development, but it is liberating—as the move from the eight-dot-three DOS file-naming convention to "long" file names (which Macintosh users had long enjoyed) was for Windows users when Windows NT and 95 came along.

Categories

Collabra goes a step beyond the implementation of display names for discussion groups (covered in the previous paragraph) by allowing groups to be optionally designated as *categorized discussion groups* when they're set up. This option replaces the traditional NNTP hierarchies with simpler, easier-to-read headings.

Suppose, for example, that people in your organization started a **pets** group, and this spawned a **pets.dogs** subgroup, which led to further categories, such as **pets.dogs.beagles** and **pets.dogs.pitbulls**. If **pets** had been set up as a categorized group, it would show up in the Message Center window as **Pets** (with no subordinate categories visible). When the group is selected and opened, however, it appears in a special Netscape Category window, shown in Figure 13.11, with hierarchical listing of categories in a pane to the left.

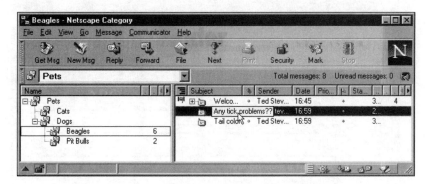

Figure 13.11 A categorized Collabra discussion group.

Like the use of display names, it's not an earth-shattering change, but it is a nice interface touch that makes Collabra discussion groups easier to navigate.

Creating Collabra Discussion Groups

One of the beauties of Collabra is that unless restrictions have been imposed by the administrator, any user can create new discussion groups from the Collabra client.

To create a new Collabra discussion group, open the Message Center window and highlight the group under which you want to start a new subgroup. (If you want it to be a top-level group, highlight the name of the appropriate Collabra server.) Then select **New Discussion Group** from the File menu. This brings up the New Discussion form in a Netscape Navigator window. If you're setting up a top (or *root*) level group, the heading will read **New Discussion under ***, as shown in Figure 13.12. (The asterisk represents the root directory.) If you selected an existing group, the heading will read **New Discussion under** *[groupname]*. In the Name: field you'll need to type a name in lowercase letters with no spaces (such as **policy**). In the Display Name: field, you can enter a name for display purposes that contains uppercase letters and/or spaces (**Company Policies**, for example). You may enter a brief description in the Description field; this is entirely optional.

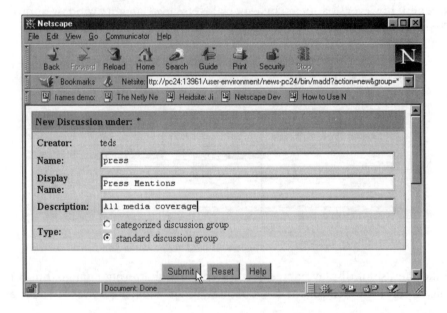

Figure 13.12 *Creating a new Collabra discussion group.*

By default, new groups are designated as Standard Discussion Groups. If you want this to be a categorized group, click the appropriate radio button below the Description field.

If at any point you change your mind about names or wording—or you've typed something incorrectly—you can clear the form fields by clicking **Reset**. When everything is to your liking, simply click **Submit** and you're done.

Creating New Categories

Users can create new categories as well. Really, it's just creating a new discussion under another name.

To create a new discussion category, you must first open a categorized discussion group. Then, highlight the header of either the main group or one of the existing categories under which you want to create a new category and select **New Category** from the File menu.

As with creating new discussion groups, a form will appear in a Navigator window headed **New Discussion under** *[categoryname]*. In the Name: field (which already contains whatever hierarchical parents this category will have, **pets.dogs.beagles**, for example), you'll need to type a name in lowercase letters with no spaces (such as **mange**). In the Display Name: field, you can enter a name for display purposes that contains uppercase letters and/or spaces (**Skin Problems**, for example). Add a **Description** if you like, then click **Submit** and it's accomplished.

SUMMARY

The Usenet is a global repository of facts and opinions organized into some 15,000 topic-based public discussion groups. At their best, Usenet newsgroups can be vibrant, noisy communities where you can keep in touch with exciting subjects. Using the Netscape Collabra discussion group tools, participating is easy: You select a set of newsgroups to follow and then regularly read the postings. If you want to respond, you can do so to the entire newsgroup or to a single user.

Inside a company or organization, Netscape Collabra discussion groups can serve as places to share research, bulletins, or other information, collaborate on work projects, or just shoot the bull. In Chapter 14, we'll delve more deeply into Collabra tools and commands.

## CHAPTER 14

Advanced Collabra Topics

Once news and discussion groups become part of your daily routine, you'll find Collabra's advanced features can speed work and add new dimensions to your activities. We'll devote this chapter to wringing from Collabra every last drop of function and performance it has to offer. Topics we'll cover include:

- Using the right-hand mouse button
- Connecting to multiple servers
- Working offline
- Intelligent navigation
- Bookmarks
- Searching and sorting

- Message management
- Virtual discussion groups

Before we launch into discussing some of Collabra's more specialized features and functions, though, we'll systematically cover all of the commands in the various toolbars and menus that apply specifically to news and discussion groups.

THE NETSCAPE MESSAGE CENTER WINDOW

The Message Center window is, of course, shared between Netscape Collabra and Netscape Messenger, but some of the commands apply specifically to Collabra functions.

Only one icon on the Navigation Toolbar relates to Collabra: The **Subscribe** button calls up the Subscribe to Discussion Groups dialog box, which we'll discuss below.

Only two of the menus, File and Edit, contain Collabra-specific commands. We'll take up each menu separately.

NOTE You should be aware that the Get Msg button on the Message Center Navigation Toolbar—or its menu equivalent, File-Get Messages—does not in fact download postings to a discussion group. It functions only to get e-mail messages.

The File Menu

Six of the commands on the File menu are specific to Collabra. They are:

- New Discussion Group
- New Discussion Group Server
- Open Discussion Group
- Get Messages
- Update Message Count
- Subscribe to Discussion Groups

We'll describe all of these functions, briefly, in the following paragraphs.

The **New Discussion Group** command lets you create a Collabra discussion group, if your organization is using the Collabra server. (It has no function in Usenet newsgroups.) Selecting it brings up a New Discussion form in a Netscape Navigator window. You enter a name for your group and perhaps a description, and the group will appear in the complete list of subscribable discussion groups.

As its name suggests, **New Discussion Group Server** lets you specify a discussion group server other than the one you listed in Preferences when you first set up Collabra (as described in Chapter 13). Unlike Netscape Messenger, Netscape Collabra lets you work with multiple servers; you can have as many as you need or want.

When you select the command, the New Discussion Groups Server dialog box pops up, as shown in Figure 14.1. Once you've entered the URL to the server you want—and checked **Secure** and/or **Always use name and password** if these apply, select **OK**, and your new server will now appear in the discussion group hierarchy in the Message Center window.

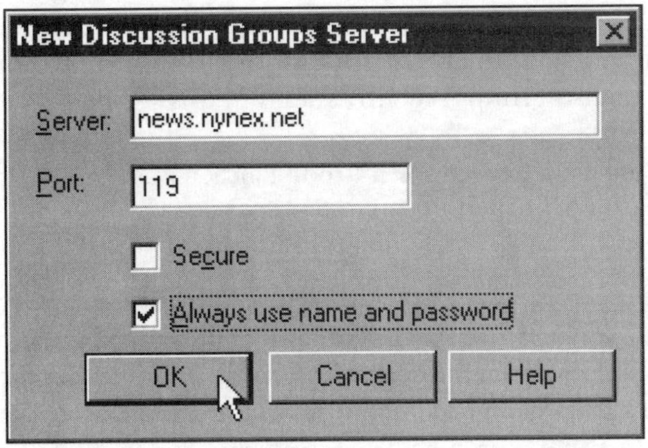

Figure 14.1 *Adding a discussion server to your list.*

Open Discussion Group opens the group currently highlighted in the Message Center window in a separate Netscape Discussion window (similar to a Netscape Messenger mailbox window).

NOTE

When you open a discussion group, the headers are automatically down-loaded—either all current headers, or the number you specified in your Groups Server Preferences.

The same result can be obtained by double-clicking the group listing in the Message Center window.

The **Get Messages** command grabs headers only, not actual messages. We'll discuss this command more fully in a later section that deals with commands in the Netscape Discussion window.

The **Update Message Count** command refreshes the tallies in the Unread and Total columns for each of your subscribed groups.

Subscribe to Discussion Groups is the command you use to scan the complete list of Usenet (and/or internal Collabra) groups, from which you can select any number to follow or *subscribe* to. It brings up a dialog box called, appropriately, Subscribe to Discussion Groups that contains three tabs. (The Subscribe button on the toolbar also calls up this dialog box.)

The **All Groups** tab accesses the comprehensive list of groups residing on or accessed through the server you've chosen. The Search for a Group tab calls up a search engine that lets you find discussions on various topics. The New Groups tab lists groups recently added to this server.

HOT LINK

The use of the **Search for a Group** function was discussed in some depth in Chapter 13.

To subscribe to any news or discussion group, highlight the group header in the list and either click the Subscribe button on the right-hand side of the dialog box or click the small green diamond in the Subscribe column next to the group name. In either case, a blue check mark indicates that you're now a subscriber.

The Edit Menu

Only two commands on the Message Center Edit menu apply specifically to Collabra:

- Delete Discussion Group
- Discussion Group Server Properties

The first of these, **Delete Discussion Group**, is quite self-explanatory: You highlight a group in the Message Center display, then select the command from the Edit menu. Collabra requires your confirmation before deleting the group from your list. The second, **Discussion Group Server Properties**, brings up a small dialog box that lists basic information about the server you're currently working with. There's no particular reason to consult this dialog box.

THE NETSCAPE DISCUSSION WINDOW

When you open a news or discussion group (as discussed in the previous section), Collabra presents it in a Netscape Discussion window that, like a Netscape Messenger window, displays headers in one pane and, optionally, shows the contents of highlighted postings in a message display pane below.

The File and the Go menus contain commands particular to Collabra. We'll look at them menu by menu.

The File Menu

There are a number of commands here that apply to Collabra. We'll run through them, devoting more space to some than to others.

Save As lets you save a downloaded posting as a text file on your hard drive for later reference.

Edit Message pulls up the currently highlighted posting in a Composition window, just as if you were composing an original message.

Open Message displays the message contents in a separate Netscape Message window. If you have the message display pane open in the Discussion window, this choice is redundant, since presumably you can already see the message contents. Another way to open postings in a Discussion window is to double-click on the header.

Get Messages actually lets you download either message headers or actual postings for the group you're currently reviewing. To clarify its function, we need to take a step back and review the basics of downloading headers.

When you open a discussion group, as described above, Collabra automatically downloads headers for the group. If there are more messages currently posted than the limit you specified when setting up your Groups Server Preferences, you'll get a Download Headers dialog box, shown in Figure 14.2. Here you're given the option of downloading all the headers or the number that you specify.

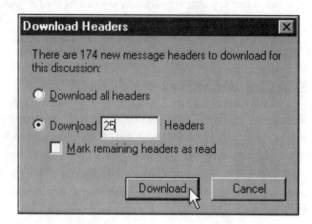

Figure 14.2 *Collabra's Download Headers dialog box.*

If you chose not to download all the headers at the outset, **Get Messages** lets you grab more. Selecting either subchoice (**New** or **Next [N]**) brings up the Download Headers dialog box, and you proceed as before.

The other two subchoices under Get Messages—**Selected for Offline Reading** and **Flagged for Offline Reading**—are for downloading actual message *contents*, as opposed to headers alone. By default, Collabra does not download news or discussion group messages to your local system unless you tell it to. It merely loads the message contents into the Message window over the network each time you select a message for viewing.

To physically download messages, you'll first need to flag each message by clicking the green diamond in the **Flag** column of the message header, then selecting **Get Messages** and the subchoice **Flagged for Offline Reading**. (The Selected for Offline Reading option is for e-mail messages.)

Go Offline disconnects you from your network or ISP if you are currently logged on. We'll discuss this and other aspects of working offline in a special section later in this chapter.

The Go Menu

The general logic of the commands here is the same as for the corresponding ones in Netscape Messenger: They let you move more efficiently through a long list of headers. But there are two commands that apply specifically to news and discussion groups. They are essentially self-explanatory, as follows:

Next Group takes you to the next discussion group in your subscription list (the list of groups you view in the Message Center window).

Next Unread Group takes you to the next group on the list that contains unread messages.

The Netscape Category Window

When you open a categorized Collabra discussion group, it is displayed in a Category window. This is similar to the Discussion window except that it has a navigation pane down the left-hand side (see Figure 13.11) and a few of the menu commands are specific to categories.

In the File menu, you'll find the command **New Category**. As you might guess, this is used to create a new category at some level within the categorized hierarchy. When you select the command, a form pops up in a Navigator window with fields for a category name (mandatory), a display name (optional), and a description (also optional).

HOT LINK

We covered the process of creating new categories in some depth back in Chapter 13. Review that section to refresh your memory on the details.

The Go menu has two Collabra-specific commands. **Next Category** and **Next Unread Category** are exactly analogous to **Next Group** and **Next Unread Group**, discussed above in the section on commands in the Discussion window.

USING THE RIGHT-HAND MOUSE BUTTON

So far, this discussion of Netscape Collabra has focused on using the toolbar and/or the pull-down menus. You can also use the right-hand mouse button as a shortcut for many functions.

Of course, Macintosh users don't have a right-hand mouse button. Mac users will use their only mouse button.

There are different choices on the right-hand mouse button menu, depending on the context. Most—but not all—of these echo the choices from the pull-down menus and the toolbar.

Right-Hand Mouse Button Commands in the Message Center

If you highlight a newsgroup header in the Message Center window and right-click, you'll get the following choices:

- Open Discussion Group
- Open Discussion Group in New Window
- New Message
- Mark Discussion Group Read
- Remove Discussion Group
- Search Messages
- Discussion Group Properties

The first two choices are quite similar: Both open a Netscape Discussion window and display headers for the selected news or discussion group. But if no Discussion window is open at the outset, they will also then open the Netscape Discussion window and display the headers. If a Discussion window is open, Open Discussion Group will open the group in that window; **Open Discussion Group** in New Window leaves the existing window intact and opens—you guessed it—a new window.

New Message brings up a Composition window with the currently highlighted group inserted in the first address line, as discussed in **Originating News Postings**, above.

Mark Discussion Group Read removes the boldfacing from the group header and removes the number from the Unread column in the header display—indicating that you've read everything in the group.

Remove Discussion Group removes the header from your list of sub-scribed newsgroups, in effect unsubscribing you. **Search Messages** brings up a Search Messages dialog box (a much simplified version of the one in the Messenger mail module) that lets you construct search queries based on the sender or subject fields.

The **Search Messages** command works only when you are connected to the appropriate Collabra or news server.

N O T E

The final choice brings up the Discussion Group Properties dialog box, from which you can make many settings that control how your system deals with the newsgroups you subscribe to. We'll look at the Discussion Group Properties dialog box in greater detail a little later in this chapter, but here, in brief, are the settings and choices you can make there:

- Receiving HTML: Choose **yes** or **no**.
- Download Settings: Use the defaults set up in Preferences or override them and download only unread messages or messages defined by date parameters.
- Disk Space: Choose to keep all messages or only messages newer than a certain date or the newest N number of messages, or only unread messages, or only the headers, discarding the messages themselves.

Right-Hand Mouse Button Commands in the Discussion Window

In the context of a Discussion window, the list of commands accessible is con-siderably longer, and generally echoes the commands in the Message menu. Here are the choices:

- Open Message
- Open Message in New Window
- Reply (to Sender, Group, or Sender and Group)
- Forward
- Forward Quoted
- Add to Address Book

- Ignore, or Watch Thread
- File, Cancel, Save, or Print Message

The first pair of choices are directly analogous to the corresponding ones in the Message Center window: If you have the message display pane open, the selected message will already be displayed there; if you choose either of these two commands, a Netscape Message window will open and the message contents will be displayed there. Note that, at this point, **Open Message** will display subsequent messages in the existing Message window, whereas **Open Message in New Window** leaves the existing window intact and creates a new window for the new message.

The Reply choices are the same as those available from the **Reply** button on the toolbar, with the exception of the irrelevant **Reply to Sender and All Recipients** variant, which is for e-mail messages. The choices for forwarding the posting are simple: Both are used to forward the posting via electronic mail, with the first sending the posting as a MIME attachment, while the second forwards the post as a quoted text message.

The next choice lets you add to your Netscape Address Book the electronic-mail address of a person who posts to a newsgroup. **Ignore Thread** and **Watch Thread** insert little reminder icons in the left-hand margin of the header list.

The final group of choices are basic file management commands. **Cancel** and **Print** are self-explanatory. **File** lets you store a message in a folder you've set up in the Message Center (this is discussed in detail in Chapter 8); **Save** lets you store it as a text file on your hard disk.

ADVANCED COLLABRA SETUP OPTIONS

A number of items in the Communicator Preferences apply directly or indirectly to Netscape Collabra and how it functions for you. We covered the basic ones in Chapter 13. Here's a brief rundown of such items, in the order in which the items appear in the Preferences tree.

In the Appearances page, there's a check box that tells Communicator to start Collabra every time Communicator starts up.

On the initial Mail & Groups page, you can make several basic choices about the appearance of Messenger and Collabra messages, including fixed- or variable-width font and how quoted material is presented. Also covered here is how Communicator handles windowing: The default is to create one Discussion window for the display of all groups reviewed in a session; the alternative is to spawn a new Discussion window for each group reviewed. The same choice is available for individual messages. The final choice, enabling or disabling an auditory alert on message arrival, relates to e-mail messages only.

On the Messages page under Mail & Groups, you can choose whether or not to send HTML-based posts as your default, and whether to automatically quote a message you're responding to. Actually, these choices will apply to both Messenger and Collabra messages. A section on Copies of outgoing messages lets you automatically save a copy of each Collabra message you send to a message folder you specify (the default is the Sent folder). Similarly, you can elect to have an e-mail copy of each outgoing message sent either to yourself or to another address.

The Groups Server page we visited when we first set up Collabra in Chapter 13. You know by now that you're not limited to using the server that's listed here. And notice again that this is where you can set one of the basic Collabra defaults: how many headers to download at once when you get your postings.

On the Offline page, you can choose **Online Work Mode** or **Offline Work Mode** as your default, or tell Communicator to check with you at each session startup. If you will be working offline (we'll discuss this topic in detail a bit later in this chapter), you'll want to click the Download page and consider the controls listed there. You can opt to download only unread messages (the typical solution), and whether to use a cutoff date. You'll also need to click the **Select Messages** button and specify which of your groups you want to download headers for on logon. To select a group, click the tiny green diamond in the Choose column (which will place a blue checkmark in the column), or press the **Choose All** button in the lower left-hand corner of the window.

Setting Discussion Group Properties

This tabbed dialog box, shown in Figure 14.3, serves as a central repository of your settings for each discussion group you subscribe to. You can access it by highlighting a group in the Message Center window and either choosing **Discussion Group Properties** from the Edit menu or clicking the right-hand mouse button and choosing **Discussion Group Properties**.

Figure 14.3 *The Discussion Group Properties dialog box.*

The General page lists the name of the group and its server location, gives you a tally of the total and unread messages, and tells you how much disk space is devoted to the group. A check box below tells Communicator that you're willing to receive HTML-based posts. As with each page of the Properties dialog box, there's a **Download Now** button.

The Download Settings page lets you make, well, download settings. You may recall that there's a general Download Settings page under Offline in Preferences (discussed above). This is where you can override those defaults for any specific group. To do so, you'll first uncheck the box that says **Use default settings** from preferences. Then, you'll make your override choices about downloading unread messages only and/or setting date limits.

CONNECTING TO MULTIPLE SERVERS

As mentioned earlier in this chapter, you can work with as many NNTP (news) and/or Collabra discussion servers as you like. This situation is different from e-mail, where you specify a single server for outgoing mail and another one for incoming mail.

To set up Collabra to work with a server that's not listed in the Message Center window, select **New Discussion Group Server** from the File menu. The command invokes the New Discussion Groups Server dialog box, which is shown in Figure 14.1. You enter the URL for the new server in the appropriate field and click **OK**, and you've set up your server. In some cases, you'll want to select the check box that tells Collabra that the server is Secure (uses SSL security features), and/or that Collabra should ask for your user name and password each time you log on. Unless you have a very good reason to change the Port field, we urge you to leave it strictly alone.

Once you click **OK**, the new server will appear in the Groups section of the Message Center window and you'll be able to access it freely.

When you subscribe to new news or discussion groups (which you do by clicking the **Subscribe** button on the toolbar or selecting **Subscribe to Discussion Groups** from the File menu), you'll notice a Server: field at the bottom of the All Groups and New Groups pages of the Subscribe to Discussion Groups dialog box; it is shown in Figure 14.4. This field is actually a drop-down list where you'll find all the servers currently set up for you to connect to. Select the server you want and Collabra will begin loading its complete groups listing.

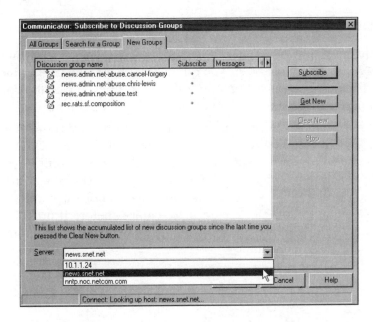

Figure 14.4 *The Select Server drop-down list in the Subscribe dialog box.*

WORKING OFFLINE

Some users will always have an active network connection. Some—such as laptop users on trains or airplanes—will not. Others, especially those using modem connections, may simply find it more convenient (and less costly) to carry out the bulk of their news and discussion group activities while not connected. Netscape Collabra's Offline Work Mode addresses the needs of users who can't be, or prefer not to be, continuously connected with their discussion servers. It may take a little while to get the hang of Online/Offline, but once you've mastered it, this feature can make you more productive and/or less poor.

 NOTE By default, Collabra assumes you're working with a continuous connection and does not download news or discussion group messages to your local system. Instead, each time you select a message for viewing, Collabra quickly loads the message contents into the Message window over the network. If you want to have postings downloaded to your hard disk, you'll have to select **Offline Work mode**.

Selecting Your Work Mode

When you make your Preferences selections (see the discussion of "Advanced Collabra Setup Options" earlier) you can select either **Online** or **Offline mode** as your default mode when Communicator starts up; you can also configure Communicator to ask you which mode to start up in each time.

Whichever mode you're in at any point in a Communicator session, you can switch to the other by going to the File menu. If you're in Online mode, you'll see the command Go Offline listed; if you're working offline, you'll see Go Online. Selecting either command brings up the Download dialog box (shown in Figure 14.5), which gives you several choices. If you're going offline, Communicator will execute these choices before it breaks the network connection; if you're going online, it will execute them immediately upon making the connection.

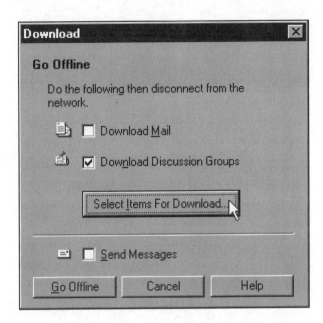

Figure 14.5 *The Download dialog box: Preparing to go offline.*

The choice that concerns us here is **Download Discussion Groups**. (Checking **Download Mail** fetches messages from your incoming e-mail server. **Send Messages** sends any messages queued in your Outbox.) If you check the **Download Discussion Groups** box when you **OK** the dialog box, Collabra will download any messages you've selected for download. (We'll return to the topic of message selection shortly.)

To specify which of your subscribed groups are downloaded, click the **Select Items for Download** button. This brings up the Discussion Groups dialog box, shown in Figure 14.6, that lists all your groups. (You've also seen this dialog box if you set up defaults under Offline in Preferences.) Groups selected for download have blue check marks in the column to the right of the group name. Click in that column to select an unselected group or deselect a selected group. If you want to download messages from all groups, click the **Choose All** button. When you're finished selecting groups, **OK** this dialog box.

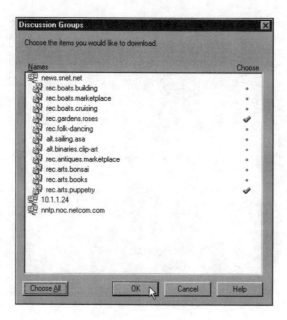

Figure 14.6 *Specifying groups to download.*

Selecting and Deselecting Messages

To download messages when changing modes, you must select them, and this is one area in which Offline mode and its subtleties can get confusing: You must clearly understand the distinction between Collabra's *unread* and *selected* status indicators.

When you first download a header in Collabra, it's rendered in boldface type and the green diamond in the Status column is big; a green arrow also points downward next to the message icon in the left margin.

But be careful: When you read the message, the green arrow and the bold-face go away and the diamond shrinks, right? The same things happen when you change the status by using the menus or clicking the diamond in the Status column, right? And you can return the header to unread status by going to the menus or clicking the Status column again, right? *Wrong!*

You can *never* bring back the green, downward-pointing arrow—the actual indicator of an unread message. Once it's gone, you can toggle the status as often as you want, but what you're doing at this point is selecting and dese-

lecting the message for download. The visual indicator for selected messages—aside from the boldface and the Status diamond—is the little red
push-pin in the message icon; this is shown in Figure 14.7. When the red push-
pin is there, the message is selected for download; when it's not there, the
message is not selected and won't be downloaded.

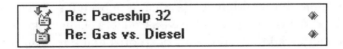

Figure 14.7 *An unread post and one selected for download.*

Physical Downloading

If you've activated one or more groups (as described above) and selected messages for download in one or more of those groups, Collabra commences to
download the message bodies for the header so selected as soon as you click
the **Go Offline** or **Go Online** (as the case may be) in the Download dialog box.

By now, you may be wondering why it's necessary to go through all of this
when Collabra downloads your messages when you log on in **Online mode.**
After all, you can read them, right? In fact, when you log on in **Online mode**,
Collabra assumes by default that you're working with a continuous connection and does not download news or discussion group messages to your local
system. Instead, each time you select a message for viewing, Collabra quickly
loads the message contents into the Message window over the network. If you
want to have postings downloaded to your hard disk, you can either select
Offline Work mode, as we've been discussing or you can *flag* and download
selected messages.

Flagging Messages for Download

When you're working in **Online mode** and you want to download messages to
your hard disk, you'll first need to flag each message. To do this, either click
the small green diamond in the Flag column of the message header or select
Flag from the Message menu. In either case, a flag icon will appear in that
header column. If you want to select all the messages currently displayed in
the Discussion window, press **Ctrl-A** or choose **Select Messages** from the Edit
menu, then select **All messages**; then select **Flag** from the Message menu.

Once you've selected your messages for download, choose **Get Messages** from the File menu, then **Flagged for Offline Reading**. Collabra will then download the postings to your hard disk.

Downloaded vs. Nondownloaded Messages

To enable you to distinguish messages that have been physically downloaded to your hard disk from those that haven't, Collabra changes the message icon in the left margin, adding a broken black horizontal line. This distinction is vital for a number of news-processing functions:

Any message with the added line can be read offline; those without it, can't. Similarly, you can respond to these posts while offline, whereas you cannot do this for nondownloaded messages.

The same holds true for filing, saving, and copying messages offline. The nondownloaded messages simply aren't there, so these operations are impossible.

You might think that the **Search Messages** feature would function offline, at least for the store of downloaded postings, but it doesn't.

Maneuvering through the Message Maze

With news- and discussion-groups, even more than with e-mail, messages can accumulate rapidly. (Of course, how rapidly depends on how many groups you actively participate in and which groups those are—some groups spawn hundreds of new messages each day; others may not generate that much give-and-take in a year.) Fortunately, Netscape Collabra gives you many cues and tools to make it faster and easier to wade through piles of postings.

For starters, let's just take a moment to review the Discussion window (in this case, for rec.gardens.roses). If you're familiar with Netscape Messenger and processing e-mail, this should look very familiar. In any case, several of the interface elements will play a significant role in your news- and discussion-group processing.

To begin with, the Subject field gives you the most important clues as to whether a given posting is something you want to read. Some Subject headers are long—too long to fit the column they're displayed in. As you'll notice in Figure 14.8, when you pass your mouse pointer over such a Subject line, Collabra displays the entire heading in a box.

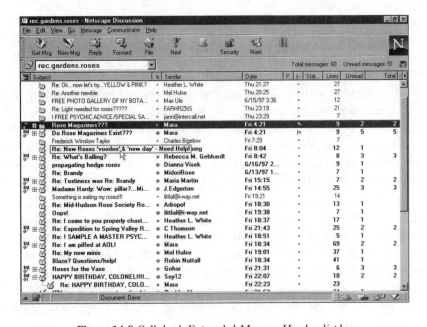

Figure 14.8 Collabra's Expanded Message Header display.

The Date field simply lets you know how long the posting has been hanging around; this can be useful in determining whether to have a look at the contents. The Flag column (to the right of the Date) lets you mark messages for any reason you choose. (We discussed one important reason you might flag messages, in the section on Downloading, above.) Even the number of Lines (listed in a column to the right of the Flag column) gives you some useful information. You may choose to glance through short messages now, while marking (or leaving) longer messages for later.

You'll notice that columns exist for Priority and Status (they're somewhat scrunched in this screen) but that they contain no information. These two designations are simply not used in news or discussion groups.

NOTE

Read and Unread Messages

Probably the most useful visual cue provided by the header display in the Discussion window is the distinction between read and unread postings. The unread messages are marked with a large green diamond (remember this practice from the discussion of Netscape Messenger?) and are displayed in bold type. For message threads—if they're displayed collapsed as they are in Figure 14.8—the Unread column tells you how many messages within the thread are unread.

The useful twist with read and unread messages is that the meaning of the designations doesn't have to be literal. When you open a message, whether you look at the contents or not, Collabra automatically changes its status from unread to read. But you don't have to open a message to make this status change: You can simply click the green diamond next to the Subject (or use the keyboard shortcut **R**). This amounts to a notation that says, in effect, "I've dealt with this."

Scrolling through and physically marking as read the messages that hold no interest is a typical first step in processing a new batch of postings. Of course, once you've marked a message (or thread) as being read, it doesn't mean that the message disappears. All it means is that the next time you're connected to the news server, Collabra won't bother to list the posting in the headers list. (And if there are no unread messages in the newsgroup, Collabra won't even list the group.)

Mass Marking

There may often be times when the most efficient way to proceed is to first read through the few postings in a batch or thread that interest you, then simply mark that whole group of messages as Read and move on.

Netscape Collabra provides several options on the Message menu that facilitate this action. Select **Mark**, and you'll find the following choices:

- As Unread
- As Read
- Thread Read
- Category Read
- All Read
- By Date
- For Later

The first two choices should be quite familiar, though this menu reminds us of the nice keyboard shortcuts U and R. Highlighting any header within a thread and choosing **Message–Mark-Thread Read** changes the status of every header in the thread. Category Read does the same for all the messages in a category; **All Read** accomplishes this for an entire group.

One refinement on this process is choosing **Mark–By Date**, which brings up a date dialog box in which you enter a date before which you want all messages marked as read. (**Mark–for Later**, incidentally, keeps a message marked as unread and moves you to the next unread message.)

NOTE Should you for any reason decide to undo the process of marking an entire thread or group as read, it's not difficult, even though there are no specific commands for this: First, choose **Select Message** from the Edit menu and then either **Thread** or **All Messages**, as the case may be (or use the keyboard **Ctrl-A** for All or **Ctrl-Shift-A** for Thread). Finish by selecting **Mark** from the Message menu and then **As Unread** from the subchoices.

Intelligent Navigation

Once you're a regular visitor to a newsgroup, your attention tends to become focused on quickly finding and scanning new material. Netscape Collabra has a number of features to help.

The Go Menu

There's a group of commands in the Go menu, for example, that's designed to whip you through a Usenet or Collabra session by taking you directly to unread material. **Next Unread Message** takes you, as you'd imagine, to the next message in your headers list that's not marked as read.

Is this convenient? Sure. Is there a better way? You bet! The newsmeister's shortcut to this command is simply to press **N**. That's right, not **Shift-N** or **Ctrl-N**; just **N** (either upper or lower case). To go the other way (to the Previous Unread Message) simply press **P**.

The **Next Unread Thread** command (keyboard shortcut, **T**) does a couple of things: It first marks as read the header you were on when you selected it, then it takes you to the next unread message—whether or not that message is part of a multimessage thread. If that message is part of a multimessage thread, it expands the headers for that thread.

When you're through with one group, just select **Next Group**. The next group on your Message Center list will load and if more headers are waiting than the maximum you specified in Preferences, the Download Headers dialog box will appear giving you the option to download all headers or just the Next (**N**).

A quicker variant of this is to select **Next Unread Group** or simply press **G**. This does the same as **Next Group**, but skips over any groups you've marked as read (using the right-mouse-button command discussed above).

The View Menu

There are a number of ways to selectively review messages in a news or discussion group, in addition to the many we've discussed in connection with the Go and Message menus. If you select **Messages** from the View menu, you'll see three relevant subchoices: **New**, **Threads with New**, and **Watched Threads with New**. Here's how they work:

View-New displays all *new* postings; that is, all posting marked as unread. **View-Threads with New** displays the entire contents of a thread if it contains any unread messages—plus all unread single messages. **View-Watched Threads with New** displays the entire contents of a thread if it contains any unread messages and has been marked as Watched, a subject we'll discuss in the next section.

Special Threads

From time to time threads may occur in your groups in which you have a particular interest: Perhaps the subject is near and dear to your heart; you posed a question or a challenge that's being digested by the group; or someone whose opinions you respect is involved in an ongoing debate. On the other hand, it's equally likely that you'll come across threads in which you're pretty sure nothing important to you will ever crop up—even though the thread may continue for a long time. It might be rehashing a topic you've been through all too many times; "that crowd of idiots again"; or just a subject in which you have zero interest.

To mark such threads, Netscape Collabra provides special symbols that you can display in the left-hand margin of the Discussion window header pane, as shown in Figure 14.9. The Watch Thread symbol is a pair of eye-glasses; the Ignore Thread symbol is the international *not* symbol—the slashed circle.

To mark a thread for watching, first highlight any message in the thread, then select **Watch Thread** from the Message menu or click the right-hand mouse button and select **Watch Thread**, or use the keyboard shortcut **W**. If you change your mind about watching the thread, you can toggle the watch symbol off by repeating any of the three alternative actions.

You can mark single messages in this way, as well as multiple-message threads. As far as Collabra is concerned, you're tagging a header, regardless of how many postings happen to be connected to it.

N O T E

The Ignore Thread symbol is toggled on and off in exactly the same way: Highlight a message in the thread; select **Ignore Thread** from the Message menu or the right-hand mouse button menu or use the keyboard shortcut **K**.

Marking a thread for ignoring also marks all the messages as read, but toggling the Ignore symbol off again does not restore unread status.

N O T E

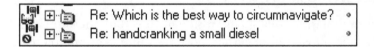

Figure 14.9 *Threads marked for Watching and Ignoring.*

If you want, you can make Ignored threads disappear from your headers list altogether. To do this, go to the View menu and select **Messages**. You should see a check mark next to one of the top four choices; the default choice is All. At the bottom of the group of subchoices, you'll see the entry Ignored. Although it's a bit illogical, when the **View-Messages** command is set to **All**, you can then toggle the display of Ignored headers on or off by selecting **View-Messages-Ignored**.

ORGANIZING AND MANAGING GROUPS

Processing the postings that show up every day takes up much time and energy, so Netscape Collabra devotes tools to daily processing tasks, but Collabra also addresses the problems of dealing with postings over time: tasks such as finding important posts from the past, zeroing in on subgroups of postings within a group, and controlling the accumulation of discussion group material on your system. We'll take a few pages to examine these tools.

Bookmarks

One way to make sure you'll be able to find an important posting quickly is to treat it like a Web page and bookmark it. To bookmark a post, grab the icon that sits in the left-hand margin next to the Subject header and drag it to the **Bookmarks Quick File** icon on the Netscape Navigator Location Toolbar. You can either just drop it on the icon (whereupon it will be added to the end of the general list) or file it in an existing bookmark folder.

To display a bookmarked posting, just select it as you would any Web site; Navigator displays it within a Netscape Message window. Collabra does not open either the Message Center window or Discussion window in order to display the post.

Virtual Discussion Groups

A handy option with Collabra discussion groups (but not with Usenet groups) is the grouping together of certain postings within a group to create a *virtual* group. Perhaps you frequent the Healthy Eaters group, and you find the comments of Jack Sprat particularly inspiring or illuminating. You'd like to be able to pull Jack's posts together in one place.

The solution begins with the **Search Messages** command under the Edit menu. Construct a search query that says **the / sender / is / Jack Sprat**, execute the search, and select **Save As**. This invokes a dialog box, where you enter a name for your virtual discussion group. Click **OK** and your new group will appear in the listing of groups under the appropriate server.

HOT LINK

For help in setting up search queries, see the section on Searching, immediately below, or the more detailed discussion in Chapter 8.

If you want a virtual subject-based group, just create a query that starts **the /
subject / is** (or contains) and proceed as for a sender-based group.

Searching and Sorting

As with e-mail messages, searching and sorting are useful ways to locate messages in the maze. These subjects are covered in depth in Chapter 8, but we'll
review the high points briefly here:

Searching

You can call up the Search Messages dialog box by selecting **Search Messages**
from the Edit menu. This option works exactly as it does in the e-mail context—you can construct complex search queries—but only the sender and
subject fields can be searched.

Also, there are a couple of conceptual problems that rather severely limit
the usefulness of this search function. As mentioned in the previous chapter,
searches in the Subject field are case sensitive: to get a hit, you must enter
your target with exactly the same case structure as in the Subject header field.
Thus the search term *boat* will not find Boat or BOAT. Perhaps worse is the
fact that searches on the Sender field actually search the e-mail address of the
sender, which often does not contain a recognizable version of the person's
real name.

In one posting we targeted with a search, the name displayed in the
Sender field was Dan, so we were quite surprised when searches on *dan* or *Dan*
failed to snag this posting. Seems Dan's e-mail address was aristotle@some-
thingorother.com (which we discovered by opening the message). Sure
enough, a search on *aristotle* did find the post.

Sorting

The header buttons in the Discussion window are sort keys, just as they are in
the Netscape Messenger window. By default, postings are sorted by date and
time of posting, but they can be sorted by any of the header fields. Probably
the most useful possibilities are to sort by Subject (just click the **Subject
header** button) or Sender (click the **Sender** button). To change the sort order
from ascending to descending, just click the button again. You can also perform sorts by selecting **Sort** from the View menu, then picking one of the
fields and choosing ascending or descending order.

Message Management

Most of what news and discussion groups are made of—the typical daily postings—is inherently more transient than your e-mail, so most groups are designed to automatically retire messages after a certain period of time. Collabra is designed the same way; it cleans out the old to make way for the new. In that respect, groups are self-managing.

Nevertheless, you will want to keep some messages on a permanent or semi-permanent basis, and Collabra makes this fairly simple.

Filing Messages

You can easily create storage folders in the Message Center filing system and keep news and discussion posts there indefinitely, just like e-mail messages. Message filing is discussed in great detail in the chapters on electronic mail, but we'll give a short reprise here.

To make a new Message Center folder, select **New Folder** from the File menu and enter a name for your folder in the New Folder dialog box. Then go to the drop-down list below the name field to specify the folder within which you want to make this a subordinate folder. (If you want your new folder to be at the top level—the same level as the Inbox—select **Local Mail**.) Then click **OK**, and you're through.

To file messages, highlight one or more, then click the **File** icon on the Netscape Discussion window Navigation Toolbar and mouse down to your folder. (If the folder you're aiming at is a subfolder, mouse to the folder it's nested in and a selection of subfolders will become available.) Release the mouse button and the message is filed. Alternatively, highlight your message(s) and click the right-hand mouse button. Select **File Message**, and follow the fly-out menu to the folder of your choice. This process is shown in Figure 14.10.

Copying Messages

If you wish to file a message in more than one folder, you can easily make copies by selecting **Copy Message** from the Message menu. A fly-out menu presents the available storage folders.

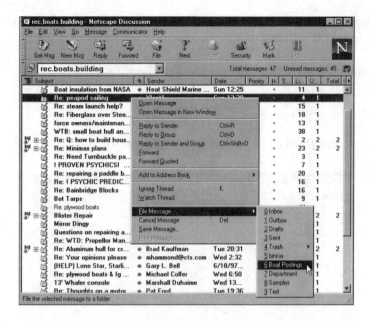

Figure 14.10 *Filing a posting using the right-hand mouse button.*

Saving Messages

If you run across messages you'd really like to keep—and be able to read outside of Communicator—you can save them using the **Save As** menu choice from the File menu (or the **Save Message** option from the right-hand mouse-button menu). This saves the message to a file; you have the option of saving the message in hypertext form (as an HTML file) or as text.

Disk Space and Message Retirement

If you kept all the group postings that entered your computer, you'd have to buy a new hard drive every few months just to store them. In fact, most posts quietly retire—that is, they're automatically deleted. Collabra gives you a number of options, however, that give some measure of control over how much disk space is used and over the details of the retirement process.

On the Advanced page under Preferences (found under the Edit menu), there's a subpage for Disk Space (shown in Figure 14.11), where you can make your default choices. In addition to deciding whether to keep both read and unread messages, or just the unread ones (via the check box at the bottom), you can choose one of the three basic options:

- Keep messages that have arrived in the past X days
- Keep all messages
- Keep only the newest X messages

(In the first and third options, X represents a number you specify.)

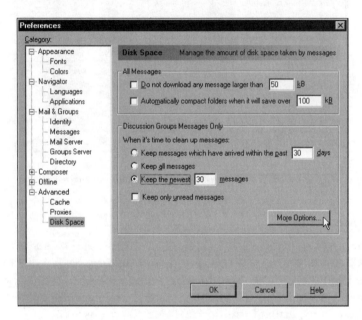

***Figure 14.11** Choices made here limit message storage.*

If you click **More Options**, you'll get another dialog box, shown in Figure 14.12, that gives you the option of discarding the messages themselves (the message "bodies") after a specified number of days, but retaining the headers for reference.

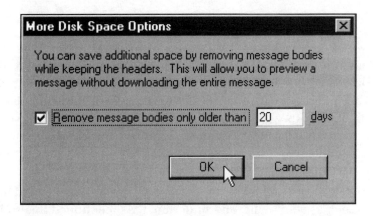

Figure 14.12 This setting lets you keep headers but discard messages.

If you're heavily involved in group discussions, it's likely that some of your groups are more important to you than others—in which case it's likely that you'll want to have different defaults for those groups. To set defaults on a group-by-group basis, highlight the group in the Message Center window, then select **Discussion Group Properties** from the Edit menu (or from the right-hand mouse-button menu). On the Disk Space tab, you'll find the same choices that we just discussed in the Preferences context—including the **More** option for discarding message bodies.

NONTEXT MESSAGE CONTENT

Collabra is a great deal more versatile than previous Netscape news readers in terms of creating and carrying rich content types. First of all, it is an HTML-based program, so it's capable of generating, sending, and receiving messages with HTML content. This means that you can take advantage of a number of text-formatting options and include graphics, tables, and links in your posts. Second, it is MIME-enabled, so you can attach binary files to your posts, thus enriching their communications potential. We'll quickly cover these Collabra options.

HTML Postings

Before you can compose HTML-based posts, you'll first have to go to **Preferences** on the Edit menu, and select **Messages** under **Mail & Groups**. There you'll need to check the box at the top of the page that says **By default, send HTML messages**. (If you've read the chapters on Netscape Messenger, this is familiar territory.) Having done this, you'll find that when you either create a new thread or reply to a post, you'll get the HTML version of the Netscape Composer window (easily identifiable by text-formatting icons on the Formatting toolbar).

In brief, this lets you choose type face, type size, type color, and text style attributes such as bold, italic, and underlined. As mentioned, it also lets you insert links, targets, graphics, horizontal rules, and tables, just as if you were building a Web page.

HOT LINK

The HTML composition capabilities of Collabra are identical with those of Netscape Messenger. For a highly detailed discussion of these capabilities and the commands that drive them, see the section on HTML-based e-mail in Chapter 8.

A moment's reflection will make it clear that much of this capability makes sense only in the context of internal Collabra discussion groups. As far as Usenet groups go, you have no way of knowing whether any of the other group participants are using HTML-capable newsreaders. You certainly can't assume this. Thus if you choose to use HTML in posting or replying to a Usenet group, you run the risk of confusing—or antagonizing—those without HTML-capable readers; they'll see all the HTML code mixed in with your message text. And of course, they won't see the HTML formatting that was the reason for your using HTML to begin with.

The one exception to this caveat is that many newsreaders are smart enough to recognize links, so you may choose to use the HTML version of the Composer window just in order to be able to easily insert links, which you can do by drag and drop, or using the tools accessed from the Composer toolbar and/or menus.

HOT LINK

Again, Collabra's commands for inserting links are essentially identical com-position to those of Netscape Messenger. Those capabilities are discussed in detail in the HTML-based e-mail section in Chapter 8.

Attaching Files and Documents

Along with its HTML capabilities, Netscape Collabra can also send binary files, such as graphics and documents, encoded as MIME attachments (or, when necessary, uuencoded). There are several ways to do so:

- Select **Attach-File** from Composer's File menu. This brings up a dialog box that lets you navigate to the file you want.

- Click the **Attach** icon on Composer's Navigation Toolbar. This brings up the same dialog box. Navigate to the file you want, highlight it, and **OK** the dialog box.

- Click the **Attach Files and Documents** tab in Composer's addressing area, then drag files from your operating system's file manager and drop them here.

If for any reason you prefer uuencoding over MIME encoding, click the **Message Sending Options** tab in Composer's addressing area and click the check box that reads **Uuencode** instead of MIME for attachments.

SUMMARY

Netscape Collabra's advanced features let you quickly and easily process the large numbers of news- and discussion-group posting that an involved newsmeister accumulates—scanning groups for interesting material, sorting and searching to locate specific messages, marking certain threads for continued attention, retiring old postings from your system, and the like.

Collabra's **Offline Work Mode** is great for those who want to minimize their online connect time and/or process discussion group material when they're not connected to the Internet. Collabra has full hyperlinking capabilities and can send and receive HTML postings, as well as carry binary file attachments, either MIME encoded or uuencoded. All, in all, Collabra is a powerful, flexible news- and discussion-group tool.

SECTION 6

Netscape Conference

You can share documents and data in several different ways with Netscape Communicator. One of the more exciting ways is Netscape Conference, which turns your Internet connection into a long-distance phone service. Chapter 15 makes up this section, which covers everything you need to know about Netscape Conference, ranging from phone calls to whiteboard and chat capabilities.

CHAPTER 15

Using Netscape Conference

Sometime in 1995, developers pushing at the limits of Internet technology figured out that they could "stream" digitized audio signals over a Net connection: send packets of audio data rapidly and steadily enough to maintain a voice conversation over the Net—at least some of the time. This led to the craze of Internet telephony.

Netscape Conference, a descendant of the first-generation telephony programs, lets you communicate with colleagues around the globe, in real time, in a variety of ways. This chapter explores the many communications capabilities of Netscape Conference. Topics include:

- Configuring Conference
- Making a Call

- The Speed Dialer
- Voice Mail
- Whiteboarding
- Collaborative Browsing
- Transferring Files
- Using Chat

HARDWARE YOU'LL NEED

To take advantage of all of Conference's features, including telephone style voice communication, your computer system must be configured with a full duplex sound card (one capable of carrying signals for two conversations simultaneously). In addition, you'll need speakers (or at least one speaker) and a microphone. If you don't have these items, they can be purchased for a modest sum (probably well under $100, although you can certainly spend much more).

Even without this hardware, you can utilize Conference's non-voice tools: Whiteboard, Collaborative Browsing, File Exchange, and Chat.

CONFIGURING CONFERENCE

Setting up the Conference module could hardly be simpler. When you start the program for the first time, a wizard steps you through the few operations you need to get up and running.

Following some preliminary remarks and instructions (such as "Have your e-mail address and information about your network connection handy"), the wizard first presents the Business Card dialog box shown in Figure 15.1. The only items that are mandatory are your name and e-mail address. The rest simply serve to identify you to other members of a conference.

NOTE   You can include a picture of yourself. To do so, click the folder icon immediately to the right of the Photo field box. This brings up a File Open dialog box that lets you navigate to the image file of your portrait.

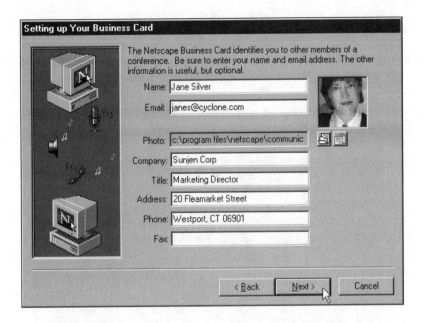

Figure 15.1 Business card info is displayed on-screen during calls.

The next screen gives you an opportunity to specify a Dynamic Lookup Service (DLS) server and a URL for an on-line phone book. Communicator provides default entries for these two items, but you're free to override these with alternative DLS servers and/or phone books. We suggest you go with the defaults.

Screen three asks what kind of network connection you have: 14,400 bps modem, 28,800 bps or higher modem, ISDN, or an LAN (local area network) connection. Just click the appropriate radio button.

The next stop on the agenda is the audio test during which Conference looks for your sound card and runs some automatic routines and enters the relevant data on the Audio page in Conference Preferences (accessed from the Call menu). You can go to this page (select **Preferences** from the Call menu, then **Audio**) to make adjustments or changes. If you don't have a sound card installed, or Conference can't communicate with your card, and the program assumes you won't be using audio. In any case, that's it. You're done.

Making a Call

Once you have started Conference (which you can do by selecting **Conference** from the Communicator menu in any Communicator module), there are several ways to dial up another Conference user. The most basic is to type in the recipient's e-mail address in the **Email address** text box on the Netscape Conference screen and click the **Dial** button, as shown in Figure 15.2.

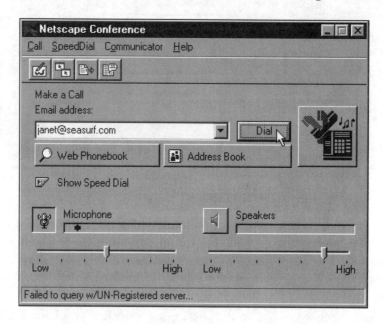

Figure 15.2 Basic calling procedure for Netscape Conference.

Conference then contacts the recipient's system via the DLS server. For a connection to occur, the call recipient must have Conference running on his or her system. If it is—and the person is not engaged in another conversation— Conference sends an invitation to the recipient to join your conversation and displays the Pending Invitation dialog box on your screen. If the recipient accepts, Conference then notifies you in return. If the other party doesn't accept—isn't at the computer, or simply chooses not to take the call— Conference lets you leave a message. (We'll discuss the Voice Mail component of Conference later in this chapter.)

If your party accepts the call, Conference will display the Business Cards of each (including photos, if entered) on the other's screen. To talk, click the **microphone** button (**Talk** button for Macintosh) and, well, talk. You'll probably need to make some adjustments in the volume controls to find optimum sound levels. (We'll take a detailed look at those adjustments in a moment.)

You can also choose among the other Conference tools: Chat, Whiteboard, File Exchange, and Collaborative Browsing. (None of these require a sound card or speakers.)

When your session is complete, click the **Hang Up** button or select **Hang Up** button from the Call menu.

SETTING CALL OPTIONS

Conference has three basic options for answering incoming calls. The default is **Always Prompt**, which means that any time another Conference user attempts to contact you, you'll have an opportunity to accept or decline the invitation. **Auto Answer**, on the other hand, automatically accepts all incoming invitations. **Do Not Disturb** is the option to choose if you don't want to accept any incoming calls.

WARNING

When you're engaged in Whiteboard or Chat sessions (which we'll discuss in detail later in this chapter), interruptions from incoming calls can cause corruption or loss of files and logs generated in these modes. It's a good idea to select **Do Not Disturb**—or, at the very least, **Always Prompt** when using either of these two Conference tools.

AUDIO ADJUSTMENTS

It may take a bit of tweaking to get a strong, clear voice signal with a minimum of extraneous noise. To this end, Conference provides audio level adjustment meters for both Record (that is, microphone) and Playback (that is, speaker) levels, as shown in Figure 15.3. The controls are pretty straightforward, but the adjustments require some understanding.

First of all, you can turn both your microphone and your speakers on or off whenever you like. The Microphone and Speaker buttons are toggles; click to activate if they're inactive or vice versa.

For the Macintosh, click **Talk** to activate your mike, **Mute** to deactivate; **Listen** to activate your speakers, and **Hold** to turn them off.

The slider controls on the Record and Playback meters work just like those on common audio components: Sliding to the right increases volume; sliding to the left decreases it.

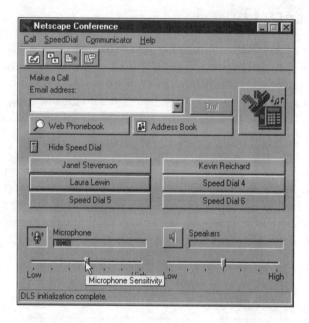

Figure 15.3 The sliders adjust record and playback levels.

The subtle part of sound-level adjustment with Conference relates to the Silence Sensor. This is a sound-level threshold below which Conference doesn't broadcast any signal. The object is to set it high enough that no transmission occurs while you are not speaking, but everything you say is transmitted when you do speak. Here are some guidelines on how to set the Silence Sensor level:

Make sure your microphone is on. Without speaking, note the sound level indicated by the green bars on the Record meter. This is your background "noise" level. Now grab the Silence Sensor bar with your mouse and drag it to the right, so it's just beyond the background noise level. Then speak, both softly and loudly. The Record meter levels should jump past the Silence Sensor indicator. In practice, it may take a bit of fiddling to get this working optimally.

ALTERNATE DIALING METHODS

Dialing by entering the recipient's e-mail address is convenient, since we tend to have the e-mail addresses of the people we communicate with regularly, but Conference lets you dial by several other methods: direct addresses—which in turn include IP addresses (such as 100.1.1.10) and qualified domain names (ted.callhost.com, for example)—and Conference's native Speed Dial feature.

HOT LINK

You can dial directly from the Communicator Address Book or your selected on-line Address Book. We'll discuss these alternatives a bit later in this chapter.

To dial a direct address, type it into the Email address box surrounded by parentheses, then click **Dial**. Alternatively, you can select **Direct Call** from the Call menu and type the direct address into the Direct Call dialog box. Click **Dial** to place the call.

Phone Book Dialing

One of Conference's conveniences it its ability to dial directly from either the Netscape Communicator Address Book or the Web Phone book. Buttons on the Conference screen link you directly to either.

The Communicator Address Book

To bring up your personal Communicator Address Book, click the **Address Book** button on the Conference screen. Once in the Address Book, select the list entry for the person you want to call, then click on the **Dial** icon in the

Address Book toolbar. By default, Communicator will use the e-mail address method of dialing.

If you don't have the person's e-mail address or you prefer to use the direct dialing method, you'll need to take one further step in preparation: Double-click on the Address Book header for the person in question to bring up his or her Card; then click the **Netscape Conference** tab (it's an icon on the Macintosh). Here you'll notice that Netscape Conference DLS server is already selected in the Address field. This is the default, and lets you dial via e-mail address without further ado. If you want to use direct addressing, you'll have to click the down arrow on the Address field list box and select **Hostname or IP Address,** as shown in Figure 15.4. This action enables the text box below, where you can now enter the person's IP address or domain name. With this task out of the way, you can now dial the person using the Dial icon on the Address Book toolbar.

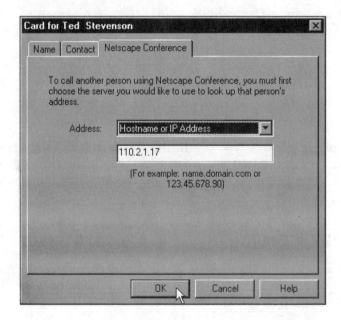

Figure 15.4 *The Address Book entry set up for an IP address.*

The Web Phone book

Clicking the **Web Phone book** icon (for Windows) or selecting **Web Phone book** from the Tools menu will launch a Netscape Navigator window and contact your default DLS server.

At the time Netscape Communicator was released, the default server was **net-dls.four11.com**. To change to another server, select **Preferences** from the Call menu and enter another DLS Server and Phone book URL in correct the boxes.

N O T E

When the Web Phone book page loads, you'll need to adopt the methodology of that particular directory. If you use the default **Four11** directory, you'll be in a special Netscape Conference section that lists other Conference users who are currently on-line. There's a search window in which you can enter a name you're looking for, or you can scan the list of all current users. Each user's e-mail address is listed, but there's also a hyperlink you can click on to dial the user directly.

If you plan to use a Web Phone book regularly, it's a good idea to register so that others can find you in the directory. You'll generally find a link on the directory's home page that you can click to register.

N O T E

The Speed Dialer

Normally hidden on the Conference screen, but accessible by a single mouse click, is a set of six Speed Dial buttons. To display the Speed Dial buttons, click the trapezoidal button to the left of the label **Show Speed Dial** (right below the Web Phone book button). You'll immediately see the Speed Dial button array, as shown in Figure 15.5.

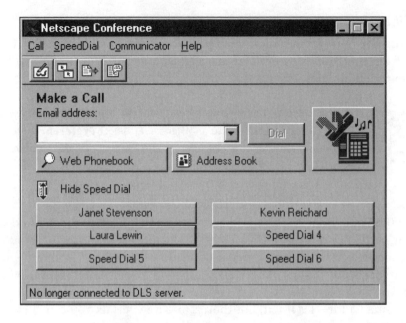

Figure 15.5 *Netscape Conference's Speed Dial buttons.*

To set up any inactive Speed Dial button either select the button number from the SpeedDial menu or click the button itself. (The latter works only on Windows and UNIX.) You then need to enter the required information in the Edit Speed Dial dialog box, as shown in Figure 15.6. The contents of the Name field will be displayed on the button, once you close. You must also enter either an **Email** address or a **Direct** address. Click **OK** and your button is programmed.

To use a Speed Dial button for calling, just click. Conference takes care of the details. To change the information associated with a button, select that button number from the SpeedDial menu, and then choose **Edit**. To clear a button, select the button number from the SpeedDial menu and then choose **Clear** .

To hide the Speed Dial buttons on the Conference screen, click the vertical pebbled bar to the left of the **Hide Speed Dial** label.

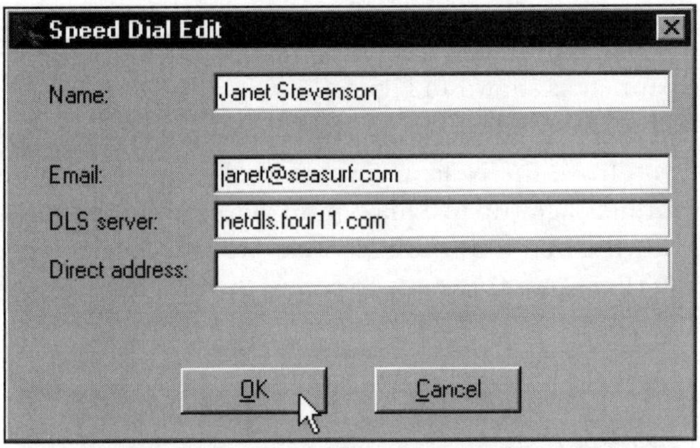

Figure 15.6 *Readying a Speed Dial button for action.*

VOICE MAIL

In addition to managing live voice calls, Netscape Conference can deliver voice mail messages to other Conference users. Conference transforms your voice input into a digital audio file and attaches this as a MIME type to a standard Netscape Messenger e-mail, which is delivered to the recipient's Messenger Inbox.

NOTE Strange as it may seem, recipients can listen to Netscape Conference voice mail messages only if they have the Live Audio plug-in installed.

When you attempt a Netscape Conference voice call but can't get through for any reason, Conference suggests sending a voice mail , but you can go straight to the voice mail step, skipping the voice call, if you wish.

To send a voice mail without first placing a call, select **Voice Mail** from Conference's Communicator menu. This brings up a dialog box in which you enter the recipient's e-mail address. When you **OK** this dialog box, you'll see the Netscape Voice Mail dialog box with your recipient's e-mail address displayed in the banner, as shown in Figure 15.7.

If you failed to make a direct voice connection but clicked the **Send Voice Mail** prompt, you'll see the Netscape Voice Mail dialog box as well. You can now record your message (up to a maximum of four minutes in length). Click the **Start** button (the one with the red circle on it) to begin recording; click the **Stop** button (the square) to end. To review the message, click the **Play** button (the triangle).

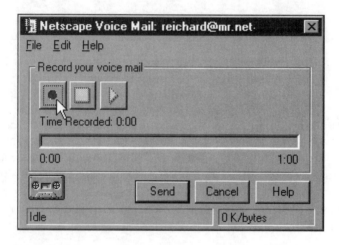

Figure 15.7 *Click the button with the red circle to Record.*

When you've completed your voice mail message, click **Send,** and you'll be taken to the Netscape Communicator Message Composition window (discussed in the chapters on Netscape Messenger and Netscape Collabra). Here you can type any text you want or need, to accompany your voice mail. When you're done, send your e-mail message in the normal manner.

The Message Composition window and all the standard procedures for sending e-mail messages are discussed in the chapters devoted to Netscape. Review Chapters 8 and 9 if you need further information on sending e-mail.

HOT LINK

Configuring Voice Mail

Although it's pretty much set up with defaults so that you don't have to fiddle with it, Conference does have a small configuration page, where you can select one of two CODECs (compression/decompression algorithms) for use in recording the message sound clip, and set a time limit for your messages.

To configure Voice Mail, select **Preferences** from the Edit menu. This calls up the Preferences dialog box, shown in Figure 15.8. The General settings include **Default Voice Mail Subject**, a text box in which you can enter a different phrase to be inserted in the Subject line of the e-mail that carries your voice mail message, and **Maximum Length (minutes)**, a self-explanatory setting to limit the length of your messages.

If you want to keep your voice mail messages to 100KB or less—not a bad idea—leave the default setting of 1 minute.

N O T E

In the **Audio Quality** area, you can choose between the two CODECs made available in Conference. The default, **higher quality**, is the higher of the two bit rates (called, oddly enough, **Low Bitrate**). If you need to record longer messages but keep the message size down, try the **Very Low Bitrate** setting. This may or may not give acceptable audio quality. If it doesn't, switch back to **Low Bitrate** and keep your messages shorter.

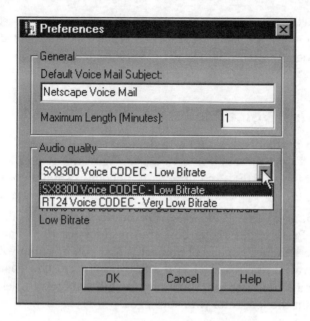

Figure 15.8 *Choosing an audio CODEC and associated Bitrate.*

THE NETSCAPE CONFERENCE TOOLS

As mentioned in the introduction to this chapter, Netscape Conference encompasses four tools in addition to audio conferencing and voice mail: Whiteboard, Collaborative Browsing, File Exchange, and Chat. Each can be accessed either from a button on the Conference toolbar or from the Communicator menu. We'll look at the four tools one at a time.

Whiteboarding

A whiteboard is analogous to the blackboards most of us had in school. It is similar in that any Conference participant can write or draw on it, and those writings or drawings can be erased. The difference, aside from the color, is that the participants don't have to be in the same schoolroom—or even the same country—to do this. Think of it as a remote-control sketch pad.

You can draw, paint, or type on the whiteboard. You can also place images there, either from files stored on your system or captured from your current desktop. The drawing and typing tools can then be used to annotate or edit image material.

NOTE   It's important to realize that image data and drawing data exist on separate "layers." This means that you can mark up an image and erase or change the marks without disturbing the underlying image. A box in the lower right-hand corner of the Whiteboard lets you switch the Edit focus back and forth between Image and Markup layers.

The Drawing Tools

If you've ever worked with an image or paint program, the drawing tools in Conference Whiteboard should look reasonably familiar to you. If you look at the buttons in the Tool palette in the left margin, you'll see a freehand marker and a freehand eraser. You'll also see tools for drawing circles and rectangles, both open and filled. You'll find a pointer tool that positions a big arrow in the whiteboard space (see Figure 15.9). The text tool is represented by the capital letter A. Below this are tools for drawing slanted and horizontal/vertical lines.

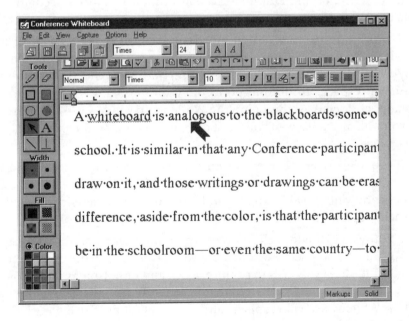

Figure 15.9 The Pointer tool can indicate anything on the canvas.

A line-width selector below the tool palette lets you choose among four line weights; below this, a fill-pattern selector provides a variety of textures to fill the interiors of ovals and rectangles. A color selector at the bottom lets you pick any of 20 colors, that can be applied to any drawing or text element.

A box in the very bottom right-hand corner of the Whiteboard screen lets you choose between **Solid** or **Clear** rendering of drawn elements. Click the box to toggle between the two settings. With the box set to Clear, some of the background image will show through the top layer.

The Image Tools

As mentioned, you can load existing GIF and JPEG images from your hard drive into the Whiteboard window. To do this, select **Open** from the File menu or click the **File open** button on the Whiteboard toolbar (immediately below the File menu). This brings up a navigation window that lets you choose the image from your file system. Once you've selected it, a position rectangle lets you see where you're placing the picture.

Alternatively, you can copy an image from another application or document and paste into the Whiteboard workspace. The commands for this operation are found on the Edit menu; a pair of toolbar buttons accomplish the same tasks.

A more unusual way of getting material onto the Whiteboard's image layer is to "capture" it from your desktop or another application, that is, to copy what's displayed on your computer monitor and paste it into the Whiteboard space. To do this, go to the Capture menu and select **Window, Desktop**, or **Region**. At this point, the Whiteboard window will minimize, leaving you with a clear view of your desktop; your mouse pointer will be a pair of cross-hairs.

If you select **Window**, move the cross-hairs to any location within the application window you wish to capture and click. In a few seconds, the Whiteboard window will reappear and a positioning rectangle will guide you in placing the image of the window on the whiteboard space.

If you select **Desktop**, click anywhere on the desktop and that image will be captured. If you select **Region**, move your cross-hairs to the upper left-hand corner of the area you wish to capture. Click and drag (that is, hold down the mouse button) to the lower right-hand corner. When you release the mouse button, Whiteboard will reappear and the positioning rectangle will let you precisely locate the image on the Whiteboard space.

Other Whiteboard Commands

Conference's Whiteboard menus contain a number of useful commands that we haven't so far seen in the context of the features discussed above. We'll go over these quickly now.

On the Edit menu, **Clear Markups** and **Clear Whiteboard** eradicate the contents of the markup layer and the entire workspace, respectively. **Synchronize Page** lets one member of the conference correct any display errors that may have occurred on the screens of other members, due to networking glitches. **Paste Bitmap, Paste Text,** and **Paste Picture** let you insert images, text sections, and vector drawings copied from other documents. **Paste Owner Display** lets you insert any display material that's been copied to the system clipboard.

The View menu contains a series of commands for zooming in or out with respect to the whiteboard canvas. To **Zoom in**, select a ratio (**1:8, 1:4,** or **1:2**), then center the cross-hairs of the magnifying glass icon over the point in the display you want to zoom in on, and click. To Zoom out, pick a ratio (**3:1, 5:1,** or **9:1**). If the chosen ratio produces a smaller image than the current size, the zoom happens automatically; if it's bigger, you'll have to click the magnifying glass icon somewhere over the image. **Original size**, of course, returns the display to the original magnification. **Refresh** redraws the screen should any display irregularities occur.

The Options menu lets you choose **Solid** or **Clear** fill, and toggle the **Erase** function between the **Markup** and **Image** layers. These commands can be executed by clicking in the indicator boxes in the lower right-hand corner of the Conference window. **Floating Toolbar** detaches the toolbar from the left-hand side of the Conference window and makes it mobile. **Hide on Capture,** the default setting, makes the Conference window disappear when you select any of the Capture commands. If you want Conference to stay on top the image during screen-capture operations, toggle the setting off. **Dither Screen Capture** lets you optimize the display of captured screens. Toggle it **off** if you care more about speed than appearance. **Compress** toggles the compression of images sent. **Pop Up on Receive** sets Conference to activate automatically when an incoming message arrives. **Canvas Size** lets you specify the extent of the Whiteboard workspace or canvas you want in pixels. On Windows and UNIX systems, you'll have to restart the system for this command to take effect.

Collaborative Browsing

The **Collaborative Browsing** tool lets conference participants share a Web browsing session by linking the operation of Netscape Navigator to Conference, presumably for the purpose of directing some aspect of a voice discussion. One member of the conference becomes the "Leader," and the contents of the Leader's browser is transmitted to the other participants.

You initiate a session by clicking the **Collaborative Browsing** button on the Conference or selecting **Collaborative Browsing** from the **Communicator** menu. This calls up the Collaborative Browsing dialog box, shown in Figure 15.10. To get the session going, click **Start Browsing.** This launches Navigator, if it's not already running, and sends "invitations" to the other participants. If the other parties accept, their copies of Navigator launch, and you're in sync.

By initiating the session, you automatically become Leader, but the lead can change hands at any time. All that's required is that the other party check this box during the course of the session. If the "follower" temporarily assumes control of his or her own browser during the session (as opposed to assuming Leadership), the Leader can bring the participants back into synchronization by clicking the **Sync Browsers** button.

To end a Collaborative Browsing session, simply click the **Stop Browsing** button (this is the same button as **Start Browsing**; it changes form once you're into a browsing session). You'll have to close Navigator independently; closing **Collaborative Browsing** does not do this.

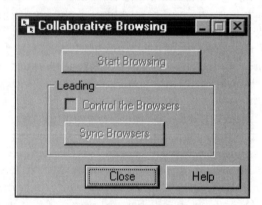

*Figure 15.10 Click **Start Browsing** to initiate a collaborative session.*

Transferring Files

Moving files around is an important computer function these days. E-mail programs (like Netscape Messenger) do it; even some fax programs do it. But being able to do it in the context of a Conference session is really handy. Conference's File Exchange tool is a breeze to use.

Launch the tool by clicking the **File Exchange** button on the Conference toolbar or selecting **File Exchange** from the Communicator menu. Either action calls up the File Exchange window, shown in Figure 15.11.

To specify files to send, choose **Add to send list** from the File menu (Windows users can also press **Ctrl+A**) or click the **Open** button on the File Exchange toolbar. This brings up the **Add File to Send List** dialog box, which lets you navigate to and select one file at a time. Each selected file then appears in the File(s) to Send portion of the split-screen File Exchange display. Repeat the action for every additional file you wish to send.

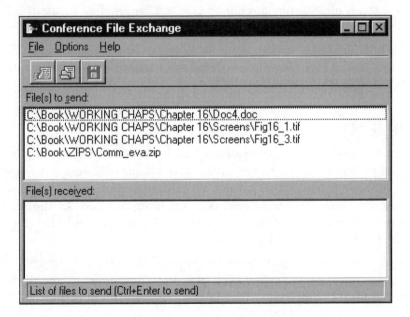

Figure 15.11 *Files ready to be sent out via File Exchange.*

When you're finished adding files, click the **Send** button on the toolbar or choose **Send** from the File menu. Off they go.

Files coming to you just show up as headers in the **File(s) received** window. To save an incoming file, click the header to select it, then click the **Save** button on the File Exchange toolbar or choose **Save** from the File menu. As with any save operation, you'll be able to specify a name and location for the file. If there's a file you don't want to save, highlight it and choose **Delete** from the File menu (**Trash** for Macintosh users).

File Exchange Options

There are all of four options for File Exchange (found under the Options menu); three if you consider that one is an either-or choice. **Compress** (the default) compresses files before transmission—and, naturally, it decompresses them on receipt. This results in fewer data packets being sent over the Internet (or intranet). To turn compression off, simply select **Compress** from the Options menu. It's a toggle.

Pop Up on Receive sets up File Exchange to launch automatically when someone sends files in your direction. As with **Compress**, to toggle this function off, just select **Pop Up on Receive** from the Options menu.

The final selections on the Options menu are **ASCII** and **Binary**. Choose **ASCII** to transmit text files; choose **Binary** to transmit executable programs, images, or other binary data files.

Using Chat

The most obvious reason to use chat (back-and-forth communication by means of real-time text messages) in an audio conferencing system is when one or both participants don't have the hardware necessary to send voice signals. Another, less obvious, reason is to maintain a record of the session. **Conference Text Chat** can indeed log the entire session and save the transcript to disk for editing and later reference.

As with the other Conference tools, you can launch Chat either by clicking the **Chat** button, or selecting **Chat** from the Communicator menu. Either action calls up the **Conference Text Chat** window, shown in Figure 15.12.

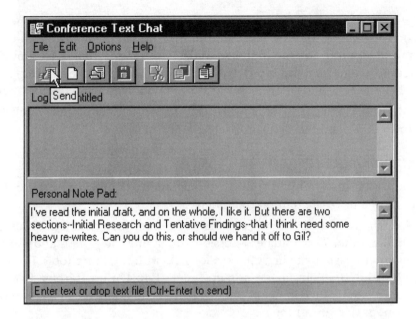

Figure 15.12 *Type your messages in the Personal Note Pad pane.*

Posting Messages

Once the Chat window is displayed, you can type a message in the **Personal Note Pad** pane of the split-screen display. To send it off, simply click the **Send** button (as shown in the Figure above) or choose **Post Note Pad** from the File menu. You can, of course, paste material into your message from the system clipboard (there are **Cut**, **Copy**, and **Paste** buttons on the toolbar) or insert the contents of a file by choosing **Include** from the File menu or clicking the **Include** button on the toolbar.

Logging Chat Sessions

As you and your chat partner trade messages back and forth, each message is appended to the session Log that accumulates in the upper pane of the Chat screen. If you want to keep this log, you can save it to disk by clicking the **Save** button or selecting **Save** or **Save As** from the File menu and giving the file a name and location. You can then save updates as you go along by clicking **Save** from time to time. Any time you want to clear the **Log file** pane and start a new log, click the **New** button on the toolbar or choose **New** from the **File** menu.

You can print a chat session log directly from the Chat module by clicking the **Print** button on the toolbar or selecting **Print** from the File menu.

Configuring Chat

There are but two humble configuration options—both available from the Options menu. We'll mention them here.

As with the other Conference Tools, you can set **Chat** to automatically pop up when another user initiates a session (or, at any rate, when another user invites you to participate in a chat session). As with the other tools, this is the default. To disable automatic pop-up, select **Pop Up on Receive** from the Options menu. (The command is a toggle; selecting it turns the feature off if it was on, or vice versa.)

If you want to select a particular font for the Chat display on your system (not that of another participant), select **Font** from the Options menu. This brings up Communicator's Font dialog box, from which you can choose any available system font, size, and style.

SUMMARY

Netscape Conference lets you make phone calls over the network, and it requires audio hardware like a sound card, a microphone, and speakers to do this. The sound quality may or may not be up to telephone quality, but Conference provides some features and functions you can't get with a conventional telephone: You can share visual materials with your conference partner, using either the **Whiteboard** tool or the **Collaborative Browsing** tool, and you can exchange files using the **File Exchange** tool. If you don't have the audio hardware to utilize real-time voice connections, you can use **Conference Text Chat** to conduct real-time text conversations.

SECTION 7

Netscape Communicator Pro Components

Netscape Communicator comes in two versions: a Standard edition (which most of you will use) and a Professional edition that comes with several components that will be used only by a small subset of Netscape Communicator users. This section covers the components that are part of the Professional edition of Netscape Communicator.

Chapter 16 covers Netscape Calendar, a tool for organizing your schedule and meshing it with other users in your workgroup.

Chapter 17 covers IBM Host on Demand, which opens a TN3270 session on a remote mainframe.

Using Netscape Calendar

If you have the Professional Edition of Netscape Communicator, you'll be able to take advantage of the rich calendaring and scheduling capabilities of Netscape Calendar. This program lets you keep track of all your meetings, appointments, tasks, and notes about your work and other aspects of your life. If your organization uses the Netscape Calendar Server, you'll also be able to schedule meetings with colleagues throughout the enterprise and reserve "resources" such as meeting rooms or audio-visual equipment. This chapter will cover the ins and outs of personal and group scheduling using Netscape Calendar. Topics include:

- An overview of Calendar
- Setting an Agenda

- Recording Tasks
- Setting Calendar Preferences
- Printing your Agenda
- Group Scheduling
- Working Off-line
- Working with Palmtops

SCHEDULING BY COMPUTER

An appointment calendar is an indispensable tool for any busy person, and software designers have been turning out computerized versions of the familiar printed appointment book for more than a decade. Along the way, they've learned that, as handy as computers are for recording, sorting, and finding data, to compete with written appointment diaries, programs need to be fast, portable, and easy to use. Netscape Calendar scores quite well on these three criteria.

In addition, a *networked* calendar program can do something that no printed appointment book can do: automate the often-arduous process of scheduling meetings among varying numbers of people. Working in combination with the Netscape Calendar Server, Netscape Calendar can handle this task across an entire organization, no matter how large or dispersed.

AN OVERVIEW OF NETSCAPE CALENDAR

Like most calendaring and scheduling programs, Calendar bases its interface on a time-slotted page that looks a lot like that of a printed page-per-day appointment book, as shown in Figure 16.1. The date is printed on a bar above the page, next to some navigation buttons. There are toolbar buttons and pull-down menus at the top; there's space on the bottom for recording notes and events that relate to the day as a whole and space on the right-hand side of the screen to record tasks you need to track.

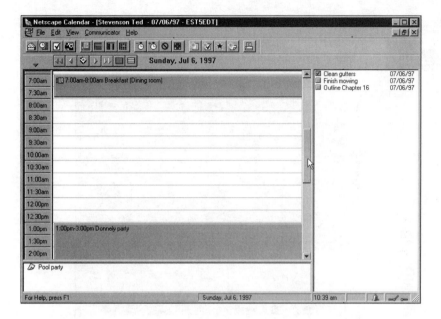

Figure 16.1 *The basic Netscape Calendar interface.*

Setting an Agenda

To use Calendar, you select a time slot and make an Agenda Entry (for things like a meeting or other event) by one of the following three methods:

- Select **New** from the File menu, then **Agenda Entry**
- Click the **New Agenda Entry** button on the toolbar (the one with the glowing plus sign over a document icon)
- Press the **F2** key (for Windows) or **-N** (for Macintosh)

Any of these actions will invoke the tabbed New Agenda Entry dialog box, shown in Figure 16.2. Type in a description of the entry in the Title field (such as **Phone Mom**), adjust the **Start time**, **Duration**, or **End time** if necessary, add **People** or **Resources**, if that's appropriate, and click the **Create** button at the bottom of the dialog box. Your entry will now appear on the Calendar page in the appropriate time slot.

MACINTOSH

The Macintosh interface uses icons instead of tabs to access the various pages of a configuration dialog. Wherever we say *tab,* read *icon* if you're a Mac user.

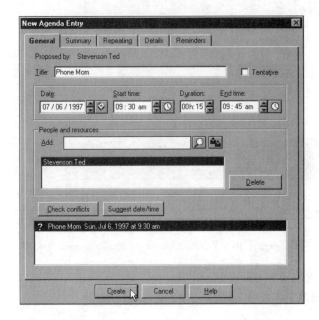

Figure 16.2 The heart of Calendar's scheduling system.

If you want to note some details about the Entry, click the **Details** tab. You can type a substantial amount of text into the Description field on this page.

To set an automatic reminder or tickler, click the **Reminders** tab. Here you can choose either a pop-up window (shown in Figure 16.3) or an Upcoming list as a reminder style, setting the timing in terms of minutes, hours, or days before the scheduled event.

Entries can also be unique (like **Donnely party**) or repeating (like **Phone Mom**, scheduled for every Sunday morning at 9:30, rain or shine). To schedule repeating Entries, click the **Repeating** tab on the New Agenda Entry dialog box. The range of scheduling choices is quite flexible, including options such as monthly on a specific date (the 5th of every month) or monthly on a specific day (second Thursday of every month). You can include or exclude Saturdays, Sundays, and holidays.

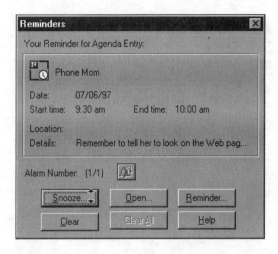

Figure 16.3 Calendar's pop-up window reminds you of scheduled events.

Recording Tasks

Netscape Calendar is equally adept at recording and tracking the tasks that make up your agenda. To enter a new task, click the **New Task** toolbar icon (the one with the check box and the glowing plus sign), select **New** from the File menu, then **Task**, or press the **F7** key (for Windows) or **⌘-T** (for Macintosh).

The New Task dialog box, shown in Figure 16.4, lets you set Due and Start dates and times, record a Completion date and the percentage that's currently completed (0% at the start, of course). You can also assign a numerical Priority to the task and set an Access level. The latter determines who else in your organization can view the details of this Entry from your on-line Agenda.

As with Agenda Entries, you can record notes or other text about a task by clicking the **Details** tab and typing in the Comments: field. Likewise, to set reminders, click the **Reminders** tab. You'll discover that you can set a reminder for both the Start time and the Due time. Very handy.

Tasks appear in the right-hand pane of the Day view, with their Due dates to the right. When you've recorded a percent completed, that's visible in parentheses. The check box for an overdue task is outlined in red. When you complete a task, simply click the check box and Calendar records it as Completed.

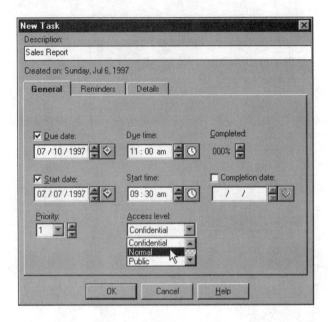

Figure 16.4 *Setting the Access level for a new task.*

Day Events and Daily Notes

If any given day contains an especially important event, or has a particular focus, you can record this as a Day Event (such as **Sales Meeting**); it will appear in the space below your individual Agenda Entries. Likewise, if you need to make a note that applies to the day generally, or to a Day Event (**Bring photos of new product line**, for example), you can use the Daily Notes option.

These options can be accessed from the File menu, like Agenda Entries and Tasks. Similarly, both have Toolbar buttons and keyboard shortcuts. Initiating a Day Event or Daily Note by any of these methods brings up a tabbed dialog box into which you enter information, pretty much along the lines we've covered for Entries and Tasks.

THE CALENDAR TOOLBAR

Most of Calendar's basic functions can be accessed from buttons on the main toolbar. The following list gives a quick rundown on these buttons and what they do—in the order in which the buttons appear on the toolbar, left to right. Where these duplicate menu commands or have keyboard shortcuts, we note these items:

- **Open In-tray** takes you to a page where meeting requests from others are queued, letting you review and act on those requests. (We'll cover this in more detail in the section on group scheduling, later in this chapter.) The command can also be accessed by selecting **Open In-tray** from the File menu or pressing **Ctrl-I** (for Windows) or **⌘-I** (for Macintosh).

- **Open an Agenda** opens your agenda or that of any other Calendar user for whom you have access rights. The command can also be accessed by selecting **Open Agenda** from the File menu or pressing **Ctrl-A** (for Windows) or **⌘-N** (for Macintosh).

- **Open Tasks** takes you to a view of all the day's tasks in a columnar display. From this you can open and edit any individual task by double-clicking.

- **Open Group Agenda** lets you create a side-by-side comparison of the personal agendas of multiple Calendar users (and resources as well), basically for the purpose of scheduling meetings. The button brings up the Selection for Group Agenda dialog box, where you enter names for people and resources. Once you **OK** this dialog box, Calendar displays the Group Agenda view, with a column for each participant and resource and a Combined column that shows whatever free time all have in common. This command can also be accessed by choosing **Open Agenda** from the File menu, then the sub-choice **A Group Agenda**. The keyboard shortcut is **Ctrl-G** (for Windows), **⌘-G** (for Macintosh).

- **Go to Entry** locates the selected In-tray entry in your Daily Agenda page.

- **View day** returns you to the Day View from whatever other Calendar view you might be in. This can also be done by selecting **Day** from the View menu or pressing **F8** (for Windows).

- **View week** returns you to the Week View from whatever other Calendar view you might be in. This can also be done by selecting **Week** from the View menu or pressing **F9** (for Windows).

- **View month** returns you to the Month View from whatever other Calendar view you might be in. This can also be done by selecting **Month** from the View menu or pressing **F10** (for Windows).

- **Decrease time slot** makes your Day View more granular by making the discrete scheduling units of shorter duration. For example, clicking the button three times would change the slots from half-hour, to 20-minute, to 15-minute intervals. Selecting **Decrease Time Slot** from the Edit menu does the same thing.

- **Increase time slot** does the reverse. You can also do this by selecting **Increase Time Slot** from the Edit menu.

- **Icons on/off** toggles the display of icons on your various Calendar views for such things as Day Events, Daily Notes, and Reminders. Choose **Icons on/off** from the View menu to do the same thing.

- **Agenda Entry Colors** lets you choose among three color-coding schemes for the Entries on your Calendar views: The Attendance Status scheme keys colors to status conditions such as Accepted, Tentative, or Refused Entries. The Importance Level scheme keys colors to the five levels of importance you (or others) can set for each Agenda Entry (on the New Agenda Entry or Edit Entry dialog boxes). The Entry Ownership scheme keys colors to whether you or others initiated an Entry and whether it is firm or tentative. The command can also be accessed by selecting **Event Colors** from the View menu.

- **New Agenda Entry**, **New Task**, **New Day Event**, and **New Daily Note**, which we've discussed in our overview, above, bring up the dialog boxes used to enter their respective data types into Calendar. All four commands can be accessed by selecting **New** from the File menu, then selecting the appropriate subchoice. The keyboard shortcuts are **F3**, **F7**, **F4**, and **F5**, respectively (for Windows) or ⌘-N, ⌘-T, ⌘-E, or ⌘-D (for Macintosh).

- **Print**, as you might imagine, lets you print any Calendar's several reports. You can accomplish this also by choosing **Print** from the File menu or pressing **Ctrl-P** (for Windows) or ⌘-P (for Macintosh). We'll cover printing in a later section.

CALENDAR'S WORKING VIEWS

One of the great advantages that an electronic appointment book provides is effortless switching among various calendar views—day, week, and month—that provide a balance between detail and the bigger picture. Netscape Calendar provides these three views; you can access them either via toolbar buttons or keyboard shortcuts (discussed above) or from the View menu.

In addition to letting you see how your time is blocked out, the Week and Month views give you a handy way to move Entries between days; you can drag and drop them from one time slot to another. We'll cover this and other manipulations a bit later in this chapter.

SETTING CALENDAR PREFERENCES

As with all other Netscape Communicator modules, the basic configuration choices for Calendar are carried out in a group of seven Preferences dialog boxes, accessed from the Edit menu. Unlike Navigator, Messenger, or Collabra, however, Calendar will work fine whether or not you make any choices here. Still, if you want to customize or fine-tune the operation of Calendar, this is where you'll do it.

The seven Preferences dialog boxes are:

- Agenda
- In-tray
- Scheduling
- Entry Defaults
- General
- Off-line
- Palmtop

We'll discuss each, at least briefly. Most of the choices—and there are a lot of them—are reasonably self-explanatory; we'll concentrate on the more important ones.

The Agenda dialog box has two tabs, as shown in Figure 16.5. One lets you set up the appearance of your calendar pages, controlling the hours covered, the granularity of your appointment time, which day of the week to start with, whether to display Saturday or Sunday, and a number of details about what's displayed in the Entry boxes. (For example, you can turn off the Start/End time display, which redundantly prints the times indicated by the graphical display.) The second tab, Notification, lets you elect to receive e-mail notifications of Entries, check automatically for new Entries from others, and automatically send e-mails to others when you make changes to your Agenda.

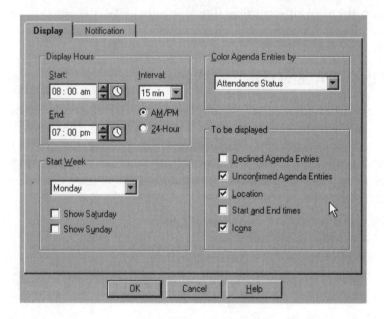

Figure 16.5 *Calendar's Agenda Preferences configuration dialog box.*

The In-tray dialog box has tabs for **New**, **Accepted**, **Sent**, and **Refused Entries**. On these tabs you set parameters for how to process the Entry type and how much Entry history Calendar should show you when you view each.

Scheduling lets you define your working day in terms of normal and extended hours for each day of the week. Optionally, you can define the hours for one day and apply them to all the rest.

The Entry Defaults dialog box has tabs for the four types of Calendar enti-ties: Agenda Entries, Tasks, Day Events, and Daily Notes. Here you set stan-dard Importance and Access Levels and set Reminders to be automatically On or Off for each type, individually.

General has three tabs. The Names tab lets you select a style for displaying user names (such as last name first, with or without middle initial, etc.), how Organizational Units and Resources are displayed, and which directory infor-mation should be included in user entries. The Date and Time tab, as you would imagine, lets you choose among a number of date styles and select the 12-hour or 24-hour clock. A Time Zones tab lets you enter your time zone and manipulate it temporarily in order to coordinate scheduling events with col-leagues in other time zones.

Those who plan to work offline will want to make settings in the Off-line Preferences dialog box, which has five tabs. **Location** lets you select (or cre-ate) a directory or folder to store your offline data. The **Download** tab lets you specify a time span for which to download schedule information and whether to download automatically, by prompt, or not at all when going on- or offline. The **People/Resources** tab is where you list those for whom you want Agendas downloaded for offline work. The **Groups** tab does the same for group Agendas. The **Reconciliation** tab lets you choose whether your offline version of an Entry or that residing on the Host will prevail when changes are detected and decide how conflicts will be handled.

The Palmtop dialog box lets you make the same decisions as does the Off-line dialog box, but with regard to an Agenda residing on your palmtop.

PRINTING

Despite the usefulness of electronic schedules kept on desktop, or laptop, or palmtop computers, many Calendar users will want to print their Agendas—and Task lists—at least occasionally. To that end Calendar provides a highly adaptable printing system that incorporates 24 styled formats, many for pop-ular printed appointment calendars such as the DayTimer, DayRunner, and Franklin Day Planner, as listed in Figure 16.6.

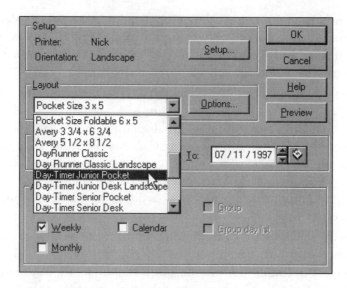

Figure 16.6 You can choose formats for many popular printed calendars.

In the Print dialog box you can also select a range of dates to print, and then opt for any or all of five views: **Day**, **Week**, **Month**, **Day List**, or **Calendar**. If, for example, you specified the dates for a week and checked the Week view, you'd get a single five- or seven-column page. If you checked Day view, you'd get five (or seven) separate pages. Day List is a nongraphical version of the daily calendar, with all appointments and tasks printed in paragraph style. Calendar is simply a rendering of the 12 months of the current year; it doesn't contain any Agenda information.

The **Options** button on the Print dialog box brings up a page on which you can customize each view. There are literally dozens of options available here, including font and margin settings. Let's take a look at some of the choices for the Day view, as an example of the kind of customization you do via the Options dialog box, shown in Figure 16.7.

First, you can include some information (Description and Location) while excluding other info (Start and End times). You can specify the time range to be included in the main Agenda display (9:00 A.M. to 5:30 P.M. in this case). That's all pretty standard stuff. But the column selectors in the middle of the dialog box let you pick and choose from a number of other useful items to include on your printed page. These include **Tasks**, **Day List**, **Calendar**, and **Note Pad**, a lined area for notes you make during the day. Click the **Preview** button and you'd see a page something like the one in Figure 16.8.

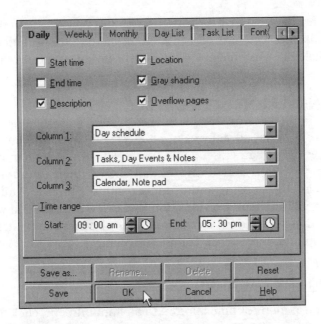

Figure 16.7 Pick and choose what to print in your personal pages.

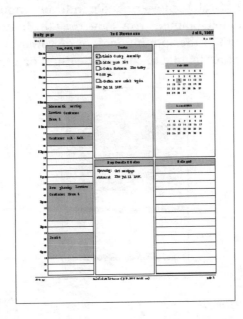

Figure 16.8 Calendar and Note Pad are useful customized touches.

Notice also that there's a Save As button. Once you've worked out the details of a layout you like, you can save it for reuse by using the **Save As** button. Calendar provides a dialog box in which you can give the layout a unique name.

DRAG-AND-DROP SCHEDULING

Another of the special advantages of an electronic appointment calendar is that you'll never need an eraser again. With Netscape Calendar, you can easily move (reschedule) Agenda Entries and change their duration by several methods, including dragging and dropping with the mouse. While these features work in all of Calendar's views, the Week view is the one in which you'll probably do these operations most often (since Entries can be dragged from day to day and time-slotted with complete accuracy).

Changing the Duration

To change the amount of time allotted to an appointment, click the box representing that Entry. It will change into a white box with a heavy blue border, as shown in Figure 16.9. In the center of the border's top and bottom are white *resizing handles*. Grab the lower handle with your mouse pointer (which will change into a double-pointed arrow) and drag the bottom border upward to decrease the length of the appointment, or downward to increase it. (You can, of course use either handle to change the duration of an Entry.)

Figure 16.9 Drag the handles up or down to change meeting duration.

To do this manually, first double-click the **Entry**. This brings up the Edit Entry dialog box. You can change the duration by altering the **Start** time, the

Duration or the **End** time. To do this, you can highlight the appropriate numbers in the time display and type in the new numbers, or use the spinners to increase or decrease the numbers. Alternatively, you can click the clock icon next to the Start or End time and use the timeline (shown in Figure 16.10) to set a new time. Either grab the big blue arrow with your mouse pointer and drag it or use the scroll arrow buttons on either end of the linear time display.

Figure 16.10 A quick, visual way to set Start or End time.

Rescheduling

To move or reschedule an Entry, first click the box, as described above, then grab the border anywhere in the blue area. The mouse pointer will change into a tiny rectangle (representing the Entry box) with arrows pointing up and down. You can now drag the Entry to another time slot in the same day or to another day's column, dropping it in the appropriate time slot.

To do this manually, double-click the **Entry** to bring up the Edit Entry dialog box. Here you may change the date, if necessary, and/or the **Start** and **End** times. The procedures are the same as described for changing the duration of an Entry, above. An alternative to entering a new date manually is to click the calendar icon to the right of the Date field. This brings up the calendar selector shown in Figure 16.11. To enter a new date, just click the button for the date of your choice.

Figure 16.11 A quick, easy way to select an Entry date.

LINKING TASKS TO ENTRIES

When you edit an existing Entry, you'll find one tab on the dialog box that you don't see when you're creating a new Entry. It's called Linked Tasks. To link a task to the current Entry, click the **New** button at the bottom of the dialog box; this invokes the Create and Link Task dialog box. You enter a Task just as you would any other Calendar Task, but it's now linked to this Agenda Entry. That's it. Although it will appear in the Task column along with your other daily Tasks, you'll always be able to check on the items that have to do with this event by referring to the tab on this dialog box.

GROUP SCHEDULING

As we mentioned above, perhaps the greatest single advantage of a networked scheduling program is its potential for automating the complex process of setting up meetings among groups of busy people. The automation centers around two distinct processes: comparing the personal Agendas of the individual participants in order to identify possible meeting times, and handling the often voluminous communications involved in inviting, declining, suggesting alternatives, and so forth. Netscape Calendar provides help in both areas.

Setting Up a Meeting

Every time you create an Agenda Entry, you have an opportunity to involve others by entering the names of people or groups in the People and resources field of the New Agenda Entry dialog box. (You can also add resources such as meeting rooms and equipment.) All the Calendar users in the organization are entered in the system directory that resides on the Calendar Server. The system administrator can create groups—Marketing or Editorial, for example—that let you address multiple people under one name.

In any case, if you enter people or groups, as described above, when you create the Entry (click the **Create** button), copies of your Entry—invitations, in essence—will be delivered to the New Entries folder located in the In-trays of the other prospective participants (those you entered). Each person invited in this way then has the opportunity to respond by opening Entry and clicking the **Reply** tab, shown in Figure 16.12.

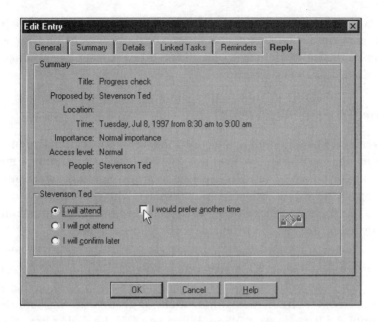

Figure 16.12 This dialog box replies to Entries you receive from others.

The three basic responses are:

- I will attend
- I will not attend
- I will confirm later

There's also a check box that lets the responder ask for another time.

E-Mail Notification

Since there's no guarantee that people will look in their In-trays regularly for New Entries, you can set up your Calendar program to automatically notify those on your participants list of new, modified, or canceled Entries via e-mail. To do this, select **Preferences** from the Edit menu, then select the **Agenda** subchoice and click the **Notification** tab.

At the top of this tab are two choices that apply to Entries Received (those initiated by others). If you want to receive e-mail notification, click the top check box. If you want Calendar to automatically check your In-tray and notify you when New Entries have come in from others, click the second check box and specify a time interval for checking. The Entries Sent Out section has check boxes that tell Calendar to e-mail the other participants whenever you Create, Modify, or Delete an Entry.

Synchronizing Agendas

Whenever it's critical that all or most of a group of participants attend a particular meeting, you can get a head start on the process of finding a mutually convenient (or possible) time by creating a Group Agenda (which might be more properly termed a Group Agenda display). This is a side-by-side rendering of the personal agendas of the participants, with a separate column that shows any open time slots in which all participants are free.

To create a Group Agenda, click the **Group Agenda** button on the main Calendar toolbar or select **Open Agenda** from the File menu, then **A Group Agenda**. Either action brings up the Selection for Group Agenda dialog box. Here you can enter the names of individual or groups, adding and deleting entries until the list is to your liking. When you **OK** the dialog box, Calendar displays the Group Agenda.

If no suitable meeting time is available on the date originally selected, you can use the Date Navigation Toolbar to check other possible meeting days.

WORKING OFFLINE

One of the barriers to a more general acceptance—and use—of electronic calendars is that it's hard to have your computer with you at all the times you might want to consult or make changes to your schedule. Laptop and palmtop systems have addressed this problem to a degree, but they bring up a new problem in the context of networked calendaring-scheduling programs: *synchronization*.

Suppose that—while on a business trip, for example—you decide to cancel an appointment that's already recorded on the Host (the Netscape Calendar Server) and make several new Agenda Entries. Furthermore, during your absence, others have made new Entries that involve you. Your Agenda is now out of synch with the rest of the organization.

Of course, you can communicate your changes next time you connect to the Host via the Internet, but then questions arise as to how to handle the changes you've made. Actually, Calendar can automate much of this, if you wish, but you'll have to make some Preferences settings.

Setting Off-line Preferences

To configure your system for offline work, select **Preferences** from the Edit menu, then the **Off-line** subchoice. This brings up the Off-line Preferences dialog box shown in Figure 16.13. Use **Location** to select (or create) a directory or folder to store your offline data. The **Download** tab lets you specify a time span in which to download schedule information and whether to download automatically, by prompt, or not at all when going on- or offline. Use the **People/Resources** tab to list those for whom you want Agendas downloaded for offline work. The **Groups** tab does the same for group Agendas.

Choose the **Reconciliation** tab to manage the process of integrating differences between your offline Agenda and the one stored on the Host. Radio buttons lets you choose whether to invoke the Reconciliation dialog box and let you resolve each change manually, or whether your offline version should automatically prevail. (That is, when you've deleted an Entry while offline, that Entry should be automatically deleted from the Host; when you've added or modified Entries, the Host should be automatically updated with this information.) Another pair of radio buttons lets you check for, or ignore, conflicts that are detected when you connect. The final check box uploads the Host-based information to your mobile system after reconciliation, so that your two versions are now in complete synchronization.

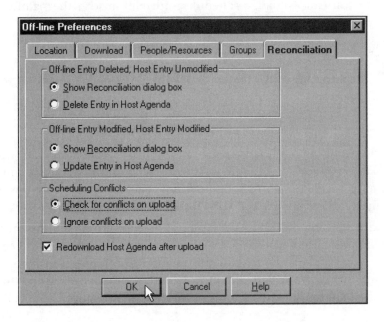

Figure 16.13 *Configure Reconciliation preferences in this dialog box.*

Going On- or Off line

To download Host Agenda information preparatory to disconnecting from the network, select **Go Off-line** from the File menu; the Agenda data defined by your preferences choices will download to your offline Calendar file. To reconnect, select **Go On-line** from the File menu. You'll be confronted by the Connect to Server dialog box, which prompts you for the User Name and Password that identify you on the system. (This is information your system administrator should supply.) If your organization has multiple servers, they will be listed in the drop-down list in the Server field. Simply mouse to the correct server name. Once you're successfully reconnected, the reconciliation processes defined in your Preferences will play themselves out, with or without your participation.

Working with Palmtops

Netscape Calendar lets you carry and modify your Agenda (and those of others) on either of two Hewlett-Packard palmtop computers—the HP-100LX or HP-200LX. (Support for other palmtops is planned for the future.) While this provides extra convenience for palmtop owners, the palmtops don't support the full scheduling power of Calendar.

Before you can exchange schedule information with the palmtop, you must install the UniLink Server software on the unit.

NOTE You'll find instructions for this procedure in the Calendar Help files: Search for **Palmtop** and display the topic **Installing the UniLink server on your HP palmtop**.

When you export an Agenda to the palmtop, you'll create a *calendar* (which is the HP-LX version of an Agenda). While working on the palmtop, you'll use the palmtop's nomenclature: Agendas will be called *Appointments*; Day Events and Daily Notes are known as *Events*; Tasks will be called *To-do's*.

As with working offline with a laptop, working with a palmtop involves a reconciliation process whenever you connect to and exchange information with the Host. The parameters for this reconciliation are set in Preferences, just as for offline work with a laptop (described above), except that you choose the **Palmtop** subchoice under Preferences instead of Off-line. As with

Off-line, Palmtop Preferences let you opt for case-by-case reconciliation or automatic updating.

SUMMARY

At its best, electronic calendaring offers features and capabilities that paper-based systems can't match. Netscape Calendar offers all the basics—such as entering and tracking appointments and meetings, tasks, and notes—in a quick, attractive, easy-to-use interface. It goes far beyond basics, however, with its flexible group scheduling capabilities. It also lets you take it with you when you're on the move, letting you work offline on a laptop or palmtop and easily reconcile your offline agenda with the version stored on the host.

In the next chapter, we'll cover the AutoAdmin capabilities in Netscape Communicator.

## CHAPTER 17

IBM Host on Demand

Connecting to mainframes, while seemingly retro, is still in demand among large corporations that also have the ability to pay lots of money for licensing many, many copies of Netscape Communicator. Hence the need for 3270 connectivity, which we'll cover in this short chapter.

MAINFRAME CONNECTIVITY

Most users won't need to worry about this, but the Professional Edition of Netscape Communicator has the ability to connect to mainframes via a TCP/IP connection.

This component is shown in Figure 17.1.

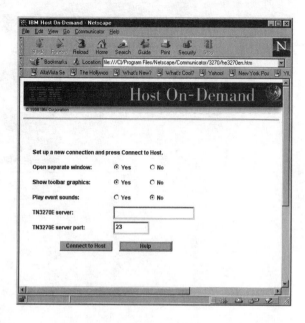

Figure 17.1 *Host on Demand*

As you can see in Figure 17.1, there's really only one field for data: the name of the host computer in the TN3270E server field. The worst that can happen is that a connection would be denied; if this happens, check with your system administrator, as you probably have the wrong name of the server.

A 3270 Session

Basically, you're using Netscape Communicator as a dumb terminal when you set up a 3270 session. You're typing input to a remote server, which then echoes the input back to you. You're working with a command line.

The one thing you will need to know is the keyboard mappings for a 3270 session. If you've used a 3270 terminal at all, you know that it features its own keyboard that doesn't match the standard PC keyboard. Table 17.1 lists the keys used in a 3270 session and their counterparts in a typical PC keyboard.

Table 17.1 *3270 Keys and PC Keys*

3270 KEYS	NETSCAPE/PC KEYS
F1-F9, 11, 12	F1-F9, 11, 12
F10	F10 (not guaranteed to work; you may need to use an onscreen equivalent)
F13-24	Shift-F1-12
Left cursor	Left arrow
Right cursor	Right arrow
Up cursor	Up arrow
Down cursor	Down arrow
Delete	Delete
Backspace	Backspace
Forward tab	Tab
Back tab	Shift-Tab
Enter	Enter
Clear	Esc
PA1	Home
End	End

SUMMARY

The IBM Host-on-Demand feature allows you to connect to IBM mainframes. This is certainly not the first action that will cross your mind in the course of a computing session, but it is certainly necessary for a small part of Netscape Communicator users, especially those in the corporate world.

In the next chapter, we'll cover security and how it relates to Netscape Communicator.

Security

The mainstream press loves to cover the more sordid aspects of the Internet—the perceived security lapses, the dangers of sharing data with other users. In this section—comprising Chapter 18—you'll learn some tools that will make your Internet computing sessions more secure.

Security and Communicator

Every few months you can count on some sensationalized account of fraud and theft on the Internet. Some of the stories are legitimate—after all, the Internet isn't quite as secure as it should be, considering that many companies are expecting to do massive business over the Internet—while others are simply not founded in fact. Because the issue of security on the Internet is of prime concern to many computer users, this chapter focuses only on security and Netscape Communicator, including the following topics:

- Public-key encryption
- Setting security preferences
- Proxies and SOCKS
- Electronic mail and security
- Java and security

519

SECURITY AND THE INTERNET

We've all heard the stories about hackers and cyberpunks: malicious computer geeks who revel at the thought of acquiring data they have no right to. This popular media stereotype is typically of a disaffected loner with few social skills and absolutely no impetus to ever leave their cubicle.

The fact is, there are hackers out there who delight in breaking into "secure" computing sites. And the fact is, there is malice among some—but certainly not all, or even a majority—hardcore computer users. This is compounded by the fact that UNIX, which really serves as the basis for the networks that make up the Internet, was designed to be as open as possible. To be honest, UNIX wasn't designed to be a secure environment to begin with, and while security enhancements have led to improvements in UNIX and networking, there are some holes that remain.

Security in Netscape Communicator is something that you should pay attention to, therefore, if you plan to send credit-card numbers and personal financial information over the World Wide Web.

NOTE There are brave new horizons of digital cash and electronic cash that are evolving rapidly—too rapidly for a discussion in this book. Until the world of digital cash evens out, the topic is something you really don't need to worry about or spend much time trying to figure out.

Secure States of Mind

Most of what passes over the Internet is not secure. This means that anyone who sits between you and the Web server can gain access to any data transfers without your knowing about it. In fact, it's quite easy to do so; ironically, many of the diagnostic tools used to create the Internet can also be used to subvert the Internet.

Netscape Communicator supports several different security methods. By far the most common security scheme is RSA public-key encryption. This is a public method that encrypts data from your computer and sends it over the Internet to a secure server, where it's decrypted. The process works both ways, so you can receive encrypted data on your computer from a secure server. Even if someone intercepts the message, they won't be able to decrypt the data if they lack a key.

Public-key technology works like this: Two keys are used by a server, a public key and a private key. When a site sends out a secure form to you, it sends along the public key. Your copy of Netscape Communicator takes the public key, encrypts the information in the secure form, and then send back the encrypted form. The server then takes the private key to decrypt the form. A public key is distributed freely, but it's worthless without the private key.

SETTING SECURITY PREFERENCES

Throughout this book a discussion of security preferences has been put off, in anticipation of this chapter. Here we'll discuss the Security dialog box—opened when you select the Security icons from the Navigator window, as shown in Figure 18.1.

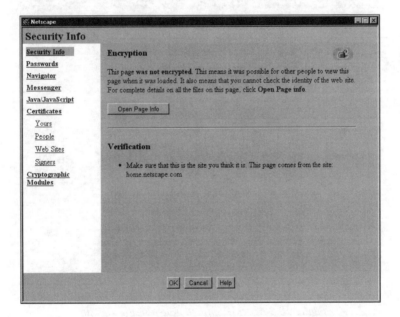

Figure 18.1 The Security dialog box.

The contents of the dialog box shown in Figure 18.1 are used to warn you when you're entering Web sites that have some sort of security mechanism intact, as well as if you're submitting a form to a Web site that may not have any security mechanism. As the commercial uses of the Web proliferate, so will the call to send credit-card information or other personal data.

Here, we've connected to a Web site without any security measures invoked. The page was not *encrypted*, which means that it was scrambled in such a way that only you and the sending party can view the page. In addition, there's no verification that the page actually came from **home.netscape.com**.

You'll notice that Figure 18.1 has a button for **Open Page Info**. This performs the same function as the Page Info selection from the Options menu, which you learned about earlier in this book.

Now look at Figure 18.2, which shows a connection to a secure Web server. You can't tell from the figure, but the padlocks on the Navigator window are both locked and surrounded with yellow shading. This indicates that you've connected to a secure server, a fact that's confirmed by the information in Figure 18.2.

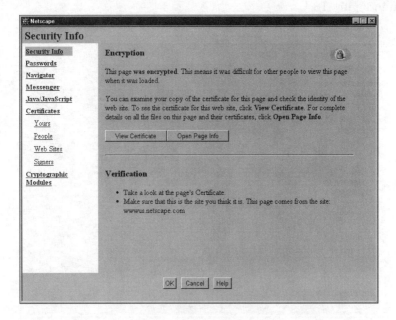

Figure 18.2 *A secure connection to a secure Web site.*

Netscape Communicator supports the Secure Sockets Layer (SSL) method of security, as do secure Netscape Communications Web servers. With this layer of security, you can transmit information and be reasonably assured that the information will be safe from any outside detection. The default for Netscape Communicator is to enable the highest SSL level, 3.0.

How do you know when a server is secure? Netscape Communicator has a few ways of telling you:

- The padlocks on the Navigator window are closed and surrounded by yellow.

- The name of the server will begin with *https://,* instead of *http://.*

- A dialog box may appear, telling you that a secure transaction is taking place.

A secure Web page is shown in Figure 18.3.

Figure 18.3 A secure page.

There may be times when you connect to a secure Web page that has some nonsecure components. The warning when you make such a connection is shown in Figure 18.4.

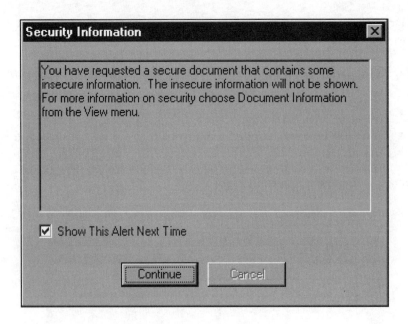

Security Information   ☒

You have requested a secure document that contains some insecure information. The insecure information will not be shown. For more information on security choose Document Information from the View menu.

☑ Show This Alert Next Time

Continue   Cancel

Figure 18.4 Mixing secure and nonsecure elements.

If you're wondering about the security level of a document, select the **Security** icon, as we showed in Figure 18.2. There, you'll learn about the server and at what level a document is secure.

N O T E   There are two levels of encryption. The basic Netscape Communicator release features 40-bit encryption. This is the version that can legally be exported under U.S. export laws (remember, software falls under the munitions portion of the law, so technically software with strong encryption is classified as banned munitions). The "strong" version of Netscape Communicator uses 128-bit encryption. The more bits, the more secure the encryption, and you can get the 128-bit version by simply requesting it from the Netscape Communications Web server and then affirming that you are a U.S. or Canadian citizen.

Site Certificates

Netscape Communicator uses site certificates that allow you to connect with other secure Web sites. When you connect to a secure Web site, you can see the certificates that make the transaction secure, as shown in Figure 18.5.

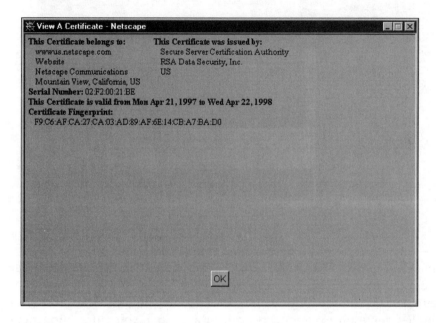

Figure 18.5 *A site certificate from a Web site.*

You can get your own Digital ID from Verisign (*http://www.verisign.com*). The ID allows you to make secure connections with other Web sites. It also allows you to encrypt your e-mail with other users who have their own Digital IDs.

After you do so, you'll get a list of sites that are cleared to make secure connections with Netscape Communicator. The standard list is shown in Figure 18.6.

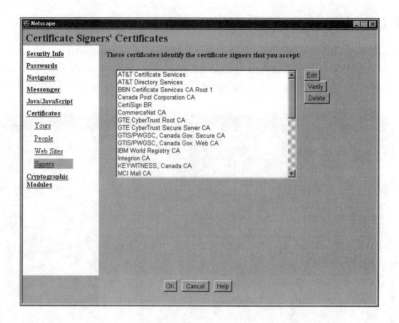

Figure 18.6 *Certificate sites.*

There's not much to do with this list of site certificates: You can delete certificates or edit them. Editing them is merely a matter of determining whether you want a warning when you enter into a transaction with a secure server, or whether you want to use a certificate at all. When you enter into situations with other vendors who may require a site certificate that you don't own, you'll be told by the vendor what to do to acquire the new certificate.

Site certificates are specific to an individual copy of Netscape Communicator. You can't use a site certificate from another person's copy of Netscape Communicator.

NOTE

NETSCAPE COMMUNICATOR, PROXIES, AND SOCKS

The Internet has been a tough sell to many corporations because of security issues. This issue has been tackled in two ways—corporations don't integrate Internet connectivity with their other networking schemes, or they set up a *firewall* between their corporate computing scheme and the Internet.

A firewall allows users to go out to the Internet, but Internet users can't get into the corporate computing system. One of the unpleasant facts about the Internet is that communications between a user and a server is basically two-way: If you go through your corporate Internet server to retrieve a document, someone else on the Internet should be able to get into your corporate Internet server. Trying to limit access with passwords will keep out the blunderers and the unsophisticated hacks, but it won't work for smart hackers (and here, we're using the term to refer to those who see a challenge in breaking into someone else's Internet site) who know security breaches in server software.

Why would anyone want access to your Internet server? Because once you're in the server, you can do just about anything. Logging in as the root or administrator on a UNIX or Windows NT system allows a person to do anything, ranging from changing file permissions and copying files to erasing files and deleting users from the user list. And if you're keeping some secure information on your Internet server, you sure don't want anyone with possibly malicious intentions rifling through your server.

That's where firewalls and the notion of keeping intruders out enter the discussions. Basically, a firewall runs alongside, and usually on a computer physically separate from, the Internet server. Firewall software, from the likes of Secure Computing Corp., oversees all access to the Internet, allowing corporate users to get out to the Internet, but keeping out all inquiries to your Internet server. In these situations, when you access the World Wide Web with Netscape Navigator, you're not going directly to the Internet—you're going to your corporate firewall, which then passes along the request to the Internet.

Or, rather, you're going to a server that is either part of the firewall software or runs separately. This server manages the requests to the Internet. As a user, you don't need to do anything differently when surfing the Web. The only thing you'll need to do is to set the address for your server, as Netscape Communicator needs to know where the proxy server is before you can surf the Web. These servers can be *proxy* (or *SOCKS*) servers.

HOT LINK

You'll learn about SOCKS in the next section. Here, we'll cover proxy servers.

Using Proxies

You can access the configuration option by selecting the **Preferences** choice in the Options pulldown menu, and then switch to the **Proxies** dialog box under the **Advanced** choice, as shown in Figure 18.7.

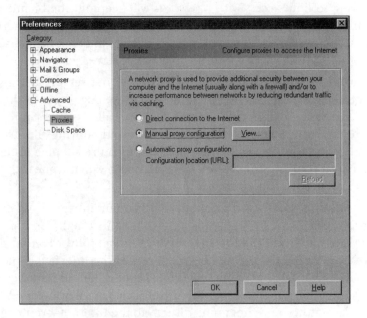

Figure 18.7 Configuring proxy servers.

If you've used older versions of Netscape Navigator, you may be surprised by what you see in Figure 18.8—instead of just giving you a series of fields to enter the names of the proxy servers, you need to tell Netscape Communicator whether you manually want to enter the proxy-server information or have it automatically set up through a document (found via a field for entering a URL address) already existing on the Web. (Don't worry if you don't have a URL address—this just means that your system administrator has set up a Web page to configure your internal proxies for you.)

Choosing the **View** button next to the Manual Proxy Configuration radio button brings up a menu containing fields for entering the information for FTP, Gopher, HTTP, Security, and WAIS proxies, as shown in Figure 18.8. In addition, you can enter a list of domains that don't need to be entered via a proxy server. You don't need to enter all the fields to enable a proxy server. You must be specific when you name the domains; you can't use wildcards to specify a range of domains, and you must use commas to separate any listings.

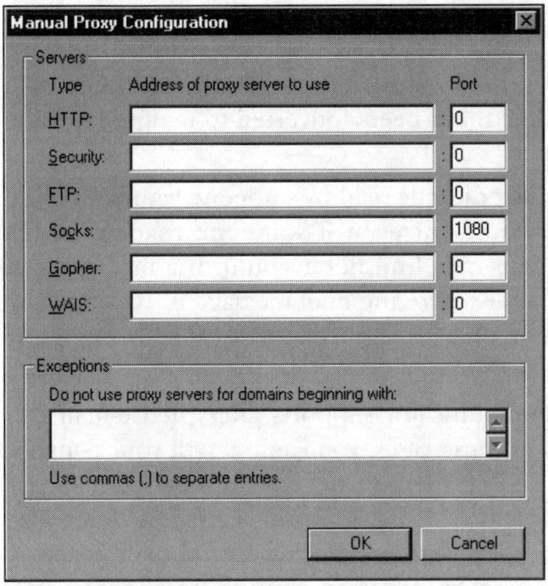

Figure 18.8 *Specifying proxy servers.*

NOTE

A proxy server protects your corporate Internet server. It does not protect your documents, such as your electronic mail. Don't assume that a proxy server is a substitute for the other security measures discussed in this chapter.

Using SOCKS

Some corporate users have incorporated SOCKS instead of proxy servers. While SOCKS servers are regarded as less efficient than proxy servers, they still have their users.

If your corporate computing environment uses SOCKS, you can still use the Proxies window to configure Netscape Communicator. As you saw in Figure 18.8, there's a line for SOCKS information, where you set the name and port number of the SOCKS host (or, more accurately, the SOCKS server). You'll need to restart Netscape Communicator to implement this new information.

Netscape Communicator supports the **socks.cstc.4.1** implementation.

MAIL AND SECURITY

Internet electronic mail is text. Even a MIME attachment to a mail message is merely a binary file that's been converted to text, to facilitate easy data transfer to the Internet.

And text can be directly read by someone who happens to intercept your mail via the Internet—or even if someone reads your mail on your own machine using your own Internet account. If a mail message stays as text, it really doesn't matter where the mail message is. It's easy enough to decode a MIME attachment, and it's easy enough to sort through a message to get at the heart of the matter.

Netscape Communicator supports encrypted e-mail if you've signed up for a Digital ID. In these cases, you can encrypt your e-mail so that it can't be read by anyone else on the Internet except the message's recipient.

N O T E   If you're using Netscape Communicator in a work situation for electronic mail, you may want to avoid using your work Internet account for any sensitive data transfer. Your employer has the total right to read through your electronic mail, either when stored on your hard disk or en route through a mail server. The law, as backed up by several court cases, is pretty clear about this, so don't even bother to try to assert any rights to privacy concerning electronic mail in the workplace.

There's also another issue that you may want to consider—e-mail forgery.

Right now there's not much e-mail forgery on the Internet. That's not to say that it couldn't happen. The protocol that oversees mail delivery, SMTP (Simple Mail Transfer Protocol), is as insecure as you can get. In theory, someone could send electronic mail under your name, making it look as though the mail was sent from Netscape Communicator. There's no way to prevent this.

What you can do is encrypt your mail to make sure that snoopers can't read it. When you sign up for a Digital ID, you also have the ability to encrypt your e-mail. This function is also covered by using the **Security** icon and selecting **Messenger**. The menu is shown in Figure 18.9.

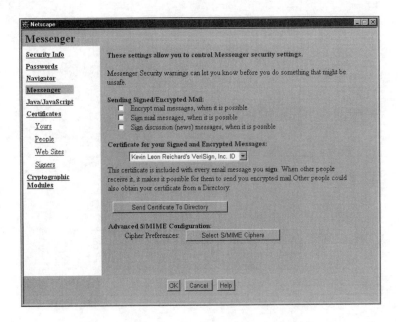

Figure 18.9 Security features for Messenger mail.

There are three choices here. If you're sending a lot of sensitive mail and are worried about its being intercepted, you should go ahead and choose to encrypt your mail when possible. Similarly, you might want to sign your mail messages when possible, in case you fear that there are situations when the veracity of your address is in question. The third option covers signing news messages and is less critical.

Passwords

Of course, all the encryption and security in the world is worthless if anyone can walk up to your computer and read your mail messages. If you're working in an office and are worried that a co-worker might want to go through your mail, you'll want to set up Passwords for Communicator. The appropriate dialog box is shown in Figure 18.10.

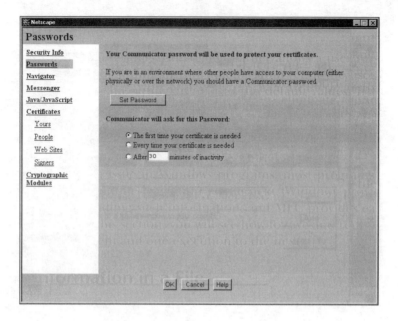

Figure 18.10 *Passwords and Communicator.*

In this situation, passwords are used a little differently than they are in the rest of the PC world, in that they apply to Communicator only when Communicator encounters another certificate and needs to send along your certificate. If this occurs, Communicator will prompt you for a password before sending along your certificate. If you're concerned about security, you should ask to be prompted *every* time a certificate is requested.

JAVA: BREWING A REVOLUTION

If you've spent any time around the Internet world, you've run across many, many references to Java, the programming language from Sun Microsystems. Visionaries have proclaimed Java as the tool that will revolutionize computing as we know it, realign world economies, and in general be a really cool thing.

So far, the hype has outpaced the reality by a wide measure, but that doesn't mean that you should write Java off as being unimportant or not worthy of attention.

The concepts behind Java are solid when looked at in the abstract: A programmer creates a small application (called an *applet*) that can be run on any type of computer—PC, Macintosh, or UNIX workstation. These applets are written in the Java programming language, which is a cousin of the C++ programming language. Since these applets are small, they can easily be embedded as part of Web pages. Therefore, you can have small applications that are transferred from Web server to Web browser on an as-needed basis.

That's the concept, which is still highly valid. The reality is something different, however. The applets we've seen released to date *have* been small and can be transferred easily. However, because of some of the limitations of the Java programming language, the applications tend to be quite slow (programmers out there will recognize why—the applets are interpreted and not compiled) and not exactly on the elaborate side. In fact, most Java applets tend to be confined to simplistic animation.

However, that's not to say that many cool things can't be created using Java. There's a whole world of potential Java applets that feature animation, sound, high-resolution graphics, and more. And while Java may be nothing more than a first-generation development tool that's superseded by other more powerful tools (already there are several next-generation Web development tools on the horizon, including one from the folks at Bell Labs who *invented* the C programming language), it's still a fun thing.

Following the Java Scent

Still, there are reason why you should take a look at Java, and why it might be fun to peruse some of the Web sites that feature Java content, security considerations aside. The best way to see Java in action is to visit one of these Java-oriented Web sites:

- The Sun Java home page (*http://www.javasoft.com*) features lots of information about Java. To see how a Java application works, load the page and look for any animation, such as a coffee cup with some steam rising. In addition, the Sun people maintain a listing of applets at *http://www.javasoft.com/applets/applets.html.*

- EarthWeb's Gamelan (*http://www.gamelan.com*), as shown in Figure 18.11, is *the* place to look for Web sites that feature Java-based content, as well as a great source for Java applets that you can download and inspect. This site also will link you with several of the other sites listed here. (A *gamelan* is an Indonesian musical instrument. Think about the history of Indonesia and you'll get the meaning behind the name of this site.)

Figure 18.11 *The Gamelan Web site.*

NOTE Java has been around for a while. It's even old enough that there are incompatible versions of Java applets floating around. Netscape Communicator can run applets created with the beta versions of Java, but not the alpha versions.

These sites should get you going with some Java applets that you can try for yourself.

Java and Security

Be warned that Java poses a security risk for your computer. Several warnings from influential monitors of computer security (including the RISKS mailing list) indicate that Java may be unacceptably risky in its current incarnation. While this point has been debated by Sun and Netscape Communications, there's enough evidence—as well as some compelling common sense—to make you sit up and take notice of any potential risks.

Most of this is due to the way Java works: Java sends a small program to your computer, where it's run locally. Your computer assumes that this program is legitimate. However, the program could be a *Trojan horse,* an evil program that can delete files or entire directories, or wreak other forms of havoc. The tools for adding security to Java are still in early development, so right now there's no effective tool for combating any Trojan horses.

A reality check here: As this book was written, there was no widespread usage of Java applets as carriers of viruses, and in fact there were very few Web sites that relied heavily on Java. In fact, there's a decent chance that you could spend a lot of time on the Web and never run across a Java applet, much less a Java applet that contained a Trojan horse. If you're really worried, go to the **Preferences** tab under the Options menu and disable Java support. This will prevent any Java applications from running on your computer—which is the best protection of all.

SUMMARY

Security and the Internet is a hot topic. That's why an entire chapter was devoted to security and Netscape Communicator, both on the good features (such as RSA data encryption, site certificates, and electronic-mail encryption) and the bad (possible Java security breaches).

For More Information

There are many other sources of information on the Internet, which expand on some of the concepts introduced in this book. Of course, the Internet itself is the best source of information about itself (a strong streak of narcissism runs through the Internet), but for those of you wanting something more permanent, here's a listing of various print resources.

BOOKS

There are far too many Internet books on the market, and most of them are of mediocre quality at best. Here are some we recommend as well as a few that were mentioned in the course of this book.

General-Interest Internet Books

The New Internet Navigator, Paul Gilster, John Wiley and Sons, 1995. This overview of all the components that comprise the Internet is encyclopedic yet accessible. The level of detail can be daunting. You're sure to find what you need here.

The Whole Internet User's Guide and Catalog, **second edition**, Ed Krol, O'Reilly and Associates, 1994. An eminently readable overview of the Internet.

The Internet Unleashed, sams.net, 1997. While not the sort of thing you'll want to read from cover to cover (its 1,000-plus pages contain some rather obvious padding), it's handy to have around for reference, and the accompanying CD-ROM contains almost every Internet utility you'll ever want.

The World Wide Web Bible, **second edition**, Brian Pfaffenberger, MIS:Press, 1996. This best-selling reference is a one-stop tutorial on the Web and the Internet.

For UNIX/Linux Users

Linux Configuration and Installation, **third edition**, Patrick Volkerding, Kevin Reichard, and Eric F. Johnson, MIS:Press, 1997. The title says it all. If you're using Netscape Navigator under Linux and are having some problems, you'll want to check out the chapters on configuring the X Window System and XFree86.

Using X, Eric J. Johnson and Kevin Reichard, MIS:Press, 1992. This book tells you how to configure the X Window System to your liking and covers issues like fonts and colors. If you're using Netscape Navigator under the X Window System, you may want to check this book out t learn more about the wonders of **.Xdefaults** and the like.

Magazines

There are a host of Internet magazines—way too many, to be honest. We're both affiliated with *Internet World* (*http://www.internet.com*), so of course we recommend that you check it out. In addition, you can go back to Chapter 4 and look through the listing of magazines in the Web sites.

APPENDIX B

Netscape Communicator and UNIX

The World Wide Web began in the UNIX world, so it's no surprise that Netscape Communicator is available for a wide variety of UNIX platforms, including:

- AIX
- BSDI
- HP-UX
- Irix
- Linux

- OSF/Motif (also known as Digital UNIX)
- SunOS 4.1.3
- Sun Solaris 2.3
- Sun Solaris 2.4

Netscape Communicator runs under the X Window System under all of these operating systems. If you're running one of these versions of UNIX under a command line instead of a graphical interface, you won't be able to use Netscape Communicator.

Basically, the UNIX versions of Netscape Communicator work the same way the Windows and Macintosh version do; throughout this book, we've noted where the UNIX versions differ.

There is one major difference, however, and it affects how certain configuration options (specifically, fonts and colors) are set up in Netscape Communicator. This has to do with the eccentricities of the X Window System.

This book won't even attempt to explain how to configure the X Window System. If you're a little fuzzy on the particulars of X Window System (or Xfree86) configuration, you may want to check out Appendix A for a list of books that can guide you through this treacherous territory.

RUNNING NETSCAPE COMMUNICATOR WITH COMMAND-LINE OPTIONS

As good UNIX hacks know, almost any UNIX application can be altered with command-line options, which you enter when you launch an application from a UNIX command line. And, like any good UNIX application, Netscape Communicator supports a number of command-line options.

The most commonly used option is `-geometry`, which sets the size and position of the Netscape Communicator window when it is launched. (For some reason, UNIX hacks tend to a tad anal about window sizes when applications are launched.) This command line supports the familiar X Window x,y window coordinates, along with width (w) and height (h). The command-line option would look something like this:

```
-geometry (w)x(h)+(x)+(y)
```

where w is width, h is height, and x and y comprise the measurement from the top left of the window in pixels. Therefore, if your line is:

```
-geometry 100x80+400+400
```

Netscape Communicator will begin in the 100×80 position. The top of the window will run 400 pixels and the sides of the window will run 400 pixels.

These measurements are all in pixels. The actual dimensions of a pixel depend on your screen measurement.

N O T E

Using the -geometry command-line options sets the geometry for the browser, mail, and news windows only; it does not affect any other windows created by Netscape Communicator.

N O T E

You can set these sizes in the **.Xresources** file. Table B.1 lists the options.

Table B.1 *Lines that can be set in the .Xresources file.*

RESOURCE	USED FOR
Netscape*Communicator.geometry: WxH+X+Y	Browser window
Netscape*Mail.geometry: WxH+X+Y	Mail window
Netscape*News.geometry: WxH+X+Y	News window
Netscape*Bookmark.geometry: WxH+X+Y	Bookmark window
Netscape*AddressBook.geometry: WxH+X+Y	Address-book window
Netscape*Composition.geometry: WxH+X+Y	Composition window
Netscape*TopLevelShell.geometry: WxH+X+Y	All of these windows

Changing Fonts

The way the X Window System handles fonts is a tricky topic, one far too involved to cover here in any depth. To learn about fonts and X, check out a good book on the subject (see Appendix A for details). If you already know about X and fonts, here's some information you can use regarding Netscape Communicator and fonts. The section of the **.Xdefaults** file that deals with fonts is the following:

```
Netscape*XmLGrid*fontList:\
    -*-helvetica-medium-r-*-*-*-100-*-*-*-*-iso8859-*,\
    -*-helvetica-bold-r-*-*-*-100-*-*-*-*-iso8859-*=BOLD,\
    -*-helvetica-medium-o-*-*-*-100-*-*-*-*-iso8859-*=ITALIC
```

Other UNIX Issues

While the UNIX version of Netscape Communicator is almost identical to the Windows and Macintosh versions, some quirks in the UNIX operating system—as well as some features that are built into it, such as mail—require things to be done a little differently under UNIX. Here are some of the things you'll want to consider; a more complete listing of these issues can be obtained directly from Netscape Communicator (select **Release Notes** from the Help menu), or go directly to *http://home.netscape.com/* and search for UNIX release notes..

Security

Because of the peculiarities of the UNIX operating system, the UNIX versions of Netscape Communicator are more susceptible to security breaches than the Windows and Macintosh versions.

If you're worried about security, check your Netscape Communicator version number (you can find it under the Help menu). If you are using version 2.0, you should consider upgrading to a more recent version. Version 2.01 added some needed security functions for UNIX.

Netscape Mail and UNIX

To be compatible with other UNIX mail readers, Netscape Communicator stores your mail in a BSD mail-folder format, which can be read by other UNIX mail tools.

By default, Netscape Mail looks for an SMTP mail server. It can also look for a mail directory (it's usually called **~/nsmail**). To use another directory, open the **~/.netscape/preferences** file and look for a line that begins with:

```
MAIL_DIR:
```

This will be followed by the name of a directory. Change it to the name of the new mail directory.

GLOSSARY

16-bit operating system: Operating system that computes data 16 bits at a time. Because of this size limitation, applications run less efficiently than under a 32-bit operating system. Windows is a 16-bit operating system.

32-bit operating system: Operating system that computes data 32 bits at a time. Windows 95 and IBM OS/2 are 32-bit operating systems.

address book: File used by Netscape Mail to store frequently used electronic-mail addresses.

anonymous FTP: Method of connecting to a public FTP server, where all you need to do is provide your e-mail address as a password.

applets: Small programs written in the Java programming language. These are transferred to your computer as part of a Web page.

archie: Tool for both indexing files stored on the Internet and the software used to search through these indices.

bookmark: A listing of your favorite Web locations.

Boolean logic: A computer-geek way of defining a choice—if this, then that.

character set: The characters needed to display information in a given language.

check boxes: Boxes in a form used to select a line of text.

client: Your computer. In the client/server model of computing, local computers run clients, and servers sit on the network and distribute information.

clipboard: Portion of your computer's memory reserved for the temporary storage of information. When you copy something to your clipboard, you can retrieve it at any time. All of the operating systems that Netscape Navigator runs under feature a clipboard.

connection: A path to the Web server. Typically, Netscape Navigator maintains several connections to a Web server, so that several files can be transferred simultaneously.

decoder software: Programs that take a real-time feed from the Internet and convert it into audio and/or video via Netscape Navigator.

dial-up Internet connection: A connection to the Internet through a modem that occurs only on demand. This is not a full-time connection, and it is only as fast as your modem.

direct Internet connection: A network link that runs through your network card to the Internet and is always active. Typically direct Internet connections are much faster than dial-up connections.

disk cache: A section of your computer's hard disk that is controlled by Netscape Navigator for the purpose of storing Web pages.

drag and drop: Method of moving data from one application to another or within applications, in which the mouse is used to drag something to another part of the screen.

electronic mail: Text messages and (possibly) attachments sent from a user to a user via the Internet.

encoding: Information that Netscape Navigator needs to display text in various languages.

encryption: Technology for scrambling data to prevent unauthorized users from reading your data.

error messages: Messages from Netscape Navigator that tell you something went wrong.

firewall: Software that sits between you and the Internet, with a high level of security designed to deter hackers.

forms: Data-entry fields in Web pages used to send information back to a Web server.

frames: Method of dividing a Netscape Navigator screen into different areas, each running individual programs and capable of loading individual Web pages.

FTP (File Transfer Protocol): A networking protocol that allows you to transfer software from a server via the Internet. Netscape Navigator allows such file transfers.

Gopher: Menuing software developed at the University of Minnesota. Gopher servers by and large have been supplanted by Web servers, although much valuable information is still accessible via Gopher servers.

helpers: Programs used to perform tasks that Netscape Navigator cannot.

history: The list of Web sites that you've recently visited.

home page: Basically, the main page of a company or a person. This is the starting point to other Web pages.

hypertext: Data format where parts of one document are linked to parts of another document (or many more documents).

HyperText Markup Language: The format that is the basis of the World Wide Web. Netscape Navigator takes pages formatted in HTML from a Web server and renders them into the pages shown on your computer screen.

Internet: A global collection of internetworked servers and computers that exchange various types of data. The Internet can best be understood when broken down into its various services: The World Wide Web, electronic mail, FTP, Usenet newsgroups, and more.

intranet: An internal network not connected to the outside world that takes advantage of Internet technology, such as Netscape Navigator. For instance, a company that uses Web servers to distribute information only to company employees is employing an intranet.

Internet Protocol (IP) address: A unique number assigned to Internet computers. They are either *dynamic* (which means they are assigned every time you login to the Internet) or *static* (which means the address is yours forever).

ISP: See *service provider*.

Java: Programming language created by Sun Microsystems used to create applets that can run on any computer. Netscape Navigator supports Java.

links: Connections from one Web page to another. Links are indicated with special formatting (different colors, underlined text). When you put your mouse over a link and press the mouse button, the page indicated in the link will be loaded into Netscape Navigator.

mail server: A computer on the Internet that handles incoming and outgoing electronic mail.

map: Graphic on a Web page that allows you to navigate through the Web. For instance, there may be a graphic showing all the products from BigCo Corporation, and if you click on the picture of the lawnmower in the map, you'll be connected to the Web page listing the lawnmowers offered by BigCo.

memory cache: A section of your computer's RAM that is controlled by Netscape Navigator for the purpose of storing Web pages.

Multipurpose Internet Mail Attachment (MIME): A format for attaching files to mail and newsgroup messages.

network: Two or more physically connected computers. This connection can either be through a network card and wire, or through a modem and telephone lines. The Internet is merely a giant, interconnected network.

network protocol: A computer-science way of describing the way computers talk to one another. The computers on the Internet use TCP/IP to talk with one another.

newsgroup: See *Usenet.*

pathname: The full name of a file, beginning with the root directory of the hard drive. Your file may be named `file` and stored in the `docs` subdirectory on the C: drive. In this case, the full pathname of the file would be `c:\docs\file`.

plug-ins: Third-party programs that extend Netscape Navigator with very specific applications (such as sound, the ability to view specific kinds of files, or audio).

Point-to-Point Protocol (PPP): Networking protocol used to connect to the Internet via modem.

POP3/IMAP mail server: Types of mail servers that Netscape Navigator connects to retrieve your electronic mail.

Port: Physical port on your computer, where your modem is connected.

postings: Messages sent to a Usenet newsgroup.

proxy server: A Web server that sits between your computer and the Internet for security reasons. This server prevents unauthorized users from entering your network, and it can also prevent you from connecting to unauthorized sites, such as *http://www.playboy.com.*

pull-down menu: A row of selectable menus that are accessed when you pull them down. Windows, Windows 95, the Macintosh OS, and UNIX (when using the X Window System) all feature pull-down menus.

push technology: Used by Netcaster to regularly update Web information in the background of the screen. Basically, push technology is regularly updated Web information in the form of channels, which are subscribed to like channels on television.

radio boxes: Selection mechanisms in a Web form, where only one selection can be active at a time.

search engine: Special Internet servers that catalogue the offerings of the World Wide Web, allowing you to search through them.

Serial Line Internet Protocol (SLIP): Networking protocol used to connect to the Internet via modem. Now largely superseded by PPP.

server: A computer hooked up to the Internet that handles requests from a Web browser or another piece of Internet software. This computer can be a personal computer running Windows NT or a workstation running UNIX. Special software (such as Netscape Commerce Server) actually handles the transactions. Web servers distribute Web documents, Gopher servers distribute Gopher menus, mail servers distribute electronic-mail messages, and so on.

service provider: A company that facilitates connectivity to the Internet, either via a direct network link or a modem dial-up connection.

signature: Text affixed to the end of mail and news messages, indicating who you are and why you're important.

site certificate: Security tool used on the Internet to verify that you're a legitimate user with legitimate access to a Web site.

SMTP (Simple Mail Transfer Protocol): Protocol used by Netscape Navigator to send mail to an SMTP mail server.

SOCKS server: A server that sits between you and the Internet, designed to provide more security than merely a straight connection.

subscribe: Tells Netscape News that you want to check a newsgroup every time Netscape News is launched.

telnet: An older networking protocol that allows you to login directly to a remote computer on the Internet. Netscape Navigator does not directly support telnet, but does provide for a third-party telnet package to be installed.

tags: Formatting codes that are sent as part of an HTML document, telling Netscape Navigator how to display text or images.

threading: Method of organizing mail and news messages so that messages on the same topic can be read sequentially.

thumbnail: A smaller representation of a larger image, used to avoid the time needed to transfer large images to your computer.

tn3270: Variant of telnet used to connect to IBM computers. Netscape Navigator doesn't support tn3270, but does allow a tn3270 client to be specified.

Transmission Control Protocol/Internet Protocol (TCP/IP): The computer language that all computers on the Internet speak.

Uniform Resource Locator (URL): Basically, the address of a page on the Web. A URL for a Web page begins with *http://*, although Netscape Navigator recognizes several different types of URLs.

Unzip: To uncompress a file using special software, such as PKZip or StuffIt.

Usenet newsgroups: Discussion groups centered on various topics, ranging from the broad (**alt.books**) to the arcane (**comp.os.lynx**).

veronica: Tool for indexing Gopher menus and resources.

Web browser: Software that takes information from the Internet and presents it on your computer screen. Netscape Navigator is a Web browser.

Web page: The document that's sent from a Web server to a Web browser.

Web server: A special computer on the Internet that distributes Web pages to users on demand.

webtop: Term used in Netscape Netcaster to denote push-technology content displayed in the background of the screen.

Win32s: Extensions to Windows 3.1 that allow the operating system to run 32-bit applications, although the computing is still being performed in a 16-bit operating system.

World Wide Web (WWW): One of the many services of the Internet. The World Wide Web is built upon Web pages formatted in the HTML language. On the Web, *Web servers* distribute *Web pages* to *Web browsers*.

X Window System: Graphical user interface for computers running the UNIX operating system.